Taxpayer Compliance

Volume 1: An Agenda for Research

Law in Social Context Series

EDITORS:
Keith Hawkins, Oxford University, Centre for Socio-Legal Studies
John M. Thomas, State University of New York at Buffalo,
  School of Management

Taxpayer Compliance

Volume 1:
An Agenda for Research

Jeffrey A. Roth, John T. Scholz, and Ann Dryden Witte, Editors

Panel on Taxpayer Compliance Research
Committee on Research on Law Enforcement
 and the Administration of Justice
Commission on Behavioral and Social Sciences
 and Education
National Research Council

University of Pennsylvania Press
Philadelphia

NOTICE: The project that is the subject of this report was approved by the Governing Board of the National Research Council, whose members are drawn from the councils of the National Academy of Sciences, the National Academy of Engineering, and the Institute of Medicine. The members of the committee responsible for the report were chosen for their special competences and with regard for appropriate balance.

This report has been reviewed by a group other than the authors according to procedures approved by a Report Review Committee consisting of members of the National Academy of Sciences, the National Academy of Engineering, and the Institute of Medicine.

The National Research Council was established by the National Academy of Sciences in 1916 to associate the broad community of science and technology with the Academy's purposes of furthering knowledge and of advising the federal government. The Council operates in accordance with general policies determined by the Academy under the authority of its congressional charter of 1863, which establishes the Academy as a private, nonprofit, self-governing membership corporation. The Council has become the principal operating agency of both the National Academy of Sciences and the National Academy of Engineering in the conduct of their services to the government, the public, and the scientific and engineering communities. It is administered jointly by both Academies and the Institute of Medicine. The National Academy of Engineering and the Institute of Medicine were established in 1964 and 1970, respectively, under the charter of the National Academy of Sciences.

This project was sponsored by the Internal Revenue Service, U.S. Department of the Treasury, under contract no. 84-0092. The contents do not necessarily reflect the views or policies of the sponsor.

Library of Congress Cataloging in Publication Data

Taypayer compliance.
  (Law in social context series)
  Bibliography: p.
  Includes index.
  Contents: v. 1. An agenda for research—
v. 2. Social science perspectives.
  1. Taxpayer compliance—United States.   2. Taxation—
Law and legislation—United States.   I. Roth, Jeffrey A.,
1945–   II. Scholz, John T.   III. Witte, Ann D.
IV. Series.
HJ4652.T396   1989   336.2'91   88-36250
ISBN 0-8122-8182-9 (v. 1)
ISBN 0-8122-8150-0 (v. 2)

ISBN 0-8122-8187-X (set)

Contents

Preface

This report explores what is known about individuals' compliance with federal income tax reporting requirements and how more can be learned about it. Strong concerns about this subject date back to the late 1970s, when articles in the financial and popular press publicized an "underground economy" in the United States, which purportedly accounted for hundreds of billions of dollars per year in untaxed economic activity. Legislators in search of painless but ethical ways to raise badly needed revenue quickly showed interest in this economy and sought ways to raise tax revenue from it. They asked the Internal Revenue Service (IRS) to estimate its size as well as the tax revenue lost as a result of its activity.

The first IRS report (IRS, 1979b) made ingenious use of existing data to provide a ballpark estimate of the amount of economic activity that was going untaxed. Although it suggested that earlier reports had exaggerated the amount of untaxed activity, it served mainly to illustrate the limited nature of data and research on tax compliance and its causes. A second, more refined study (IRS, 1983f) placed the "tax gap" due to noncompliance with federal income tax laws by individuals and corporations at about $90 billion for 1981.

When legislators and tax administrators began to search for information to assist them in developing policies to recover the revenue lost to noncompliance, they found little help in social science research. Although economists had been building theoretical models of taxpayer compliance since the early 1970s, these models were derived mainly from literature on the economics of crime and reflected too few of the unique aspects of taxpaying to provide useful policy guidance. There was also substantial work by survey researchers who obtained taxpayers' self-reports of previous noncompliance with tax laws and related them to measures of attitudes, beliefs, and sociodemographic characteristics. But the measures of compliance in these survey studies were very general, and the explanatory variables were usually related only indirectly to policy variables that might be used to stimulate higher levels of compliance.

Even without much information to guide them, legislators proceeded vigorously in their attempts to recover the revenue lost to noncompliance. They based major portions of the 1982 Tax Enforcement and Fiscal Responsibility Act on the supposition—supported by some economic models but not others, some research within the IRS, and some survey research—that higher penalties would lead to fuller compliance. The Deficit Reduction Act of 1984 closed off certain tax shelters and broadened information reporting, the mechanism through which interest payments, dividends, and some other types of income are reported directly to the IRS before tax returns are filed.

By that time, academic researchers outside the IRS had begun to publish articles using data collected by the IRS. Econometricians were primarily concerned with how tax rates and IRS administrative actions, particularly audits, affected compliance by individual taxpayers. Results suggested that lower tax rates and higher audit rates might indeed stimulate compliance. Economic theorists began to model some important aspects of the tax environment, such as features of the Internal Revenue Code and the interaction between the taxpayer and the taxing agency. Researchers from other disciplines sought to understand other important aspects of the process, such as appeals to morality, patriotic motives, the disapproval of peers, and imperfect knowledge of compliance requirements. This work, although best regarded as pioneering rather than definitive, illustrated for both researchers and the IRS the potential benefits to be gained from cooperation.

Some might question the scholarly propriety of such cooperation. Some of the lowest compliance rates occur among small-scale entrepreneurs, people in need of income from part-time jobs, family farmers, and other generally law-abiding citizens—causing some to wonder whether noncompliance with tax laws requires the attention of researchers outside the IRS.

But noncompliance with tax laws raises some serious social problems. Tax evasion by people who may have special opportunities to conceal income is unfair to others who pay their full share. Public knowledge that successful evasion occurs may encourage further evasion, leading eventually to more coercive tax collection methods. And a large underground economy may encourage attitudes of guardedness among acquaintances, dishonesty in financial transactions, and alienation from government.

Taxpayer noncompliance presents intellectual as well as social problems. It offers fertile ground for the refinement and testing of theories from a host of social sciences. Such concepts as maximization of expected utility, game theory, social sanctions, guilt neutralization, social networks and social fields, decision heuristics, and bounded rationality have all been used in efforts to conceptualize the process of taxpaying. Empirical research in the area raises exceedingly difficult problems of measurement and inference—problems that challenge social scientists and produce competing claims and methodological qualifications that frustrate policy makers in search of definitive conclusions.

Seeing the potential value of research but confused by often conflicting statements, the IRS Research Division in 1984 asked the National Academy of Sciences to convene a panel to assess the current state of knowledge regarding taxpayer compliance and to recommend promising areas for future research. In response, the Committee on Research on Law Enforcement and the Administration of Justice created the Panel on Taxpayer Compliance Research. The panel was a diverse group that included a former commissioner of internal revenue, leading tax lawyers and accountants, and social scientists from the major disciplines with research bases that relate to compliance—anthropology, economics, political science, criminology, psychology, and sociology (see Appendix D for brief biographies of panel and staff members). Although all panel members were respected members of their disciplines and professions, some had not previously considered tax compliance issues in depth. Fortunately, every panel member recognized that the expertise of the others was needed to encompass the diverse and complex issues related to taxpayer compliance.

To fill in possible gaps and to extend the panel's knowledge, we commissioned a number of papers on specific topics; these were presented and discussed at a conference held at South Padre Island, Texas, January 15–17, 1986 (see Appendix C for the program and list of participants). Rather than simply reviewing the literature on compliance, most of the papers sought to extend knowledge by drawing insights from work being done in other areas. Eight of the papers appear as Volume 2: Social Science Perspectives.

Two of the papers are concerned entirely with methodology and are included in this volume. The paper by Peter Schmidt (Appendix A) extends recent multivariate statistical work to deal with important aspects of taxpayer compliance analysis. The paper by Robert F. Boruch (Appendix B) suggests ways experimental and quasi-experimental designs can be used to inform taxpayer compliance research.

The papers in Volume 2 vary widely in terms of approach and disciplinary orientation. Several are reviews of literature from subfields of several disciplines—decision psychology, social psychology, economics, and deterrence research—highlighting issues that have received too little attention in previous taxpayer compliance research. Others present new conceptual frameworks for compliance, and three contain original research—a microeconomic model that incorporates tax advisers, an ethnographic study of noncompliance in one occupational setting, and a history of recent federal tax and budget legislation that has defined the options available to the IRS for tax administration.

Because of their disciplinary orientations and personal interests, panel members placed different levels of emphasis on the information and ideas developed at the symposium, in other prepared background materials, in meetings with compliance researchers, in extensive panel discussions, and in early drafts of this report. Some placed more emphasis on alternative theories of decision making under uncertainty. Others believed it is more important to recognize that compliance is embedded in the social, cultural, and financial sociocultural aspects of taxpayers' environments and to study how those environments develop. The tax practitioners, administrators, and policy analysts were occasionally bemused by the social scientists' arcane discussions. They regularly reminded the group of the legal, administrative, and institutional structure that defines taxpaying. "What does this debate mean for policy?" was a frequent question.

Despite their differences in emphasis, panel members were in general agreement that existing economic theory reflected the institutional, legal, and administrative structure surrounding taxpaying too poorly to serve as a basis for policy. We also noted the lack of rigorous theory related to compliance from other disciplines and concurred in recognizing the need to develop more informed theories of compliance. In developing our list of important aspects of taxpayer compliance behavior, we drew on compliance research in regulatory fields. We also believe that both ethnographic and experimental research should be used to inform theory and to provide preliminary tests of models of compliance.

The panel found existing empirical work flawed, but we agreed that some consistent insights regarding compliance have emerged from this work. More sophisticated empirical work on better, more current data is urgently needed. Improvements are urgently needed in compliance measurement at the individual level.

In recommending promising areas for future research, the panel shared a hope that results would cumulate to form a firm base for tax policy and tax administration, at the same time contributing to basic knowledge in several disciplines. Some of this accumulation should occur spontaneously, as independent scholars seek to fill the knowledge gaps that are pointed out in

Chapters 2 and 3. Additional important knowledge can be developed through the more applied tax administration research illustrations that appear in Chapter 4; these will require closer cooperation among researchers, tax administrators, and tax practitioners. The IRS will no doubt continue to play a central role in taxpayer compliance research, as it provides compliance research data and other forms of support.

While different panel members would place different weights on various conclusions and recommendations, overall censusis was achieved. Panel members agreed that carefully designed randomized field experiments with policy innovations, when feasible, could produce the firmest conclusions about influences on compliance. Beyond that, some panel members would emphasize deductively derived theory tested by multivariate statistical analyses of audit-based data, while others would place more emphasis on exploratory and ethnographic research as a means of refining theory. As the panel's work progressed, all of us gained respect for disciplinary and administrative perspectives that were new to us.

The dedicated efforts of the staff have been central to the work of the panel. Jeffrey Roth, study director from the inception of the panel, made a very substantial contribution to the panel's activities. He skillfully managed the affairs of the panel, drafted large segments of the report, guided the panel through an extensive report review process, and revised (many times) all report materials. John Scholz, whose association with the panel began shortly after its inception, was responsible for drafting significant segments of the panel report, particularly the material developed in Chapters 3 and 6. Like Jeff, John has reviewed and helped to revise various sections of the report many times. The panel also benefited considerably from the administrative and secretarial work of Gaylene Dumouchel and Teresa Williams of the National Research Council and Helen Graham of Wellesley College.

Early drafts of the report were reviewed by many people. The panel and staff are grateful to members of the Commission on Behavioral and Social Sciences and Education, members of the Committee on Research on Law Enforcement and the Administration of Justice, and selected outside reviewers (Harold Grasmick, Karyl Kinsey, Robert Mason, Daniel Nagin, and Louis Wilde). Their valuable comments were all seriously considered and helped us to sharpen our thinking. Nearly all sections of the report were revised in major ways to reflect important new insights and clarifications as a result of these individuals' comments on our work.

The task of editing the large volume of material assembled by the panel has been considerable. Christine McShane, editor of the Commission on

Behavioral and Social Sciences and Education, not only sharpened our language but also challenged our assertions when they were insufficiently developed or documented. In doing so, she made an excellent and important contribution to the report.

An important feature of the panel's work has been the support and encouragement of the sponsor, the Research Division of the Internal Revenue Service. As the IRS contracting officer's technical representative, William Lefbom kept in close touch with the panel throughout its work and provided valuable encouragement, insights, and information. Patricia White, a member of his staff, prepared useful computer analyses and provided other information. Roscoe Egger, commissioner of internal revenue during much of the panel's life, deputy commissioner John Wedick, and assistant research director Irene Sherk also provided general encouragement and support for our efforts.

Sadly, as this report was in final preparation, IRS research director Frank Malanga passed away. Frank understood the sometimes serendipitous ways in which social science research might improve tax administration, he respected the panel's needs for independence and time to reach consensus, and he valued a broad range of research perspectives. He will be missed by the compliance research community.

Ann Dryden Witte
Chair, Panel on Research on Taxpayer Compliance

Summary

According to Internal Revenue Service (IRS, 1988) estimates, individuals failed to report between $70 and $79 billion in federal taxes due on legal income they received in 1986, amounting to nearly 20 percent of federal personal income taxes due and 40 percent of the federal deficit in that year. Other forms of noncompliance—for example, by organizations, by those who fail to pay the income tax they do report, and by those who receive illegal income—probably push the annual "noncompliance tax gap" above $100 billion.

Since the IRS manages to recover at most an estimated 10 to 15 percent of the noncompliance tax gap through all its enforcement activities (IRS, 1986b), it has a pragmatic interest in learning why some people comply with reporting requirements, while others fail to do so. The question has also intrigued scholars from several disciplines, as well as the community of practitioners who prepare tax returns and advise clients concerning tax matters. The panel of scholars and other profesionals responsible for this report was created in response to an IRS request to the National Academy of Sciences to critically review previous research on the factors that influence taxpayer compliance with reporting requirements. The panel was asked to state the conclusions that can be drawn from this literature, to identify the gaps in knowledge that future research may be able to fill, and to suggest how the needed research might be carried out.

Defining Taxpayer Compliance

Compliance with income tax reporting requirements involves accurate reporting of taxable income, accurate claims of subtractions such as income adjustments and itemized deductions, correct computation of tax liability, and timely filing of the tax return. These tasks require reading and arithmetic skills, record-keeping effort, and judgments that challenge the capabilities of many taxpayers. Therefore, although noncompliance with tax reporting requirements sometimes results from deliberate choices, it may also occur because of carelessness, errors, and misunderstandings of requirements related to keeping records and filing returns.

For this reason, the panel adopted a definition of compliance that implies no assumptions about taxpayers' motivations:

> Compliance with reporting requirements means that the taxpayer files all required tax returns at the proper time and that the returns accurately report tax liability in accordance with the Internal Revenue Code, regulations, and court decisions applicable at the time the return is filed.

Against this standard, noncompliance includes both overreporting and underreporting of tax liability. It includes both deliberate underreporting that is punishable by criminal sanctions and underreporting due to misinformation, misunderstanding, negligence, or some other cause. It does not include the structuring of one's financial affairs within the law so as to reduce taxes, perhaps in ways that were not intended by lawmakers. It also does not include situations lacking a clear legal precedent, in which compliance status is ambiguous.

Patterns and Trends in Taxpayer Compliance

Taxpayer compliance is notoriously difficult to measure. But, according to the IRS Taxpayer Compliance Measurement Program (TCMP) for individual returns (see Chapter 1, Supplementary Note B, for more explanation of this program, which involves audits of randomly sampled returns) and other IRS (1979b, 1983f, 1988) studies, the following rudimentary picture of taxpayer compliance and noncompliance patterns emerges.

1. Taxpayer noncompliance is widespread: In nearly half of all 1979 TCMP audits, the auditor recommended tax changes because of apparent noncompliance, and at least one change in an itemized deduction was recommended for 88 percent of taxpayers who itemized.

2. Unreported income accounts for about 75 percent of the amount of individual noncompliance with reporting requirements, overstated subtractions account for about 13 percent, nonfiling for about 10 percent, and arithmetic errors for the remaining 2 percent.

3. Not all noncompliance is in the taxpayer's favor: of taxpayers who misreport income about 12 percent overreport, of those who misreport subtractions about one-third fail to claim all to which they are entitled, among nonfilers about 40 percent have already had enough tax withheld and many would receive refunds if they filed.
4. Most noncompliance involves fairly small amounts: the 1982 TCMP cycle found that 48 percent of all returns had precisely correct reports of taxable income, 70 percent were deemed accurate within $50, and 90 percent within $1,000.

As a compliance measurement device, auditors' recommendations are subject to two kinds of errors. First, TCMP audits detect less than $1 of every $3 of unreported income that is not subject to withholding or third-party information reporting (e.g., Form 1099 for interest and dividends), according to the IRS (1988). Second, they overstate noncompliance that auditors do detect by at least 12 percent, the fraction of recommendations that are reversed on appeal; some potentially successful appeals are presumably not undertaken because of the cost and uncertainty involved.

Tax Administration Strategies and Social Science Research

The IRS pursues four basic strategies for administering tax laws. First, it can pursue deterrence and revenue recovery objectives either by applying resources to detect noncompliance or by designing the taxpaying process to make noncompliance easier to detect. The agency uses labor and computer resources to do such things as audit tax returns, match third-party information reports, and conduct detailed investigations. Tax administrators and legislators can make noncompliance easier to detect by such structural measures as making income more visible through information reports or by raising the minimum threshold (e.g., as a percentage of adjusted gross income) for deducting an expenditure such as medical costs. Previous research clearly demonstrates that structural measures encourage compliance and suggests that audits and computerized examinations of tax returns slightly improve compliance, both by taxpayers who are directly contacted and by those who learn about the experiences of others. But estimates vary of how responsive compliance is to strategies of deterrence and revenue recovery.

Second, lawmakers and the IRS can decrease the taxpayer's cost of compliance by making compliance easier: by simplifying the tax laws, by defining compliance requirements in terms of information that taxpayers may routinely record for other purposes, by simplifying tax forms and instructions, by providing informational publications, by answering telephone inquiries about compliance requirements, and by providing assistance in resolving taxpayers' problems. Research has begun to measure compliance costs, and some preliminary evidence suggests that efforts to reduce compliance costs may encourage compliance somewhat. But there are no firm estimates of how responsive compliance is to these costs or to IRS or congressional efforts to make compliance easier.

Third, the IRS can encourage normative support for compliance, encouraging taxpayers to reframe their compliance decisions in a more positive light—by personalizing the process, by reminding taxpayers of social commitments, or by reminding taxpayers of the tax-supported services they receive, for example. Evidence of the compliance effects of these techniques is too sketchy at present to permit conclusions.

Fourth, some IRS programs may encourage compliance less directly through tax practitioners, who interact with many taxpayers. Over half of all returns each year are affected by lawyers, accountants, and others who prepare returns or offer advice about tax matters. These practitioners review far more returns each year than the IRS does, and they are subject to penalties for helping their clients evade taxes. Yet they are also obligated to interpret arguable positions on behalf of their clients rather than the government. Research evidence is beginning to suggest that practitioners' actions may encourage compliance with straightforward requirements and may discourage compliance with more ambiguous ones. However, the issue is far from settled.

Integrating these four components into a coherent approach to tax administration is difficult, particularly since they must compete for limited resources. Furthermore, pursuit of one strategy (e.g., deterrence through fear of penalties) may inhibit the success of another (e.g., increasing commitment to comply). And some policies are two-edged swords that may encourage compliance by some taxpayers but stimulate noncompliance by others.

Tax administrators are better placed than social scientists to address many of the questions that arise in the course of refining tax administration policy—for example, estimating administrative costs and assessing political constraints. But social science research offers great potential to estimate the compliance effects of policy changes, which administrators usually overlook precisely because they are difficult to measure. Research can also point to characteristics of taxpayers and their environments that are beyond IRS reach but that influence compliance and should therefore be considered in developing policy.

Even though taxpayer compliance research is no more than twenty years old, it has already established rather strong findings about a few factors that affect compliance. Yet knowledge is still limited because of the fragmentation of academic disciplines, the difficulties of measuring compliance and of gaining access to some of the most useful IRS data, and the difficulty of developing theory and designing empirical research that adequately capture many of the institutional realities of taxpaying. The next major section summarizes the major findings from previous research on taxpayer compliance and suggests questions that researchers should address in extending this work. The following section introduces some ideas that have proven useful in understanding other kinds of human behavior and suggests ways to apply them to taxpayer compliance.

Taxpayer Compliance Research: Findings and Prospects

Research to date tends to support tax administrators' long-held conjectures that financial incentives, social sanctions, and moral commitment may all affect taxpayer compliance with reporting requirements. But much more empirical and theoretical work is needed to confirm the existence of these relationships, to measure the strength of their influences on compliance, and to learn how these factors are themselves influenced by taxpayers' environments.

FINANCIAL SELF-INTEREST AND COMPLIANCE

Using both survey research and econometric techniques, many researchers have studied how compliance is affected by several elements of financial self-interest: the probability that a noncompiler will be detected, the penalties for noncompliance, the tax rate structure, and the level of income. The following sections summarize conclusions from research to date and pose questions that would be valuable for scholars to pursue in the future.

DETECTION PROBABILITIES FOR NONCOMPLIERS.   Previous research suggests that:

  1. Income that is more visible to the IRS (e.g., through withholding or information reporting) is likely to be more fully reported than other income.

2. Experiencing an audit may slightly increase future compliance, at least if the audit discovers all unreported taxes and the taxpayer feels the outcome is fair.
3. For at least some classes of taxpayers, higher audit rates in local geographic areas may increase compliance slightly by signaling others that they are vulnerable to audits—a general deterrence or ripple effect stemming from awareness of an IRS audit presence.
4. The IRS succeeds to some extent in concentrating its audit resources on taxpayers who are least compliant.

These findings leave many questions unanswered. Many of the relevant studies are based on data that describe behavior more than fifteen years ago, and so they do not indicate how compliance has changed since then because of refinements in IRS allocation of resources and procedures for detection of noncompliance. The studies rely on audit rates as proxies for the probability that a taxpayer's noncompliance will be detected; but that probability is unknown to both the taxpayer and the IRS, and almost nothing is known about how taxpayers assess detection risks using information they have. Perhaps most important from a policy standpoint, no sound estimates are available of the magnitudes of these effects—of how responsive compliance is to enhanced information reporting, to previous audits, or to changes in audit rates.

Two extensions of existing lines of research can help to fill these gaps in knowledge.

1. Updating the 1969 data base on which most of the conclusions about general deterrence are based, if a more adequate compliance measure can be developed and validated; and
2. Measurements at multiple points in time of taxpayers' perceptions of the risk that noncompliance will be detected, and ethnographic and survey research on how those perceptions form and change in response to changes in financial circumstances, IRS contacts, and other events.

OTHER ELEMENTS OF FINANCIAL SELF-INTEREST.   Research to date provides even less firm conclusions about how other elements of self-interest affect compliance. The panel recommends that existing lines of economic and econometric research in three areas be extended to improve understanding of these relationships.

1. *Noncompliance penalties.* Most studies have failed to demonstrate that higher penalty rates encourage compliance. A few studies have found such an effect, at least when the probability of imposing the penalties exceeds

some minimum threshold level. Research is needed on the level of the threshold compared with the actual probabilities of severe penalties for noncompliers. Recent increases in prescribed penalties and fines present opportunities for before-and-after studies that could clarify how penalties affect compliance.

2. *Tax rates*. Some research suggests that lower tax rates may improve compliance by reducing the rewards for evasion. But other empirical research fails to confirm that effect, and there are sound reasons to doubt this finding. Since the tax structure links the rates to income levels, it is difficult to disentangle tax rate effects from income effects. Analyses of experience before and after the Tax Reform Act of 1986, which changed the tax structure, may lead to more clear-cut conclusions about how changes in tax rates affect compliance.

3. *Income*. Neither theoretical nor empirical findings about the relationship between true income and compliance are at all clear-cut. Achieving more understanding will require analyses of individual-level data on changes in income level and composition, experience with IRS contacts, use of tax practitioners, and compliance. Collecting and analyzing these data over a time period that includes changes in tax rates would make it easier to distinguish income effects on compliance from tax rate effects.

4. *Microeconomic theory*. To design future econometric studies, microeconomic models of compliance should incorporate the multiple roles of tax practitioners and recognize the different costs of compliance and risks of noncompliance detection and punishment that are associated with different return items. Models with these features can address how compliance is affected by the timing of income receipts and tax payments (e.g., through withholding, estimated tax payments, and refunds), and by various costs of compliance and noncompliance. Eventually, these theoretical models may provide a basis for empirical models that distinguish more adequately the contributions of taxpayers, taxing agencies, and tax practitioners to compliance.

SOCIAL SANCTIONS AND COMPLIANCE

A few surveys of self-reported compliance suggest that social sanctions—disapproval by friends and acquaintances—may discourage noncompliance, perhaps even as effectively as legal sanctions for some taxpayers. However, because survey data reflect what respondents tell interviewers rather than actual compliance, they are not sufficient to establish this proposition. Individual-level data over time are needed that link measures of the threat of social sanctions to measures of compliance constructed from tax returns or audit results. There is also a need for research on why members of different groups approve or disapprove of others' noncompliance.

MORAL COMMITMENT AND COMPLIANCE

Not surprisingly, survey research has consistently found that taxpayers who report high moral commitment to obey tax laws are unlikely to report cheating on their taxes. However, it is not clear whether this pattern reflects actual behavior or merely a desire to report behavior that is consistent with one's proclaimed attitudes. Again, survey data alone are not sufficient to establish this proposition. Rather, data are needed that link measures of social commitment to nonsurvey compliance measures.

Studies of how taxpayer compliance and commitment are related to attitudes toward law generally, toward government, toward tax laws, and toward enforcement methods have produced inconsistent results. Research is needed not only on how these attitudes relate to compliance, but also on the experiences and circumstances that shape these attitudes over time.

DEMOGRAPHIC PATTERNS OF COMPLIANCE

Older taxpayers appear to have higher levels of compliance. However, it is not clear whether taxpayers grow more compliant as they age, or whether successive cohorts of taxpayers are becoming less compliant. Distinguishing between aging effects and cohort effects is essential for predicting future compliance levels but requires compliance measures collected over time for individuals whose ages and other relevant characteristics are known.

Compliance rates are higher for women than for men. There is also some evidence that compliance is higher among whites than nonwhites, but the differences are small and depend on details of individual studies.

Expanding the Framework of Compliance Research

Previous compliance research has focused almost exclusively on the four kinds of influences just discussed: financial self-interest, social sanctions, moral commitment, and demographics. But several characteristics of taxpaying and tax administration may also affect compliance and should be more fully recognized in future research.

Tax administration blends the characteristics of criminal and administrative law enforcement. Although criminal punishments are available in certain circumstances, taxpayer noncompliance does not arouse social condemnation of the sort that is triggered by many street crimes, and the victim of noncompliance is diffuse and thus not salient to most taxpayers. The objective circumstances that structure taxpaying arise from two-way interactions between taxpayers and their social environments, particularly their coworkers and others with whom they carry out financial transactions. Taxpayers are only partially informed about their own objective circumstances, including the requirements and costs of compliance and the risks and rewards of noncompliance. Their methods of coping with uncertainty and misinformation may introduce erors into perceptions and decisions, which in turn contribute to noncompliance. Individual taxpayers place different moral values on compliance; these values may be influenced by such factors as childhood socialization to obeying rules, the values of friends and business acquaintances, and taxpayers' personal experiences with the tax system.

These observations point to several kinds of studies that have been underused in previous taxpayer compliance research and that the panel believes should be more widely used by researchers in the future:

1. Laboratory experiments to study how tax returns are affected by the various routines that taxpayers use to cope with the complexity and uncertainty of taxpaying;

2. Ethnographic studies of individuals to learn how they form their understandings of compliance requirements, their perceptions of the financial and social risks and rewards of compliance, and the moral values they place on compliance; and

3. Ethnographic studies of social and occupational networks of individuals to learn how patterns of financial transactions develop that encourage or discourage compliance, how information (and misinformation) about compliance requirements and contacts with tax administrators are communicated, and how values concerning compliance are exchanged.

These three kinds of compliance research are perhaps best carried out by individual scholars with only minimal coordination with tax authorities. In addition, the differences between tax laws and most criminal laws suggest that tax authorities adopt a broader approach to their own research. As a start, there is a need for tax administrators to examine how changes in enforcement methods affect compliance, not merely the revenue yield from enforcement. There is a need to examine how compliance responds to features of the tax system that are influenced by the tax legislators and administrators who construct it and by the lawyers, accountants, and other tax practitioners who help taxpayers interpret and use it. This research will require much closer coordination between researchers, tax administrators, and the other communities.

To illustrate this broader orientation to tax administration research, the panel selected three programs that could produce substantial benefits to tax administration and to the understanding of taxpayer compliance. The three programs concern: (1) responses to changes in tax laws and their administration, with special emphasis on the Tax Reform Act of 1986; (2) tax practitioners and their relationships to taxpayer compliance; and (3) the compliance effects of IRS contacts with taxpayers. There are, of course, other excellent tax administration research opportunities, including ethnographic research in conjunction with programs such as these three.

RESPONSES TO CHANGES IN TAX LAWS AND ADMINISTRATION

By substantially changing the tax structure, the Tax Reform Act of 1986 (TRA86) offers a remarkable opportunity for learning about taxpayers' responses to changes in the incentives that may affect compliance, to efforts to improve the perceived fairness of the tax system, and to legal changes that affect the complexity of compliance requirements. A research program on these matters should contain the following elements:

1. A comparative analysis of individual-level 1985 and 1988 TCMP data, to learn how compliance changed in response to the changes in incentives created by TRA86;
2. A survey of how taxpayers sought information about the changed compliance requirements and how TRA86 affected their use of tax practitioners' services;
3. Survey research to analyze how TRA86 affected perceived fairness of the tax system, combined with a study of how compliance changed in response to changes in perceived fairness; and
4. Organizational studies of how IRS procedures adapted formally and informally to requirements and constraints imposed by TRA86.

The panel recommends that the IRS develop a permanent data collection and analysis capability to take advantage of similar research opportunities that future changes in tax laws and administrative procedures will present.

TAX PRACTITIONERS AND COMPLIANCE

The influence of practitioners on taxpayer compliance has only recently begun to attract broad research attention, and very little is known about their effects on compliance. A research program on this subject should include the following components:

1. Cross-sectional and panel surveys on the motivations, circumstances, and events that affect taxpayers' use of practitioners and their choices of particular practitioners;

2. Research on how different types of practitioners affect compliance, through analyses of individual-level TCMP data, through further organizational studies of practitioners and their interactions with clients, and if the necessary cooperation can be obtained, through analysis of the effects of an "exemplary practitioner" program administered jointly by the IRS and appropriate professional societies; and

3. Experimental studies of how specific practitioner interactions with clients (e.g., a simple probe for unreported income) affect their clients' compliance.

TAXPAYER CONTACTS AND COMPLIANCE

Although taxpayer audits and the annual mailing of tax forms and instructions are perhaps the most visible ways in which the IRS contacts taxpayers, there are others. These include contacts with individuals initiated both by the IRS (e.g., computerized notices of arithmetic errors and other discrepancies, outreach classes, publications) and by taxpayers (e.g., telephoned questions, letters of inquiry, requests for problem resolution). Also included are mass media campaigns to encourage compliance through news articles and advertisements. These contacts may indeed affect compliance, but virtually no measures are available of those effects. To measure the effects of such programs, the IRS should consider adopting a more systematic approach to evaluation and innovation. The panel recommends an approach that involves:

1. Evaluating the compliance effects of current practice using quasi-experimental designs that exploit natural variation over time and across districts in the timing, coverage, and quality of taxpayer contact programs;

2. Using laboratory experiments to design and pretest innovations in taxpayer contacts to remedy problems discovered in evaluations; and

3. Testing promising innovations in contacts using randomized experimental designs in the field wherever possible, to measure compliance effects and revenue yields more accurately.

Various psychological theories suggest some specific tactics for improving the effectiveness of IRS communications. These include personalizing letters by providing a named IRS staff member, reminding taxpayers of instructions that may apply to their particular situations and that may reduce their tax liabilities, and calling attention to compliance motivations that may appeal to taxpayers as good citizens. Besides potentially improving tax administration, laboratory and field experiments involving techniques such as these would provide further tests of the relevant psychological theories.

Data Needs in Taxpayer Compliance Research

Much taxpayer compliance research requires data on large samples of taxpayers, including measures of compliance and of other variables that may help to explain compliance. Suitable data bases have been produced in four ways:

1. The TCMP Survey of Individual Returns Filed, an IRS program conducted every three years, which involves comprehensive audits of random samples of about 50,000 tax returns in each cycle;
2. Taxpayer surveys that collect self-reports of previous compliance and data on relevant taxpayer characteristics and attitudes;
3. Experimentally generated data bases, in which the compliance effects of a randomized treatment are measured as the average difference between the treatment and experimental groups in year-to-year changes in tax return items; and
4. A 1969 aggregate cross-sectional file (IRS Project 778) that contains, for each three-digit zip code area, an estimate of the aggregate compliance level, data on IRS activity, and demographic and socioeconomic characteristics of the area.

Each kind of data has particular strengths but fails in some way to adequately support research on the determinants of taxpayer compliance. To enhance the value of these four data collection approaches, the panel makes six recommendations.

1. *To expand the research uses of TCMP,* we recommend that the IRS consider modifying the TCMP check sheet to include a more detailed description of the preparer who signs the return, information on others whose advice may have affected the return, information on the taxpayer's primary and secondary occupation and industry, and information on the issues underlying changes the auditor recommends on the return.

2. To improve the *timeliness of TCMP data* for all its uses, we recommend that the IRS formally consider restructuring the program from a three-year cycle to an annual or a biennial cycle (with a fraction of the entire sample audited in each year) and search for ways to reduce the three- to four-year delay in file development.

3. To enhance the *value of taxpayer surveys* for reseachers and tax administrators, we recommend that the IRS and others who undertake surveys expand their research focus—to include the relationships between values, perceptions, and compliance; to give greater emphasis to the processes, circumstances, and events that affect the relevant values and perceptions over time; and to provide more resources for the replication of findings.

4. To strengthen the *foundations of survey research* on taxpayer compliance, we recommend a research program to improve the interpretation of self-reports of noncompliance and to ascertain whether and how the specificity and validity of self-reports can be improved through the randomized response technique, innovations in questionnaire design, and repeated interviews.

5. As a possible *basis for more current information* about the general deterrence effects of IRS activity, we recommend that the 1969 aggregate cross-sectional data base (Project 778) be updated and refined if the reliability of the compliance measure can be demonstrated for a more recent year.

6. To provide a *basis for stronger inferences* about the compliance effects of administrative activities, we recommend that the IRS and external researchers increase their use of randomized experiments in both field and laboratory settings.

Taxpayer compliance research, including several projects recommended in this report, raises very difficult questions about how to provide useful knowledge without jeopardizing taxpayer privacy, other generally accepted rights of research subjects, and the IRS mission. To deal with these matters, the panel recommends long-term cooperative efforts—involving the IRS and the broad research community—to deal with three issues:

1. To develop and implement policies governing access by researchers to compliance research data, especially external use of sensitive IRS data.

2. To develop and implement policies to foster compliance research within the IRS that uses the most methodologically sound research techniques, including randomized experiments when needed, to ad-

dress problems in tax administration while protecting research subjects from unfair burdens and risks.

3. To formally and thoroughly consider the feasibility and desirability of arranging for the deposit of sensitive IRS data in an independent secure repository.

A standing authority should be established to interpret and monitor these policies and arrangements in light of evolving research ideas, changes in compliance requirements and forms of noncompliance, innovations in tax administration, and advances in statistical matching techniques. Additional resources should also be provided for the IRS Research Division to continue and expand its technical effort to support external researchers' use of IRS data bases through public-use files or special tabulations.

A Look Ahead

Much has been learned in twenty years of taxpayer compliance research—but much remains to be learned that is of intellectual and policy interest. The understanding of taxpayer compliance can best be advanced through the involvement of an intellectually exciting community of researchers that extends across the tax professions and social sciences. While such a community has already begun to form, its growth can best be encouraged by a diverse array of organizations—including private foundations, federal research sponsors, and the tax policy community, as well as the Internal Revenue Service.

The IRS can continue its major role in compliance research by improving the research potential of its data bases, facilitating expanded research use of its data, integrating research and evaluation more fully into its policy deliberations, and strengthening the infrastructure that supports the research community.

To assist the IRS in these efforts and to provide a structure for sustained communication with the research community, we recommend that it form and regularly convene a Compliance Research Advisory Group that brings external experts in taxpayer compliance research together with agency administrators to regularly review research priorities and revise them as conditions change. Consideration should also be given to the possible need for new organizational arrangements to strengthen and broaden the compliance research community. These arrangements might include a center for compliance research, a consortium of sponsors supporting a range of activities, or a looser federation of cooperating institutions. It is essential, of course, that any such organization not divert significant resources from original research, and that it serve to complement and facilitate the work of individual researchers, existing tax research centers, and established data centers.

1. Paying Taxes

This report is concerned with why people comply with federal income tax reporting requirements—a question of both intellectual and policy interest. Policy interest has grown dramatically in the last decade, in an environment of large budget deficits, reluctance to raise taxes, and the discovery of a large "underground economy" and other forms of noncompliance. The Internal Revenue Service estimates that for 1986 the "tax gap" arising from individuals' failure to report federal income taxes due was $70 billion— about 40 percent of the federal deficit (IRS, 1988). Noncompliance with other federal income tax requirements—by corporations, by those who receive illegal income, and by those who fail to remit taxes due, for example—probably pushed the total tax gap above $100 billion.

Noncompliance of this magnitude raises important issues of equity between citizens who pay their taxes fully and those who do not. For some, it also raises questions about the future viability of the primary system for supporting federal services. In recent years the IRS and other institutions in the tax policy community—other units within the Department of the Treasury, the tax committees of Congress, the General Accounting Office (GAO), the Tax Section of the American Bar Association (ABA), and the American Institute of Certified Public Accountants (AICPA)—have all undertaken projects concerned with improving compliance. At least one 1988 presidential candidate highlighted improved compliance as a means of reducing the federal deficit.

This rising tide of concern contributed to the passage of statutes in 1981, 1982, and 1984 that were intended to strengthen tax law enforcement and culminated in the Tax Reform Act of 1986. These legislative initiatives sought to improve compliance through a variety of tools: new and increased penalties for various forms of noncompliance, expanded requirements for information reporting to the IRS (e.g., reporting of interest and dividends by banks and brokerage firms), new restrictions on tax shelters, and changes in compliance requirements that removed some taxpayers from the tax rolls and reduced the number who could benefit from itemizing deductions. To improve its ability to cope with noncompliance, the IRS has initiated administrative innovations on a variety of fronts: the use of computers to compare reports of transactions on tax returns with information reports, simplification of forms, and refinement of the statistical algorithms used to select returns for audit. The implicit rationale for this legislative and administrative activity seems to be that simplicity, equity, and fairness of the tax code, combined with efficient but unobtrusive enforcement,[1] are keys to improving taxpayer compliance (see Dubin, Graetz, and Wilde, 1987c; Steuerle, 1986; and Scholz, Vol. 2, for more complete discussions of trends in tax administration).

For the scholar, understanding the broad range of behaviors involved in taxpayer compliance requires the intellectual tools of many social science disciplines and provides ample empirical material for applying the most recent scientific advances and for challenging current paradigms. Researchers in different disciplines have attempted to understand taxpaying in different ways. Sociologists and anthropologists have studied questions about compliance effects of social status, communication of experiences and values through social networks, the cultural environment of taxpayers, and the structure of financial transactions. Economists understand taxpayers' compliance behavior to reflect a calculus comparing the expected benefits of evasion with the expected costs, including the possibility of being punished. Social psychologists focus on social norms in trying to account for changes in compliance. Paying taxes imposes complex decision-making demands on taxpayers, and psychologists have raised questions about systematic biases in taxpaying arising from the decision-making shortcuts that individuals use in uncertain, complex situations.

This array of influences on taxpayer compliance illustrates both the wealth of topics that researchers from many disciplines could investigate and the potential value of applying knowledge from all these disciplines to tax policy and administration problems. Current interest in taxpayer compliance, especially individuals' compliance with federal income tax laws, has already stimulated a large number of academic studies, several multidisciplinary literature reviews, and some broader research programs. The IRS, the ABA, the Arthur Young Foundation, and other organizations have indicated their commitments to encourage compliance research by sponsoring research projects, by organizing seminars that bring together the academic and tax policy communities, and by facilitating the use of sensitive or unwieldy data sets. Recognizing the richness of taxpaying as a domain for building and testing theories of human behavior, the National Science Foundation has begun sponsoring independent research on the topic.

Until recently, research on taxpayer compliance has been hampered by unduly narrow disciplinary and methodological boundaries, by researchers' ignorance about the institutions of taxpaying and tax administration, and by restrictions on access to the rich data resources within the IRS. Consequently the body of compliance research has only recently begun to grow rapidly, to integrate insights drawn from practical experience and diverse theories and methodologies, and to address the questions of tax administrators with some understanding of their current problems and response options. As interest in the issue grows, the time is opportune for tax administrators and policy makers, researchers, and research sponsors to discuss what is already known and what future research directions are likely to produce further knowledge and insights that may help to improve tax administration. This report is intended to contribute to that discussion.

Scope of the Panel's Inquiry

The Panel on Taxpayer Compliance Research was convened in response to an IRS request to the National Academy of Sciences to synthesize existing knowledge about influences on taxpayer compliance and to recommend future research that offers the prospect of augmenting that knowledge base. The scope of the panel's report is, of course, shaped by both the nature of the request and the state of existing research.

Although taxpayers and noncompliance come in many varieties, published research and working papers have examined only some of them. Published hypotheses about taxpayer compliance are nearly all grounded in theories of the behavior of individuals—as maximizers of their own self-interest under uncertainty, or members of social groups, or actors in an environment that structures their financial transactions—rather than corporations, partnerships, and other enterprises. When compliance researchers make any explicit assumption about the tax base, they usually consider income taxes rather than sales, excise, personal property, payroll, or other taxes. Of the three major noncompliance categories—failing to *file* the return, failing to *report* tax liability accurately on the return, and failing to *remit* taxes owed—most theoretical work has focused on the reporting of tax liability. To the panel's knowledge, no models consider explicitly how compliance with income tax laws is affected by the legality or illegality of the income being taxed.

In published empirical research, all taxpayer surveys known to the panel concern individual rather than organizational taxpayers, and most of them differentiate between nonfiling, inaccurate reporting, and nonremittance. But, with only a few exceptions, available nonsurvey data permit analyses of compliance only with requirements for accurate reporting of tax liability on filed returns, not with filing or remittance requirements. With a few exceptions that deal with state taxes (e.g., Groves, 1958; Mason and Calvin, 1978, 1984; Klepper and Nagin, 1987b), most empirical research on taxpayer compliance is concerned with the federal income tax.

In short, most existing taxpayer compliance research is concerned with accurate reporting of tax liability on legally earned income by individual filers of federal income tax returns. The panel therefore focused primarily but not exclusively on that subject.

It would of course be of interest to develop theoretical models of return filing and tax remittance and to generalize the models of reporting described there to other tax structures and to organizational taxpayers. In virtually all cases, it is an open and interesting question whether the findings we report apply to compliance in these other contexts. But in developing explicit research recommendations, the panel concentrated on extending existing lines of research and studying the effects of other related but understudied influences—changes in compliance requirements, the effects of tax practitioners, and the psychological framing of compliance requirements—on individual reporting of federal income tax liability. This choice reflects the interests and expertise of the panel members, as well as the relative magnitudes involved. Because of differences in the taxable income involved, the tax gap due to individual underreporting of tax liability on legal income is estimated to be about seven times the gap associated with illegal income, ten times the tax remittance gap, eleven times the corporate noncompliance gap, and twenty-three times the gap associated with individuals' failure to file returns (IRS, 1983f). Nevertheless, the panel strongly supports theoretical and empirical research on taxpayer compliance in these other contexts.

In reviewing and synthesizing previous research, the panel attempted to consider all theoretical and empirical research on taxpayer compliance that had been published in the United States by the end of 1987. It also commissioned a number of papers on special topics related to taxpayer compliance: two methodological papers are included as appendices to this volume, and eight others appear in a separate volume. In addition, the panel considered a number of other documents that came to its attention, including unpublished working papers and conference presentations on taxpayer compliance, pertinent published literature from other fields, internal IRS memoranda, and foreign research literature on taxpayer compliance. While our reviews of these other categories are by no means comprehensive, pertinent items from them are cited throughout this report.

Defining Compliance

Accurate reporting of tax liability can be treated as having four components: (1) accurate reporting of income subject to tax; (2) accurate claims of subtractions such as income adjustments, itemized deductions, exemptions, and tax credits; (3) timely filing of tax returns; and (4) correct computation of tax liability. Thus, unlike compliance with many criminal laws, which require only that individuals refrain from certain proscribed activities, compliance with reporting requirements requires a series of actions that may involve substantial effort, reading and computational skill, and judgment. For this reason, noncompliance may occur in a variety of ways and for a variety of reasons other than a deliberate decision to understate tax liablity.

This variety complicates the problem of defining noncompliance in either behavioral or legal terms. In Volume 2, Kidder and McEwen define a typology of noncompliance that attempts to illuminate the different forms of behavior involved. Their definitional scheme includes such terms as *procedural noncompliance* (e.g., a failure to observe some detail of filing rules that may or may not affect the accuracy of the report) and *lazy evasion* (e.g., an underreport of tip income that may be deliberate but is motivated more by the effort required to record taxable income accurately than by a calculated intention to evade taxes).

The Internal Revenue Code defines a legal taxonomy of noncompliance by distinguishing between evasion—the criminal offense of willfully attempting to escape tax liability (26 U.S.C. 7201)—and negligence—failure to make a reasonable effort to comply (26 U.S.C. 6653).[2] But, as noted by the American Bar Association's Commission on Taxpayer Compliance (American Bar Association, 1987) and by Smith (1986), the boundaries are fuzzy between evasion, negligence, and legal but controversial positions that reduce tax liability. The fuzziness arises because even neutral, fully informed experts sometimes disagree about what the compliance requirements are in a particular situation. This potential for disagreement is reflected in the use of such terms as *substantial authority* and *reasonable basis* in regulations that are intended to define the boundaries.

Thus, both behavioral and legal definitions of noncompliance invoke assumptions about taxpayers' motivations. Discovering the nature of these motivations is precisely the task that compliance researchers undertake, and it is extraordinarily difficult. Consequently, the panel found it more straightforward to adopt a compliance definition that minimizes the role of required assumptions and to define noncompliance as any departure from that standard, regardless of the explanation. Therefore, in this report:

> *Compliance* with reporting requirements means that the taxpayer files all required tax returns at the proper time and that the returns accurately report tax liability in accordance with the Internal Revenue Code, regulations, and court decisions applicable at the time the return is filed.

When the taxpayer's return reports a tax liability less than the accurate amount, we use the term *underreporting*. Similarly, we use the term *overreporting* when the taxpayer reports a liability greater than required. Underreporting and overreporting are both forms of *noncompliance,* as the panel uses the term.[3] Under this definition, *misclassifications,* in which the taxpayer uses the wrong return item to report a transaction but the error does not affect the reported tax liability, are treated as compliant rather than noncompliant.

Choice of this definition does not deny the broad range of phenomena that may lead a taxpayer to report income tax liability incorrectly. For some taxpayers, failure to comply results from a willful act of tax evasion. For others, noncompliance may result from ignorance of tax laws or from simple mistakes in following instructions on the tax forms or in calculating taxes. Between these two extremes, noncompliance may be due to misinformation or misunderstandings about the tax laws. Taxpayers obtain misinformation from such sources as friends, acquaintances with whom they deal financially, tax preparers or advisers, and IRS staff who respond to telephone inquiries. Misunderstandings may reflect inattention, lack of interest, or acceptance of conventional wisdom about compliance requirements within a taxpayer's network of acquaintances; they may persist despite a sincere effort to find the appropriate interpretation of a confusing issue. Some misunderstanding undoubtedly reflects a willingness, sometimes to the point of negligence, to assert aggressive interpretations of the tax law that may reduce the taxpayer's tax liability, whether or not they are based on a reliable authority. Thus, willfulness, aggressiveness, carelessness, ignorance, good-faith reliance on misinformation, and acceptance of acquaintances' judgments are all of interest as possible explanations of failures to comply—but we have excluded these judgments about the intentions and psychic state of the taxpayer from the definition of compliance.

Although this definition of compliance avoids the difficulties associated with inferences about taxpayers' states of mind, it cannot escape the problem of ambiguity, which may arise when neither statutory nor case law has anticipated a particular set of circumstances. In that situation, the law does not precisely define compliance requirements, and even fully informed neutral experts may disagree about how the law should be applied. When it is necessary to designate taxpayers' reports that fall within this range of disagreement, we refer to them as *ambiguous*. For the most part, however, the panel treats ambiguous reports as compliant reports.

Ambiguous cases create a fuzzy boundary between (noncompliant) underreporting and (compliant) reduction of tax liability. The term *tax reduction* is used to mean compliant behavior that reduces one's tax in a way that may be unintended by tax legislators but is permissible under the statute. It is accomplished by structuring transactions so as to minimize tax liability within the limits of the law and is legally permissible even in cases that may be morally objectionable to some people (for example, when wealthy individuals carry out advantageous transactions that produce no tax liability). Aggressive tax reduction may rely on currently unestablished legal interpretations that vary in their plausibility and possibility of being accepted by the courts.

Beyond the limits of ambiguity, favorable interpretations that are asserted by taxpayers without a legal basis constitute noncompliance. In filing noncompliant reports, taxpayers may simply neglect to ascertain requirements. Or they may deliberately assert specious legal arguments or assert that ambiguity exists to disguise intent. If the underreporting is legally proven to be intentional, it constitutes tax evasion, a criminal offense.

Although the panel did not treat ambiguous reports as noncompliant, there are several ways in which ambiguity may aggravate noncompliance. Exploitation of ambiguity and assertions of ambiguity by high-income, well-informed taxpayers may stimulate resentment and noncompliance by other taxpayers. The existence of ambiguity may encourage some taxpayers to use specious legal arguments in an attempt to claim that an unsupportable interpretation of compliance requirements lies within the range of ambiguity. Legislators or tax administrators, in attempting to reduce ambiguity, may increase the complexity of legislation or regulations through requirements that increase the volume of record keeping, the burden of computations, the difficulty of interpreting regulations, or the difficulty of imputing values in noncash transactions. The increased complexity may aggravate noncompliance. One indicator that complexity may affect compliance is the fact that substantial fractions of noncompliers overreport rather than underreport their tax liabilities. It seems likely that at least some of the overreporting is due to errors that result from complexity.

Even this brief explanation of the compliance definition adopted by the panel has hinted at the broad array of attributes—of taxpayers, of their financial and social environments, and of the federal income tax and its administration—that may affect compliance. Distinguishing knowledge about those relationships from suppositions was the panel's task. Before proceeding to that discussion, however, it is useful to describe what little is known about the extent of compliance and to summarize the administrative techniques that the IRS uses to administer the tax laws.

The Extent of Compliance

The extent of taxpayer compliance is known very imperfectly. Because noncompliance cannot be directly observed, its magnitude must be inferred, usually through analyses of taxpayer audit results, discrepancies in official economic statistics, and specially collected data, such as surveys of tipping practices. The necessary data are expensive to collect, and assumptions are needed to derive the compliance estimates. Because of these difficulties, estimates are prepared infrequently and are also imprecise and controversial. The panel's primary concern was with understanding compliance rather than measuring it. Therefore, we did not critically review the available estimates, and our recommendations in Chapter 5 concerning compliance measurement address the quality of individual-level compliance measurement, for research purposes, not the accuracy of measures of the aggregate tax gap due to noncompliance. Nevertheless, while imprecision and controversy surround the aggregate estimates, it is useful to summarize them in this section as a context for our report. A more complete discussion appears in Supplementary Note A to this chapter.

Taxpayer audits are a basic source for many compliance estimates, especially those that attempt to describe noncompliance patterns rather than merely totals. Under its Taxpayer Compliance Measurement Program (TCMP), the IRS regularly audits samples of taxpayers and uses discrepancies between taxpayers' reports and the TCMP auditors' assessments as a measure of noncompliance. This measure is used both in developing statistical rules for selecting tax returns for audit and in producing aggregate noncompliance estimates. The TCMP program is described more fully in Supplementary Note B to this chapter.

Even though TCMP audits are conducted with special care and are generally acknowledged to provide the most accurate estimates available, auditor-taxpayer discrepancies—or recommended changes—measure noncompliance only imperfectly. Auditors fail to detect an unknown fraction of unreported tax liability, especially tax due on casual income that is not reported to the IRS by the income sources themselves through withholding and information reporting, such as on forms W-2 and 1099. For tax year 1976, the IRS (1983f, 1988) has estimated that for every $1 of unreported casual income that it detected, more than $3 of casual income was actually unreported. But there is controversy over that estimate, and the fraction should have decreased since then because of administrative improvements. Auditors also sometimes overassess tax liability, through error or because they interpret an apparently ambiguous report differently from the taxpayer. According to the IRS (1988), about 12 percent of the tax assessments by auditors are successfully challenged on appeal. But that correction misses auditors' overassessments that are not appealed because of the associated cost and uncertainty.

Interest outside the government in measuring noncompliance first became apparent during the 1970s, when estimates appeared of an underground economy that involved several hundred billion dollars of unreported economic activity annually (Feige, 1979, 1980; Gutmann, 1977; see Henry, 1983, for a detailed comparative history of aggregate compliance measurement). Even if these estimates are accurate, they would dramatically overstate unreported taxable personal income because they fail to subtract legitimate deductions. Most of the estimates of unreported taxable personal income for 1976, one commonly used reference year, cluster between $75 and $100 billion (see Supplementary Note A, Table 1). However, the IRS (1983f) estimate was $118 billion for that year, and others offer even higher estimates.

For this report, the more pertinent concept is the individual income tax reporting gap, that is, the federal income tax liability that is not reported on timely filed tax returns. The IRS (1979b, 1983f, 1988) has published three sets of estimates of this figure, using successively more refined data and methods, that have led to lower estimates. The 1988 estimates were $26.3 billion for 1976, $46.3 billion for 1982, and $70.1 billion for 1986, after appeals (successful appeals reduced the estimate based on auditors' assessments by about 12 percent). In each year about 90 percent of the gap was attributable to discrepancies on filed returns and about 10 percent to nonfilers. These estimates are somewhat lower than earlier (IRS, 1983f) estimates, which are reported in Supplementary Note A, Table 2. While none of the figures should be considered very precise, they suggest that at least 80 percent of estimated true tax liability is being reported by taxpayers on timely returns. Nevertheless, the tax gap due to noncompliance involves substantial sums.

For understanding compliance and developing policies to improve it, it is useful to know how widespread noncompliance is. One such measure is the prevalence of noncompliers—the fraction of taxpayers who fail to comply—according to the panel's definition. Prevalence has been estimated based on TCMP audit results and on surveys in which taxpayers are asked to report their own noncompliance in previous years.

On the basis of 1979 TCMP audits, noncompliance is believed to be quite widespread (Supplementary Note A, Table 3). Nearly half of all TCMP audits found discrepancies or changes in taxpayers' reports of income items, with underreports exceeding overreports by a factor of 7 to 1. Fewer returns had changes in subtraction items—only 7 percent of all returns had changes in adjustment items, such as employee business expenses, and 25 percent in itemized deductions. But those rates do not reflect the fact that income items are reported on virtually all returns, while adjustments or itemized deductions are used on only some returns. As a fraction of only the returns using these items, the noncomplier prevalence rates are over 50 percent for adjustment items, and 88 percent for deductions. For subtraction items, changes that lead to underreports of taxable income exceed overreports by a factor of only 2 or 3 to 1.[4]

In addition, for 1979 fewer than 6 percent of all households failed to file required returns according to the IRS (Supplementary Note A, Table 3). Of these, nearly one-third would have either received a refund or had no balance due if they had filed as required. In short, all three elements of noncompliance—involving income items, subtraction items, and filing itself—sometimes injure the taxpayer rather than the government, suggesting that errors and oversights may help to account for the behavior.

According to taxpayer surveys, only 12–22 percent of respondents acknowledge ever underreporting income, and 5–25 percent acknowledge "overstating deductions," the usual survey wording for reducing tax liability by overreporting subtraction items (Supplementary Note A, Table 5). As one might expect, these are low compared with estimates based on audits—especially considering that the audits relate to only one tax year as a reference period, while the surveys use much longer reference periods, usually "ever" or "within the past five years." The lower values are to be expected, of course, because respondents acknowledge only instances of noncompliance that they recognize, recall at the time of the interview, and are willing to reveal to an interviewer. Most surveys that use special techniques (e.g., randomized response and locked-box approaches) to reduce respondents' sensitivity to the question by preserving their anonymity report higher prevalence estimates than other surveys.

Compliance measurement through audits permits analyses that are more detailed in terms of both dollar amounts and the return items on which noncompliance occurs. For example, Supplementary Note A presents tabulations of the 1982 TCMP data performed for the panel, demonstrating that most cases of noncompliance concern fairly small dollar amounts (Table 6). While only 48 percent reported the total of their income items exactly correctly according to TCMP auditors, 70 percent reported within $50 of the auditor's assessment and 90 percent reported accurately within $1,000. This pattern is even more striking with respect to deductions: while only 8 percent of taxpayers who itemized deductions calculated them precisely according to the auditor, 52 percent were within $50 and 85 percent were within $1,000.

Those tabulations also make clear that compliance depends on the structure of tax return items. The visibility of income to the IRS through withholding and information reporting has a substantial effect. While 95 percent of all taxpayers correctly reported their wages and salaries subject to withholding, only 70 percent reported all dividends (which are subject only to information reporting), and only 47 percent reported all tips. Easy access to records also seems to encourage compliance, which is better for mortgage interest paid to financial institutions (which usually provide annual summary reports) than for mortgage interest paid to individuals (who frequently do not).

Possible effects of ambiguity and complexity on compliance are also suggested by statistics on the underreporting and overreporting of particular return items (Supplementary Note A, Table 6). Compliance is less prevalent for return items that involve burdensome record keeping and interpretations of complex rules than for other items that are similar in terms of visibility to the IRS and access to records. For example, underreporting is somewhat more common for Schedule E income (rent, trusts, royalties, other) than for capital gains, but so is overreporting. These and other return item patterns are generally consistent with those that appear for the voluntary reporting percentage (VRP)—an estimate of the fraction of dollars being accurately reported rather than the fraction of filers who are accurately reporting (Table 6). Additional compliance patterns are described in Supplementary Note A.

Tax Administration and Taxpayer Compliance

In defining compliance and describing its magnitude in the preceding two sections, it was useful to introduce concepts that have meaning only in the context of a system of tax administration. These concepts include the visibility of income to the IRS and the complexity and ambiguity of compliance requirements. The need for such concepts illustrates that taxpayer compliance cannot be understood without being related to the system of tax administration. As factors that help to define compliance, they also draw attention to tools of tax administration, such as third-party information reporting of income and simplification of compliance requirements, which can be expected to affect levels of taxpayer compliance. Because the tax administration system is so important in understanding and influencing taxpayer compliance, it is useful to describe that system in more detail before proceeding further.

IRS activities could be classified in a number of ways. Instead of grouping administrative programs by organizational units, in this discussion we group them by compliance strategies: (1) increasing the probability that noncompliance will be detected, either by changing the tax structure so as to make noncompliance more visible or by increasing the resources devoted to detecting and penalizing noncompliance; (2) decreasing the costs of compliance; (3) encouraging compliance through public communications; and (4) regulating tax practitioners. The section concludes with brief discussions of the activities of the IRS Research Division and the role of research in developing policies for increasing compliance.

INCREASING THE PROBABILITY OF DETECTION
One way to encourage compliance is to increase the probability that noncompliance will be detected and penalized. This can be done in two ways: by structuring taxpaying so as to make noncompliance more visible to authorities and by devoting more resources to detecting noncompliance.

INCREASING THE VISIBILITY OF NONCOMPLIANCE. If all the information needed to correctly calculate an individual's taxes were readily available to the IRS, noncompliers would face an enormous risk of getting caught. Indeed, the availability of such information would obviate the need for taxpayers to file tax returns, and, in such a formless society, compliance with reporting requirements would be automatic. Although society is far from formless for all taxpayers, the system of reporting that has been developed since withholding requirements on wages were enacted in 1942 has brought us close to that goal for the nearly 20 percent of all taxpayers who file short forms (IRS, 1987). The income tax due on wages is subject to withholding by employers. Information reports are filed by third parties for such income as interest and dividends from stocks and bonds, state income tax refunds, miscellaneous income such as employer-paid moving expenses, fellowships and royalties, and payments to independent contractors involving more than $500. Information reports are also required for certain subtraction items, such as the adjustment for contributions to individual retirement accounts (IRAs).

In the current system of tax filing, a computerized Information Reporting Program (IRP) uses the third-party information reports to verify corresponding items on taxpayers' returns. The IRS received over 900 million information reports in its 1987 information returns program. The 1987 IRP generated 2.2 million notices of potential discrepancy between information documents and taxpayers' returns, and another 2.5 million taxpayers were sent notices of apparent failure to file tax returns. These figures reflect the importance of the programs but overstate the extent of noncompliance they discover, since some of the discrepancies that trigger notices are due to errors on information returns or to taxpayers' misclassifications that do not affect tax liability.

In the narrowest sense, IRP is clearly cost effective, since the cost of mailing the computerized notices is low compared with the expected revenue returned in response to them. Through general deterrence, IRP may also encourage compliance by other, unnotified taxpayers who hear about IRP notices from acquaintances who receive them. However, there are possible secondary consequences that make the outcome less clear. Taxpayers who receive erroneous notices may become resentful and therefore make less effort to comply in the future. Also, some taxpayers will ignore their notices or will dispute the alleged discrepancies, thereby confronting the IRS with the need to decide whether to begin more extensive follow-up procedures. Failure to follow up may cause taxpayers to lower their estimates of the probability that noncompliance will be pursued and penalized. Their revisions may encourage future noncompliance, by both them and their acquaintances who may hear about the experience.

For these reasons, an IRS follow-up decision that is based solely on a comparison between cost and expected direct revenue yield will ignore large and potentially counterproductive effects on future compliance. But even though estimates of these compliance effects could be obtained through fairly straightforward applications of standard methods, the necessary research has not yet been undertaken.

The effectiveness of IRP depends on the quality of information reported to the IRS. Thus, compliance with information-reporting requirements by income sources such as banks is an important part of the program. The 1981 and 1982 tax acts increased IRS authority to gain compliance with information-reporting requirements. In 1984, a Payer Master File was established to track information reporters; it identified 50,000 who apparently stopped reporting some type of information. Better understanding of this group might be valuable in encouraging compliance efficiently: there are fewer information reporters than taxpayers, they frequently have incentives to keep track of the requested information as the basis for claiming a business expense, and, for many of them, payments to others leave more visible audit trails than most taxpayer transactions. These possibilities are considered by Kagan (Vol. 2).

The visibility of noncompliance can also be increased in other ways. The 1982 Tax Enforcement and Fiscal Responsibility Act (TEFRA) increased the visibility of tip income, a known area of low compliance, by requiring that restaurant owners report 8 percent of their gross receipts as a proxy for the actual tip income received by their employees. Tax forms now require that taxpayers seeking deductions for alimony payments and interest payments to individuals must report those individuals' identities; the receivers' returns can be checked to ensure that payments were reported. Computer match programs also keep track of items that are limited over taxpayers' lifetimes, such as the one-time exclusion of gain on a residence or the maximum residential energy credit for home improvements. Other less direct strategies to increase the visibility of transactions, such as discouraging the use of cash transactions, may be feasible but are not being seriously considered for tax administration purposes at this time (see Feffer et al., 1983; Kagan, Vol. 2).

The strategy of making noncompliance more visible is pursued somewhat differently in the case of subtractions from income, such as adjustments for professional expenses or deductions of medical expenses. Unlike some income-producing transactions, these transactions are always visible to the IRS because they are reported on the tax return. But verifying their compliance status requires revenue agents to examine the taxpayer's documentation. Because these examinations are costly to the IRS and to taxpayers, they are frequently not undertaken unless a large subtraction arouses concern. Therefore, the compliance status of many small transactions remains invisible to the IRS. By raising the fraction of income that items such as medical expenditures must exceed before they can be subtracted, the Tax Reform Act of 1986 made it cost effective for the IRS to examine a larger fraction of these subtractions. Therefore, their compliance status became more visible, on average, to the IRS.

INCREASING RESOURCES FOR NONCOMPLIANCE DETECTION.   The most costly and familiar enforcement function of the IRS is the examination, or audit, of tax returns. More than one-third of the IRS budget is used for this function, which involves over 16,000 revenue agents who handle complex corporate and individual returns and 3,100 tax auditors who conduct taxpayer audits in IRS offices (IRS, 1987). The percentage of returns audited has dropped steadily over the last decade. In 1987, about 1,100,000 individual returns were audited, only 1.09 percent of the individual returns filed. This represents a drop from 2.3 percent in 1975 (see IRS, 1975). High-income returns are audited at higher rates: 1.4 percent of taxpayers with total positive income in the $25,000–50,000 range, 2.2 percent of those with income over $50,000, and nearly 4 percent of those with income over $100,000 who file Schedule C were audited in 1987. In addition, a statistical Discriminant Index Function (DIF) is used to score all returns with an indicator of the potential yield from audit (see Supplementary Note B for further explanation of the DIF system).

Although the fraction of returns examined has decreased in recent years, use of the DIF system has clearly improved the IRS's ability to select the returns for which audits are most likely to result in tax changes. Together with improved auditing techniques, the improved selectivity has also increased the average revenue yielded per audit. In 1975, 81 percent of revenue agent and 76 percent of tax auditor audits resulted in tax changes; audits by revenue agents yielded an average of $2,584 in recommended tax change and penalty, and audits by tax auditors yielded an average of $220. In 1987, 88 percent of revenue agent and 86 percent of tax auditor audits resulted in tax changes, with an average tax change and penalty of $5,922 for revenue agents and $1,020 for tax auditors (IRS, 1987, Table 8, adjusted to 1975 dollars).

But the revenue yield from audits is only part of the story. Their yield amounts to only a small fraction of the noncompliance tax gap, and there are limits to the extent that this fraction can be increased. As explained more fully in Supplementary Note A, the IRS (1986b, Table 2) estimates that audits and IRP matches of individual taxpayers together yielded $3.2 billion in additional taxes and penalties on individual returns for 1985—about 5 percent of the amount underreported by return filers. The same report also estimates that only about $28 billion—about 31 percent of the individual noncompliance tax gap including nonremittance—could be recovered through all IRS enforcement programs combined, even if they were increased to the extent possible without incurring marginal costs in excess of their marginal revenue yield. As explained by John Scholz (Vol. 2), the IRS has found it impossible to augment its budget sufficiently to achieve this economically feasible limit.

The limited ability of the IRS to recover revenue lost to noncompliance suggests why it should be concerned with maintaining and increasing the compliance that occurs without agency follow-up—"voluntary compliance," in the agency's terminology. Taxpayer contacts through IRP notices and audits potentially improve compliance by informing taxpayers of compliance requirements and by increasing their concern about the penalties associated with noncompliance. Taxpayers who are suspected of noncompliance face the penalty of lost time and other costs associated with the audit itself. Taxpayers whom the IRS determines to be noncompliant may receive civil negligence penalties of 5 percent of the underreported tax or, more rarely, civil fraud penalties of 75 percent plus half the interest due (26 U.S.C. 6653). For reasons that will become clearer in Chapter 2, little is known about the extent to which audits encourage compliance, either by informing taxpayers or by stimulating fear of these penalties.

In addition to routine examinations, the IRS has established special programs that use other investigatory techniques to focus on taxpayers in known problem areas, such as construction contractors specializing in home improvements and recipients of tip income. These programs led to the examination of over 26,000 returns and assessed almost $140 million in additional taxes in 1985 (IRS, 1986a). Other recent special programs involving individual tax returns have focused on those who have purchased tax shelters deemed abusive by the IRS (141,000 examinations in 1985 produced $2.5 billion), tax protesters, and those who overclaim exemptions on W-4 forms.

Criminal penalties for evasion and other tax offenses, which are sought and imposed very rarely, serve two primary purposes. One, carried out under the General Enforcement Program, is to publicly condemn tax evasion and deter it by punishing the most egregious offenders. The second, carried out under the Special Enforcement Program, is primarily to augment the punishment and investigative capability available with regard to an offender who is charged with another federal crime, by adding tax evasion as a secondary charge. Criminal penalties, unlike the civil penalties imposed by the IRS, require a court conviction and involve other institutions, primarily the U.S. Department of Justice. They also usually require extensive preindictment investigations, which are carried out by the IRS Criminal Investigation Division. These costs keep the annual number of criminal sentences for Internal Revenue Code violations quite small— 1,515 cases excluding narcotics-related issues in 1985.

The Criminal Investigation Division sometimes undertakes special projects, investigating groups of persons who are suspected of similar evasive activity (e.g., fraudulent refund claims by prisoners, failure by banks to file reports of large cash transactions, understatement of cash receipts by catfish farmers). On the basis of case studies of several such investigations (IRS, 1978b), the division concluded that the widely publicized arrests, indictments, trials, and convictions that followed these investigations appeared to produce at least temporary decreases in levels of these activities. Recently the Criminal Investigation Division, reflecting general IRS policy, has focused on cases involving illegal tax protesters (302 convictions) and fraudulent tax shelters (55 convictions). To date, the heavy requirements for investigative and prosecutorial resources have constrained criminal prosecutions for use as a narrowly focused deterrence weapon. Considerable research would be needed to learn whether public information about criminal investigations and prosecutions encourages compliance by taxpayers who are unlikely to become targets of such efforts.

Decreasing the Costs of Compliance

A number of IRS activities are aimed at decreasing the costs imposed on taxpayers in determining and reporting tax liability. The IRS expects lower cost to decrease the likelihood that taxpayers will simply fail to file or fail to report a particular item because of the complexity involved. The IRS tries to reduce compliance cost by simplifying tax forms and instructions, by providing publications and telephone-answering services, and by offering personal help to assist in filing and to resolve problems taxpayers may encounter in dealing with the IRS. There are no reliable estimates of how these activities affect compliance.

The Tax Forms and Publication Division of the IRS aims to develop forms that are simple and likely to lead to accurate calculations. The development of the simplified 1040EZ form is only one of many changes made to simplify forms during the past decade. As part of this program, comments about forms are encouraged through hearings and requests to affected groups and tax practitioners. Procedures for field testing hypothetical problems on sample audiences have been developed recently. The success of simplification efforts is limited by annual deadlines for incorporating the large number of changes imposed by amendments to the tax code: 200 of the division's 375 forms are revised on an annual basis (IRS, 1985b:23). In addition to this time pressure, a tax form coordinating committee must approve all changes. Representatives from other divisions on the committee are usually more concerned with other enforcement aspects of the form, such as accuracy of interpretation or the usefulness of the information requested for enforcement. Other efforts to simplify filing requirements include research into a magnetic tape filing system, which would reduce the number of individuals required to file returns on paper.

The Taxpayer Services Division provides assistance to the public about the requirements of the tax law and about the status of a taxpayer's account. During 1987, the IRS responded to about 54 million calls, including nearly 11 million handled by a recently installed system of recorded messages (IRS, 1987). An internal probe found an overall accuracy rate of 93 percent on these calls. However, the U.S. General Accounting Office (1987a) reported an accuracy rate of only 79 percent in its probe, and further study of the matter is planned. Following widespread complaints about taxpayer confusion following the Tax Reform Act of 1986, the IRS announced that it would not assess penalties for noncompliance that taxpayers could demonstrate occurred because of errors by taxpayer service representatives.

In 1987, the Taxpayer Services Division offered personal assistance in 411 permanent locations, and the IRS voluntary income tax assistance (VITA) and tax counseling for the elderly programs trained about 57,000 volunteers who assisted 1.7 million taxpayers. Finally, 8.6 million questions about taxpayers' accounts were answered in 1987. Although rough estimates of the compliance effects of these activities could probably be obtained using fairly standard research techniques, the panel is aware of only one planned attempt to do so.

The IRS and its chief counsel provide written interpretations of the tax code through regulations, revenue rulings, and private letter rulings, which affect most taxpayers primarily by informing tax practitioners. In addition, over 2 million technical referrals a year are handled through taxpayer services. Finally, the problem resolution program intervenes to resolve errors and misunderstandings between the IRS and the taxpayer, resolving 407,000 problems for taxpayers in 1987. Although the General Accounting Office (U.S. GAO, 1987b) found that special assistance through the problem resolution program increased levels of taxpayer satisfaction, it also expressed concern about the quality of the feedback the IRS obtains through its efforts to evaluate the program. What is more important from the panel's perspective, very little is known about the effects of these programs on compliance.

Encouraging Compliance Through Public Communications

The IRS has increased its efforts to encourage compliance through public communications. In 1987 outreach and educational efforts included the distribution of materials to nearly 4 million students, the training of 4,000 teachers, and the distribution of six 15-minute films through the "Understanding Taxes" program. In addition, the IRS and the General Counsel's office organized or participated in workshops for 47,000 small business owners, institutes for 36,000 tax practitioners, and student tax clinics at twelve law and graduate accounting schools. The IRS participated in seventeen televison and seven radio tax clinics during 1987, with estimated total audiences of over 17 million. In total the IRS received about $45 million in free advertising from publications, radio, and television (IRS, 1987). The Public Affairs Division constantly deals with the media and professional organizations, particularly to inform them of changes in laws, regulations, and practice. Little is known about the role of communication in encouraging compliance, and considerable investigation is needed to learn how to combine communication strategies effectively with enforcement programs.

Regulating Tax Practitioners

Tax practitioners—lawyers, accountants, and others who prepare tax returns or advise clients about tax matters—provide an important component of the tax system. Since they prepare nearly half of all individual tax returns each year, they affect a much larger proportion of returns than IRS examiners. They are more easily monitored than taxpayers since they are a much smaller group. In many ways, they are more vulnerable to punitive actions by the IRS or by professional organizations to which they belong, since the loss of credentials and reputation could eliminate their source of livelihood. Good relations with IRS officials are probably useful to their work. They may probe for unreported income, question implausible claims, and encourage compliance by their clients in other ways. Or, by encouraging taxpayers to play the odds against being audited or hinting at what is difficult for auditors to detect, they may encourage noncompliance. Only recently have researchers begun to study how compliance is affected by return preparers and by other practitioners who offer advice and structure transactons so as to maximize after-tax income.

One source of IRS control in this area comes from its authority to administer and enforce regulations governing administrative proceedings within the IRS. Although attorneys and certified public accountants are automatically authorized to practice by the Agency Practice Act of 1965, over 31,000 other "enrolled agents" have been authorized by the IRS. Their duties and responsibilities are governed by Treasury Circular 230, and they can be disciplined by suspension or disbarment for such acts as false and misleading advertisement, bribery, submission of fradulent returns, or fraudulent opinions relating to abusive tax shelters. Legislation over the years has provided penalties for preparers, many of whom are not lawyers, certified public accountants, or enrolled agents. These provisions provide civil penalties for abuses such as not signing a return, filing false returns, and so on. Abuses are discovered during routine examinations when preparers are discovered to be involved with an incorrect return. Files kept in district offices and service centers are used to identify consistent abusers, whose other clients' returns are then flagged for examination. In the late 1970s, about 5 percent of all examinations were related to this practitioner program (U.S. GAO, 1976), although a cost-saving decision not to record preparers' identification numbers on computer files in the early 1980s decreased the IRS's ability to request examinations in this way (U.S. GAO, 1982).

ACTIVITIES OF THE IRS RESEARCH DIVISION

Although several IRS divisions carry out research and related activities, the center for guiding most research on compliance by individual taxpayers is the IRS Research Division. The Research Division employs a staff of about sixty professionals and controls an annual budget of just over $4 million for purchasing equipment, supplies, and services under the general heading of research and development. Its functions may be classified in five categories.

1. *Taxpayer Compliance Measurement Program coordination*. The Research Division plans and coordinates the entire TCMP program.[5] This coordination, which requires two to three professional staff years annually, is only

a small fraction of the full cost of TCMP, which the IRS estimates at $128 million for the 1985 survey.[6]

2. *Compliance measurement.* Using TCMP and other data sources, the Research Division prepares and updates measures of the amount and composition of the noncompliance tax gap. This effort requires seven to eight staff years plus a small contract budget.

3. *Management studies.* This category includes workload projection, resource allocation, development and testing of computer-based strategies for detecting unreported taxable income, DIF development, expert systems development, evaluation of forms simplification efforts, and analysis of specific statistical problems encountered in tax administration. These efforts require about forty-two staff years annually, plus perhaps $2 million in contractual costs.

4. *Surveys.* Surveys of taxpayers and, recently, tax practitioners require about two staff years of Research Division personnel, plus about $500,000 in contractual costs.

5. *Liaison with the research community.* Although such activities as annual research conferences, responses to researchers' requests for data and questions concerning interpretation, and others consume only one to two staff years of Research Division time, they require programming and legal support from other parts of the IRS and perhaps $500,000 per year in contractual costs.

These figures make clear that TCMP dominates the IRS investment in individual taxpayer compliance research, costing about sixteen times as much as all other Research Division activities. The primary justification for TCMP is its use in development of the rules for selecting returns for audit; these rules have been demonstrated to improve the net yield from audits by far more than the TCMP program cost. Similarly, most of the projects in the management studies category are either efforts to ensure that staffing is adequate in all locations or tests of enforcement innovations intended to increase the net cost effectiveness of enforcement activity. By reducing the incidence of breakdowns in processing returns, appeals, and refunds and by discriminating between effective and ineffective programs for revenue recovery, these studies pay for themselves in quite visible ways. The benefits of long-range compliance research activities—compliance measurement, taxpayer surveys, and liaison with the research community—are less visible and more speculative. Therefore, it is not surprising that the investment in these activities is less than 2 percent of the cost of TCMP and the management studies.

Policy Analysis and Social Science

Not all successful social science research on taxpayer compliance will be useful to the IRS policy makers who operate these programs or to others in government who legislate or carry out tax policy. Nor should it be. But there are some natural areas of overlap between the policy concerns of the tax community and the intellectual questions that intrigue scholars. In discussing potential areas of overlap, it is useful to begin by listing some of the considerations that will be weighed by tax administrators considering a change in program (i.e., in tax laws or administrative procedures):

1. *IRS/administrative costs.* Changes in IRS resources required to set up and implement a new program.

2. *Private-sector costs.* Changes in the costs incurred by taxpayers, third-party information reporters, and tax practitioners for such activities as the maintenance of records, the filing of reports and returns, and the time involved in IRS contacts and appeals.

3. *Intangible social costs.* Changes in taxpayers' perceptions of the intrusiveness of enforcement—the need to keep records to document legitimately deductible expenses, reluctance to entrust the government with personal financial information, fear and psychic costs evoked by contacts with the IRS, awareness of being watched by an impersonal and mysterious bureaucracy.

4. *Political costs and constraints.* Reactions by the public, Congress, public interest groups, and budget makers that may thwart a program. Examples include reactions against the 1984 statute and subsequent regulations requiring contemporaneous record keeping for vehicles used for business and pleasure, reactions against laws requiring banks to withhold taxes due on interest paid, recurrent battles to increase IRS computer capabilities and budget.

5. *Direct revenue effects.* The revenue yielded directly by new or expanded enforcement programs (e.g., audits, matching of information returns, new computer technologies) or the net revenue effects of reallocating resources from one enforcement activity to another.

6. *Compliance-based revenue effects.* The revenue effects of policy changes that occur indirectly, through changes in compliance. For example, a well-publicized shift in criminal investigations from catfish farmers to promoters of abusive tax shelters may deter investments in such shelters but encourage noncompliance by catfish farmers. A decision to waive penalties incurred because of mistaken advice from a taxpayer services representative

may strike some taxpayers as fair but aggravate others' resentment of complexity. A tax amnesty may induce some taxpayers to clear their consciences, while angering those who have routinely complied and causing others to question their perception of the IRS as an omniscient tax collector.

Of these six considerations, the last is the one for which social science can be most helpful. As the examples of compliance-based revenue effects were selected to show, policy instruments tend to be swords with at least two edges. The diverse theories that underlie the various branches of social science can call attention to these edges, and empirical research can measure their sometimes conflicting effects on compliance.

At present much of the potential of social science for informing legislators and policy makers about the compliance effects of their actions remains unrealized. There are several reasons. First, taxpayer compliance research is quite recent (i.e., of the last ten to fifteen years) because, outside the IRS, the subject has received extensive research attention only since the existence of a large purported underground economy in the United States was publicized in the late 1970s. Second, although researchers have begun to cross traditional disciplinary boundaries in the last few years, most existing research is quite fragmented. As a result, a central concern of one discipline—which may reveal the second edge of a policy sword—may be ignored by a researcher from another. Third, while researchers have discovered a variety of statistically significant correlations between compliance and other variables, very little can be concluded about the magnitudes of the compliance differences found. In part, this imprecision exists because the field is new. But it also reflects the difficulty of measuring compliance and of gaining access to recent useful data—some of the most recent research is based on data for 1969. And it reflects the fact that the IRS frequently fails to take advantage of changes—in the law, in administrative procedures, and in resource allotments—as opportunities to measure compliance responses. Fourth, research has only begun to progress in reflecting important institutional realities of taxpaying. This beginning reflects progress on two fronts: the development of tractable theoretical and empirical models that can cope with such complexities and enhanced communication among the communities of tax administrators, tax practitioners, and social scientists.

In developing its recommendations, the panel has tried to provide an agenda that balances the concerns of immediate policy relevance and those of long-term understanding, that respects the privacy concerns and rights of taxpayers, and that promises results commensurate with the administrative costs and political risks involved. In suggesting research we have tried to ensure that it is within acceptable bounds for equal treatment of classes of taxpayers and that it is likely to inform policy debates.

Our research agenda and recommendations for its execution are influenced by additional organizational priorities and constraints extending beyond data-base development and disclosure. Of fundamental importance are the differences between organizations such as the National Science Foundation, established to support basic or general applied research, and the research arms of mission agencies such as the IRS. The former organizations can be guided primarily by assessments of likely scientific payoffs from proposed research. However, the latter must also weigh the prospects of visible contributions and costs in terms of the agency's primary mission. This basic difference will sometimes lead the two kinds of organizations to place different priorities on a given research question. It is therefore incumbent on advocates of particular lines of research by mission agencies to make their case primarily in terms of their practical policy implications.

Even when a research question is acknowledged to have broader scientific implications, the research design will be influenced by more immediate considerations. For example, in assessing the feasibility of a particular randomized experiment, the IRS must consider whether it will stimulate legal challenges, ethical objections, overt public opposition to the agency (with possible adverse effects on compliance), or less visible social delegitimization of the agency that could aggravate noncompliance. For these reasons, in developing its recommendations the panel attempted to emphasize questions having both scientific and policy interest, to explain the practical significance of the proposed research, and to advocate approaches yielding generalizable results while recognizing organizational and resource constraints.

Plan of the Report

In this chapter, we have offered a definition of compliance with federal income tax reporting requirements and discussed available estimates of the magnitude of noncompliance. In Chapter 2, we review and synthesize previous theoretical and empirical research on factors that may affect taxpayer compliance, and we recommend promising extensions of several existing lines of work. In Chapter 3, we argue that several new lines of research should be opened, to study how compliance is affected by the social and financial environments that people find themselves in, and by the mental processes through which they make sense of these complex and uncertain environments. These matters suggest that various components of the tax system itself may be important influences on compliance and that they should receive more research attention than they have to date. To illustrate the point, in Chapter 4 we suggest useful research on how three components—legislative and administrative change, tax practitioners, and IRS taxpayer contact programs—affect compliance.

In Chapter 5 we recommend a number of innovations for improving the quality of compliance research data and making it more accessible to compliance researchers, while protecting the rights of citizens as taxpayers and research subjects and the security of confidential IRS enforcement information. Finally, in Chapter 6 we argue that knowledge about taxpayer compliance can best be accumulated by a diverse group of independent researchers who communicate actively among themselves and with the IRS, and we recommend a number of institutional innovations to facilitate interaction and cooperation.

Supplementary Notes

A: PATTERNS AND TRENDS IN TAXPAYER COMPLIANCE

The panel's interest in compliance measurement was primarily in the compliance of individuals. Measures of aggregate noncompliance were of some interest, however, as a context for our work. This note focuses primarily on the aggregate noncompliance estimates that were available when the panel began its work at the end of 1984. While these studies were concerned with different time periods, many of them happened to include estimates for the year 1976; therefore, for comparability, much of the following discussion focuses on that year.

At the outset it should be emphasized that the estimates reported in this note are subject to very large potential errors. In addition, seemingly trivial differences in concept definitions or in the wording of survey questions can increase or decrease estimates by factors of 2 or 3. Chapter 5 of this report contains several recommendations for improving the individual-level compliance measures to be used in future empirical research. Some of those recommendations, if implemented, might eventually improve the accuracy of the aggregate estimates. But the panel did not critically review the aggregate estimates nor attempt to develop recommendations to improve them.

In interpreting aggregate noncompliance estimates, at least five different concepts should be distinguished. The first two are concerned with taxable income, and the rest are concerned with income tax.

The first concept is the so-called underground economy, the value of all economic activity that is unrecorded in national income accounts and is presumably untaxed. Estimates of the size of the underground economy were made by Feige (1979, 1980), Gutmann (1977), Henry (1975, 1976, 1983), and Tanzi (1980, 1982). Although their studies differ in details and underlying assumptions, the basic strategy is to count money in circulation, estimate the share of that money used in recorded transactions, and to assume that the rest is being used in unrecorded activity. As shown in Table 1, the 1976 estimates differ substantially, from Henry's range of $40–$65 billion to Feige's estimate of $369 billion annually. All these estimates are analogous to the national income accounting concept of gross national product, because they are intended to include the value of all goods and services produced but not recorded. But the outputs of some producers in the underground economy are sold to other producers in intermediate transactions; if these other producers were reporting their income for tax purposes, they would first deduct intermediate transactions as allowable business expenses. Consequently the underground economy concept is overly inclusive as an indicator of income that is untaxed because of noncompliance with federal income tax laws.

The second concept, unreported taxable personal income, excludes the value of intermediate transactions and income earned by organizations rather than individuals. As shown in Table 1, two estimation approaches have been used. Kurtz and Pechman (1982) have derived an indirect estimate for 1976 of $78 billion from discrepancies in personal income accounting statistics. The IRS (1979b, 1983f) has compiled direct estimates of between $100 and $154 billion by adding up estimates of components (e.g., unreported tips, overstated deductions, failure to file returns) obtained using a variety of methods.

The third concept, the income tax noncompliance gap, is a measure of the tax revenue lost because of all forms of noncompliance by taxpayers. Estimates by the IRS (1983f) for several years, summarized in Table 2, amount to about $43 billion for 1976 and about $90 billion for 1981. The gap includes the taxes due on unreported taxable personal income plus two other components: the corporation tax gap and the remittance gap—the failure of employers to deposit all taxes withheld on their employees and the failure of taxpayers to remit all taxes due along with their returns.

The fourth concept, the individual income tax reporting gap, conforms

TABLE 1   Estimates of Aggregate Unreported Taxable Personal Income for 1976

Concept and Source	Originally published ($ billions)	Adjusted[a] ($ billions)	Percent of personal income[b]
Underground economy			
Feige (1979, 1980)	369	157	12
Gutmann (1977)	176–240	61–93	5–7
Tanzi (1980, 1982)	138–199	78–124	6–9
Henry (1975, 1976, 1978)	40–65	72	5
Unreported taxable personal income			
Indirect estimates:			
Kurtz and Pechman (1982)	78	77	6
Direct estimates:			
IRS (1979b)	100–135	61–96	5–7
IRS (1983f)	154	119	9

[a] Reflects adjustments by Henry (1983) to achieve conceptual uniformity and further adjustment for the panel's use to remove illegal income, estimated at $26 million by Simon and Witte (1979).
[b] 1976 personal income estimate of $1,351 billion is from Bureau of Economic Analysis (1981, Table 8.7).
Source: In all estimates except IRS (1983f), originally published estimates are taken from Henry (1983). IRS (1983f) originally published estimates are the sum of filers' unreported income (Table III-1, p. 12) and nonfilers' balance due (Table C-5, p. 79).

most closely to the scope of the panel's inquiry. It is computed by subtracting from the estimated income tax noncompliance gap the components associated with corporations, nonremittance, and illegal activity. As shown in Table 2, the IRS (1983f) estimates that the reporting gap amounts to about 75 pecent of the overall income tax noncompliance gap—$32 billion in 1976 and $68 billion in 1981.

The fifth concept, the net individual income tax gap, is the portion of the individual income tax reporting gap that remains after IRS administrative actions. It was estimated by the IRS (1986b) for 1981 by subtracting from the individual gap the estimated $8–$11 billion of revenue yielded directly by checking arithmetic errors, matching tax returns to information reports, auditing returns, collection activities, and criminal investigations. This estimate, of course, takes no account of secondary or "ripple" effects of these activities on compliance by taxpayers who are not contacted directly through these programs. Compared with a 1981 gross (preenforcement)

Table 2   Income Tax Gap, 1973–1981 ($ billions)

	1973	1976	1979	1981
Legal-sector tax gap				
Total	28.8	39.2	62.3	81.5
Corporation tax gap, total	3.5	4.6	6.4	6.2
Individual tax gap, total	25.3	34.6	55.9	75.3
Individual income tax reporting gap:				
Total	23.8	32.2	50.6	68.5
Nonfilers' income tax liability				
(Net of prepayments and credits)	0.9	1.4	2.0	2.9
Filers' income tax liability:	22.9	30.8	48.6	65.6
Unreported income	17.3	24.2	38.4	52.2
Overstated business expenses	2.1	3.4	4.7	6.3
Overstated personal deductions[a]	3.4	3.0	5.0	6.6
Net math error	0.1	0.2	0.5	0.5
Individual income tax remittance				
gap, total:	1.5	2.4	5.3	6.8
Employer underdeposit of				
withholding[b]	1.1	0.9	1.8	2.4
Individual balance due after				
remittance	0.4	1.5	3.5	4.4
Illegal-sector tax gap (partial)[c]	2.1	3.4	6.3	9.0
	(0.8)	(1.3)	(2.2)	(3.2)

[a] Includes itemized deductions, personal exemptions, and statutory adjustments.
[b] Includes a small amount for underreported withholding by employees and a small negative amount for underclaimed withholding by individuals.
[c] Includes income from illegal drugs, illegal gambling, and prostitution only. Figures in parentheses are standard errors.
Source: IRS (1983f, Table I-1, p. 3).

individual income tax gap of $75 billion, the net gap was estimated at $64–$67 billion.

THE UNDERGROUND ECONOMY AND UNREPORTED TAXABLE PERSONAL INCOME.   In the absence of any means of direct measurement, estimates of underreported taxable income have been produced for a variety of purposes under a variety of assumptions. The various approaches are described in some detail in Henry (1983). Because all of them are difficult and time consuming, they are not available on a regular basis. Many of the authors report estimates for tax year 1976, and Henry (1983) applied the methods of others to derive estimates for that year. These 1976 estimates are summarized in Table 1. The table reports both the authors' original estimates and estimates adjusted by Henry that are intended to compensate for conceptual differences in the figures estimated by the original authors.

The estimates summarized in Table 1 are categorized as "indirect" or "direct," depending on the estimation approach used. All the estimates of the underground economy are indirect, obtained by inferring the unmeasurable unreported income from data on measurable quantities—components of the money supply (Feige, 1979, 1980; Gutmann, 1977; Tanzi, 1980, 1982; Henry, 1975, 1976, 1983) or of the national income and product accounts (NIPA) (see Kurtz and Pechman, 1982).

Indirect estimates. Indirect estimates of unreported economic activity are derived from discrepancies that emerge in reconciling economic statistics that should be related by definition in the absence of noncompliance. They have been calculated by analyzing monetary data and by comparing adjusted gross income (AGI) totals from individual tax returns with AGI estimates computed by the Bureau of Economic Analysis (BEA) for the national income and product accounts. The latter are based primarily on business tax returns, which are considered more reliable (Parker, 1984).

The monetary indirect estimates are based on the presumption that most unreported economic activity takes place in cash. Econometric techniques are applied to data from an earlier period to estimate the relationship between the value of currency in circulation and some other statistic, such as demand deposits (i.e., checking accounts) or national income. The estimated relationship is used to project the expected value of currency for a later period, and the excess of actual currency over expected currency is assumed to be producing unreported taxable income. As noted by Henry (1983), these estimates have been widely criticized on technical grounds—failure to adjust for increased overseas holdings of American dollars, failure to model the effects of increased use of credit cards (which might affect the ratio of currency to checking accounts regardless of trends in unrecorded activity), and failure to test the sensitivity of the estimates to alternative estimates of the velocity of money (i.e., the value of transactions per year per dollar in circulation) and of currency lifetimes, which are themselves subject to great uncertainty. An additional problem in terms of the panel's scope is that the indirect monetary estimates include income earned in illegal activities such as drug trafficking and prostitution; adjustments to remove the illegal components are difficult to make. Finally, the estimates include the income of persons who are not required to file, which should not be included in estimates of noncompliance.

The indirect noncompliance estimates based on discrepancies between national income account estimates produced by the BEA and personal incomes reported to the IRS have been used as noncompliance benchmarks for many years. They are only approximations, however, because the discrepancies arise from several causes other than taxpayer noncompliance. First, the BEA estimates do not reflect allowable adjustments to income such as moving expenses but do include income earned by persons who are not required to file. Second, BEA approximations to components of income that are not routinely captured by the bureau's data collection systems (e.g., interest to individuals, individual capital gains) are themselves open to question.

Direct estimates. The IRS (1983f) direct estimate of unreported taxable income reported in Table 1 includes three components: overstated subtractions from income by return filers ($20.8 billion), unreported income of return filers ($131.5 billion), and net taxable income of nonfilers ($2.1 billion). The estimates of overstated subtractions and some kinds of unreported income for filers are derived from the 1976 cycle of the IRS Taxpayer Compliance Measurement Program, which is described more fully in Supplementary Note B to this chapter. The estimates of nonfilers' taxable income were computed from discrepancies between individuals' IRS master file records and their Social Security Administration and Census Bureau income reports.

The IRS considers the TCMP audit a relatively accurate device for measuring overstated subtractions; it is usually straightforward to determine whether the taxpayer has the documentation needed to support an adjustment to income or an itemized deduction. For this reason, unadjusted 1976 TCMP results were used to estimate overstated subtraction items by taxpayers who filed returns. Unreported income is considered more difficult for auditors to establish, because they must first discover its existence. Today, information reports such as forms W-2 and 1099 help to identify unreported wages, interest, dividends, and other categories of income. But in the 1976 TCMP cycle, auditors did not have access to the information reports, and a special study (IRS, 1983f, Appendix B) found that for the income categories subject to information reporting, those reports established far more unreported income than did the TCMP auditors. Although the multiple (the ratio of estimates from information reports to estimates from audits) varied substantially by type of income, unreported taxable income was estimated by multiplying the TCMP estimates for most categories of unreported income (i.e., all categories except tips, informal suppliers' income, and certain types of capital goods, dividends, alimony, and business income) by a common factor, 3.5. The validity of this adjustment is subject to question, and the most recent estimate (IRS, 1988) is based on a factor of 3.28. Since unreported income accounts for nearly 80 percent of the total estimate of unreported taxable personal income, that estimate should be interpreted with great caution.

For some categories of income, TCMP audit results, even adjusted on the basis of information reporting, were not considered sufficiently accurate. Therefore, TCMP-based estimates of unreported income were supplemented by estimates from special studies of certain types of unreported income, including unreported tip income and unreported income of undocumented aliens and informal suppliers, such as street vendors and firewood purveyors with no fixed business address. These special studies are described elsewhere (IRS, 1983f).

The last major component of the IRS direct estimates for 1976 was the taxable unreported income of citizens who failed to file tax returns as required and therefore could not have been selected for TCMP. Nonfiler estimates were obtained using "exact match" data files for 1972 and 1977 that contained information about individuals from the IRS master file (including an indicator whether a return had been filed), the Census Bureau's Current Population Survey, and Social Security Administration administrative records. Individuals with Social Security or Census Bureau records indicating receipt of taxable income, but no matching IRS record, were flagged as potential nonfilers. Their income levels and other relevant information were checked to see if they should have filed a tax return. For individuals who apparently should have filed on the basis of their income and employment status, estimates of taxable income were added to the underreporting estimates for nonfilers. Over 4.2 million nonfilers were estimated for 1976. However, nearly 1.8 million of them would have received a refund or owed no additional tax because of prior withholding. Therefore, only about 2.4 million nonfilers avoided tax liability, and the net contribution of nonfiling to total unexpected income was only $1.4 billion. Questions have been raised concerning errors in the construction of the exact match files, and these errors may have created inaccuracies in the estimates of unreported income by nonfilers.

THE INCOME TAX NONCOMPLIANCE GAP. Another commonly reported measure is the noncompliance tax gap—the tax loss associated with unreported taxable income and uncollected tax by individuals and corporations. This measure has been calculated for tax year 1976 (IRS, 1983f) and projected forward to 1981 under the assumption that taxpayers reported constant fractions of the components of taxable income and subtractions throughout that period. Both the 1976 and 1981 tax gap estimates are reported in Table 2, which is reproduced from IRS (1983f:3). The 1981 estimates are subject not only to the problems discussed above in estimating the components of unreported income for 1976, but also to errors that may stem from changes in compliance behavior between 1976 and 1981.

According to the IRS estimates for 1981, about $90.5 billion, or 20 percent, of corporate and individual income tax liability was not collected without IRS intervention. Of this amount, corporate returns accounted for $6.2 billion, and returns involving illegal income accounted for $9 billion. Both measures involve major problems that undermine their validity but are not considered further because corporate and illegal sector compliance are beyond the scope of this report. Another $6.8 billion, the remittance gap, was reported but not paid.

THE INDIVIDUAL INCOME TAX REPORTING GAP. The remaining amount in Table 2, a 1976 individual income tax reporting gap of $32.2 billion, measures the concept of noncompliance that corresponds most closely with the scope of the panel's inquiry (IRS, 1983f). It represents about 75 percent of the entire estimated income tax gap. For 1981 the estimated reporting gap was $68.5 billion, of which $65.6 billion was attributed to inaccurate filed returns and the rest to nonfilers. This amounts to an estimated 17 percent of true tax liability. While it is important not to attribute great precision to the estimates, they suggest that somewhat more than 80 percent of true tax liability is accurately reported by compliant taxpayers without being contacted by the IRS. Nevertheless, the 1981 noncompliance tax gap amounts to approximately 87 percent of the federal deficit in that year and 37 percent of the average annual deficit since then.

As this report was in final preparation, the IRS (1988) released new estimates of the individual income tax reporting gap over the period 1973–1992. The latest estimates are said to be more accurate than those in IRS (1983f) because of refinements in the adjustments for unreported income not discovered by TCMP auditors and in the computations of the tax rates that apply to the unreported income. Unfortunately, IRS (1988) does not contain any estimate for filers only for 1981, but the estimate for 1982 is only $51.9 billion, of which $46.2 billion was attributed to filed returns— lower than the 1981 estimates in IRS (1983f). IRS (1988) projects an individual income tax reporting gap of $79.3 billion for 1986, a decrease to $63.5 billion in 1987 because of the Tax Reform Act of 1986, and a trend upward to $82.6 billion in 1991, not adjusted for inflation.

THE NET TAX GAP. To complete the story, we need to consider how much of this noncompliance is caught and corrected through IRS enforcement actions. A recent study of the net tax gap (IRS, 1986b) estimated that the program for securing returns from delinquent nonfilers caught $287 million, or 10 percent, of the $2.9 billion in unreported taxes from nonfilers in 1981 and yielded an additional $66 million in interest and penalties. Of the $65.6 billion tax-reporting gap for individuals who filed in 1981, $458 million in taxes due (0.7 percent) was discovered by the computerized arithemetic error checking program, $490 million (0.7 percent) by matching against information reports, and $2.7 billion (4.1 percent) in the examination program. Thus, only an estimated 6 percent of the $68.5 billion tax gap from individual reporting errors was discovered through various enforcement programs. The same study notes that "about $28 billion could potentially have been recovered with current sources of information and current IRS enforcement programs funded for operation at their highest economically feasible levels" (IRS, 1986b:1; the figure includes returns from collections activity and amounts to about 31 percent of the $10.5 billion noncompliance). Although the assumptions required to generate such an estimate preclude putting much confidence in it, this estimate suggests that at best only something like 30 percent of the total tax gap could be collected efficiently by enforcement actions, and much of that would be collected from corporations. The relatively small percentage of the individual tax gap that is actually caught by enforcement actions underscores the potential importance of compliance, in contrast to the revenue yield from enforcement, in reducing the tax gap.

OTHER NONCOMPLIANCE MEASURES. Although estimates of aggregate noncompliance are useful for describing the magnitude of the tax compliance problem, other statistics can provide additional insights into the nature of compliance and can further inform the development of policies for encouraging compliance. The IRS regularly reports additional data on patterns of noncompliance: the prevalence of noncompliers in the population, the extent of certain disaggregated categories of noncompliance for specific types of taxpayers, and trends in noncompliance of certain types. These data are described in the following sections.

Prevalence of noncompliers. After presenting estimates of the noncompliance tax gap, it is logical to ask whether the gap is accounted for by a few taxpayers, each of whom underreports a large amount of taxable income, or whether a broad cross-section of the taxpaying population underreports by small amounts. The fraction of the population that fails to comply may be called the prevalence of noncompliers. Estimates of noncomplier prevalence are available from a variety of sources. As a first step in reporting these estimates, it is important to distinguish between current prevalence—the fraction that fails to comply in a single tax year—and cumulative prevalence—the fraction that fails to comply at least once during an observation period of several tax years. Because a multiyear observation period presents more opportunities to fail to comply, cumulative prevalence should always equal or exceed current prevalence for any group of taxpayers. Moreover, cumulative prevalence should increase with longer observation periods. However, these distinctions have usually been ignored in comparisons of prevalence statistics across studies (see, e.g., Westat, Inc., 1980f; Kinsey, 1984).

Estimates of both current and cumulative noncomplier prevalence can theoretically be based either on the results of IRS audits or on self-reports of surveyed taxpayers who are asked whether they have failed to comply. However, even leaving aside measurement errors arising from such sources as auditors' errors and survey respondents' distortions, prevalence estimates derived in these two ways are not strictly comparable. Even candid survey respondents can acknowledge only noncompliance of which they are aware, and so will fail to report noncompliance arising from complexity or misunderstandings, unless the instances are brought to their attention by the IRS. In contrast, prevalence statistics based on TCMP audits reflect noncompliance for any reason and should therefore be larger than survey-based estimates in any sample, even if survey respondents have no memory lapses and make no effect to conceal noncompliance.

In addition to this conceptual difference, operational problems have so far made it impossible to produce comparable prevalence estimates from TCMP and taxpayer surveys. With the exception of a panel study involving small samples of taxpayers between 1969 and 1973, TCMP cycles have involved cross-sectional samples whose tax returns for only a single year are examined. Because a sample of taxpayers cannot be repeatedy audited without affecting compliance behavior, the TCMP program as currently structured cannot produce estimates of cumulative prevalence over a multi-year observation period. In contrast, survey researchers, probably as a means of reducing respondent sensitivity to questions about non-compliance, have nearly always probed for noncompliance during such multiyear periods. Consequently, except for the 1978 current prevalence estimates of Aitken and Bonneville (1980), all surveys of noncompliance have produced only cumulative prevalence estimates, which are of course not comparable.

Audit-based noncomplier prevalence estimates for 1979. Table 3 presents 1979 prevalence estimates for nonfilers, misreporters of income, and misreporters of subtractions from taxable income. The estimates for nonfilers were computed in the exact match study previously discussed, and the estimates for filers are derived from the 1979 TCMP survey.

Table 3 indicates that according to IRS (1983f), 5.6 percent of all persons who were required to file a 1979 tax return failed to do so. The majority of these, 3.2 percent, if they had filed, would have shown a balance

TABLE 3   Prevalence of Noncompliant Taxpayers based on TCMP Measures, 1979 (percentage)

	Current prevalence	
Type of noncompliance	*All filing taxpayers*	*Taxpayers meeting preconditions*[a]
Failure to file return[b]		
With balance due	NA	3.2
With refund or zero balance	NA	2.4
Misreporting income[c]		
Underreporting taxable income	42.3	42.3
Overreporting taxable income	6.0	6.0
Misreporting subtractions from income[c]		
Adjustments to income resulting in[c]		
Underreporting taxable income	4.4	32.2
Overreporting taxable income	2.5	18.5
Itemized deductions resulting in[c]		
Underreporting taxable income	17.5	61.0
Overreporting taxable income	7.8	27.1

NA = not applicable.
[a] Taxpayer base is restricted to exclude taxpayers who could not have engaged in a specific form of noncompliance. For rows 1,2,3a and 3b, the respective bases are: all persons required to file, all filers reporting income, all filers reporting adjustments to income, and all filers itemizing deductions.
[b] Source: Nonfiler estimates from IRS (1983f, Table C-4, p. 78) include delinquent nonfilers plus enforcement-secured returns. Base includes nonfiler estimates plus count of files.
[c] Source: American Bar Foundation analyses of 1979 TCMP data files prepared by the IRS Research Division. Item misclassifications that do not affect tax liability are excluded from counts of noncompliers. Base for "all taxpayers" measure is filed returns. Adjustments include subtractions such as moving and business expenses and payments to IRA or Keogh retirement accounts. Itemized deductions include allowable medical, interest, charitable, and other Schedule A expenses.

due despite withholding and prepayments during the tax year. But a sizable minority, 2.4 percent, would have shown a refund due.

Table 3 also presents 1979 prevalence estimates for specific forms of noncompliance on filed returns. These estimates are abstracted for the panel from K. W. Smith's (1985) tabulations of 1979 TCMP data. According to those data over 50 percent of all returns correctly reported all income items; of the 48 percent with reporting errors, 42 percent involved under-reporting taxable income and 6 percent involved overreporting.

Prevalence estimates are also reported in Table 3 for taxpayers who over- and underreport two kinds of subtractions from income: adjustments to income, such as employee business expenses, and itemized deductions. In interpreting these statistics, it is important to note that the majority of returns filed do not involve these items. In 1979 only 14 percent of returns included adjustments and 29 percent itemized deductions. Therefore, the fraction of noncompliers is reported both as a fraction of all filing taxpayers and as a fraction of taxpayers meeting preconditions (e.g., the number who failed to adjust income accurately is divided by the number for whom adjustments were an issue, according to either the taxpayer or the TCMP auditor).[7] It is significant that of the taxpayers meeting preconditions, 18 percent misreported adjustments to income and 27 percent misreported itemized deductions in such a way as to overstate their taxable income. These large figures suggest that, relative to reporting income, subtracting allowable adjustments is even more subject to errors and misunderstandings.

Noncomplier prevalence by return item. Table 4, which is also based on tabulations of 1979 TCMP data by Smith (1985), reports noncomplier prevalence by return item, for all items that were used, or that auditors thought should be used, on at least 2 percent of all filed returns. Each prevalence estimate is expressed as a fraction of taxpayers who met preconditions, i.e., taxpayers who either reported a nonzero amount for the return item or should have done so according to the TCMP auditor. (The fractions meeting preconditions, which also provide some indication of the policy significance of noncompliance on the specific return items, are reported in the last column of the table.) Return items are grouped into categories of income and subtractions from income and are listed in order of the prevalence of taxpayers who underreport taxable income.

Three sets of prevalence estimates are reported: the fraction that under-reported taxable income by any amount, the fraction that underreported taxable income by more than $50, and the fraction that overreported

TABLE 4   Noncomplier Prevalence by Return Item (percentages)

Return	Underreporting taxable income[a]		Overreporting taxable income	Meeting preconditions
	Any amount	$51+		
Income items				
Total	42.3	NA	6.0	100.0
Farm income (Sch. F)	66.9	62.5	14.3	2.8
Proprietor's income (Sch. C)	65.2	60.3	11.1	10.9
Rents/royalties	47.4	42.1	14.1	9.0
Tips	45.4	29.9	1.4	3.1
Interest	39.8	14.2	3.3	79.3
Other income (Sch. E)	29.9	23.7	4.1	10.0
Capital gains (Sch. D)	26.7	22.1	12.1	10.3
Partnership income	26.4	25.0	5.5	3.2
Taxable dividends	25.8	16.5	8.9	11.8
State/local tax refund	18.3	13.8	3.3	15.8
Wages/salaries	6.6	5.3	1.0	89.2
Subtraction items				
Total adjustments	32.2	NA	18.5	14.1
Total itemized deductions	61.0	NA	27.1	28.7
Nonpremium medical expenses	60.5	44.6	24.4	9.4
Casualty losses	53.3	48.7	7.5	2.2
Political contributions credit	46.5	11.1	5.5	3.0
Employee business expenses	43.9	39.8	22.1	7.6
Misc. deductions	36.0	27.1	12.7	23.3
Cash contributions	33.4	26.1	12.7	25.3
Child care credit	30.6	19.0	20.7	4.4
Residential energy credit	29.9	13.5	11.1	4.9
Other state and local taxes	29.9	16.3	24.3	28.2
Nonmortgage interest	29.8	20.8	19.3	24.3
Noncash contributions	24.4	17.3	13.7	7.2
Real estate taxes	18.9	13.7	9.2	25.1
Medical insurance premiums	18.5	11.9	7.8	16.8
Investment credit	17.4	11.6	39.2	7.1

Mortgage interest	11.1	8.9	7.5	22.7
State and local income taxes	10.1	7.1	11.1	24.1
IRA contributions	9.6	8.4	2.8	2.6
Self-employment tax	8.2	NA	59.5	2.2
Interest penalty (early withdrawal)	4.2	2.6	29.8	2.1

[a] Base is returns reporting item per taxpayer's or auditor's interpretation. Numerator includes those found to have illegally reported zero income in category or claimed unentitled subtraction.
Source: Derived from American Bar Foundation analysis of 1979 TCMP tabulations.

taxable income.[8] The pattern is consistent with at least two hypotheses about taxpayer compliance: it is discouraged by greater complexity of calculations and judgments needed to compute the item, and it is encouraged by greater visibility of transactions. For three income items for which noncompliers are very prevalent—farm income, properietor's income, and rents/royalties—taxpayers are expected to understand complicated regulations, to keep detailed records, and to perform fairly extensive calculations. For all three items, some gross receipts are offset by allowable expenses, and noncompliance can occur either because records or the interpretation of regulations fails to support the expenses claimed or because evidence is found of unreported income. In addition, some income in each of those categories may come in the form of cash, which lacks documentation that is immediately visible to the IRS. In contrast, the three income items with the lowest prevalences of noncompliers—dividends, state and local tax refunds, and wages and salaries—are largely precalculated for the taxpayer, and two of the three are made visible to the IRS through information reports (forms W-2 and 1099) from their sources. Compared with income items, subtraction items are more visible to the IRS because the taxpayer carries the burden of documenting their existence. Nevertheless, it may be significant that the five items for which noncompliance is the most widespread involve judgments about the allowability of expenditures, while the five with the least widespread noncompliance leave little to interpretation.

Table 4 also demonstrates that overreporting of taxable income occurs for all items and is fairly widespread for some. Since presumably few taxpayers want to pay more taxes than necessary, they may be having difficulty in interpreting complex regulations and performing calculations, or they may fail to claim a subtraction that they believe is legal but likely to arouse IRS suspicion. The three income items for which underreporting is most prevalent are also among the items for which overreporting is most prevalent—presumably an effect of the complexities mentioned above with respect to those items.[9] The fact that the prevalence of overreporting is generally higher for subtraction items than for income items is consistent with both possible explanations. The regulations governing investment credits, employee business expenses, and the like are complex, and tax-payers may be reluctant to claim such rare deductions because of an expectation that the claim would trigger an IRS audit.

Survey-based noncomplier prevalence estimates. Another approach to estimating the prevalence of noncompliance is through surveys that ask respondents if they have failed to comply in the past. Even if survey-based measures were error free, they could be expected to differ from audit-based measures because of auditors' errors that may over- or understate noncompliance, and because of unsettled differences between auditors and tax-payers over complex or ambiguous matters. But surveys are also subject to errors because of noncompliance that respondents do not recognize, forget about, or wish to conceal from interviewers. Very little is known about the magnitudes of these discrepancies, for at least two reasons. First, most surveys measure noncompliance over a reference period of several years and so are not comparable to audit-based measures, which relate to a single year. Second, in the United States, IRS concern over taxpayer privacy has prevented researchers to date from comparing audit and survey results for a common sample of taxpayers. When such a comparison was carried out in the Netherlands, however, Hessing, Elffers, and Weigel (1986) found essentially a zero correlation.

Table 5 summarizes the major survey-based U.S. prevalence estimates. Because of the uncertainties just discussed, the estimates should be treated as very tentative. Most of them are also reported by Kinsey (1984), who provides specific methodological critiques of the estimates.

Table 5 summarizes survey-based prevalence estimates for "general" noncompliance—including both understanding income and overclaiming subtractions—and for each of those categories separately.[10] Within each section, estimates are listed for the most part in order of reference period for the prevalence estimate from longest to shortest—lifetime, five years, and current (one year). If all the samples represented the same population, the shorter reference periods should of course be associated with smaller estimates. For general noncompliance (Table 5, Section A), survey-based

TABLE 5   Noncomplier Prevalence Estimates Based on Surveys

Prevalence	Study	Prevalence estimate (%)	Method
A. Estimates for general noncompliance			
Cumulative, lifetime	Grasmick and Scott (1982)	25 (1979) 28 (1981)	Sealed envelope responses of 350–400 persons interviewed in person in 1979 or 1981 (Oklahoma City)
Cumulative, 5 year	Scott and Grasmick (1981)	20	Sealed envelope responses of 329 persons interviewed in person in 1980 (Oklahoma City)
Cumulative, 5 year	Tittle (1980)	12	Responses to direct questions by 1,993 persons interviewed in person in 1972 (Oregon, Iowa, New Jersey)
Cumulative, 3 year	Minor (1978)	12	Responses to direct questions by 274 persons interviewed in person in 1975 (Tallahassee, FL)
B. Estimates for underreporting income			
Cumulative, lifetime	Spicer (1974)	22	Responses to direct questions by 130 household heads interviewed in person in 1974 (Ohio suburbs)
Cumulative, lifetime	Yankelovich et al. (1984)	16	Responses to direct questions by 2,208 primary taxpayers interviewed in person in 1983 (United States)

TABLE 5   *(cont.)*

Cumulative, lifetime	Westat, Inc. (1980f)	12–15	Responses to direct questions by 348 primary taxpayers interviewed in person in 1979 (San Jose, CA, and Smith Bend, IN). Estimate higher when interview scheduled by appointment.
Cumulative, 5 year	Mason and Lowry (1981)	17	Responses to direct questions by 801 primary taxpayers interviewed in person in 1980 (Oregon)
Cumulative, 5 year	Mason, Calvin, and Faulkenberry (1975)	15	Responses to direct questions by 800 primary taxpayers interviewed in person in 1975 (Oregon)
Cumulative, 5 year	Habib (1980)	12 (randomized response)	Responses by 172 primary taxpayers interviewed in person by 1980 (Multinomah County, OR)
Current	Aitken and Bonneville (1980)	26 (locked box: how often?)	Responses by 3,588 primary taxpayers interviewed in person in 1979
		21 (randomized response) 12 (locked box: yes/no)	
C. Estimates for overstating deductions			
Cumulative, lifetime	Spicer (1974)	25	See entry in Section B.

Cumulative, lifetime	Habib (1980)	16 (randomized response 5 (direct question)	See entry in Section B.
Cumulative, lifetime	Yankelovich et al. (1984)	7	See entry in Section B.
Cumulative, lifetime	Westat, Inc. (1980f)	6–7	See entry in Section B.
Cumulative, 5 year	Mason and Lowry (1981)	6	See entry in Section B.
Cumulative, 5 year	Mason, Calvin, and Faulkenberry (1975)	5	See entry in Section B.
Current	Aitken and Bonneville (1980)	11 (randomized response) 4 (locked box: yes/no)	See entry in Section B.

cumulative prevalence estimates follow this pattern: they lie in the ranges of 22–25 percent for a lifetime reference period and 12–20 percent for a five-year reference period. The single study to use a three-year reference period reports a prevalence of 12 percent.

For underreporting income (Table 5, Section B), the range of lifetime estimates extends from 12 to 22 percent, and the range of five-year estimates is only slightly smaller, from 12 to 19 percent. Interestingly, the 26 percent single-year prevalence estimate obtained by Aitken and Bonneville (1980) using the locked-box technique is higher than any of the multiyear estimates, most of which were obtained using direct questions. This suggests that sensitive question techniques have at least partial success in eliciting admissions of noncompliance. However, even this estimate is well below the 42 percent estimate derived from the 1979 TCMP and reported in Table 4.

For overstating deductions, all but one of the cumulative estimates obtained using direct questions lie in a lower range, 5 to 7 percent of all respondents. The Aitken-Bonneville current prevalence estimate obtained using the randomized response technique is 11 percent—higher than most of the survey-based cumulative estimates. Adjusting this estimate for the fact that only 28.7 percent of all taxpayers itemize deductions, the estimate is comparable to the prevalence estimates obtained from TCMP as a fraction of all itemizers.[11] This suggests that the randomized response technique was relatively successful in eliciting admissions of the overstatement of deductions in one study. While Habib (1980) obtained a conflicting result, the technique may have potential for future taxpayer compliance research, especially since it can be used as the dependent variable in multivariate analyses (see Fox and Tracy, 1986). In addition, the fact that those current prevalence estimates are no lower than the cumulative estimates obtained by other researchers who generally used direct questions suggests that the usual survey-based estimates obtained using direct questions may substantially understate cumulative noncomplier prevalence; that is, respondents appear to answer in a similar manner whether a one-year or multiple-year reference period is used. Chapter 5 contains recommendations for a program to improve both TCMP and surveys as compliance measurement techniques.

OTHER MEASURES.   Besides tax gap and prevalence estimates, TCMP data can be used to compute other statistics that measure compliance with tax reporting requirements. Two of them, the voluntary compliance level (VCL) and voluntary reporting percentages (VRPs), measure compliance in relative dollar terms—the ratio of amount actually reported by taxpayers to the amount that should have been reported. In the TCMP data base, amounts that should have been reported reflect auditors' assessments and are not adjusted to reflect appeals.

VCL measures the amount of tax liability reported by taxpayers "voluntarily" (i.e., after IRS computerized arithmetic error correction but before any other enforcement contact) as a percentage of corrected tax liability as determined by TCMP examination.[12] According to Fratanduono (1986), VCL for the 1982 cycle was 91.8 percent; that figure represents at least the temporary interruption of a steady downward trend in VCL, from 94.3 percent in 1965 to 91.0 percent in 1979. In contrast to the prevalence statistics indicating that noncompliance is widespread among taxpayers, the high levels of VCL reflect a high compliance level as a percentage of taxes owed. The contrast reflects the fact that most cases of noncompliance involve rather small dollar amounts. Fratanduono's estimates are not adjusted for unreported income that is not discovered by TCMP auditors.

VRP is analogous to VCL but measures compliance separately for each return item: VRP is the ratio of the amount reported by taxpayers to the correct amount as determined by the auditor. For income items, VRPs below 100 percent reflect underreports of tax liability. For subtraction items, VRPs that exceed 100 percent (i.e., overstated adjustments and deductions) reflect underreports of tax liability. Special tabulations from the 1982 TCMP survey were made available to the panel by the IRS Research Division. These were used to construct Table 6, which displays compliance patterns by return item, in terms of VRPs, prevalence rates, and other compliance measures that highlight different aspects of taxpayer compliance.

As Table 6 shows, VRPs vary widely across return items in patterns that suggest some conjectures about causation. For example, compliance is generally high according to the VRP measure for income items that are largely computed for the taxpayer and that are subject to withholding or information reporting, such as salaries, pensions, and interest income.[13] VRP is low for items that are not subject to withholding and for items that require interpretations of complex regulations—tips, proprietors' income, and other (Schedule E) income are examples. Among subtraction items, taxpayers fail to take full advantage of only two—the investment credit and the adjustment for interest penalties for early withdrawal of certificates of deposit. Conventional wisdom within the IRS is that many taxpayers are unaware of the interest penalty adjustment, and that the investment tax credit is not used by many eligible taxpayers who fail to report the income from small, low-visibility businesses. Compliance is high (i.e., VRP only slightly exceeds 100 percent) for deduction items such as IRA contributions and state and local taxes; compliance is much poorer for items that require judgments as to allowability (e.g., political contributions), imputations of amounts (e.g., casualty losses), or extensive documentation (e.g., employee business expenses).

As an alternative compliance measure, Table 6 also contains complier prevalence estimates by return item from the 1982 TCMP survey. While 95 percent of all taxpayers correctly reported their wages and salaries (most of which are subject to withholding), only 70 percent reported all dividends (which are subject only to information reporting), and only 47 percent reported all tips. Easy access to records also seems to encourage compliance, which is better (using both VRP and prevalence) for mortgage interest paid to financial institutions than for mortgage interest paid to individuals. Complier prevalence rates of course increase as the underreporting tolerance is increased. But even when tax increases as large as $1,000 are ignored, complier prevalence is low for items such as proprietor's income (65 percent) and farm deductions (74 percent).

Table 6 also displays the percentage of overreporting, the fraction of taxpayers who misreport items in ways that overstate tax liability.[14] Rea-

TABLE 6 Compliance for 1982 by Return Item

		Complier prevalence				
Return item	Voluntary reporting[a] (%)	No tolerance (%)	$50 underreport tolerance (%)	$1,000 underreport tolerance (%)	Overreporting taxable income (%)	Average item change[b] (%)
Components of taxable income						
Total	96.9	47.6	70.8	89.5	9.6	1,610
Wages/salaries	99.9	95.3	96.8	99.1	0.9	844
Pensions/ annuities[c]	97.9	90.5	91.8	96.7	1.7	879
Interest income	97.0	56.1	81.6	98.2	3.2	311
Gross farm income (Sch. F)[d]	97.0	20.4	72.5	86.3	5.8	3,272
Taxable dividends	96.5	70.0	84.2	97.7	7.8	644
Capital gains (Sch. D)	93.5	68.0	84.6	94.1	9.9	1,809
State and local tax refund	90.9	83.0	88.6	99.7	1.5	208
Unemployment compensation	90.0	74.7	82.3	94.3	3.9	333
Alimony income	86.1	80.1	85.1	89.9	3.2	990
Proprietor's income (Sch. C)	67.6	22.2	37.8	65.4	10.3	3,694
Tips	59.8	47.0	54.2	88.3	0.4	1,924
Other income (Sch. E)[b]	22.3	50.1	66.6	85.3	11.7	2,253

TABLE 6 (*cont.*)

Subtractions from taxable income or taxes

Total itemized deductions	105.5	7.6	52.3	85.3	26.3	1,019
Total tax credits	105.6	43.3	84.1	99.2	12.5	212
Total adjustments	106.3	71.9	87.4	95.3	8.4	1,036
Interest penalty	84.4	66.6	97.7	99.9	2.0	126
Investment credit	99.0	44.5	86.1	98.1	16.8	*e*
IRA contributions	101.1	93.6	96.2	98.3	1.1	962
State and local income taxes	101.4	80.6	92.1	98.7	7.2	494
Mortgage interest (financial institution)	101.8	83.8	91.9	97.2	4.6	1,031
Total farm deductions (Sch. F)	103.0	16.4	49.0	74.3	18.0	2,234
Real estate taxes	103.0	75.6	88.6	98.9	6.7	317
Mortgage interest (individuals)	104.0	75.0	86.3	93.4	4.9	959
Other state and local taxes	104.4	50.5	85.1	99.6	19.9	494
Other interest	105.0	56.3	81.7	97.1	15.2	538
Residential energy credit	105.0	37.0	91.0	99.8	9.8	
Noncash contributions	108.6	67.2	85.1	99.4	5.4	350

TABLE 6 (*cont.*)

Cash contributions	109.7	55.9	74.3	98.1	8.8	346
Medical/dental expenses	113.4	37.7	71.0	95.6	16.1	441
Other misc. deductions	119.7	53.4	74.7	97.3	9.6	173
Child/dependent care	122.7	42.0	76.7	99.7	12.4	
Employee business expenses	128.9	28.2	57.6	83.8	9.6	1,239
Political contributions	145.0	39.9	91.1	100.0	2.3	
Casualty losses	145.7	17.2	51.1	89.3	4.1	893

[a] For income items, VRP less than 100 percent implies understatement of taxable income. For subtraction items, VRP less than 100 percent implies overstatement.

[b] For income items, table reports mean increase for returns with an increase. For subtraction items, table reports mean decrease for returns with a decrease.

[c] Includes fully and partially taxable pensions.

[d] Prevalence based on net farm income.

[e] Tax credit item. Changes for credit items are not comparable to changes for income, adjustment, and deduction items.

Source: Calculated from IRS tabulations of 1982 TCMP data for individual filers.

soning that such misreports are unlikely to be intentional, Klepper and Nagin (1987a) have used overreporting as a proxy for the complexity and ambiguity of an item. Some income items, such as income from schedules C and E, which have low values of VRP, have high rates of overreporting, suggesting that they involve difficult compliance requirements. On subtraction items, high overreporting may reflect some taxpayers' failure to itemize deductions when it is to their advantage (e.g., deductions for state and local taxes, interest, and medical expenditures), lack of awareness (e.g., child/dependent care credit), or concealment of income (e.g., the investment credit).

Finally, Table 6 reports the "average item change,"[15] for returns on which the auditor changed the taxpayer's report. This measure is an indicator of the average revenue yield from discovering a misstatement that caused an understatement of tax liability. On income items the average item change generally tracks VRP except on items such as farm income and capital gains, which frequently involve large amounts but are used by few taxpayers.

The compliance measures for an item are not always correlated with its contribution to the tax gap, because some items are used so much more frequently than others. For example, underreporting of wages contributes about five times as much to the noncompliance tax gap as overclaiming of all credits, despite the values of their compliance measures, since credit items are relevant to few taxpayers. For the same reason, even though tips, alimony, and unemployment compensation are poor-compliance items, they contribute less than one-fifth as much to the reporting gap as wages, pensions, and interest. Some items, of course, reflect poor compliance according to all measures and also make a large contribution to the noncompliance tax gap. These include income from Schedule E (rents, royalties, trusts, etc.) and Schedule C (proprietorships), the adjustment for employee business expenses, deductions for medical expenses, and miscellaneous deductions (mostly deductions for home offices and educational expenses).

TRENDS IN NONCOMPLIANCE.   As previously discussed, there is great uncertainty about the aggregate level of noncompliance for any given tax year. Noncompliance trends are even harder to measure, since the definitions of income and compliance and the nature of the measuring devices have all changed over the years. Probably the best information on long-term compliance trends is a compilation by Holland and Oldman (1984) for the period 1946–1976 of VRPs for certain major components of

TABLE 7 Trends in Voluntary Reporting of Income, 1946–1982

Income category	Voluntary reporting percentage by year							
	1946	1952	1959	1966	1976 (H-O)	1976 (IRS)	1979	1982
Wages and salaries	94	95–96	97	97	97–98	100⁻	100⁻	100⁻
Business and professional income								
Nonfarm	—	78–85		86	—	81	76	68
Farm	—	34–41		40	—	49	35	—
Subtotal	70	70–71	72	78	60–64	77	72	
Interest	34	36–39	66	77	84–90			
Dividends	80	85–87	92	93	84–92	97	96	97
Rental income	50	59	—	44	50–65			
Total	86	90	—	93	92–94	97	96	97

Note: —Not reported.
100⁻ = VRP rounds to 100 percent.
Sources: Estimates for 1946–1966 and for 1976 (H-O) are reported by Holland and Oldman (1984). Estimates for 1976 (IRS), 1979, and 1982 are reported by Fratanduono (1986).

taxable income. Projections of these VRP trends to 1982 are available in an IRS report (Fratanduono, 1986). These statistics are reported in Table 7.

Table 7 suggests that compliance with reporting requirements improved between 1946 and 1966, according to the figures of Holland and Oldman (1984). In attempting to assess trends since 1976, it is first important to note that for return items in common, the IRS estimates for that year are higher than the Holland/Oldman estimates—an indication of the great uncertainty that surrounds the measures. Since that year, reporting of wage and salary income on which taxes are withheld has consistently approached 100 percent.[16] Taxpayer reporting of interest and dividends, which are subject to information reporting, has remained about 96–97 percent. Compliance with reporting requirements has deteriorated in both the nonfarm and farm components of business income, for which compliance is perennially poor.

With respect to subtractions from income, Fratanduono (1986:21) reports substantial variations in VRP across cycles of TCMP, with some fairly pronounced trends. Overstatement of adjustments to income, especially business expenses, jumped substantially between 1965 and 1969 and has continued to increase since that time, while compliance improved for other categories of adjustments. Overstatements of most itemized deductions generally decreased between 1965 and 1982. Overclaiming of exemptions has increased during the period primarily in the category of children at home; this may reflect disallowances of exemptions claimed for children of divorced couples during a period of increasing divorce rates.

This admittedly very shaky evidence suggests that compliance with reporting requirements increased between the end of World War II and the mid-1960s, at least for many components of taxable income. These trends apparently began a moderate decline in the late 1960s or early 1970s. The underreporting of taxable income probably grew at an average annual rate that exceeded the growth of reported personal income by at least 1 percent and perhaps as much as 5 percent per year.

B: Taxpayer Compliance Measurement Program

The Taxpayer Compliance Measurement Program was begun by the IRS in 1962. It originally included three phases or surveys, each of which measured compliance with a different set of requirements: payment of taxes owed by individuals, timely filing by nonfarm businesses, and accurate reporting on returns by individual filers. Of the three original phases only Phase III, the Survey of Individual Returns Filed, is still being regularly conducted; the ninth replication or cycle of Phase III is concerned with tax year 1985 and is still in process. At various times since 1962, however, additional phases have been conducted to measure other aspects of compliance: the accuracy of returns filed by small corporations, for estates, by tax-exempt organizations, for employee pension plans, and for partnerships.

TCMP Phase III is the source of virtually all aggregate statistics on unreported taxable income of individuals. Its primary justification, however, is to support development of the Discriminant Index Function (DIF), which is used to rank returns in order of expected noncompliance. And TCMP data have been used in various ways to support research on compliance with reporting requirements. Because of its importance for many of the analyses described in this report, this note contains a short explanation of TCMP Phase III and its uses in compliance measurements and research. More detailed descriptions are contained in IRS (1984n).

TCMP Phase III (hereafter TCMP) involves audits of randomly selected return filers. Since 1973 a replication or cycle has occurred every third tax year, and a stratified random sample of about 50,000 returns has been drawn for each cycle. Since 1979, strata or "return classes" are defined in terms of income and return complexity: these are measured, respectively, by total positive income (TPI)—the total of all income before offsetting losses against income or other subtractions—and by the forms and schedules filed with the return. Sampling probabilities within strata are set to achieve predetermined precision levels in estimates of unreported taxable income and to produce an expected yield of at least 500 noncompliant tax returns in each stratum, for purposes of DIF development.

Each selected taxpayer undergoes an intensive, comprehensive audit by a specially trained examiner. On a check sheet for each audit, the examiner records values for each item (i.e., components of income, deductions, credits, exemptions, and computation of tax) on the tax return as reported by the taxpayer and as adjusted by the auditor. Codes are also entered on each check sheet to describe the taxpayer's occupation (and industry for returns with schedules for business or farm income) and whether a paid preparer signed the return.

TCMP audits differ from other audits in that they involve examinations of all tax return items, rather than only selected items that have attracted an auditor's attention. TCMP auditors are specially selected and trained to scrutinize returns especially thoroughly, and the check sheets are thoroughly reviewed. Despite these special precautions, inaccuracies are thought to remain. For example, TCMP audits are generally thought to overlook substantial portions of unreported income that is not subject to withholding or information reporting, and information reports have been provided to TCMP auditors only since the 1979 TCMP cycle. Other forms of auditors' errors no doubt occur, and of course some discrepancies between taxpayers' and auditors' assessments reflect unsettled differences of interpretation.

The IRS administers TCMP as a program of tax law enforcement rather than of research. Therefore, the agency bills the taxpayer for additional tax liability discovered by the auditor plus applicable interest and penalties. Like other audits, TCMP audits can lead to criminal investigations of the taxpayer and penalty assessments against the paid preparer. Taxpayers can appeal the results of TCMP audits. However, appeals and their results are not recorded on TCMP check sheets, where they would be readily available for research purposes. Under a statute of limitations, TCMP audits, like other audits, must normally be completed within three years after the return is filed. The taxpayers selected for TCMP audits are not afforded any special protection as research subjects; however, the audit results and tax returns are afforded all the legal privacy protections afforded to all tax-payers under 26 U.S.C. 6103.

The primary IRS use of TCMP data is to develop statistical rules for selecting returns for audit in future years on the basis of the expected tax change that such an audit would produce. By applying statistical methods akin to discriminant analysis to the TCMP check sheets, the IRS estimates DIF formulas, with the auditor's recommended tax change as the dependent variable and nonlinear functions of return items as reported by the taxpayer as predictor variables. Once estimated, the DIF formulas are used to score incoming returns in future years as part of normal return processing. To regulate examiners' workloads across districts, DIF score thresholds are set, and incoming returns with DIF scores that exceed the threshold set for the district office are manually reviewed for audit potential. To improve the accuracy of DIF scores as predictors of audit potential, separate DIF formulas and selection rules are created for predetermined audit classes, which are defined in terms of income ranges and return characteristics (e.g., 1040EZ, 1040A, 1040, 1040 including schedules C or F). In recent TCMP cycles, from seven to twelve audit classes have been used.

Because the DIF formulas play a role in selecting 60 to 70 percent of all returns that are audited, the formulas and their elements are a closely guarded secret within the IRS. Out of concern that others might attempt to replicate the DIF formulas, the IRS also restricts access to TCMP records for all purposes, including research. In fact, the agency has engaged in protracted litigation to prevent research access to TCMP data used in DIF development (*Long* v. *Internal Revenue Service,* 1984). To facilitate research that it wishes to support, however, the IRS has occasionally produced tabulations of TCMP and carried out statistical analyses of TCMP according to external researchers' specifications.

Several of these special analyses have been used in research that is discussed in this report. For example, several columns of Table 6 were derived from tabulations of 1982 TCMP data performed at the panel's request. Table 4 summarizes data from special tabulations that were prepared for researchers at the American Bar Foundation. Machine-readable tabulations of compliance measures for categories of taxpayers (e.g., by occupation, by IRS district office, by preparer type) have been prepared and distributed to researchers. One specially requested analysis— tabulations of aggregate compliance measures and other data by return item, as calculated from 1982 TCMP data—was used by Klepper and Nagin (1987a) to analyze how compliance is related to characteristics of the return items.

TCMP data from the 1969 cycle were used in creating the compliance measure for one aggregate cross-sectional data base that was used for several taxpayer compliance studies discussed in Chapter 2. The desired compliance measure was an estimate of voluntary compliance level (VCL—the ratio of tax liability as reported to tax liability as adjusted by the auditor) for each of seven audit classes for each zip code area in the United States. To produce this measure, the first step was a set of multiple regression analyses—one for each audit class—of the 1969 TCMP data to estimate the relationships between DIF scores and the absolute values of tax change established by TCMP audits. This regression relationship was applied to the DIF score on every return filed for tax year 1969 to compute a predicted tax change. Then, by tabulating the IRS master file, two figures were computed for each audit class in each zip code: total tax liability reported by taxpayers and total predicted tax change. Then the desired VCL estimate was computed as the ratio of tax liability to tax liability plus tax change. In addition, by tabulating the IRS master file by audit class and zip code, measures of IRS activity in the zip code area were computed, such as the fraction of taxpayers audited or contacted in various ways by the IRS. These data have been used in research by Dubin and Wilde (1988) and by Beron, Tauchen, and Witte (1988).

The TCMP program is time consuming and costly. Each cycle requires almost five years for design of check sheets and sample, selection of returns, conduct of the audits, and preparation and cleaning of the automated file of TCMP check sheets. The 1985 TCMP cycle is expected to require direct labor of 1,096 staff years, for a cost of $42 million. In addition, there is an opportunity cost because the TCMP audits of randomly selected returns yield less revenue than other audits. For the 1985 cycle, the IRS estimates the opportunity cost at $86 million, for a total cost of $128 million. The IRS justifies this cost on the basis of the improved efficiency of return selection made possible by DIF. TCMP data are also a very important resource for taxpayer compliance research. The panel makes several recommendations in Chapter 5 for further enhancing both the operational and research value of the TCMP Survey of Individual Returns Filed.

Notes

1. As relatively unobtrusive and inexpensive computerized notices of suspected noncompliance sent to taxpayers have become more prevalent, the use of more expensive and obtrusive in-person audits has declined, from 2.5 percent of returns in 1976 to 1.1. percent 1986.
2. Negligence, which is punishable with civil penalties, should not be confused with tax reduction—the structuring of financial affairs so as to legally reduce taxes owed.
3. The panel's concept of compliance has a similar meaning to the IRS term *voluntary compliance,* which refers to compliance status before the taxpayer is subjected to any enforcement actions. However, such compliance is legally coerced, in the sense that it occurs under the threat of legal sanctions. To avoid implying a judgment about taxpayers' motivations for compliance, the panel adopted the term *compliance* rather than *voluntary compliance.*
4. Note that underreports of income items lead to underreports of tax liability. But for subtraction items, such as exemptions, adjustments, deductions, and credits, the opposite is true: overreports of the items lead to underreports of tax liability. To avoid confusion, throughout this report noncompliance that concerns subtraction items is always described in terms of its effect on reported tax liability, rather than as a simple overreport or underreport.
5. The entire program includes not only the survey of individual filers, but also other surveys intended to measure compliance by corporations, tax-exempt organizations, nonfilers, partnerships, and other categories of taxpayers.
6. The direct labor required was estimated at 1,096 staff-years, primarily for revenue agents to conduct the audits and record the results—the equivalent of $41.8 million in direct cost. In addition, because the TCMP returns are sampled randomly, the audits yield less revenue on average than audits of returns selected on the basis of expected revenue yield. The IRS estimates the oppor-

tunity cost of the lower average yield at $86 million, for a total cost of $127.8 million.

7. The issue of meeting preconditions is of negligible importance with respect to income reporting, since nearly 100 percent of returns report income.

8. For income items, "underreporting taxable income" means that the auditor increased the item above what the taxpayer reported. For subtraction items, "underreporting" means that the auditor reduced the item below what the taxpayer reported; it includes instances in which the entire subtraction was disallowed. Note also that the auditor's reduction of a credit item increases the tax liability by the same amount; with deduction items, the increase is calculated by multiplying the auditor's change by the applicable tax rate.

9. The relatively high prevalence of overreporting for capital gains must be interpreted somewhat differently. These overreports include the treatment of some current income as capital gains in order to take advantage of the capital gains exclusion that was allowed until the 1986 tax legislation.

10. All surveys that are specifically concerned with subtractions from taxable income have asked about "deductions." The researchers' expectations, which seem reasonable, are that respondents tend to group itemized deductions with statutory adjustments, exemptions, and tax credits in formulating their answers.

11. If 28.7 percent of the respondents itemized deductions, then 38.3 percent (i.e., 0.11/0.287) of those who itemized reported "overstating deductions" using the randomized response technique. The comparable range for TCMP estimates (see Table 4) is between 32.2 percent who overstate adjustments and 61.0 percent who overstate deductions.

12. There are actually several variations of the VCL concept. The one reported in this supplementary note is the ratio of tax reported to tax that should have been reported. A common variation is to add up the absolute values of all positive and negative changes and to compute VCL as the ratio of tax reported to tax reported plus the sum of absolute changes.

13. IRS staff members believe that a large fraction of unreported wages paid in cash escapes auditors' attention and therefore is not counted in the denominator of the VRP. Therefore VRP for this item may be best considered a compliance measure for only the wages and salaries subject to tax withholding.

14. For income items, "percent overreporting" is the number of taxpayers who had the item reduced by the auditor, as a fraction of all taxpayers who used the item. For subtraction items, "percent overreporting" is the number of taxpayers who had the item increased by the auditor, as a fraction of all taxpayers who used the item or could have used it, according to the auditor.

15. Here, "change" is defined as an increase by the auditor for income items and a decrease by the auditor for subtraction items.

16. This estimate applies only to wage and salary income paid by employers who submit W-2 information returns. It does not apply to wages earned by employees of organizations whose economic activity is unrecorded.

2. Understanding Taxpayer Compliance: Self-Interest, Social Commitment, and Other Influences

Summary of Existing Research Findings

Social scientists from a variety of disciplines have sought to discover, through theoretical and empirical research, why people comply or fail to comply with federal income tax reporting requirements. The research suggests that considerations of both self-interest—including both financial incentives and social sanctions—and moral commitment affect levels of compliance. And empirical research has revealed certain demographic and socioeconomic compliance patterns that may be interpretable in terms of self-interest and moral commitment. Much more work is needed to quantify the magnitudes of these relationships, to measure the compliance effects of IRS activities, and to understand how taxpayers form their perceptions of the risks and rewards of noncompliance and their personal values concerning compliance.

FINANCIAL SELF-INTEREST

Simple economic theory predicts that compliance increases as the detection of noncompliance becomes more probable. Consistent with this prediction, there is strong evidence that income from sources that are more visible to the IRS is more likely to be fully reported. Visibility is enhanced by withholding, by information reporting by third parties such as banks, and by other records.

Evidence also suggests that experiencing an audit may slightly increase future compliance, at least if the audit discovers all noncompliance and the taxpayer feels the outcome is fair. But even that conclusion is based on old data, and individual-level data over time on IRS contacts, changed perceptions, and compliance would be needed to reach more definitive conclusions. In addition, little is known about the actual detection probabilities for different forms of noncompliance and about how taxpayers form perceptions of these probabilities.

Analyses of a 1969 data base suggest that, in some taxpayer audit classes, higher audit rates may increase compliance slightly by signaling members of those classes that they are vulnerable to audits. This is sometimes called a "deterrence" or "ripple" effect stemming from awareness of a salient IRS audit "presence." They also support the long-held contention that the IRS succeeds to some extent in concentrating its audit resources where taxpayers are the least compliant. More current estimates of these effects and of the compliance effects of new computer-based technologies should be quite important for IRS resource allocation. Updating the 1969 data base should be a high priority if a more valid compliance measure can be developed.

Most microeconomic models predict that higher penalty rates applied to evaded tax would increase compliance, but most empirical studies have failed to find such an effect. A few support the prediction, at least when the probability that the penalties will be imposed exceeds some minimum threshold. Research is needed on the psychologically relevant threshold levels and on the sanctioning process for noncompliers to learn more about determinants of the probability that severe legislative sanctions will be imposed in practice. Recent increases in prescribed penalties and fines present opportunities for before-and-after studies that could reach more clear-cut conclusions.

Some empirical research suggests that lower tax rates improve compliance by reducing the rewards for evasion. But since it is usually difficult to isolate tax rate changes from income changes, those results are open to question. Analyses of experience before and after the Tax Reform Act of 1986, which changed the tax rate schedule, will provide an opportunity to reach more clear-cut conclusions about how tax rates affect compliance.

Neither theoretical predictions nor empirical findings about the relationship between true taxable income and compliance are at all clear-cut. Achieving more understanding will require analyses of individual-level data on changes in income level and composition, experience with IRS contacts, use of tax practitioners, and compliance. Collecting these data over a time period that includes changes in tax rates would make it easier to distinguish income effects from tax rate effects.

Theories are beginning to be developed about how compliance might be affected by variations in the costs of compliance (e.g., understanding complex compliance requirements, filing returns) and noncompliance (e.g., discounts for cash, extraordinary fees to promoters of abusive tax shelters). Some progress is also being made in measuring these costs. But empirical research on how compliance responds to changes in the costs is almost nonexistent and should be a high priority.

SOCIAL SANCTIONS

A few studies suggest that social sanctions—disapproval by friends and acquaintances—may discourage noncompliance, perhaps even as effectively as legal sanctions for some taxpayers. However, confirming this suggestion requires individual-level data on measures of the threat of social sanctions and on compliance measures obtained through techniques other than surveys.

SOCIAL COMMITMENT

Existing survey research has consistently found that taxpayers who report high moral commitment to obeying tax laws are less likely to report cheating on their taxes. However, it is not clear whether this reporting pattern reflects actual behavior. Studies examining how general attitudes toward law, government, tax laws, and the enforcement of tax laws are related to both commitment and compliance have produced less consistent results, and research suggests that the relationships among various attitudes may be quite complex.

TAXPAYER CHARACTERISTICS

As with other laws, compliance with tax laws has been found to increase with age. Compliance is apparently higher for women than men. It may also be higher among whites than nonwhites, but the apparent differences depend on methodological details. Socioeconomic status, indicated particularly by income and education levels, has a more complicated and less consistent relationship to commitment and compliance. The methodological problems, the inconsistencies of some results over a number of studies, and the lack of research on important topics does not allow us to draw firm conclusions about most of these relationships at this time.

Perspectives on Taxpayer Compliance

CONVENTIONAL VIEWS

Since income tax affects the lives of so many citizens, it is not surprising that most people have their own views about why people do or do not comply with the law. A discussion of common elements in these views provides one way of introducing the many factors affecting compliance. The following quotations from group discussions of tax compliance (Westat, Inc., 1980c:9–65) reflect the spectrum of beliefs, some more accurate than others, that are frequently heard when conversations turn to tax matters.

One common element in discussions of compliance involves fears of dealing with the IRS and of being caught cheating. In part this fear is based on the amount of information the IRS has about individuals and their ability to use it to track down noncompliers; in part it is based on the terror some feel when confronted with the institution of the IRS:

> I don't think that you can get anything past the IRS. Eventually, somewhere in that system, the complicated maze that has been worked on to perfection over the years . . . (p. 19).
> In Boulder, Colorado, they have a big computer bank that runs about twenty blocks long where they have everything recorded. Your name is there from the day you were born, your Social Security number, your Army serial number, every time you work it is recorded there. Every medical expense you've ever had that you have claimed on an income tax form is recorded there and what they do each year, they have a group of actuaries who will go over these things yearly and set up an average and they will set the machines, the computers, at this average. If anything goes above this average, I think it is by three points, then they kick it out. The machine is automatically set to kick it out (p. 22).
> If you get a letter in the mail and it says IRS, you say, "Oh my God, what do we do?" (p. 11).
> I don't think the audit in and of itself is any sweat, you know, that's no big deal. I think the thing that is troublesome is there's this big aura surrounding something of uncertainty because nobody's too darn sure about what's going on, even when you make contact. . . . When both sides are uncertain, but yet one side is the authority, you know, the audit becomes some uncertain, big intangible thing (p. 28).

Of course, not all taxpayers are as impressed with the ability of the IRS to track down noncompliers:

> I was just wondering, you know, when I list all my children's names down and thinking how the heck do they know that I have six kids. I could put seven kids and put another name down (p. 23).
> When you stop to think of all the dividend checks and bank deposit slips and getting it going to the income tax—IRS—I wonder if they got enough help to put that in (p. 24).

A taxpayer's fear of getting caught and punished depends in part on structural characteristics of his or her financial environment that make noncompliance more or less difficult to detect. Environments that make noncompliance easy to conceal provide strategic taxpayers with more incentives to cheat:

> If I don't get the form [W-2], I don't file. . . . I'll say c'est la vie . . . that's my money (p. 60).
>
> I switched occupations because in my new work . . . I can take off [personal] car expenses, entertainment expenses, etc., which I couldn't do before (p. 57).
>
> I've got the condominium, which is legal and I charge all kinds of things to it. I paint my house, write down the address of the condominium. That's probably illegal, but it's the only kind of way I can get ahead (p. 60).
>
> I get tips individually, to myself, see. I just put it in my pocket. . . . This is why I don't know [how much to report] (p. 61).
>
> You really don't worry about making that [estimate of tip income] very accurate, so the way you do it is figure something that sounds about reasonable (p. 61).

But fear and strategic considerations are not the only motivating factors most people associate with taxpaying. Social commitment to what people perceive to be right and wrong is involved, and so are their perceptions of informal sanctions—the results of acting in ways that others are likely to see as wrong:

> It's a question of how much pain you're going to feel. I mean, if you understate your income tax by failing to report $18 worth of interest on a savings account, it's wrong; but it's not going to bother you. If you try to make a statement on your income tax that you contributed $1,000 to the United Fund and you don't have any cancelled check or any back-up on that, then you're taking a risk. They're both wrong. But you know, the degree of conscience is going to be a problem because the person who sticks his neck out that far is going to be embarrassed (p. 38).
>
> If you can afford to pay, [income] $30,000 plus, you should pay. If you don't, that's cheating. If you make less than $30,000 any shortcuts to save money are fine (p. 38).
>
> I don't know, embezzlement is embezzlement. You know, a rose is a rose is a rose. And I can't separate them (p. 39).
>
> Outright cheating is where you just put down the wrong figure or don't report income or make up a deduction. A shortcut is where it's the law, but you interpret it one way, even though you're pretty sure that's not the way it's interpreted. . . . But it's worth the gamble trying it (p. 41).

The people that sit on the tax court are human beings and this one judge in one state . . . will rule this way and you'll read the *Wall Street Journal* three months later, you know, and this other judge . . . rules another way. . . . You look at both of them and you think well, wait a minute, that doesn't sound right to me, you know. So you begin to get, you know, common morality mixed up, well, what do you think's right and what do you think's wrong (p. 40).

I tell you, the average American cheats every way they can on the government. That's the truth. But they do it the honest cheating way (p. 42).

Finding a way of going outside the boundaries, you know, reading what the boundaries are, seeing about satisfying my particular need, and then say well I think I can get away with going outside these boundaries and I'm going to take my chances and therefore I'm going to cheat on purpose. I don't think that many people overtly do that (p. 42).

Views about fairness of the tax burden, citizenship duty, and what the government does with tax money also affect some people's perceptions about taxes:

What bothers me about the IRS is the unfairness of it. It's the little guy that's always paying because the very wealthy people have the CPAs and the attorneys that get the loopholes. And they end up paying much less tax than maybe an average income person that's raising a family and that is absolutely unfair (p. 48).

I'd like to see the big people pay their share, but I don't resent taxes. I mean I don't mind paying taxes, as long as we do it equitably and do it in some consistent manner so that it's understandable (p. 48).

You get right down to it, we voted all these things in. . . . So we can sit here and groan all we want, but we're gonna pay . . . (p. 47).

I wouldn't mind it so much if I could designate where my tax dollars went to. I resent having to find out why frogs in South America croak and things like that . . . (p. 46).

The majority of the time that you and I pay taxes, we don't know what it's going for. I feel that we have wasted a lot of our taxes going to somebody else that doesn't deserve or even want our help and the minute they get it, they stick their middle finger at us. Forget it (p. 47).

Social Science Perspectives

The comments above reflect a broad range of notions that people have expressed about paying taxes and about compliance with laws governing the federal income tax. Some of them suggest motivations, personal circumstances, and characteristics of compliance requirements that may plausibly affect compliance. But more is needed to learn the conditions under which these suggestions are actually borne out in taxpayers' behavior and to discover other influences on compliance that taxpayers may be unable or unwilling to divulge to others—in short, to test the accuracy of conventional wisdom about the determinants of taxpayer compliance.

Explaining complex human behavior is the objective of the social sciences. While different social sciences use quite different methods to advance knowledge, they generally share three basic objectives: building, testing, and refining theories of human behavior. In building theory, social scientists draw on some combination of fundamental assumptions about human behavior, advanced mathematics, logical reasoning, and the experiences of themselves and others to generate hypotheses—that is, formal and testable predictions about behavior under different conditions. To test these theories, they gather information—audit records, tax returns, survey responses, logs of the results of experiments, notes on observations, for example—on actual or hypothetical behavior under a range of conditions. By applying appropriate methodologies, the social scientist then tests the hypotheses. Ideally, when the empirical results fail to support the underlying theory, they are used to revise the theory and to structure subsequent tests of the refined theory.

The theories of different social sciences tend to emphasize different processes in attempting to explain taxpayer compliance. While the boundaries are not hard and fast, economists emphasize how individuals' choices are affected by incentives—in the case of tax compliance, the rewards and risks of underreporting tax liability—in an uncertain situation. Sociologists and anthropologists tend to emphasize how compliance is influenced by other factors: fear of social disapproval, practices among colleagues, morality, commitment to the larger society and its rules, and the structures of rules and financial transactions that define options for those who receive income. Psychologists have emphasized the emotional and thinking processes by which individuals cope with complexity and uncertainty; develop their perceptions of compliance requirements, risks, and rewards; and experience guilt from breaking rules or exhilaration from "beating the system." Recently researchers from all these disciplines and from the tax practices of accounting and law have begun to focus on how practitioners affect nearly all these factors—by shaping risks and rewards, transmitting compliance-related values, and coping with complexity.

Most existing research on taxpayer compliance has focused on the inhibiting effects of the three factors discussed by Wrong (1961): fear of legal (i.e., formal) sanctions, fear of social (i.e., informal) sanctions, and moral commitment to legal behavior. This chapter reviews research on the compliance effects of these three factors. In the discussion, several basic themes emerge.

First, because compliance is difficult to measure and alternative explanations of compliance abound, there are many theories but very little firm empirical knowledge about why compliance is greater for some return items and taxpayer categories than for others. Second, no single study (or program of studies) will soon produce the unambiguous knowledge that social scientists and tax administrators would like. Instead, large numbers of specialized studies will be needed to refine existing theories so that they can be used to structure meaningful tests, to identify theories that fail to explain actual behavior, and to verify that the more promising theories hold up against rival explanations, among different taxpayer groups, and under changing compliance environments. Third, because research to date has refuted so few of the possible explanations for compliance with federal income tax laws, none of the social sciences can yet be said to have a monopoly on wisdom in this field. Therefore, progress in understanding taxpayer compliance is likely to come most rapidly through research that draws on the theories and methods of all the social sciences concerned with the issue.

To illustrate the way in which social science research can incorporate social commitment and deterrence factors, consider one of the earliest and most widely cited field experiments in tax research. In face-to-face interviews, Schwartz and Orleans (1967) presented two different questionnaires, one emphasizing social commitment and the other emphasizing deterrence, to randomly selected middle-income taxpayers a month before the 1961 income tax filing date. The social commitment questions were designed to arouse motives for taxpaying ranging from guilt to a patriotic desire to support the government. The deterrence questions asked about the likelihood of being audited and punished, reminding respondents about the potential costs and fearful consequences of cheating. The experiment randomly assigned respondents to three different groups: the first group received only the basic questionnaire, the second group was given the basic questionnaire plus the social commitment questions, and the third group was given the basic questionnaire plus the deterrence questions.

After the respondents filed their returns, aggregate data on income, deductions, and taxes for each group were provided by the IRS from tax returns for that year and the preceding one. Schwartz and Orleans then tested the differences between reports for the three groups. Since the groups were randomly assigned, all groups would be expected to report approximately the same year-to-year average change in tax return items in the absence of the three treatments. Both groups that were presented the additional questions reported more tax due in the second year, although only the group receiving the social commitment questions was significantly higher by standard statistical tests (at the .05 level of confidence). The social commitment group exceeded the control group in both income reported and taxes paid. Schwartz and Orleans concluded that normative appeals appear to increase levels of compliance, while deterrence threats have little or no effect on compliance levels of the population in the experiment.

These conclusions have been criticized for a number of methodological reasons (Friedman and Macaulay, 1977:324–330). First, the levels of statistical significance are low even for the social commitment group, and findings for the deterrence hypothesis were not fully consistent. Second, the entire sample differs from an untreated comparison group, particularly in deductions claimed, and may not have been representative. Third, individuals were dropped from both interviewed groups because no interview was obtained. If those who refused interviews differed systematically from those who were interviewed in terms of their responsiveness to deterrence- or commitment-based appeals, the validity of findings may have been affected. In particular, the test of the deterrence hypothesis is certainly inconclusive, and even the positive findings for social commitment appear to depend on the increased reporting of some—not all—of the group. Replication of the study with more attention to these possible difficulties would be very desirable.

Despite these concerns, this study remains a landmark for at least two reasons. First, it is still the only study in which a randomized experiment was used to test compliance theories on actual tax reporting behavior. All subsequent empirical work has relied on weaker designs and has therefore produced results more open to question on methodological grounds. Second, it is one of the few studies that examined the compliance effects of both sanction threats and appeals to morality in a common framework, using comparably strong measures of both. The Schwartz-Orleans compliance measure—called the return-based measure—still holds great promise today, as a complement to measures based on audit results or taxpayer self-reports.

The rest of this chapter reviews theoretical and empirical research on taxpayer compliance that has been carried out since the Schwartz-Orleans study. Most of that research has examined patterns of compliance that can be explained in terms of self-interest, moral commitment, or demographic characteristics. Figure 1 offers one possible organizational structure for discussing this research. Since that structure has been adopted for the rest of this chapter, the figure may provide a helpful map for the discussion that follows. Sections with titles keyed to items in the figure discuss the current state of knowledge and suggest promising directions for future work.

Some readers will note that Figure 1 omits a number of additional factors that seem intuitively to offer some possible explanations for compliance patterns. Such factors include the complexity of tax laws, the decision processes that people use to cope with complex situations, the development of personal values related to compliance, and the use of tax practitioners' services, for example. For the most part, the theories that might relate such factors to taxpayer compliance have been developed and tested in other contexts. To date, they have received little attention from researchers concerned with taxpayer compliance. For this reason, Chapter 2 is concerned with the findings of previous taxpayer compliance research—concerning self-interest, commitment, and demographic patterns—while discussion of the broader framework is deferred to Chapter 3.

Theories of Financial Self-Interest

Research interest in the relationships between self-interest and compliance with tax laws has been triggered by theoretical and empirical questions within both economics and sociology. This section reviews theories concerning these relationships in both disciplines.

MICROECONOMIC THEORIES

Microeconomic theoretical models of taxpayer compliance have evolved directly from Becker's (1967) pioneering model of criminal choice. Although Becker mentioned tax evasion as a possible area of application for the model, the first to carry out such applications were Allingham and Sandmo (1972). As suggested above, these models treat taxpayer compliance as a problem in maximizing expected utility and analyze it using approaches that were originally developed by von Neumann and Morgenstern (1947).

FIGURE 1. Self-Interest, Social Commitment, and Demographic Factors in
Previous Compliance Research

Theories of Financial Self-Interest
    Microeconomic Theories
        Static random-audit models
        Modeling interactive audit strategies
        Multiperiod dynamic models
        New directions in microeconomic modeling
            General theoretical refinements
            Specific theoretical refinements
    Sociological Theories
Formal Legal Sanctions
    Previous Legal Sanctions
    The Probability of Detection
        Measuring actual and perceived detection probabilities
        Perceived sanction probabilities and self-reported compliance
        Audit rates and estimated compliance measures
        Transaction visibility and detection probability
    Severity of Legal Sanctions
Informal Social Sanctions
Other Compliance Benefits and Costs
    Tax Rates
    Income
    Compliance Costs
Social Commitment
    The Relationship Between Commitment and Compliance
    Attitudinal Influences on Commitment
        General attitudes toward law and government
            Attitudes toward law
            Attitudes toward government
        Specific attitudes toward tax laws
            Perceptions of equity
            Perceptions of complexity and ambiguity
        Attitudes toward tax administration and enforcement
            Attitudes toward the IRS
            Attitudes toward enforcement
            Attitudes toward enforcement effectiveness
Demographic and Socioeconomic Factors
    Demographic Characteristics
        Age
        Sex
        Race and ethnicity
    Socioeconomic Status

In this framework, taxpayers are assumed to make compliance choices in the following context. If the tax liability on the return is accurate (tax liability reported is always assumed to be paid), then the taxpayer receives some level of utility from the after-tax income. If the return reports less than the true taxable income—after subtracting legal exemptions, adjustments, deductions, and credits—then the outcome is uncertain because the IRS may or may not discover the unreported income. If it is not detected, then the taxpayer is better off than if he or she had reported accurately. But if the unreported income is detected, then he or she is worse off because the tax due is collected together with a penalty. Therefore, the expected utility of underreporting a given amount of taxable income depends on the taxpayer's total income,[1] the tax rate structure that applies to that income, the probability of detection of unreported taxable income, and the penalty for failing to report taxable income accurately. Using advanced mathematics, microeconomists derive hypotheses about how the taxpayer's income report would be altered by changes in these factors if they were recognized and if the taxpayer were trying to maximize expected utility.

This simple model can be enriched to reflect many real-world complexities. Examples include other costs of accurate reporting (e.g., ascertaining compliance requirements) and of underreporting (e.g., discounts for cash), the discontinuous bracket structure of U.S. income tax rates, the time costs of being audited, a "guilt discount" for income retained through evasion, and informal sanctions that may be experienced by noncompliant taxpayers because of social disapproval. As these and other complexities are introduced into the model, the mathematics required to derive specific hypotheses about their effects on compliance behavior becomes more difficult. Despite this difficulty, microeconomic models of taxpayer compliance behavior have evolved substantially over the last two decades.

These theories are useful for thinking about compliance and about the relationships between the taxpayer and the IRS, but their predictions are virtually never sufficient as a guide to policy. The models rarely predict relative magnitudes of effects, and the predictions are frequently conditional on behavioral assumptions (e.g., decreasing aversion to risk as income increases) that cannot be independently verified. Nevertheless, both the conditional and unconditional predictions of such models can be used to structure empirical research. And as demonstrated below, the newest models, which capture institutional realities of tax administration more accurately, call attention to some relevant considerations for tax administrators.

The evolution of microeconomic models of taxpayer compliance can be discussed in terms of three generations: static random-audit models, models of interactive audit strategies, and multiperiod dynamic models. These are explained in the following sections, which are followed by a discussion of promising new directions in microeconomic models of taxpayer compliance.

STATIC RANDOM-AUDIT MODELS.   The earliest microeconomic models of taxpayer compliance are reviewed by Witte and Woodbury (1983) and by Cowell (1985c). Following the original work of Allingham and Sandmo (1972), important contributions were made by Srinivasan (1973), Yitzhaki (1974), Weiss (1976), Andersen (1977), Pencavel (1979), Isachsen and Strøm (1980), and Sandmo (1981), among others. This first generation of models are frequently characterized as random audit, since all taxpayers are assumed to face the same audit rate (and the audit is assumed to detect all unreported taxable income), regardless of the nature of their tax return or compliance status.

These models were used to generate hypotheses about how variations in four elements of taxpayers' financial self-interest—noncompliance penalties, noncompliance detection probability, income, and tax rate—would affect compliance if taxpayers knew their values and behaved as strategic maximizers of expected utility. Until quite recently, they were used to structure all the econometric research on taxpayer compliance.

Many hypotheses generated by the random-audit models are consistent with the commonsense notion that increasing the risks of noncompliance encourages compliance. For example, most models since the pioneering work of Allingham and Sandmo (1972) have predicted that increasing the audit rate would cause an increase in reported income. Later, Isachsen and Strøm (1980) introduced the notion of a two-sector economy—a legitimate sector with a high audit rate, and a hidden economy with a low audit rate. Their model allowed for the possibility that if the two rates were different enough, further increases in the audit rate in the legitimate sector could cause so many workers to shift to the hidden economy that aggregate reported income could actually fall.

Predictions about how reported income is affected by changes in true income or in penalties for underreporting taxes depend critically on underlying assumptions about the relationship between income and aversion to risk (see, for example, Cowell, 1985c). The most common assumption in modeling many risky decisions is "decreasing absolute risk aversion"—that is, that increases in income cause an increase in dollars allocated to risky assets. In the context of taxpayer compliance, the implication is that unreported income increases as true income increases. More stringent assumptions can be made about relative risk aversion, that is, the fraction of dollars allocated to risky assets; as summarized by Cowell (1985c:172), "an increase in income will increase/leave unchanged/decrease the proportion of income concealed from the tax-man according as relative risk aversion is, respectively, decreasing/constant/increasing."

Most random-audit models provide no basis for presuming that compliance can be increased by decreasing tax rates.[2] If the underreporting penalty is a constant fraction of the unreported income, then a decrease in the tax rate presumably decreases the incentive for underreporting. But it also increases after-tax income, which will increase underreporting under the common assumption of decreasing absolute risk aversion, so that the net effect is ambiguous (Allingham and Sandmo, 1972). However, as noted by Yitzhaki (1974), in the United States and Israel, civil penalties are levied as a fraction of the unreported tax, so that a decrease in the tax rate has precisely offsetting relative effects on the risks and rewards for evading tax. But the rate decrease also increases after-tax income; therefore, lower rates should reduce compliance if absolute risk aversion decreases with income.

Slemrod (1985a) examined the relationship between tax and compliance in the context of a progressive tax rate structure. He hypothesized that the closer a noncompliant taxpayer's income is to the top of the next lower bracket, the more likely he or she is to underreport income still further—by enough to get into the lower bracket. If confirmed, this theory would suggest that the IRS use proximity to the top of a bracket as a factor in selecting returns for audit.[3]

MODELING INTERACTIVE AUDIT STRATEGIES.   A natural criticism of the random-audit models is that audits are not equally likely for all taxpayers. It is well known that the IRS selects many returns for audit using an interactive strategy—selection is based on characteristics of the return that are associated with substantial income underreporting. (See Chapter 1, Supplementary Note B, for a more complete description of the IRS strategy, which is called DIF selection.) This fact and its possible consequences for empirical research were recognized several years ago (see, e.g., Clotfelter, 1983; Witte and Woodbury, 1983, 1985; Lansberger and Meilijson, 1982). However, interactive IRS selection strategies were not incorporated into single-period theoretical models of taxpayer compliance until 1985 by Reinganum and Wilde. This work is summarized by Graetz,

Reinganum, and Wilde (1986), by Cowell (1985c), and by Tauchen and Witte (1986).

To model the interaction between a strategic taxpayer and a strategic IRS, researchers have used two game-theoretic approaches: the principal-agent model and the Nash equilibrium model. In the principal-agent model (e.g., Reinganum and Wilde, 1985b), the IRS is taken to be the principal who is seeking to control the behavior of the taxpayer (agent). The IRS asks the taxpayer to report income and, on the basis of this imperfect information about true income, decides whether to audit the return. The taxpayer is assumed to try to maximize his or her own expected after-tax income. Reinganum and Wilde showed that an audit cutoff strategy—in which a report of taxable income below some threshold always triggers an audit and a report above the threshold never does—raises revenue for the tax agency at least as efficiently as a random-audit strategy, so long as taxpayers are risk neutral. The IRS DIF selection system is an example of a complex cutoff strategy.

As explained by Graetz et al. (1986), one difficulty is that the principal-agent model assumes that the tax agency announces its strategy in advance. Realistically, with advance knowledge of the audit cutoff strategy, tax-payers would anticipate and attempt to defeat it—if the cutoff income were known to be $12,000, strategic noncompliant taxpayers would always report at least $12,001, for example. The tax agency would then be forced to abandon the audit cutoff strategy. Not surprisingly, therefore, the actual DIF formula is one of the most closely guarded secrets in the IRS.

Under the Nash equilibrium approach (Graetz et al., 1986), the tax agency and the taxpayer are treated more symmetrically and are assumed to play against each other without preannouncing their strategies. In its most widely explored form (Graetz et al., 1986), the Nash model allows tax-payers to earn one of two incomes, called "high" and "low." The taxpayer maximizes expected net income by reporting either high or low income, and the tax agency audits some fraction of the taxpayers who report low income.

Under these assumptions, the model predicts that increases in the penalty rate, the differential between low and high income, and the tax rate will all increase the probability of true reporting. As noted by Graetz and Wilde (1985), it is important from the standpoint of tax policy that neither these interactive models nor most of the random-audit models offer any theoretical support for the presumption that compliance can be improved by reducing tax rates.

A concern remains that, as with the random-audit models, the behavioral predictions of the interactive models depend on rather heroic simplifying assumptions. For example, although they require no assumption about risk aversion, they do assume that only two income levels can be reported and that the IRS budget is unconstrained. But theoretical recognition of the interaction between taxpayers and the IRS is an important advance for structuring econometric research.

Interactive models are not only important for structuring empirical research on taxpayer compliance; they also offer theoretical support for certain strategies of tax administration, some of which would be innovations. For example, Reinganum and Wilde (1985b) suggest that within any fairly homogeneous group of taxpayers, reported tax revenue will be maximized if the IRS audits the returns that report the lowest levels of taxable income; this contrasts with a strategy of auditing returns with high levels of income to maximize the expected revenue from audit. Their work also suggests that among returns that report the same income, it is most productive to audit those that suggest the greatest income potential, as reflected in occupation, address, and other information on the tax return. As summarized by Graetz et al. (1986), their work also extends to tax administration the notion that under certain conditions[+] higher penalties encourage compliance more cost effectively than greater efforts to detect violations (Polinsky and Shavell, 1979).

MULTIPERIOD DYNAMIC MODELS.   In contrast to interactive models, which all relate to a single return-filing period, multiperiod models have begun to consider more complex timing and audit selection strategies. For example, Lansberger and Meilijson (1982) first showed that at least under certain conditions, maximizing tax revenue over a taxpayer's lifetime would require the IRS to vary the audit probability from year to year. Some of the more recent models suggest specific innovations that would increase tax revenue under idealized theoretical conditions, which might be of value in more realistic situations. For example, Greenberg (1984) derives a revenue-maximizing audit selection strategy in which each taxpayer faces one of three different audit probabilities, depending on the results of audits in previous years.

Green and Laffont (1986) recognize explicitly that, before establishing audit selection rules, the IRS can sample from all returns. For example, under conditions outlined in their working paper, it would be optimal for the agency to analyze all returns prepared by a given practitioner in developing audit rules for clients of that practitioner. Besides the direct advantage of using this additional information, announcement of such a strategy would give practitioners an incentive to examine the quality of their potential clients' records before accepting them as clients.

NEW DIRECTIONS IN MICROECONOMIC MODELING. Although microeconomic theories of taxpayer compliance have advanced substantially in recent years, they still fail to incorporate many institutional realities of taxpaying. One of the most basic is differences among return items in detection probabilities, penalties, compliance costs, and, until recently, tax rates. The other is the role of tax practitioners in providing information and altering the incentives for compliance and noncompliance.

Future theoretical models should recognize these influences on compliance. These more refined models should be used to explore the ways compliance is affected by the following four factors, among others: the timing with which different types of income are received and taxes are paid out during the year, costs of compliance such as preparing returns and undergoing examinations, the errors of taxpayers in preparing returns and IRS staff in examining them, and ignorance about penalties and errors in estimating the chances of getting caught cheating.

General theoretical refinements. Until recently, microeconomic theories of compliance have ignored two important institutional aspects of taxpaying—the different categories of income and subtractions from taxable income and the roles of tax practitioners. Two important next steps in the evolution of microeconomic theories of taxpayer compliance are to incorporate these phenomena.

Nearly all microeconomic models treat income as a homogeneous quantity, yet nearly all components of self-interest that are theoretically related to taxpayer compliance depend on the form in which income is received. As explained in Chapter 1, many kinds of unreported income are far less likely to be detected than overstated subtractions.[5] Within the category of unreported income, the probability of detection is greater for types that are subject to tax withholding, information reporting, or some special IRS enforcement program. In contrast, the probability that a given subtraction will be questioned depends on its plausibility in view of other taxpayer characteristics, and the probability that it will be disallowed depends in part on the quality of the taxpayer's record keeping. The severity of noncompliance penalties can also be expected to vary by return item. For items whose application to a given taxpayer's circumstances can be construed as ambiguous, noncompliant taxpayers can plead ignorance and probably receive relatively mild negligence penalties instead of the more severe fraud penalties.

Klepper and Nagin (1987a) have taken an important first step in disaggregation by characterizing return items in terms that are related to the probability of audit and the severity of penalties. They argue, for example, that noncompliance is less likely to be detected if it involves items that are less *traceable* through withholding or information reporting. Severe criminal penalties are less likely when intent is more *deniable* (e.g., because many taxpayers make errors) or requirements are more *ambiguous* (as indicated by more legal controversy). They then use a microeconomic model to predict how those characteristics affect compliance. The next logical step is to allow these item-specific characteristics to depend also on taxpayer characteristics such as occupation. But even the current state of disaggregation permits the additional complexities discussed below to be addressed theoretically.

The other fundamental omission from nearly all microeconomic models of compliance is the tax practitioner. As explained more fully in Chapter 3, practitioners directly affect the compliance status of at least half of all returns filed each year. They also potentially affect nearly all the institutional complexities mentioned above: the cost of compliance, the detection probability for noncompliance, the severity of penalties, and taxpayers' error rates. By advising clients how to structure their financial affairs to maximize after-tax income, tax practitioners can affect the allocation of some taxpayers' true income across sources. Because practitioners' compliance incentives may differ from those faced by taxpayers (e.g., they face severe penalties for negligence and fraud but may substantially increase their incomes by creating a reputation for establishing and successfully defending novel interpretations of law that benefit their clients), they can be expected to alter reported income from the levels reported by a strategic taxpayer working on his or her own behalf.

Yet even though practitioners should theoretically influence nearly all aspects of taxpayer compliance, they have been incorporated in only a few microeconomic models to date (see, for example, Klepper and Nagin, 1987b; Mazur and Nagin, 1987; and Scotchmer, Vol. 2). Together with disaggregation of taxable income, incorporation of practitioners is essential if microeconomic models are to address institutional complexities such as those considered in the next section.

Specific theoretical refinements. By recognizing that different return items are reported and examined differently, economic theorists can extend their models in at least four important ways.

First, the timing of income receipts and tax payments is affected by tax withholding and appears to have substantial effects on taxpayer compliance. Focus group reports (Westat, Inc., 1980e) and persistent overwithholding suggest that taxpayers may psychologically concede withheld taxes to the government and value after-tax income more highly if it is received as a tax refund than if it is received in regular paychecks through-out the year. However, the compliance implications of this pattern have not been explored theoretically. For example, Alexander and Feinstein (1986) have used "rejoicing and regret functions" to allow for the possibility that taxpayers value dollars gained from noncompliance more or less highly than dollars acquired in other ways. It would be useful to allow these functions to be affected by the timing of earnings and taxes.

Second, as explained more fully later in this chapter, the fundamental assumptions of the von Neumann-Morgenstern model of expected utility maximization under uncertainty are being challenged on theoretical and experimental grounds by both economists and psychologists. Many of the challengers have proposed alternative assumptions about how the probabilities of alternative outcomes enter the expected utility function. The alternatives are reviewed by Machina (1987), and their applications to criminal behavior are reviewed by Lattimore and Witte (1985). There is a need to explore theoretically the implications of these alternative assumptions for predictions about how a taxpayer maximizing expected self-interest would respond to changes in the relevant risks and rewards for noncompliance.

Third, as noted by Slemrod (Vol. 2), there is a need for future theoretical models of compliance to incorporate other taxpaying costs besides taxes and penalties. He notes that tax laws require positive actions and hypothesizes that the more costly these are, the greater is the incentive to avoid the costs altogether by failing to file. Models recognizing such effects could potentially explain nonfiling and consistent overreporting of tax liability in more satisfactory terms than taxpayer error. Relevant variables might include the costs of determining compliance requirements and the costs of maintaining the records that an auditor would require to document an adjustment or deduction. Since these costs clearly vary across tax return items, compliance would also be expected to vary.

While filing and record-keeping difficulties provide a major source of compliance costs, the other major source arises in the course of reducing uncertainty about the tax liabilities for nonroutine transactions. The effect of uncertainty on compliance is not clear. Uncertainty may increase under-reporting of tax liability to the extent that the loss from errors of over-reporting is greater than the expected penalties (net of benefits) associated with errors of underpayment (Slemrod, Vol. 2), thus inviting taxpayers to err on the side of evasion (Scotchmer, Vol. 2). Slemrod concludes, however, that uncertainty is likely to increase compliance for an individual considering a specific act of noncompliance because of the costs of an audit associated with errors of understated taxes. Klepper and Nagin (1987a) note that the potential for uncertainty makes imposition of civil rather than more severe criminal penalties more likely for certain items, which then become targets for noncompliance. Further analysis is needed to understand when uncertainties lead to greater search for certainty (through the investment of the taxpayer's time in hiring the services of a third party) and what the consequences of such search may be (Scotchmer, Vol. 2). Such analyses should also consider the simultaneous effect of uncertainty on the IRS, since uncertainty is equally likely to affect enforcement costs and efficiency.

A compliance cost that calls for much more theoretical attention than it has received to date is the cost to the taxpayer of undergoing an audit. Despite empirical evidence to the contrary,[6] most microeconomic models of compliance implicitly assume that only noncompliant taxpayers are audited and that auditors always discover all unreported tax liability. From the standpoint of empirical research, the effect of ignoring auditors' errors has been acknowledged—and modifications to estimation techniques proposed—by Alexander and Feinstein (1986), Beron et al. (1988), and Schmidt (Appendix A to this volume). In the absence of an underlying theoretical framework, none of these investigators has modeled the errors explicitly; incorporation of auditors' errors into theoretical models would therefore advance empirical research on compliance. To advance the state of multiperiod theoretical models, it would be useful to model the effects of auditors' errors on both taxpayer compliance and IRS strategic behavior in subsequent years.

Fourth, most microeconomic models of taxpayer compliance assume that taxpayers have precise knowledge of the relevant detection probabilities and penalties, even though there is empirical evidence discussed later in this chapter that, in general, individuals make systematic errors in estimating low probabilities. There is a need to refine the models by incorporating systematic over- and underestimates of probabilities into compliance calculations. In interactive and dynamic models, it would be useful to incorporate alternative assumptions about how the relevant probabilities are learned through repeated cycles of taxpaying and to examine how predictions about compliance are affected by alternative assumptions about this process.

Finally, of course, it is important to test these models empirically and to use the results to suggest further useful refinements.

SOCIOLOGICAL THEORIES

Sociologists concerned with how sanctions inhibit illegal behavior frequently distinguish among three inhibiting mechanisms: (1) fear of formal sanctions—the punishment delivered by a legal or administrative system; (2) fear of informal sanctions—the disapproval of one's peers; and (3) internalization of legal norms, a moral commitment to legal behavior that may be enforced by internally produced guilt (Wrong, 1961). The hypothesis that more certain or severe legal sanctions will encourage compliance with the law is consistent not only with the economic theories discussed above, but also with exchange theory in sociology.

As summarized by Grasmick and Green (1980), a crucial explanatory variable in theories that relate social sanctions to compliance is whether a person's friends or respected acquaintances engage in noncompliance. Through the mechanism of social sanctions, taxpayers with noncompliant friends (and, in the taxpaying context, acquaintances with whom one deals in earning and spending income) should tend to be noncompliant themselves.[7] There is dispute about how social and legal sanctions interact in deterring illegal behavior. If the major effect of legal sanctions is to expose the offender to others' disapproval, then legal sanctions are likely to deter noncompliance only when there is a substantial perceived threat of social sanctions. Alternatively, if social sanctions represent a strong threat, then only a small amount of noncompliance would exist in the first place, and so one would expect weaker deterrence effects from legal sanctions (see Zimring and Hawkins, 1971; Tittle and Logan, 1973; and Grasmick and Green, 1980, for more complete expositions concerning this debate). Because of remaining questions about the nature of this interaction, and because the certainty and severity of legal and social sanctions are likely to be correlated, empirical compliance research needs to account for both types of sanctions.

It is sometimes hypothesized that, for several reasons, social sanctions should be a less important deterrent to taxpayer noncompliance than to other illegal behaviors involving similar amounts of money. First and as noted previously, unlike the laws against burglary, for example, which require only refraining from prohibited behavior, compliance with tax laws requires a taxpayer to follow a procedure that is complex and subject to uncertainty; peers may be unlikely to condemn failure to comply under these conditions. Second, as noted by Klepper and Nagin (Vol. 2), incidents of noncompliance with tax laws rarely become public unless the IRS pursues criminal sanctions or the taxpayer contests civil penalties in court. The former rarely happens unless fraud or other serious, more widely condemned crimes are also involved, and the latter suggests an honest difference of opinion between the taxpayer and the IRS, which is unlikely to be socially condemned. Third, noncompliance with tax laws may be unlikely to be socially condemned, because it produces no individual identifiable victim and because sizable fractions of the population believe the tax laws are unfair anyway (see, e.g., Yankelovich et al., 1984).

However, there are reasons to question whether in fact social condemnation is as unimportant as these considerations would suggest. As noted by Kinsey (1984), the crime seriousness ratings obtained for tax evasion seem to depend on what other illegal acts are used for comparison and on the wording used to describe evasion. In a national survey of crime seriousness, the relative rating for tax evasion (compared to auto theft, passing bad checks, and robbery) depended on whether a specific dollar amount was named (Wolfgang et al., 1985); the results suggested that in the absence of a specific dollar amount, respondents tended to assume that tax evasion involved larger amounts than the other crimes. The level of social condemnation for taxpayer noncompliance seems to depend on the specific behavior. According to the IRS (1985j), 26 percent of the respondents to the survey by Yankelovich et al. (1984) preferred jail sentences for "cheating by large amounts," and 42 percent preferred "heavy fines." But many believe that the IRS should ignore certain types of unreported income altogether, such as income from barter transactions (53 percent), tips (42 percent), and cash payments for services (28 percent).

Taken together, sociological theory and empirical evidence suggest that it is important to test how legal and social sanctions interact to inhibit noncompliance with taxpaying requirements.

Empirical Evidence on Formal Legal Sanctions

The preceding section discussed theories of how taxpayer compliance is related to formal legal sanctions and informal social sanctions. The rest of this chapter is concerned with empirical rather than theoretical research. This section reports findings from research on the compliance effects of formal legal sanctions. The remaining sections are concerned with empirical research on informal sanctions, other costs and benefits of compliance, social commitment, and demographic characteristics that researchers have found to be correlated with compliance.

In studying the relationships between the threat of formal legal sanctions and taxpayer compliance, researchers have usually measured sanction threat in one of three ways: previous experience with sanctions for noncompliance, the perceived probability of such sanctions, and their perceived severity. Firm conclusions on how these threats affect compliance are rare because of three primary difficulties: measuring sanction threat and compliance accurately, sorting out directions of causality between sanctions and compliance, and eliminating other competing explanations of empirical correlations.

The research discussed in this section suggests that, at least for some taxpayers and for some forms of noncompliance, a higher perceived probability of detection for noncompliance is associated with more complete compliance. In addition, taxpayers who perceive greater severity of sanctions for noncompliance are more likely to express intentions to comply, at least above some threshold of perceived probabilty that the sanctions will be imposed. Research has not established the effect of taxpayer audits on subsequent compliance, although this question is important both to test specific deterrence and rehabilitation hypotheses and to help develop audit strategies.

The research findings are quite sensitive to the underlying assumptions. Reaching conclusions with more confidence and specificity will require future researchers to analyze the sensitivity of findings to assumptions more systematically, to improve their measures of sanctions and compliance, and to develop and analyze data that describe taxpayers' sanction perceptions and compliance at multiple points in time.

This section discusses the results of researchers' attempts to estimate relationships between measures of compliance and three measures of legal sanctions: (1) the occurrence of previous sanctions, (2) the probability of detecting noncompliance, and (3) the severity of legal sanctions.

EFFECTS OF PREVIOUS LEGAL SANCTIONS

In criminological literature, legal punishment for noncompliance is usually hypothesized to improve an individual's future compliance through two mechanisms: specific deterrence, which operates by arousing fear of future punishment, and rehabilitation, which operates by educating offenders or modifying their attitudes to heighten commitment to compliance. In the context of taxpayer compliance, tests of this relationship have nearly all focused on the effects of taxpayer audits, asking the question: Are taxpayers who have been audited in the past more compliant? Contrary to a deterrence or rehabilitation hypothesis, most studies of this question have reported that previous audits are correlated with poorer compliance. But their designs confound the compliance effects of audits with the effects of IRS audit strategy, which attempts to select returns of the least compliant taxpayers.

Even in studies that control for selection effects, however, only small apparent deterrence and rehabilitation effects have usually been found. Their size and direction may depend on specific conditions, such as the audit outcome, taxpayer satisfaction, and other circumstances that have not been controlled in most published research to date. Testing such speculations requires research designs that capture pre- and postaudit measures of compliance, perceived detection probabilities for noncompliance, and commitment to compliance. The details are discussed in the following paragraphs.

Most studies of the relationship between audits and compliance have sought to relate a measure of compliance in one year to indicators of routine audits in previous years. One approach has been cross-sectional surveys, in which respondents were asked to report previous noncompliance and previous audit experience. Contrary to a deterrence hypothesis, most of these surveys found previous audits associated with poorer self-reported compliance, at conventional levels of statistical significance (Spicer and Lundstedt, 1976; Westat, Inc., 1980f; Yankelovich et al., 1984).

In the one nonsurvey study using this design, the IRS (1973) used indicators of taxpayers' calendar 1967–1969 audit histories as explanatory variables in a multiple regression analysis of the 1968–1969 change in reported tax liability. Since the analysis also controlled for the 1968–1969 change in adjusted gross income, the compliance measure could reflect only behavior with respect to deductions and credits. For three of the four medium- and high-income classes, for which deductions and credits are most relevant, the previous audits were associated with decreases in reported tax liability—the opposite of expectations under a deterrence hypothesis. Only in the low-income classes, for which deductions and credits are less important, were the results consistent with a deterrence or rehabilitation effect.

There are several reasons to doubt that these findings actually describe the effect of audits on subsequent compliance. First, the IRS attempts to concentrate its audit resources on taxpayers it suspects of noncompliance. If compliance behavior tends to be stable from one year to the next, that strategy will lead to a spurious counterdeterrence effect in simple correlations between audits and subsequent compliance. Second, despite the IRS selection strategy, fully compliant taxpayers are sometimes audited. For these taxpayers the audit may serve to reinforce existing behavior (i.e., to show "no effect" in the analysis). Or it may trigger resentment or a recalculation that future audits are unlikely, either of which could lead to future noncompliance (i.e., showing a counterdeterrence effect). Third, some audits of noncompliant taxpayers miss at least part of the unreported tax liability. Responses to these errors of omission may produce a true counterdeterrence effect by reducing the taxpayer's expectation that future noncompliance will be detected. Since auditors' errors are unobserved by the researcher, their effects on behavior are not isolated in the analysis.

Several kinds of evidence suggest that the anomalous positive correlations in these studies do in fact arise from the IRS selection process. On the basis of a simultaneous equation analysis of the data from Yankelovich et al. (1984), Kinsey and Smith (1987a) suggested that noncompliance increased the probability of audit. However, their analysis also suggested that the audit experience decreased the perceived probability of reaudit and left expectations unchanged about the nature of sanctions; therefore, no specific deterrence effect was observed.

Additional evidence concerning the specific deterrence effect comes from analysis of a TCMP panel study, in which some subjects of 1969 TCMP audits were audited a second time in the 1971 TCMP. Because TCMP subjects are selected randomly, the confounding effect of IRS audit selection strategies on the correlation is eliminated. On the basis of its analyses of the TCMP data for three audit classes in both years, the IRS (1975b) reported that for the taxpayers who were audited twice, the voluntary compliance level—the ratio of self-assessed tax liability to tax liability assessed by the TCMP auditor—was greater in 1971 than in 1969, while VCL for the entire 1971 sample was lower than for the entire 1969 sample.[8]

This finding suggests that the first TCMP audit had a deterrence or rehabilitation effect, but recent reanalyses of a partial subsample in a working paper by Long and Schwartz (1987) suggest that the effect is rather limited. They find decreases between the first and second audits (from 2 to 10.4 percent, depending on taxpayer category) in the fraction of panel subjects who allegedly underreported their tax liability by more than $25. But they also find slight increases (between 0.3 and 1.8 percent) in the fraction who overreported tax liability. And while the average amount of tax deficiency assigned by the auditor decreased in four of five of the taxpayer categories used by the researchers, the decreases were small and not statistically significant.

One laboratory experiment does suggest a specific deterrence effect from audits. After ten simulated periods of earning income and paying taxes, with subjects audited according to a random strategy so as to remove possible audit selection effects, Spicer and Hero (1985) reported that higher numbers of audits during the first nine periods were associated with less evasion in the tenth round.

Survey researchers have asked repondents how their subsequent taxpaying was affected by an actual previous audit (Westat, Inc., 1980f) or would be affected if an audit took place (Aitken and Bonneville, 1980). Both surveys suggest that some taxpayers experience a deterrence effect. The majority (80 percent in the Westat survey, 70 percent in the Aitken and Bonneville survey) reported no change. Of those who reported a change, the most common reponse was to be more careful (69 percent in Westat,[9] 70 percent in Aitken and Bonneville); while *careful* was probably intended to mean "more careful to comply," it may have been interpreted to mean "more careful to take advantage of legal tax reduction opportunities" or even "more careful to conceal taxable income." Smaller numbers (14 percent in Aitken and Bonneville) responded "be more honest" (Westat didn't include this response). A few respondents (one in the Westat survey and 1 percent of the Aitken and Bonneville respondents) gave answers indicating they would be less honest in the future. The latter effect could have resulted either from failure of the audit to detect some unreported tax liability or from adverse effects on commitment—causes with quite different policy implications—but was rare in any event.

THE PROBABILITY OF DETECTION

One question that has long been recognized as an area for empirical research on taxpayer compliance is whether variations in the probability of sanctions affect levels of illegal behavior. The question is also of great policy significance, because IRS enforcement efforts may have broad ripple or presence effects that are large compared with their direct revenue yields. Sound estimates of these effects would be extremely useful in allocating IRS resources.

Research to date has yielded few firm conclusions about the compliance effects of variations in detection probabilities that occur because of changes in enforcement resources. Surveys that ask taxpayers to estimate probabilities and to report noncompliance produce results that are consistent with a deterrence hypothesis for reporting of one's own noncompliance, but the results may not carry over to actual noncompliant behavior. Econometric studies also provide limited support for a deterrence hypothesis. But the compliance measures are too questionable, and the results are too sensitive to details of the analysis, to serve as a basis for firm conclusions. In any event, most of the results were obtained using a data base constructed for 1969, and many relevant changes in tax laws and tax administration technology have occurred since then. One consistent result is that structural characteristics of the tax system that increase the probability of noncompliance detection (e.g., by increasing income visibility or reducing the role of taxpayer discretion in interpreting regulations) have a rather strong deterrent effect on noncompliance.

Further progress in describing these relationships will require conceptual work on the measurement of compliance and the relevant detection probabilities and on specifying the reciprocal relationships between compliance and detection probabilities. Progress would be facilitated by an updated and improved version of the 1969 data base used for most of the econometric analyses, as well as by taxpayer surveys that provide validated measures of compliance and the relevant perceived probabilities at multiple points in time. In the sections below we explain these issues further and review empirical knowledge about:

1. Perceived chances that noncompliers will be detected;
2. Relationships between perceived probabilities and self-reported compliance;
3. The relationships between audit rates and taxpayer compliance; and
4. The compliance effects of other influences on noncompliance detection probabilities.

MEASURING ACTUAL AND PERCEIVED DETECTION PROBABILITIES. The measurement of both actual and perceived detection probabilities for noncompliance is still in its infancy, in part because of conceptual confusion about what is being measured. The portion of returns audited in 1983 was only 1.27 percent, far below the detection probabilities estimated in taxpayer surveys. But the audit rate understates the detection probability because noncompliant returns are more likely than others to be audited and because audits are only one means of detecting noncompliance. Survey results clearly indicate taxpayers' recognition that failure to report all taxable income increases the chances of an audit, especially when large amounts are involved. In addition, in focus groups and surveys, taxpayers express beliefs about specific return characteristics that increase the chances of audits. However, very little is known about how these impressions are formed. Work is needed to refine the probability construct and to increase understanding of how perceptions about it are formed.

Estimates of the perceived and actual probabilities that noncompliance will be detected vary from study to study, because of differences in the wording of questions. For example, between 80 and 90 percent of respondents to the Westat, Inc. (1980f, Table 29) survey estimated that a $500 understatement of tax liability would be detected less than half the time. But when respondents to the taxpayer survey by Yankelovich et al. (1984) were asked to estimate the chances that someone trying to cheat by a "small" amount (which on average they considered to be $307 in tax liability) would be detected, only 54 percent placed the probability at less than half. For a "large" amount (which they placed at a mean of $16,000 and a median in the $1,001 to $4,999 range), only 23 percent placed the chances so low. The difference between the studies indicates possible artifacts of question structure, since response options in the Westat questionnaire emphasized low probabilities and options in the Yankelovich questionnaire emphasized high probabilities.

When respondents to the Aitken and Bonneville survey were asked to estimate the audit rate per return at their own income levels, answers ranged from 0 to over 50 percent, with a mean of 43 percent. These and other survey-based estimates are sometimes dismissed as substantial overestimates of the true noncompliance detection probability, based on comparisons with actual audit rates—only 1.27 percent of returns for tax year 1983, the year preceding the Yankelovich survey (IRS, 1984a).

But there are several reasons why the overall audit rate may not be the right benchmark. First, the rate varies substantially by audit class—from 0.29 percent for short-form filers with income below $10,000 to 5.3 percent for Schedule C filers (businesses) with gross receipts over $100,000 (IRS, 1985). Second, the audit rate fails to incorporate the rate at which noncompliers are found through computerized matching of tax returns against information from other sources, such as interest and dividend reports; these reach far more taxpayers each year than audits. Third, the audit and contact rates distort detection probabilities because of two types of errors—missed noncompliance and erroneously alleged noncompliance—that occur at unknown rates in audits and computerized matching.

Fourth, the audit or contact rate as a fraction of all returns may be quite different from the rate for noncompliant returns.[10] Because of DIF selection and other procedures, noncompliant taxpayers are presumably more likely than others to be examined. If taxpayers are aware of this selectivity, they may weigh their perception of the rate per noncompliant return more heavily than the perceived rate per return. But efforts to measure how these selective strategies increase the audit and contact rates for noncompliant returns are still in their infancy, so there is no sound basis for adjustment.

Fifth, even if estimates of the relevant rate could be constructed, they would no doubt depend on the amount and type of noncompliance. Unreported tips are less likely to be discovered than unreported interest from a commercial bank that files information returns, and a questionable $100 charitable contribution is less likely to trigger an audit than a questionable $10,000 contribution.

For all these reasons, it is not possible at this stage to assess the accuracy of taxpayers' perceptions of the probability that noncompliance will be detected, and there is a need to develop disaggregated and conceptually different measures of both perceived and actual probabilities that noncompliance with tax laws will be detected.

Information is also quite scattered on how perceptions of sanction probabilities are formed. Under the "availability heuristic" of Tversky and Kahneman (1973), events are judged to be objectively more probable if they come more readily to mind, and one laboratory test in the context of taxpayer compliance finds supportive evidence for this heuristic. Spicer and Hero (1985) find that simulated taxpayers who were audited more frequently during the first nine rounds of an earning and taxpaying game reported more of their income during the tenth round.

Outside the laboratory, much more interference affects the communication channels for information about tax audits. The IRS publishes but does not highly publicize its audit rates, and it is legally prohibited from publicizing individual audit results. Therefore, it would seem that personal experience and word-of-mouth reports by friends must be primary sources of information. But the number of individuals with direct audit experience appears to be relatively small, with prior self-reported contacts with IRS auditors ranging from 33 percent of the sample (Westat, Inc., 1980f, quoted in Cahalan and Ekstrand, 1980) to only 18 percent (Aitken and Bonneville, 1980:55). These fractions do of course increase in the audit classes with greater exposure to audit—29 percent for itemizers and 38 percent for taxpayers with incomes exceeding $50,000—but do not approach a majority.

Consequently, information from friends and acquaintances about their audit experiences must provide a major source of information. But this channel allows considerable selection and freedom of interpretation in reporting the results of audits to others, and the data suggest that this interference tends to reduce both the availability of audit information (in the Tversky and Kahneman sense) and the perceived probability that unreported tax liability will be detected even if an audit occurs. Fewer respondents in the Westat survey (Cahalan and Ekstrand, 1980) reported knowing of friends that had been audited than reported having been audited themselves (Westat, Inc., 1980f); among compliers, 30 percent were audited but only 26 percent reported that their friends were audited, and among noncompliers the percentages were 45 and 40 percent, respectively. If on average an individual's friends are as likely as the individual to be audited, the percentage for friends should be considerably greater. Apparently, either many friends do not mention the fact that they were audited, or individuals' own experiences remain salient over a longer time period. If the few acquaintances who are willing to talk about their experience are those wishing to brag about how they outsmarted the IRS, then the information will tend to reduce the subjective probability that underreported tax liability will be discovered even if an audit occurs. These conjectures suggest strongly that research on the frequency and content of communication about experiences with IRS contacts would be of value in understanding how perceptions are formed of the probabilities that are relevant to general deterrence hypotheses.

PERCEIVED SANCTION PROBABILITIES AND SELF-REPORTED COMPLIANCE. With very few exceptions, surveys using a variety of analytical techniques have found that respondents who perceive higher probabilities of legal sanctions or who express higher fear of those sanctions are more likely than others to report that they comply with tax laws (see, e.g., Vogel, 1974; Spicer and Lundstedt, 1976; Westat, Inc., 1980f; Mason and Calvin, 1978; Mason and Lowry, 1981; Grasmick and Bryjak, 1980; Grasmick and Green, 1980; Grasmick and Scott, 1982; Waerneryd and Walerud, 1982; and Yankelovich et al., 1984). These findings may mean that high probability estimates deter noncompliance; alternatively, taxpayers who experiment with noncompliance may lower their estimates if they escape detection. Higher perceived detection probabilities may also deter the reporting of one's own noncompliance, though not the noncompliance itself.

Survey studies support deterrence hypotheses fairly consistently. For example, in a discriminant analysis, Mason and Calvin (1978) found that respondents with higher detection probability estimates were significantly ($p < .05$) less likely to report ever having overstated deductions, underreported income, or failed to file a return for the Oregon state income tax. In the Westat Inc. (1980f) pilot survey, there were small but statistically significant ($p < .01$) differences in probability estimates between self-reported compliers and noncompliers. Among noncompliers, for example, only 4 percent thought that taxpayers who reduced their tax liabilities by $500 by underreporting income were more likely than not to be caught, compared with 11 percent for compliers. In a discriminant analysis, Yankelovich et al. (1984) found fear of getting caught to be the most statistically significant variable in explaining self-reported tax cheating.

Two survey studies have found partially conflicting findings. For a sample of 130 Ohio households, Spicer and Lundstedt (1976) found no statistically significant correlation between the perceived probability of detection and an index of self-reported tax evasion; they did, however, find a negative correlation ($r = -.17$) between the perceptions and a scale of propensity to evade taxes. For a sample of 426 Swedish male adults, Waerneryd and Walerud found no statistically significant differences in probability estimates between self-reported compliers and noncompliers.

In interpreting these findings, it is important to recall that they all relate reports of past compliance to present perceptions of sanction probabilities, based on surveys at a single point in time. As noted by Paternoster (1987), it is impossible with this design to distinguish between two alternative explanations of the findings presented above: the deterrence hypothesis, that high perceived probabilities discourage taxpayers from failing to comply, and the experiential hypothesis (Saltzman et al., 1982), that taxpayers begin by overestimating detection probabilities and those who fail to comply lower their estimates if they succeed in avoiding detection.[11] Paternoster (1987) reports that so-called panel studies that measure compliance with other laws (e.g., petty theft, marijuana use, shoplifting, writing bad checks) and probability perceptions at multiple points in time nearly all find that such experiential effects dominate deterrence effects, which turn out to be fairly weak. No such panel studies have been conducted in the taxpayer compliance field.

Sorting out experiential from deterrence effects is of more than academic interest. If taxpayer compliance is subject to a strong experiential effect of the type described above, more audit attention should be directed to new taxpayers in their first few years of filing and to taxpayers who have experienced sudden and substantial shifts in their financial circumstances that might cause them to contemplate forms of noncompliance that were previously remote (e.g., deducting a fictitious home office immediately after buying one's first home). To try to distinguish between these two effects, serious consideration should be given to designing a two- or three-wave panel of data on taxpayers' detection probability estimates, their IRS contact experience, and their compliance.

AUDIT RATES AND ESTIMATED COMPLIANCE MEASURES.   There have been several econometric tests of the general deterrence hypothesis for audits. The tests do not provide conclusive results. Most of them have analyzed an aggregate-level cross-sectional data base for tax year 1969. Some results have been consistent with the hypothesis that higher audit rates are associated with higher compliance levels, and some have supported the long-held conjecture that compliance levels also affect audit rates as the IRS attempts to allocate more auditors to areas where compliance is poorest. Because the results vary substantially depending on audit class, details of model specification, and interpretation of coefficients, they provide limited and inconsistent support for the general deterrence hypothesis. Neither these nor other econometric studies provide usable estimates of the ripple or presence effects of audits on compliance.

Most econometric tests of the deterrence hypothesis have used versions of a single data base, which was constructed by the IRS for tax year 1969 (IRS, 1978a; Witte and Woodbury, 1984, 1985; Dubin and Wilde, 1988; Beron et al., 1988). As explained in Chapter 1, Supplementary Note A, the file contains a record for each of seven audit classes in each three-digit zip code area. Each record contains an estimate of voluntary compliance level for tax year 1969 returns. In the original file, explanatory variables in each record included audit rates per 1,000 tax returns for three previous years, rates of other enforcement activities (e.g., civil fraud penalties, criminal investigations and sentences), and various demographic and socioeconomic characteristics of the zip code area. Researchers using the file have since expanded the set of explanatory variables.

If the econometric problem were only to identify characteristics of areas that are correlated with compliance levels, then ordinary least squares regression analysis of VCL on the characteristics (i.e., estimation of a reduced form equation) would suffice. But efforts to test for general deterrence effects using aggregate data face methodological problems similar to those faced by a long line of deterrence researchers during the 1970s. That large body of research was reviewed by the National Research Council's Panel on Research on Deterrent and Incapacitative Effects (Blumstein, Cohen, and Nagin, 1978). The panel noted that any negative association between crime rates and sanction probabilities could reflect either a deterrence effect or a reciprocal causal effect: that jurisdictions may be less likely to impose sanctions because they have higher crime rates. The reciprocal effect could occur through saturation if, for example, enforcement resources became overburdened and therefore less effective in pursuing offenders. If such a reciprocal effect exists but is not incorporated in empirical models, then estimates of the general deterrence effect will be statistically inconsistent and potentially completely misleading. Incorporating the reciprocal effect requires an identifying restriction, in the form of at least one variable that affects sanction probabilities but not crime rates directly (see Fisher and Nagin, 1978, for a detailed discussion of these issues).

In the context of taxpayer compliance, the random-audit assumption is equivalent to assuming that compliance rates in a region have no causal influence on audit rates. Under this assumption, a positive correlation between the audit rate and VCL is interpretable as a general deterrence effect or, in IRS lexicon, a positive ripple or presence effect. In reality the ripple effect of audits on VCL may interact with reciprocal effects of VCL on audit rates, and the interaction could produce positive or negative correlations. A saturation effect could cause a positive correlation between VCL and audit rates if declining compliance in an area triggered more thorough audits but no increase in audit resources, thereby necessitating a decrease in audit rates. Alternatively, under more responsive resource allocation, decreasing compliance in an area could cause the IRS to transfer auditors to an area in order to increase audit rates, causing a negative correlation between VCL and audit rates.[12] If either effect exists but is not incorporated into the model of compliance, estimates of ripple effects will be statistically biased and misleading about the existence and magnitude of general deterrence effects.

The first analyses of the 1969 data set that were widely disseminated outside the IRS were conducted by Witte and Woodbury (1982, 1984, 1985).[13] Although they recognized the possibility of reciprocal causal relationships between audit rates and VCL, they adopted the random-audit assumption as a reasonable first approximation and estimated a separate equation for each of seven audit classes. In their 1984 working paper, each equation included eleven measures of sanction rates,[14] and the estimated coefficients varied in sign and significance depending on audit class, sanction type, and year. In 1985 they summarized the results for three audit classes, in the form of elasticities computed using only the statistically significant coefficients ($p < 0.1$). Consistent with a general deterrence effect, the estimated elasticities for audit rates were positive but small,[15] but they were negative for the civil fraud penalty rate and approximately zero for the criminal sanction rate. Ignoring the possibility of biases because of the random-audit assumption, the results are consistent with a general deterrence effect only for audits and do not suggest a very sensitive response.

The Witte and Woodbury analysis was later criticized by Dubin and Wilde (1988) on several grounds, of which the random-audit assumption is most important. Instead of the random-audit assumption, Dubin and Wilde assumed that a taxpayer's odds of an audit depend both on how the IRS selects returns for audit (based on return characteristics) and on IRS audit resources in the taxpayer's geographic area. They assumed that taxpayers form expectations about the odds of an audit based on some impressions about the IRS selection rules but no information about IRS resources. Taxpayers' compliance was assumed to be determined by the expectations of audit odds plus sociodemographic indicators of tastes and preferences. Dubin and Wilde (1986; 1987a,b; 1988) reanalyzed the same basic 1969 data set as Witte and Woodbury, augmented with published state-level data on IRS budget per taxpayer (for use as an identification restriction for the deterrence relationship) and on the fraction of tax not subject to withholding, as a measure of income visibility. In the published paper, Dubin and Wilde (1988) report that VCL affected audit rates through return selection effects in five of the seven audit classes. In two of those five, the results also suggested a deterrence effect (higher audit rates were associated with higher VCL). But in two others, the coefficient suggested no deterrent effect, and in the fifth, the results were consistent with a counterdeterrent effect. In the two audit classes in which they found no return selection effect, Dubin and Wilde (1988) estimated coefficients that were consistent with a deterrence effect from audit.

Tauchen and Witte (1986) later advanced a somewhat different model of the taxpayer's compliance decision. They argued that rather than forming perceptions of the audit odds, taxpayers form perceptions of how the odds are marginally affected by specific personal characteristics that are known to the IRS, including their areas of residence and items on their tax returns. Under this assumption, if taxpayers' perceptions are accurate, they argue that compliance is a function of the estimated parameters of the audit odds function rather than realized or fitted values of the audit odds themselves, as specified by Dubin and Wilde.

In attempting to test the Tauchen-Witte model using an augmented version of the 1969 data base, Beron et al. (1988) found that the aggregate nature of the data prevented them from obtaining satisfactory estimates of the audit-odds parameters. Therefore, their model specified both reported adjusted gross income (AGI) and reported tax liability as functions of the audit odds, measures of income visibility, and various socioeconomic characteristics. They justified their choice of reported items rather than a compliance measure on two grounds. Most theoretical economic models generate predictions about reported income rather than about noncompliance. Moreover, while the taxpayers' reports are directly measurable, the compliance measures are subject to measurement error because of auditors' mistakes, and very little is known about the distribution of that error.

Like others who have analyzed the 1969 data base, Beron et al. (1988) estimate coefficients that are consistent with modest deterrence effects for audits (e.g., elasticities of about 0.2 for reported tax liability with respect to the audit odds) but are statistically significant in only some audit classes. They also find that specific results are very sensitive to details of model specification.

Taken together, analyses of the 1969 aggregate cross-sectional data set provide little persuasive evidence concerning either deterrence or resource allocation effects. The results on these effects are inconsistent across audit classes and sensitive to details of coefficient interpretation and model specification. These limitations appear to stem largely from the loss of individual variation inherent in aggregating the data, from the difficulty of specifying and estimating the IRS audit function with publicly available data, and from the difficulty of measuring compliance.

One econometric study has analyzed in 1978–1985 time series of state-level data on a noncompliance measure, audit rates, and other variables (Dubin et al., 1987a). The noncompliance measure is the ratio of tax and penalty yield from IRS audits to total IRS collections, adjusted for inflation. The analytical technique is instrumental variables regression analysis of the compliance measure on detection probability as measured by the audit rate in the preceding year, on income, and on several other control variables. As in their cross-sectional analysis, the authors exclude the IRS budget per return as their identifying restriction for the noncompliance relationship. Consistent with their cross-sectional findings for most audit classes, the results here suggest that compliance affects audit rates through a resource allocation effect. The audit rate coefficient, which is intended to measure the deterrence effect of audits on compliance, has the expected sign but is statistically significant at only $p < 0.2$. They also find that IRS budget per return is the most important determinant of audit rate.

There are at least two reasons for doubting that the audit rate coefficient in the regression equation for compliance is a consistent estimate of the deterrence effect. First, unlike TCMP audits, which are intended to be performed uniformly as a compliance measurement device, routine audits are a revenue collection device that varies greatly in terms of quality, as reflected in the number of return items examined and the intensity of the examinations. Therefore, the findings here are also consistent with the hypothesis that when the IRS has more resources per return, it performs higher-quality audits, which yield more tax and penalties. Second, over the 1978–1985 period, there were major legislative changes in noncompliance penalties and coverage of information reporting, as well as efforts to upgrade computerized matching and taxpayer services. These changes are captured imperfectly at best in the time trend variable included as an explanatory variable. To the extent that the upgrades in other areas drew resources away from maintaining audit rates, they would partially account for the negative estimated coefficient on audit rate. Therefore, because the estimated coefficient is statistically insignificant and may be explained by other relationships, it does not provide evidence that higher audit rates are associated with greater compliance.

Even though econometric analyses to date have painted an inconclusive picture concerning the general deterrence effects of IRS audits, the question is too important for both scientific and policy purposes to give up at this stage. In particular, improved cross-sectional estimates could be obtained using an aggregate cross-sectional data base that describes a more recent year and contains several improvements. There is a need to include data on rates of computerized notices triggered by mismatches between tax returns and other sources. The aggregate audit rates need to be replaced by rates of audits that produce, respectively, tax increases, decreases, and no change, since these outcomes presumably affect perceived risks in different ways. There is also a need for the updated data base to include multiple versions of validated compliance measures so that researchers can distinguish between over- and underreports of tax liability.[16] There is also a need for more extensive data on IRS resource allocation and other variables that could serve as plausible identification restrictions for estimating compliance relationships.

TRANSACTION VISIBILITY AND DETECTION PROBABILITY.   The strongest evidence that a higher noncompliance detection probablity is associated with higher compliance relates to the visibility of different sources of income. When income is recorded in a manner that makes it potentially visible to an inquisitive enforcement official, the probability of being caught for underreporting income increases with the ease with which the enforcer can get access to and act on the records (Feffer et al., 1983; Kagan, Vol. 2; Klepper and Nagin, Vol. 2). Studies using very different methodologies support the hypothesis that the higher detection probabilities associated with greater income visibility encourage more complete reporting of income. While the question is not yet well explored with respect to subtractions from taxable income, the small amount of available evidence supports the hypothesis in that context as well.

Feffer et al. (1983) place income in four categories, in decreasing order of visibility: (1) income subject to withholding, (2) income subject to information reporting, (3) income that appears in other taxpayers' auditable records, and (4) cash income. Using the real estate and construction industry as an example, they propose a number of administrative innovations to increase income visibility. Kagan (Vol. 2) proposes a more complex hierarchy of income visibility and demonstrates using examples from the house-painting industry how the visibility of income depends not only on how it is earned but also on characteristics of the taxpayer, such as scale of operations.

Evidence that greater income visibility increases compliance appears in Table 8. The TCMP data summarized there show that the percentage of returns with substantial underreports of income is lower for income that is subject to information reporting or withholding than for income such as proprietorships, rents, and capital gains, for which records are less accessible to the IRS. Several internal IRS studies have documented increases in VCL following the introduction of computer matching programs and information reporting that increases the visibility of income from particular sources.

Five of the six econometric analyses that have examined the issue also offer evidence of a statistically significant and empirically important link between compliance and income visibility, using visibility measures such as the fractions of income received as wages, dividends, or interest (Clotfelter, 1983); employment in manufacturing (in which wages are subject to withholding) as a fraction of all adult employment in a jurisdiction (Witte and Woodbury, 1985; Dubin and Wilde, 1988; Beron et al., 1988); amount of capital gains income and filing of a Schedule C (proprietorship income) or F (farm income) (Alexander and Feinstein, 1986); and a dual measure—the coefficient of variation for a reported item and whether the item is subject to information reporting (Klepper and Nagin, 1987a).[17] Only Slemrod (1985a) did not find a statistically significant relationship,

TABLE 8   Noncompliance by Type of Income, as Detected by 1979
TCMP Audits

Type of income	Returns with unreported income of $500 or more (%)	Returns with unreported income $2,001 or more (%)	Returns with item in exam (%)	Estimated number of returns
Schedule F[a]	45.7	24.0	2.8	627,620
Schedule C[b]	42.3	22.3	10.3	2,126,880
1120S distr[c]	27.2	15.3	0.8	116,690
Rents/royalties	22.6	6.8	8.7	545,490
Form 4797[d]	20.5	11.0	1.6	166,720
Partnership distr	16.9	8.5	3.1	244,140
Schedule D[e]	12.9	5.3	9.4	455,080
Tips	11.8	4.9	2.3	102,350
Estates, trusts	5.0	2.9	0.9	22,660
Dividends	4.8	1.8	10.9	184,610
Interest	2.1	0.4	65.4	251,580
Wages/salaries	2.3	0.6	89.1	512,640

[a]Farm income.
[b]Income from trade or business.
[c]Income from Subchapter S partnership.
[d]Capital gains on certain business property.
[e]Capital gains
Source: Kagan (Vol. 2, Table 1).

although the sign of his estimated coefficient was consistent with the
hypothesis.

Most survey-based compliance studies also support the relationship
between visibility of income source and compliance, with self-employed
respondents (Vogel, 1974; Aitken and Bonneville, 1980; Mason and
Lowry, 1981; Groenland and van Veldhoven, 1983; Yankelovich et al.,
1984) and employees not subject to withholding (Mason and Lowry,
1981) more likely to admit noncompliance than salaried employees.
Madeo, Shepanski, and Uecker (1985) found that expert judgment by
accountants also weighted the source of income (salary versus cash) as the
most critical factor affecting compliance. These differences were not found
in one Swedish study (Waerneryd, 1980), however. In addition, one U.S.
study found the proportion of income received as wages, salaries, or pensions to be positively correlated with a scale of the propensity to evade taxes
but not with an index of actual previous evasion (Spicer and Lundstedt,
1976). Some of the differences in compliance for different income sources

may, of course, be attributed to different levels of commitment toward compliance associated with different kinds of income (Hotaling and Arnold, 1981), particularly for more marginal sources of income. But the available evidence clearly supports the hypothesis that the higher probability of detection associated with more visible income sources is associated with greater compliance.

The visibility hypothesis has not yet been tested as thoroughly with respect to subtraction items such as deductions and credits, but two studies offer supportive empirical evidence. Beron et al. (1988) find reported tax liability to be positively correlated with two measures of higher visibility—higher levels of employment in manufacturing and lower levels of employment in services. Klepper and Nagin (1987a) hypothesize that tax authorities will find it more difficult to establish a given percentage of illegal subtractions than to establish the same percentage of unreported income subject to withholding, but that unreported income in other forms is harder yet to establish. In a multiple regression analysis of a return-item tabulation from the 1982 TCMP, they estimate that the percentage noncompliance by return item varies consistently with this hypothesis, but the estimated coefficient is not statistically significant. They also hypothesize that noncompliance is harder to trace (i.e., less visible) for income and subtraction items with larger coefficients of variation (a measure of dispersion relative to the mean value), because the large relative dispersion makes deviations from normal amounts harder to detect. They estimate a statistically significant coefficient that is consistent with this hypothesis. They also find that increases in the amount of low-visibility income are associated with decreases in the percentage of noncompliance on more visible subtraction items—a correlation they interpret as a substitution of noncompliance on less visible items for noncompliance on more visible items.

Future studies of the impact of visibility on compliance need to consider several issues. First, nearly all previous large-sample studies of the question have focused either on the source of income or on characteristics of the taxpayer, and there is a need for further work on how those sets of factors interact to determine the visibility of a given transaction and, in turn, compliance with respect to the transaction. Investigation of these issues will require individual-level data with compliance measures for specific return items. Second, there is a need to examine how individuals' compliance changes over time—as the visibility of their transactions is altered by changes in the composition of their income and expenditures, by changes in their family and other personal circumstances, and by changes in tax administration procedures such as information reporting. Third, there is a need to know more about the social organization in occupations dominated by low-visibility transactions and how that organization affects the perception, evaluation, and responsiveness of objective sanction threats.

SEVERITY OF LEGAL SANCTIONS

Most studies that have examined the question conclude that variation in the severity of sanctions does not affect the level of taxpayer compliance. However, a few studies suggest a possible interaction between the probability and severity of sanctions: that when the perceived probability is sufficiently high, increases in severity may increase compliance.

We recommend further study of the relationship between compliance and sanction severity in the context of an interaction with sanction probability. Such studies would provide an opportunity to test competing theories of decision making under uncertainty about low-probability risks. They are also of potential policy interest because, within limits, increases in the severity of penalties and fines may be achievable at less administrative cost (e.g., for additional appeals) than increases in the probability that they will be imposed. This approach is limited, of course, by the unwillingness of legislatures to enact, and authorities to impose, punishments that seem harsher than violators deserve.

Recent changes in the legislatively prescribed civil and criminal sanctions for some specific forms of noncompliance may provide an opportunity to reach more definitive conclusions about how sanction severity affects compliance. We recommend that the opportunity be taken to study how these changes affect the enforcement and adjudication of cases of tax avoidance and evasion, and to learn how changes in legislatively prescribed sanctions affect the distribution of sanctions actually imposed.

The relationship between compliance and the severity of punishment has been examined using survey and econometric techniques, and most of the studies have found no evidence of a relationship (see, e.g., Spicer and Lundstedt, 1976; Westat, Inc., 1980f; Witte and Woodbury, 1985).

As noted by Grasmick and Bryjak (1980), there are two grounds on which to question most survey findings about severity and compliance with laws. First, severity measures that involve actual objective sanctions assume that a given punishment has the same meaning to all respondents. To test for the compliance effects of variations in perceived severity, they recommend use of a subjective measure of how severe respondents think the punishment would be (e.g., very severe, not so bad) rather than the nature of the punishment. Second, variations in punishment severity may affect compliance only among respondents for whom the perceived probability is above some threshold level. The failure to find severity effects may be due to the low probability levels involved.

There are several kinds of evidence that support the threshold hypothesis. In their survey data, Grasmick and Bryjak (1980) find the expected relationship between behavior and severity only for respondents with a high subjective probability of punishment. Reanalyzing the same data, Grasmick and Green (1980) find a positive correlation between illegal behavior and a joint severity/probability scale, even controlling for a measure of social sanctions. In their regression analysis of percentage of noncompliance by return item according to TCMP, Klepper and Nagin (1987a) estimate coefficients for their severity measures[18] that are consistent with a deterrence hypothesis. But the coefficients become statistically significant only when their strongest detection probability measure (the coefficient of variation measure described previously) is removed from the equation.

These findings suggest that increases in the severity of civil and criminal sanctions may encourage compliance, at least if the probability that they will be imposed exceeds some threshold. Opportunities to reach more definitive conclusions on this question may have been presented by legislative changes between 1981 and 1986 in the civil penalties applicable to some specific forms of noncompliance (see Dubin et al., 1987c, for a summary of these changes) and by changes in the criminal penalties for evasion prescribed by new federal sentencing guidelines, which took effect in November 1987. Before-and-after comparisons of the compliance effects of these changes may provide an opportunity to test alternative theories of decision making under uncertainty (see reviews of these theories by Lindzey and Aronson, 1985; Machina, 1987). The results would also be of potential policy importance. Within the limits of deserved punishment, relatively small expenditures (e.g., for enacting legislation, for processing appeals) are needed to increase the severity of (nearly always monetary) penalties for noncompliance once it is detected, while increasing the detection probability through more enforcement efforts is relatively expensive.

An important related question, however, is whether the more severe penalties prescribed by law will actually be imposed with high enough probabilities to affect compliance. The pertinent probability thresholds, if any, are not known. But Long (1980a) has documented the low rates at which the IRS seeks civil and criminal penalties even when they are apparently applicable, and the IRS (1968) has remarked on the reluctance of judges to impose severe criminal penalties on tax evaders who otherwise are perceived as solid citizens. It is not clear that the probabilities can be increased, even if they are currently too low for the new prescribed sanctions to affect behavior. The IRS would need additional resources to raise noncompliance detection probabilities by an appreciable amount, and its requests for budget increases are not always successful (see Scholz, Vol. 2).

Even if detection probabilities could be increased, it is not clear that the increase in statutorily prescribed severity would lead to an increase in the severity of penalties actually imposed. A comprehensive review of the effects of changes in criminal sentencing structure found that such changes rarely affect the sanctions actually imposed, because of adaptations by prosecutors and judges in case processing at stages prior to adjudication (Cohen and Tonry, 1983). As explained more fully in Chapter 4 in the context of the Tax Reform Act of 1986, we recommend research to examine whether such adaptation also occurs in response to the legislative changes in prescribed sanctions for various forms of noncompliance.

Empirical Evidence on Informal Social Sanctions

The theoretical discussion earlier in this chapter explained ways in which informal social sanctions may interact with formal legal sanctions to increase compliance. Because of the difficulty of obtaining measures of the threat of social sanctions and linking them to audit results, empirical knowledge about the effects of social sanctions on taxpayer compliance is sparse and comes entirely from surveys. All surveys that have examined the question find that measures of the threat of social sanctions are positively correlated with self-report compliance measures. These correlations are consistent with the hypothesis that social sanctions encourage compliance. However, they may also reflect methodological artifacts that are intrinsic in the use of self-reports to measure compliance. A more definitive test of the hypothesis would require measuring correlations between threats of social sanctions and compliance measures obtained from tax returns or audits.

Spicer (1974), Vogel (1974), and Westat, Inc. (1980f) all report that taxpayers with noncompliant friends, relatives, or acquaintances are more likely to report previous noncompliance themselves. Because this correlation could arise through reverse causation—taxpayers who have failed to comply in the past may be more likely to associate with other noncompliers—some researchers have preferred to measure noncompliance in terms of future intentions. Using this measure, Tittle (1980) has found that respondents with friends who engage in illegal behaviors including tax evasion are more likely to report future intentions to engage in those behaviors themselves.[19]

Two studies have examined how illegal behavior including tax evasion is related to indices of legal and social sanctions.[20] Using indices of eight illegal behaviors, Grasmick and Bryjak (1980) found results that were consistent with a stronger deterrence effect for social sanctions than for legal sanctions. Using a self-reported previous noncompliance measure, they found that the strength of deterrence by legal sanctions was not affected by the level of social sanctions. But using measures of future intentions, they found that legal sanctions have a stronger deterrence effect when the index of social sanctions is lower. Using the same index of social sanctions in multivariate analyses, Grasmick and Scott (1982) found that social sanctions, legal sanctions, and moral commitment together explained more of the variance in self-reported tax evasion than in self-reported petty theft or grand theft. Their estimated coefficient for social sanctions was double that for legal sanctions, but half that for self-imposed guilt.

There are two reasons for caution in interpreting these findings. First, fear of social or legal sanctions could deter the reporting of previous tax evasion without deterring the underlying behavior. Second, for any of a number of reasons—to reduce cognitive dissonance, to neutralize guilt, or to appear consistent with the behavior of others—respondents who evade taxes (or expect to in the future) may report greater numbers of noncompliant friends or acquaintances. Eliminating these alternatives would require more resource-intensive research methods. One approach would involve longitudinal designs, in which reports of changes in the number of noncompliant friends and acquaintances could be correlated with subsequent return-based measures of noncompliance.[21] Ethnographic studies would also be valuable for interpreting correlations and refining theories of how compliance is related to social and legal sanctions.

Other Compliance Benefits and Costs

In the self-interest model of compliance, the benefits derived from an illegal act provide the primary incentive not to comply. A number of studies have argued that systematic differences in benefits explain observed patterns of noncompliance. For example, Tittle and Rowe (1973) found cheating on tests to be more prevalent among students with lower grades who had more to gain. Feest (1967) noted that the decreased benefit (increased risk) of running a stop sign when cross traffic was present accounted for most compliant stopping at stop signs. Ehrlich (1973) argued that the positive association he found between income inequality and crime rates demonstrated that the lack of legitimate opportunity made crime more attractive. Similarly, Witte and Woodbury (1985) found that tax compliance was significantly higher in growing areas with low rates of unemployment and poverty, where job opportunities were better.

The most obvious benefit of evasion is the amount of taxes saved. For a given amount of underreported taxable income, the amount saved increases as the applicable tax rates increase. But as noted earlier, both the utility of the evaded tax and the taxpayer's willingness to take risks to acquire it are traditionally assumed to depend on the level of (after-tax) income. Also as noted earlier, other costs of compliance—ascertaining compliance requirements, maintaining records, filing returns—and of noncompliance—large fees to promoters of abusive tax shelters, discounts for payments in cash—may affect taxpaying behavior. The following sections review the empirical evidence concerning the compliance effects of variations in tax rates, income, and compliance cost.

TAX RATES

Three of five econometric studies have found higher applicable tax rates to be associated with lower compliance. One study found no statistically significant relationship, and another found higher state income tax rates to be positively correlated with higher compliance with federal taxes. The relationship remains in doubt, in part because of past difficulty in separating the effects of variations in tax rates from variations in income. Because the Tax Reform Act of 1986 changed the tax rates faced by most taxpayers, it provides a one-time opportunity to study the compliance effects of a change in tax rates.

Empirical evidence about how variations in tax rates affect compliance is of particular intellectual interest because, as discussed previously, different assumptions lead to different predictions about this relationship. Estimating the compliance effects of variations in tax rates—independently of variations in income—has been very difficult, since the progressive federal income tax structure ties the tax rate to income level (Cox, 1984). Econometricians have sought with only limited success to exploit variations over time in the federal tax rates and variations across states in the total state plus federal tax rate and to relate the variations to measures of compliance.

Three of five econometric studies of the question suggest that, contrary to some theoretical predictions but consistent with many observers' expectations, higher tax rates are associated with poorer compliance. Clotfelter (1983) augmented individual-level 1969 TCMP data with information on state tax rates and found that higher total tax rates (state plus federal) were associated with greater tax changes imposed by TCMP auditors. Poterba (1987) analyzed trends over time in the aggregate fraction of capital gains reported according to TCMP auditors in the six TCMP cycles between 1965 and 1982—a period when the applicable statutory maximum tax rate varied between 20 and 35 percent. Using two measures of the tax rate, he found statistically significant elasticities suggesting that increases in the applicable rate were associated with less complete reporting of realized capital gains. In an analysis of 1982 TCMP data Alexander and Feinstein (1986) used estimation techniques that were intended to adjust for taxpayers' errors that lead to noncompliance and for auditors' errors that cause either an erroneous tax deficiency assessment or an oversight of noncompliance. They found that, when the amount and type of income are controlled, a higher tax rate is associated with a higher probability of noncompliance and, in two of the three estimated models, with a higher amount of evaded tax.[22]

Slemrod (1985a) found no statistically significant relationship between marginal tax rates and a compliance measure derived from a 1977 sample of tax returns. He notes that because of the step nature of tax brackets (at the time his data were generated), noncompliant taxpayers have an incentive to underreport tax liability by just enough to fall into a lower bracket; their returns, therefore, should tend to cluster near the upper limits of brackets. He did find disproportionate concentrations of tax returns in the top quartiles of brackets but, in a multivariate analysis, did not find a statistically significant relationship between marginal tax rate and position within the bracket.

Doubts have been raised about the usual finding—that higher rates are associated with lower compliance. Dubin and Wilde (1988) note that because audit rates are omitted from Clotfelter's model and are likely to be correlated with both marginal tax rates and compliance, his estimates of the compliance effect of variation in tax rates may be biased. Analyzing their own 1977–1985 panel of data Dubin et al. (1987a) estimate that higher state tax rates are associated with higher compliance with federal income tax laws. As indicated previously, there are questions about whether their dependent variable measures compliance or the effectiveness of audits. Despite these reservations, the finding suggests caution in presuming that compliance can be increased by reducing tax rates.

The Tax Reform Act of 1986, by raising the marginal rates faced by some taxpayers and lowering those faced by others, presents an opportunity to reach more clear-cut conclusions about how changes in tax rates affect compliance. In Chapter 3, the panel recommends such an analysis as part of a larger research program focused on this legislation.

INCOME

Correlations between income and compliance can be expected to reflect a variety of causal links operating simultaneously. Because empirical analyses have differed in the extent to which they control or account for these links, the results are quite inconsistent across studies. Therefore, the empirical relationship between income and compliance should be considered unresolved.

Predictions about the relationship of income to compliance are quite difficult to make. In the simplest microeconomic models, holding other conditions constant, variations in income are predicted to affect compliance through their effects on aversion to risk and on the marginal utility of evaded tax. But other relevant conditions are not constant. During the period when most of the research was carried out, the progressive tax system introduced a relationship between income and tax rate that made it impossible to distinguish income effects from tax rate effects. In addition, the composition of income and expenditures is likely to interact with the amount of income, in ways that doubtlessly affect compliance but are only partially understood: as examples, the proportion of income received in cash, the complexity of transactions, and the availability of savings that could be used to purchase tax shelters can all be expected to depend on the level of income. Finally, in theoretical models that incorporate interactions between taxpayers and the IRS, the probability that noncompliance will be detected is assumed to depend on either the level of reported income (Graetz et al., 1986) or the difference between reported and true income (Klepper and Nagin, 1987a).

Given this multiplicity of relationships involving income and compliance, it is not surprising that empirical studies using different approaches have reached quite different conclusions about how they interact. Among survey studies, for example, Mason and Calvin (1978) did not find income correlated with the prevalence of any form of self-reported noncompliance except failure to file a return—high-income taxpayers were more likely to comply by filing returns. But even that relationship was called into question in a subsequent survey by one of the same investigators, when Mason and Lowry (1981) found failure to file most prevalent in the $5,000–$9,999 and $30,000–$39,999 ranges. Both Westat, Inc. (1980f) and Yankelovich et al. (1984) found misstatements on filed returns to be more common at higher-income levels.

Different econometric analyses reach different conclusions about the income-compliance relationship depending on whether they use aggregate or individual data; what other variables are controlled in the analysis; and whether they use relative (e.g., VCL, or the percentage of taxable income not reported), absolute (e.g., dollars of taxable income not reported), or prevalence (e.g., fraction reporting all taxable income) measures of compliance. Witte and Woodbury (1984) found higher mean income associated with higher VCL in six of seven audit classes in their analysis of the 1969 aggregate cross-sectional data base.[23] But the data base did not permit them to control for tax rate effects. In his analysis of individual-level 1969 TCMP data, which did control for tax rate, Clotfelter (1983) found that in eight of ten audit classes, higher after-tax income was associated with larger amounts of unreported adjusted gross income. Analyzing 1982 individual-level TCMP data and controlling for tax rate, Alexander and Feinstein (1986) found that the effect of income on the amount of unreported income was quite sensitive to the analytical technique; but controlling for both taxpayer and auditor errors, they found higher after-tax income associated with smaller amounts of unreported taxable income.

There are also some conflicts in findings about how compliance is related to other measures of financial status. Higher unemployment is found to be correlated with lower compliance levels for all audit classes by Dubin and Wilde (1988) and for some audit classes by Witte and Woodbury (1984, 1985). Yet in two surveys (Vogel, 1974; Mason and Lowry, 1981), respondents who said they were better off financially than they were five years before were more likely to report previous noncompliance.

Clearly there is much to be learned about how compliance is related to income. Research that might clarify the picture would be facilitated by collection of longitudinal data on individual taxpayers. Such data would permit analyses of how taxpayers alter their compliance after transitions in their level and composition of income. If the data collection period spanned a change in tax rates, it could be used to distinguish income effects more clearly from tax rate effects.

COMPLIANCE COSTS

As indicated by Slemrod (Vol. 2), an important yet neglected factor in taxpayer compliance research is the cost in time, effort, and psychic energy required for any given level of compliance. Tax laws require positive actions for compliance, but noncompliance with a particular requirement may impose higher or lower costs than compliance. Although Slemrod (Vol. 2) provides a theoretical model relating costs and compliance, and an IRS-sponsored project has produced estimates of these costs, there has been little empirical research on the relationship between compliance costs and compliance. The issue is an important one because the Tax Reform Act of 1986 is widely thought to have reduced compliance costs for some tax-payers, while increasing them for others.

Despite the sparseness of empirical research, there is some sketchy evidence that high compliance costs act as a barrier to compliance. Over 70 percent of the respondents to a 1973 survey commissioned by H&R Block agreed that tax forms then in use were too complicated for the average person (cited in Ekstrand, 1980). And circumstantial evidence supports the notion that the difficulty of the basic forms imposes higher costs on less educated persons: nonfilers tend to have low educational attainment (U.S. GAO, 1979).

Empirical Evidence on Social Commitment

Political analysts have long considered citizen commitment to obey the law an essential ingredient of national survival. Even Machiavelli, who is associated with the espousal of government use of coercion, argued that no prince can govern long unless most citizens willingly obey the laws of the land. Comparative research on national development has argued that nations whose people generally support government policies progress more rapidly than nations in which obedience must be coerced (Almond and Verba, 1963; Easton, 1965). Since revenues from income tax have become the primary source of support for many Western democracies, civic commitment to comply with tax laws is viewed in this perspective as an important national asset.

Commitment to obey the law refers to the individual's perceived moral obligation to obey, based on internalized beliefs and attitudes. In the framework of cognitive developmental psychologists, moral development passes through several stages: considerations of self-interest, considerations of the standards of others and legal standards, and considerations based on general moral principles (Piaget, 1932; Kohlberg, 1976, 1984). Commitment refers to the later stages in this process and is distinct from an individual's concern with being punished or held in low esteem by others for breaking social norms, which were discussed earlier in this chapter in the section on self-interest. While the boundary between social norms and internalized norms is not clearly demarcated, the distinguishing factor about commitment is that it is effective even when only the individual knows about his or her actions. The incentive for living up to one's perceived moral obligation may be considered to be the positive reinforcement of self-esteem or the negative reinforcement of guilt, but in either case the motivation comes from the individual's own judgment of her or his behavior.

Knowledge about the role of commitment in tax compliance, however, is not well established. As Lewis concluded in his extensive review of tax attitude research, "We can be confident in our general prediction that if tax attitudes become worse, tax evasion will increase, although a more precise statement about which attitudes are reflected in behavioral intentions . . . and in actual tax evasion is not yet within our grasp" (Lewis, 1982a:177). The majority of studies designed to test the importance of commitment in determining compliance have indeed found significant relationships but have also demonstrated the limits of current knowledge about the complex interactions between commitment and taxpayers' beliefs and attitudes, their social, political, and economic environments, and tax policy and administration. We begin our discussion by reviewing evidence about the relationship between compliance and taxpayers' commitment to comply. We then consider the relationships that link taxpayers' commitment, their general beliefs and attitudes, and their social environments.

EVIDENCE THAT COMMITMENT SUPPORTS COMPLIANCE
The most consistent series of studies conforming the effect of commitment on tax compliance has been undertaken to expand and test the deterrence model of compliance by Tittle (1980), Grasmick and various associates (Grasmick and Green, 1980; Grasmick and Scott, 1982; Scott and Grasmick, 1981; Grasmick, 1985), and Thurman, St. John, and Riggs (1984). These studies measure commitment by asking survey respondents to rate what they think about tax cheating on a multipoint scale ranging from "It is never wrong to do it" to "It is always wrong to do it" (Grasmick and Scott, 1982) or to rate how much guilt they would feel if they failed to

report certain income or claimed undeserved deductions (Thurman et al., 1984). When so measured, moral commitment was significantly related to self-reported tax compliance (Grasmick and Scott, 1982; Scott and Grasmick, 1981; Thurman et al., 1984). The significance of moral commitment has been found in studies of compliance with other laws as well (Tittle, 1980; Grasmick and Green, 1980, 1981). The relationship remains significant even when perceived threats of legal and social sanctions are included in the analysis. Commitment appears in these studies to have a consistent positive relationship with (self-reported) tax compliance.

Two other surveys found the relationships between commitment and compliance with different commitment measures to be statistically significant. The 1979 Westat, Inc., pilot survey found that self-reported noncompliers were more likely (chi-square test) to evaluate three forms of evasion as less serious than compliers (Cahalan and Ekstrand, 1980). The most extensive survey, by Yankelovich et al. (1984), asked respondents to rate the acceptability of sixteen noncompliant acts ranging from not reporting the income equivalent of a barter arrangement to stretching medical deductions by including nonmedical expenses. Coefficients for this index of acceptability and an index of disaffection from government were both found to be statistically significant in a regression analysis of admitted underreporting of income (Smith, 1987).

Experimental studies have produced further support for the significance of commitment in explaining tax compliance. The Schwartz and Orleans (1967) experiment described earlier in this chapter demonstrated the effectiveness of questions emphasizing normative reasons to comply in producing higher income reports. The results suggest not only that commitment is important, but also that it is subject to changes determined by the kinds of messages that attract the taxpayer's attention.

Beginning with the work of Friedland, Thibaut, and Walker, (1973) and Thibaut, Friedland, and Walker (1974), a series of laboratory experiments have probed the effect of factors related to commitment on compliance in hypothetical income tax situations. Different situations are assigned randomly to subjects (primarily university students) to test the effect of these situations on the subject's willingness to understate income taxes on the hypothetical return. Significant differences in compliance levels have been found to relate to enforcement methods differing in fairness (Friedland et al., 1973), different redistribution of tax revenues (Thibaut et al., 1974), and different perceived inequities in tax rates (Spicer and Becker, 1980). Presumably the manipulated perception of fairness and equity of the tax system altered the subject's commitment to honest reporting, again confirming the importance of commitment in determining who complies and who does not.

While the overall weight of the evidence from the various kinds of studies supports the view that commitment plays a role in supporting compliance, three methodological problems raise some questions requiring further resolution. First, the relationship between self-reported compliance in surveys and actual compliance is unclear. Klepper and Nagin (Vol. 2) argue that self-reported noncompliance is low compared with TCMP and other estimates in part because respondents provide the socially accepted and consistent answers that they disapprove of cheating and they personally do not cheat. If true, the effect of this biased response would be to overestimate the relationship between commitment and compliance. By contrast, audit-based measures classify misreports that the taxpayer assumed to be correct as noncompliance. Since commitment is expected to influence only conscious noncompliance, a reliable survey measure would be conceptually more valid.

Second, the individuals in a survey sample who cannot be contacted, refuse to be interviewed, or do not complete interviews provide another source of potential bias. If noncompliers reluctant to admit to an act that they recognize as morally repugnant constitute an important part of these nonrespondents, then eliminating such high-commitment noncompliers from the data will result in an overestimation of commitment effects based on individuals who did participate in the survey (Klepper and Nagin, Vol. 2). More serious tax evaders with little compunction about the morality of their evasion are also likely to refuse to discuss their tax affairs, since doing so might increase their risk of being caught. The absence of this group in the survey data would bias results in the opposite direction. Nonresponse rates vary in different surveys and are not always reported, but the implications for tax research do not appear to be different from those for other survey research. Research on the characteristics of nonrespondents in tax-related surveys would be useful to clarify this potential bias.

Third, collecting cross-sectional survey data from a single time period makes it difficult to determine the dynamics of the relationship between commitment and compliance, even if we accept that the relationship is positive. Attitudes and behavior may evolve independently in the same direction because of social and economic factors associated with noncompliance (Ekland-Olsen, Lieb, and Zurcher, 1984), for example, when tax noncompliance requires continuing links with a network of suppliers or employees who are also noncompliant. Or attitudes may be determined by behavior, rather than behavior by attitudes. For example, Paternoster et al. (1982a,b) found that the impact of perceived penalties on compliance with other laws that appears in cross-sectional data disappears when the conditioning effect of previous noncompliance on perceived penalties is controlled for. The connection between commitment and compliance, for example, may reflect the rationalization process of taxpayers who have many chances of cheating without being caught. They may cheat because they can get away with it and then develop consistent attitudes justifying low commitment to comply. The reversal of causation may be a particular problem in the Thurman et al. (1984) argument that guilt neutralization strategies allow even respondents who believe that cheating is wrong to cheat without feeling guilty. For example, respondents who agree with the statement, "It is okay to claim an undeserved deduction when you are not really sure what the rule is," can use the denial of responsibility strategy to reduce guilt they otherwise would feel. However, the statistically significant relationship found by Thurman may primarily reflect retrospective rationalization rather than prospective neutralization.

Several other methods may be useful in identifying the direction of causal relationships. Thurman et al. (1984), Grasmick and Green (1980), and Tittle (1969), for example, asked for future intentions to comply rather than past behavior in order to resolve the logical problem of explaining prior behavior with current attitudes. Future intention has been shown in one study to be a good predictor of actual subsequent criminality, and the factors that predict future intention are essentially the same as those that predict subsequent criminality (Murray and Erickson, 1987). However, future intention is also more subjective and possibly more likely to be related to commitment because of the respondent's interest in appearing consistent. Furthermore, since past behavior is likely to be highly correlated with future intention, methods must be found to control for the impact of past behavior on commitment and on guilt neutralization when their effect on future intention is analyzed.

Panel studies following the same people over time provide a more powerful design for analyzing the direction of causal influence (Paternoster et al., 1982a,b), since changes in noncompliance between interviews can be used to analyze impacts on commitment and related beliefs. Of course, panel studies are considerably more expensive and introduce another potential source of bias through attrition.

As explained by Boruch (Appendix B), experimental studies in laboratory and field settings avoid several problems encountered with other methods, particularly because the random assignment of treatments under controlled circumstances ensures that significant differences in compliance are caused by the experimentally manipulated factors. However, it is difficult to maintain randomization in field settings. In the laboratory, the main issue is external validity: Do the experimental game and the subject population represent the essential features of taxpaying situations sufficiently well to allow for generalization of conclusions from the laboratory to the real world? And even if the compliance effects are generalizable, are they large enough to be of practical significance outside the laboratory, where competing influences may dilute relationships? Applications of field and laboratory experiments are rare in tax administration and taxpayer compliance. Previous applications are summarized by Boruch (Appendix B), suggestions for future applications appear in Chapter 4, and the ethical issues raised by field experiments are discussed in Chapter 5.

In sum, although the small number of studies and the problems associated with each leave many questions unanswered, the overall weight of the evidence supports the basic hypothesis that commitment plays a significant role in explaining tax compliance behavior. It is not clear just how important commitment is in relation to self-interest factors, nor how the two are related. Neither set of factors has explained more than a small part of the variance in compliance behavior in existing studies, suggesting that compliance behavior is considerably more complex than the simple views explored so far.

We now expand our review of studies involving commitment to consider a broader range of factors likely to affect commitment and how it is related to compliance behavior. We should note, however, that we do not review the larger literature on fiscal psychology, which deals with how people think about tax policy but generally is not concerned with commitment or compliance. This literature is reviewed by Lewis (1982a). The taxpayer compliance research we review has focused primarily on two sets of factors: one relating to the taxpayer's attitudes and beliefs related to taxes, and the other relating to the social and economic conditions affecting the socialization of the individual.

ATTITUDINAL INFLUENCES ON COMMITMENT

The established psychological concept of consistency (Lindzey and Aronson, 1985) suggests that a taxpayer's normative commitment to comply with tax laws should be consistent with his or her general attitudes toward logically related subjects such as law and the government and also with more specific attitudes toward tax laws and the actions of tax administrators. For example, we might expect higher levels of commitment to compliance with tax laws from taxpayers with well-established commitments to obey other laws and with favorable attitudes toward the government, the fairness and equity of the tax system, and the fairness of their treatment by tax administrators. However, the bulk of psychological as well as tax literature (Lewis, 1982a; Sears and Citrin, 1982) suggests that related attitudes on any given subject may be inconsistent in a number of ways. The connections among an individual's attitudes and beliefs on a given subject differ across different groups, are frequently inconsistent with expert opinion and logical analysis, change over time, and are influenced by different frames of reference.

Sociologists and psychologists offer slightly different approaches to explaining how potentially inconsistent attitudes and beliefs affect the relationship between commitment to comply and actual compliance behavior. For example, certain attitudes and beliefs may directly affect compliance by providing situation-specific justifications for not following a recognized moral commitment (Thurman et al., 1984). Schwartz (1977), in analyzing why individuals perform altruistic acts (e.g., donating blood, rescuing a drowning swimmer) despite personal costs, develops the theory that commitment to altruism requires two conditions to be activated: a recognition of personal responsibility to act and an awareness of the harm that would result from not acting. If two people have the same commitment to altruism, the one who is less aware of harm being prevented would therefore exhibit less of the relevant altruistic behavior. Schwartz argues that altruistic acts are motivated by the need to fulfill recognized moral obligations in order to maintain self-esteem, but only when the harm prevented by altruism is commensurate in some way with the altruistic individual's cost. Schwartz reviews experimental evidence in support of the mediating role of awareness of harm on commitments, which was also confirmed in studies of citizen responses to energy conservation programs (Black, Stern, and Elworth, 1985) and other environmental actions (Stern and Oskamp, 1987).

Sociologists working in a different tradition identified specific attitudes about responsibility and consequences that, according to their research, allowed delinquents to commit acts they would otherwise have considered morally reprehensible by neutralizing their guilt. Sykes and Matza (1957) hypothesized that these attitudes provided justifications to reduce the loss of esteem or the guilt that would otherwise result from participating in the act. As noted earlier, Thurman and others (1984) investigated the impact on tax compliance of an expanded list of guilt neutralization attitudes developed from Minor (1981), including the denial of responsibility, denial of injury to any victim, defense of necessity, condemnation of the system, and appeal to higher loyalties. The study found all guilt neutralization attitudes to be significantly ($p < .05$, logit analysis) related to self-reported tax compliance, after controlling for perceived commitment and social and legal sanctions. The previously discussed problem of whether this relationship reflects rationalization for past noncompliance or neutralization of guilt concerning future intentions remains to be solved, but the results at least suggest that such attitudes may be important in understanding the relationship between commitment and compliance.

GENERAL ATTITUDES TOWARD LAW AND GOVERNMENT.   The small research base that we review below provides only partial clues about other attitudes that are consistently related to commitment and compliance in the tax domain.

Attitudes toward law. Since tax laws are just one of many types of laws, the consistency hypothesis suggests that the commitment to obey different components of tax laws would be closely related to a commitment to obey tax laws generally as well as other laws. Some evidence supports this hypothesis. Both Tittle (1980) and Grasmick and Green (1980) found that a commitment scale combining responses to taxes with responses to other laws proved more robust in explaining self-reported compliance than the sum of commitment measures for the other laws, suggesting that commitment to obey tax laws followed from a general commitment to obey. This suggests that a more general commitment attitude affecting compliance with social as well as legal norms is being tapped.

By contrast, the Westat survey found that, while self-reported tax compliers differed substantially from self-reported noncompliers in commitment to obey tax laws, they did not differ in commitment to laws against larceny involving the same amount of money (Westat, Inc., 1980f). Complicating this picture even further, individual taxpayers differed in their commitment to obey different parts of the tax laws. For example, the Yankelovich (1984) survey found that only 23 percent rated failure to report the income equivalent of exchanges between neighbors of goods and services as unacceptable, compared with 60 percent who rated failure to report small outside income as unacceptable and 88 percent who rated stretching medical deductions to include nonmedical expenses as unacceptable. Available analyses have also not considered how commitment to law in general interacts with attitudes toward specific laws in influencing compliance with those particular laws. Nor do we have any evidence about the stability over time of general or tax-specific commitment to comply.

Attitudes toward government. A government's lack of legitimacy almost by definition diminishes the moral justification for obeying its laws (Easton, 1965). Within the American context, however, attitudes about the broad legitimacy of government have seldom been found correlated with tax commitment or compliance. General attitudes toward government, feelings of disenfranchisement, and patriotism measures showed no significant relationship with either reported compliance or an index measuring commitment to comply in the Yankelovich survey. Westat, Inc. (1980e) found that political concerns were mentioned in focus group studies of compliance, but attitudes toward the government and the IRS did not differ significantly among self-reported compliers and noncompliers (Cahalan and Ekstrand, 1980). Voting behavior studies have found party affiliation and ideology to be important determinants of voting patterns, but studies testing the hypothesis that Republicans or conservatives are more likely to resist taxes have not found party affiliation to be significantly related to commitment (Spicer and Lundstedt, 1976; Song and Yarbrough, 1978; Lewis, 1979).

While attitudes toward government do not appear to affect commitment and compliance directly, they may affect them indirectly through their impact on general attitudes toward taxes and tax policy. Furnham (1983:125) argues that conservative ideology (virtue will be rewarded, success is attendant purely upon effort, and the poor and unemployed are to blame for their plight) is associated with negative attitudes toward taxes, on the basis of a small survey in England. A simple analysis of public opinion trends (Darnell and Gallaher, 1985) noted that fairness ratings of the federal income tax system appeared to change with popularity ratings of the president. But fluctuations in perceived tax fairness were not related to periods of major policy changes or to fluctuations in trust in government, even though both have generally declined during the previous two decades. No statistical tests for significance were used to verify these observations. One study (Song and Yarborough, 1978) did find several attitudes toward government (politicians waste time, politicians manipulate people, perceived political efficacy) had significant ($p < .05$) simple correlations with a measure of commitment (tax ethics). But only the taxpayer's perception of political efficacy remained significant in explaining commitment when other factors were controlled for.

SPECIFIC ATTITUDES TOWARD TAX LAWS. *Perceptions of equity.* Attitudes about tax law and administration, particularly attitudes relating to the perceived equity of the tax system, have been found to be more closely related to commitment and tax compliance than are more general attitudes toward law and government. This is consistent with findings in other domains (Ajzen and Fishbein, 1980) that links between attitudes, intentions, and behavior are strongest for attitudes most closely related to the behavior being studied.

Surveys have measured taxpayer perceptions of several dimensions of tax law equity. The term *exchange equity* refers to the perceived relationship between taxes paid and benefits received and is measured by agreement or disagreement with such statements as, "The government spends little on me," "There are many services I use," "My tax payments are about right, taxes are reasonable for the number of services provided" (Scott and Grasmick, 1981), "Government wastes too much money, Too much is spent on welfare" (Mason and Lowry, 1981). *Vertical equity* refers to perceptions of the taxpayer's tax burden relative to individuals in higher- and lower-income groups and is measured by responses to statements like, "The tax system benefits the rich and is unfair to the average taxpayer" (Yankelovich et al., 1984) and, "The poor pay too much in taxes." *Horizontal equity* refers to perceptions of the taxpayer's tax burden relative to others in the same income group. It is measured by asking respondents whether they pay more or less than others making the same income and whether others like them get more tax breaks.

Interpreting the results of existing studies is difficult because survey questions do not always fall into the categories of exchange, vertical, and horizontal equity. Furthermore, analyses differ in the techniques of testing relationships and the factors controlled for in multivariate analysis, and results are not fully consistent. The existing evidence suggests that perceptions of tax law equity do affect commitment as well as the relationship between commitment and compliance but that a broader scope of analysis is required to unravel the intricacies.

Exchange equity was positively related to both commitment and self-reported compliance in a small survey (Spicer and Lundstedt, 1976). A larger national survey (Yankelovich et al., 1984) found exchange equity (index of objections to government spending) to be more strongly related to self-reported compliance than to commitment. The Yankelovich survey found no significant relationship to commitment or compliance for questions tapping vertical or horizontal equity. The small survey by Thurman and others (1984) reported that attitudes of exchange and horizontal inequity were significantly ($p < .05$) related to noncompliance even after controlling for the general effect of commitment, but Scott and Grasmick (1981) found no similar relationship. The relationship of equity measures with commitment was not reported.

Scott and Grasmick (1981) hypothesized that negative attitudes toward equity motivate people to consider noncompliance and suggested that the inhibiting effect of commitment (and other variables) would be most clearly observable when there were such attitudes. Their survey results supported the hypothesis: the effect of commitment (as well as of perceived social and legal sanctions) on compliance was greater when perceived equity was low than when it was high. From the analysis it cannot be determined whether low equity judgments act as a motivator for noncompliance that is then inhibited by commitment, as Scott and Grasmick imply, or whether existing commitment is inhibited by perceptions of inequity. The interaction between fairness and commitment that Scott and Grasmick found but Thurman et al. did not suggests an important avenue of research on commitment that needs further exploration; it also cautions against testing only simple linear relationships between attitudes, commitments, and compliance.

A laboratory experiment (Spicer and Becker, 1980) also found horizontal equity to be important, since subjects informed that their assigned tax rates in a simulated tax problem were higher than average complied at significantly lower rates than those informed that their tax rate was lower than average. Indirect support for the importance of perceived equity comes from survey findings suggesting that most respondents thought fairness was related to compliance. The most common response to the question of why other people cheat was that the tax system is unfair (Yankelovich et al., 1984). However, two Oregon surveys (Mason and Calvin, 1984; Mason and Lowry, 1981) and the pilot Westat survey (Ekstrand, 1980) found no relationships between equity measures and self-reported compliance. Mason and Calvin speculated that fear of sanctions may have inhibited noncompliance by all subjects in their sample, including those who consider the system unfair.

Perceptions of complexity and ambiguity. As noted previously, excessive complexity theoretically reduces compliance by increasing compliance costs and decreasing the chances of severe criminal punishment for noncompliance. But respondents in several surveys did not list complexity among the major problems with the tax system (Song and Yarborough, 1978; Westat, Inc., 1980f; Yankelovich et al., 1984).

It appears that the ambiguity of the tax law and its impact on perceived equity is more closely related to taxpayer commitment than complexity. In Westat, Inc.'s (1980e) focus group discussions, moral latitude arising from gray areas and ambiguity in tax laws emerged as a major motivation for noncompliance. Of the seven guilt neutralization mechanisms investigated by Thurman et al. (1984), the justification, "It is okay to claim an undeserved tax deduction when you are not really sure what the rule is," was the most widely accepted and most consistently related to compliance. An early IRS (1968) study speculated that people cheat by small amounts because they believe that all doubts should be resolved in favor of the taxpayer, not the government. This sentiment is probably a major factor for the consistent finding that very few taxpayers think petty cheating should be punished with fines (ICF, Inc., 1985).

ATTITUDES TOWARD TAX ADMINISTRATION AND ENFORCEMENT. *Attitudes toward the* IRS. Just as specific attitudes toward the tax laws are likely to be more closely linked to tax compliance than general attitudes toward law, so also are attitudes toward tax administration (by the IRS for federal income tax) likely to be more closely linked than general attitudes toward government. Research in a number of fields has demonstrated that individuals who feel that they have been treated fairly by a government agency are more likely to comply with its decisions, even when they go against the individual's self-interest (McEwen and Maiman, 1984; Tyler, 1986). Tyler in particular argues that the perceived procedural legitimacy of interactions between individual and government agency affects satisfaction and intentions to comply with agency rules and regulations.

Surveys have reported public opinion about the honesty, integrity, and efficiency of the IRS to be positive, in the sense that the average respondents choose evaluations above the midpoint in the evaluation scale (Yankelovich et al., 1984; Aitken and Bonneville, 1980). However, a 1984 Roper survey found that the ratio of favorable to unfavorable responses was lower for the IRS than for any of the other federal agencies included in the survey, presumably because most other agencies provide services more popular among their recipients than does the IRS. The relationship between attitudes toward the IRS, commitment, and compliance remains untested for the most part. The Yankelovich et al. (1984) survey found no relationship between evaluations of the IRS and either commitment or compliance. A reanalysis by Smith (1987), however, suggests that attitudes toward the IRS affect compliance indirectly by affecting attitudes toward tax laws.

Attitudes toward enforcement. A growing literature has debated the impact of cooperative and coercive enforcement approaches on citizens' attitudes and compliance (Hawkins and Thomas, 1984; Scholz, 1984). In the tax domain, one laboratory experiment compared the effects of coercive strategies (in which subjects had no incentive except possible penalties to cooperate with the tax authority) with cooperative strategies (in which money was refunded to taxpayers in proportion to the number of compliant taxpayers) (Thibaut et al., 1974). Compliance levels were higher under cooperative rules. When the tax rules affecting payments were less clearly specified at the beginning of the experiment, compliance increased in the coercive setting but decreased in the cooperative setting. Furthermore, subjects in the cooperative situation judged the outcomes to be more reasonable and more just and the agency to be fairer, more honest, and more cooperative, independent of actual payoffs.

A comparative study of European tax systems, based on surveys of 1,000 persons in Britain, Germany, France, Spain, and Italy (Schmölders, 1970), examined the effects of different enforcement styles on compliance and attitudes. The more intrusive German collection system achieved greater compliance than the British system, but at the cost of more negative attitudes toward the tax system in general and its degree of justice and equity. The British achieved only slightly lower levels of general compliance but more positive attitudes through a "rich reservoir of loopholes" and less intrusive accounting and auditing requirements. The worst situation was found in countries that faced both difficulties, when crude assessment methods were ineffectual in securing compliance yet provoked considerable resentment against tax collectors. Particularly in these situations, "the discrepancy between tax law and reality, the arbitrary assessment and insecurity as to one's legal obligations, lead to a deterioration of attitudes" (Schmölders, 1970:303).

Thus, the relative efficiency of enforcement may affect attitudes differently in different national contexts. Increasing enforcement effort may increase commitment by reducing the discrepancy between laws and reality and by confirming the social obligation to pay taxes, as hypothesized initially. Alternatively, increased enforcement may aggravate negative attitudes and resistance to the tax system, perhaps including normatively motivated tax protest and deliberate tax evasion (Kidder and McEwen, Vol. 2). There is no evidence about the strength of these effects or how they might interact with deterrence effects discussed previously.

Attitudes toward enforcement effectiveness. It is a common perception among enforcement officials that some people always obey the law, some always try to break the law regardless of what enforcers do, and most people obey as long as enforcers catch and punish at least some of the lawbreakers (Bowles, 1971). Similarly, tax and other compliance studies have consistently found commitment and compliance to be lowest among those who perceive noncompliance as widespread (McGraw, 1985; Fincham and Jaspers, 1983).

This connection has several possible explanations that have not yet been adequately separated in tax studies. A belief that noncompliance is widespread could simply affect perceptions about the likelihood of getting caught and the expected social penalties, as discussed earlier in the section on self-interest. In addition, the belief could affect commitment through negative confirmation from society and from authorities that compliance with a particular law is unimportant. Or the belief could provide a justification for ignoring a general commitment to obey the law in a specific context, since even good citizens do not want to be the only "suckers" who fully pay their taxes. These three effects are not mutually exclusive, but the magnitude of each in any given setting may be quite important because they have very different implications for tax administration, especially for public information strategies.

A number of studies provide indirect evidence about the extent to which a citizen's commitment to obey laws is contingent on the ability of the state to ensure through enforcement that others will comply as well. The IRS (1968:31) analysis of its first commissioned survey, for example, speculated that petty cheating was encouraged by the perception that many others get away with it. In Sweden, 74 percent of respondents agreed that "since tax evasion is so common one cannot be blamed for evading taxes" (Vogel, 1974:512). In America, respondents chose the statement, "Think everyone else does it," as the third most frequent reason why people cheat, after, "Think tax system is unfair" and, "Think they can get away with it" (Yankelovich et al., 1984).

Yankelovich et al. (1984) found that an index combining perceptions of tax cheating with measures of perceived integrity was the strongest predictor of compliance and the second strongest predictor of commitment. A Westat survey (Ekstrand, 1980) also found that noncompliers were significantly more likely to respond that cheating is common and has increased in the past ten years. This finding, if true, is particularly significant, since national surveys have found that the number of people agreeing with the statement, "Almost every taxpayer cheats a little," increased from 36 percent in 1966 (IRS, 1968) to 44 percent in 1979 (Aitken and Bonneville, 1980) to 48 percent in 1984 (Yankelovich et al., 1984). But the evidence is not fully consistent, since one laboratory experiment found that different information about the level of cheating by others had no significant effect on the amount of cheating by subjects (Spicer and Hero, 1985).

The adequacy of enforcement toward one's social peers appears to be less of a concern to taxpayers than enforcement toward wealthier entities or blatantly criminal actions, although these perceptual issues are not well understood. Respondents in the Yankelovich et al. (1984) survey incorrectly perceive illegitimate write-offs of business expenses and overclaimed deductions by individual taxpayers to be as important a source of cheating as underreported income. Finally, a Roper survey in 1984 found that 74 percent said strict enforcement of tax laws affecting businesses was very important, compared with 57 percent for personal taxes.

Surveys also suggest that people care more about penalizing flagrant violators than petty cheaters. The number of respondents in national surveys preferring heavy fines for small amounts of cheating decreased from 25 percent in 1966 to 7 percent in 1984, while the number favoring the collection of merely taxes owed and interest increased from 37 percent in 1966 to 50 percent in 1984 (ICF, Inc., 1985). Respondents willing to impose jail sentences for tax cheating by large amounts increased from 3 percent in 1966 to 26 percent in 1984 (ICF, Inc., 1985), indicating an increasing condemnation of major evaders. Responses to a 1982 Roper survey question on preferred methods of closing the tax gap indicated a similar viewpoint: while only 7 percent preferred to give the IRS additional collection tools (e.g., withholding on interest) and 6 percent preferred to give IRS resources to hire additional auditors, 24 percent preferred that the IRS prosecute more evaders (ICF, Inc., 1985).

Since legal penalties signal the state's judgment about the seriousness of a particular violation, penalties may affect compliance indirectly by influencing attitudes as well as directly through self-interest concerns. The simple correlations reported in Scott and Grasmick's (1981) study indicated that commitment was less related to equity ($r = .29$) than to perceived legal ($r = .43$) and social ($r = .60$) sanctions. The "omnipotence of the IRS" measure in the Yankelovich et al. survey (1984:65,67) appears to explain more of the variance in their commitment measure than in compliance, again suggesting that punishment credibility and commitment are related. One cluster of taxpayers, labeled "strategic noncompliers" by Yankelovich et al., had relatively low scores on both commitment and perceived sanctions, suggesting a strong relationship for at least some taxpayers.

The effect of perceived penalties on commitment may depend on other factors as well. For example, Schwartz and Orleans (1967) found that higher-status taxpayers in the experimental group that received the questionnaire emphasizing penalties expressed stronger commitment to compliance than the control group, while lower-status taxpayers expressed less.

Empirical Evidence on Demographic and Socioeconomic Factors

In addition to measures of incentives, commitment, and other variables of theoretical interest, many researchers also incorporate certain demographic and socioeconomic characteristics of taxpayers into their models of compliance. Examples include sex, race or ethnicity, age, education, occupation, and socioeconomic status. Researchers have repeatedly found rather strong correlations between these variables and compliance measures. But these variables are commonly designated as merely indicators of tastes or statistical control variables, and few serious efforts have been made to interpret the correlations.

Researchers have fairly consistently found age, sex, and race to be correlated with reported noncompliance, with younger males from minority groups reporting lower levels of compliance. Survey researchers have found noncompliance measures that are positively related to socioeconomic status, as measured by income and education.

An analysis of one national survey (Yankelovich et al., 1984) found that personal demographic and socioeconomic characteristics provided almost as good a predictor of self-reported noncompliance as did specific tax-related attitudes, although neither explained much variance (5 percent for social characteristics compared with 7 percent for attitudes). However, personal characteristics were far less closely related to taxpaying commitment than specific attitudes were, with social characteristics explaining only 14 percent compared with 58 percent for attitudes. Since commitment itself is a type of attitude, this is not surprising. The relatively weak explanatory power underscores the need to understand the more complex relationship between the taxpayer's socioeconomic environment, tax-related attitudes, and behavior.

DEMOGRAPHIC CHARACTERISTICS
AGE.   Taxpayer age has been found to be related to commitment (Vogel, 1974; Spicer and Lundstedt, 1976), to self-reported compliance (Mason and Calvin, 1978; Aitken and Bonneville, 1980; Westat, Inc., 1980f;

Mason and Lowry, 1981; Yankelovich et al., 1984:85—underreporting only), and to audit measures of compliance in TCMP (Clotfelter, 1983). Mixed results have been obtained in analyses of the 1969 cross-sectional data base (Witte and Woodbury, 1985; Dubin and Wilde, 1988; Beron et al., 1988), in which compliance is measured in the aggregate and age is measured as the proportion older than sixty-five. In most of these studies, commitment or compliance is generally low in the early work years and higher in other age groups. Two other surveys did not find a significant linear relationship between age and commitment (Song and Yarbrough, 1978) or compliance (Spicer and Lundstedt, 1976). Although both income and education explained more of the variance in self-reported compliance than age in one study (Yankelovich et al., 1984), another survey found that the compliance effects of income and education became insignificant when controlled for age (Cahalan and Ekstrand, 1980:15).

Tax cheating appears to shift from nonfiling and underreporting income for younger taxpayers to overstating subtractions from income for older ones (Yankelovich et al., 1984:85), which can be explained in terms of available opportunity (Mason and Lowry, 1981). Younger taxpayers have fewer records of prior taxes or of financial transactions that could be used to find them, are more likely to work in marginal jobs not subject to withholding, and may have no previous experience with tax forms. Older taxpayers have more expenditures to be itemized and perhaps overstated as deductions. Other possible connections between taxpayer aging and compliance with tax laws are developed by Kagan (Vol. 2), and the issue is developed in terms of a hypothetical "tax career" in Chapter 3.

However, the age-compliance correlation has only been measured with data sets collected at a single point in time. With only cross-sectional data of this type, it is impossible to distinguish effects of taxpayer aging from cohort effects, in which cohorts of taxpayers born earlier comply more fully than do later-born cohorts (Kinsey, 1984; Kidder and McEwen, Vol. 2; Schmidt, Appendix A). The decline in many measures of trust in government during the last two decades (Darnell and Gallaher, 1985) may signal attitudinal changes in the baby boom generation or responses to particular events like the Vietnam War and the Watergate crisis.

Kidder and McEwen (Vol. 2) suggest that another interpretation is that the age-compliance relationship is an effect of particular historical periods. For example, cyclical economic conditions might create identifiable tax compliance problems unique to taxpayer generations coming of working age in depressed regions; young workers for whom cash jobs are the only option in depressed, heavy-industry towns may retain attitudes learned in the informal economy even when prosperity returns and they move on to regular jobs. To the extent that occupational and community structure brings individuals of a similar age together (e.g., age-related housing location), the historical period effect on individuals would become magnified and stabilized through social interaction.

Distinguishing among aging, cohort, and period explanations of the age-compliance correlation is extremely important from a policy standpoint, because the demographic alternatives have radically different implications for the future. The aging explanation implies that aggregate compliance may improve in the future, as the baby boom generation grows older. The cohort explanation implies that compliance may deteriorate over time if new cohorts entering the work force continue past trends. If particular historical periods have produced the age-compliance correlation, then that explanation offers no demographic basis for future projections. To distinguish among the alternative explanations, actual or synthetic panel data bases (i.e., individual-level data on compliance over time) will be needed (see Schmidt, Appendix A). Data requirements are discussed further in Chapter 5.

SEX.   Survey evidence has found significant relationships between tax compliance and taxpayers' sex, race, and socioeconomic status. This evidence is less consistent than the evidence for the age relationship, and as noted earlier, none of the indicators is a very powerful predictor of compliance.

In taxpayer surveys, women generally have reported more compliance than men (Yankelovich et al., 1984; Tittle, 1980; Aitken and Bonneville, 1980; Mason and Calvin, 1978; Vogel, 1974). In the one econometric study to examine the issue, Beron et al. (1988) found higher compliance for audit classes with more complex returns in areas with more female-headed households. The relationship has been explained in several ways. Richards and Tittle (1981) found that women perceive the chances of getting caught as much higher than men do and suggest that closer parental supervision (at least in earlier generations) socialized women to develop a greater stake than men in conformity and a greater concern with visibility to the community. Tittle (1980) also emphasizes the socialization of women into more conforming life-styles. Grasmick, Finley, and Glaser (1984) hypothesize that as women's careers become more like men's both in terms of early socialization and of occupational choices, commitment and compliance behavior will also become more similar. Their study found that women with nontraditional views of sex roles as well as women employed outside the home (54 percent of the sample) were much closer to men's levels for tax noncompliance and other economic crimes than to women with more traditional views, even after age was controlled for. Further indirect evidence for a transition in sex-related differences was presented in Mason and Lowry (1981), who found that the significant relationship between sex and compliance in the 1975 Oregon survey was not repeated in the 1980 survey, possibly reflecting changes in women's role in the labor force.

RACE AND ETHNICITY.   Research offers some evidence that both compliance with tax laws and expressed commitment to compliance are higher among whites than among nonwhites. But the magnitudes of interracial differences are small in most studies and depend on details of the analytical approach.

The largest race differences have been found in studies of indices of commitment to compliance. Song and Yarbrough (1978), who analyzed a 100-point scale of tax ethics, reported a mean of 64 for whites and 50 for blacks, in a sample from a small town in North Carolina. Race explained 19 percent of the scale variance by itself, and an unreported but statistically significant share when other relevant variables (e.g., income, education, and measures of alienation and perceived political efficacy) were statistically controlled.

The results of Yankelovich et al. (1984:64–67) concerning race are impossible to interpret fully, but they suggest that race has a smaller association with self-reported previous compliance than with an index of attitudes condoning noncompliance. Their white-nonwhite indicator showed a negative correlation ($r = -.16$) with the index and a smaller positive correlation ($r = .06$) with self-reported noncompliance. The indicator, however, is not defined in the report. The correlations seem unimportant in any event, since the indicator explains only 1.5 percent of the variance in the index and 0.4 percent of the variance in noncompliance. In the survey by Aitken and Bonneville (1980), race differentials in self-reported compliance are sensitive to the wording of questions. More blacks than whites (39 versus 25 percent) acknowledged being less than absolutely honest on their previous return, and more (6 versus 2 percent) acknowledged claiming a dependent to which they were not entitled. But an identical fraction of blacks and whites, 8 percent, acknowledged stretching the truth to pay less on their previous return.

Econometric results also do not find strong relationships between race and compliance. In their multiple regression analyses of estimated voluntary compliance levels, Witte and Woodbury (1982) found statistically significant negative coefficients on "percent nonwhite" in two audit classes but insignificant coefficients in the other five. Dubin and Wilde (1988) report statistically significant negative coefficients in all seven classes. The estimates imply that each 1-point increase in the percentage nonwhite is associated with a 0.4- to 4-point decrease in VCL, depending on audit class. Controlling for adjusted gross income, Beron et al. (1988) find a significant negative coefficient on percentage nonwhite for only one audit class in their regression analysis of reported tax liability. They report negative coefficients on percentage foreign born in two audit classes.

SOCIOECONOMIC STATUS

Socioeconomic status, as indicated by income and education, has been found to be related to noncompliance, but so many factors are interrelated with these variables that such interpretations are fairly speculative. Clotfelter's (1983) analysis of individual TCMP data suggested that income was negatively related to the fraction of income reported, even when other factors were controlled. Others have suggested that noncompliance is most common at the highest and lowest levels of income and social status, perhaps because there are more possibilities for successfully hiding income in those ranges and for overstating deductions at the highest levels; middle-income groups are more likely to have wages and salaries subjected to withholding and reporting. A few studies have found evidence for this pattern based on self-reported previous noncompliance (Mason and Lowry, 1981), estimated VCL for geographic areas (Witte and Woodbury, 1985), and other government data (Simon and Witte, 1982).

The other primary indicator of status, level of formal education, has consistently been found to be negatively related to self-reported previous compliance in surveys (Yankelovich et al., 1984; Mason and Lowry, 1981; Aitken and Bonneville, 1980; Vogel, 1974) and to estimated VCL in aggregate-level econometric studies (Witte and Woodbury, 1985; Beron et al., 1988). Yankelovich et al. (1984) and Vogel (1974), however, found that respondents with a higher level of education were more likely to assert greater commitments to comply.

Thus, research offers some support to the thesis that higher socioeconomic status leads both to greater commitment to obey laws and to greater opportunities to commit economic crimes (Sutherland, 1939; Geis and Meier, 1977). According to the first hypothesis, as an individual becomes integrated into community life, the process of socialization increases internalized commitment to obey community laws and fear of condemnation by others in the community for individuals with considerable stake to lose. In conformance with this hypothesis, other measures reflecting an individual's integration into the community, such as length of time in the community and home ownership, have also been found to be positively related to taxpayers' compliance (Mason and Lowry, 1981:16–17).

According to the second hypothesis, the general law-abidingness of high-status individuals makes those who do disobey less subject to harsh treatment by the legal system. Grasmick et al. (1983) found that high-status individuals perceive less likelihood of punishment than low-status individuals and argued that this accounted for higher admitted noncompliance even when the individuals asserted commitment to comply. In the tax arena, this perspective would suggest the plausible argument that high-status taxpayers have greater access to low-risk opportunities, more ability to learn how to conceal their evasion, and less likelihood of being punished than low-status individuals. In addition, unlike street crimes, tax cheating is not generally made known to the community and is not as strongly condemned as other kinds of crimes. These factors are argued by some (Klepper and Nagin, Vol. 2) to overwhelm the compliance effects of commitment for high-status individuals.

Conclusion

As this chapter has shown, although researchers have found many correlations between taxpayer compliance and other variables, they have developed very few hard facts. Taxpaying seems only loosely connected to the incentives and attitudes that are expected to govern it. Correlations between compliance and taxpayer characteristics seem to raise nearly as many questions as they answer. And research to date offers surprisingly little evidence even about how IRS activities affect compliance.

Some promising extensions of previous lines of research have been suggested in the previous pages. But substantial progress in understanding compliance may also require theoretical and empirical attention to some questions that compliance researchers have only recently begun to consider. How do taxpayers shape their financial circumstances, and how do those circumstances shape the incentives and values that influence compliance? How do taxpayers make sense of a tax system with complex compliance requirements and uncertain risks and rewards for failing to comply, and how do their shortcuts affect compliance? When and how do citizens seek help concerning tax matters, and how do tax practitioners affect their clients' perceptions and attitudes pertaining to compliance?

Because questions such as these have attracted very little research attention to date, almost nothing is known about their answers. But approaches that have been successfully used with similar questions in other settings may offer useful perspectives and methods. These matters are taken up in Chapter 3.

Notes

1. Generally, income is assumed to have "decreasing marginal utility"—that is, each additional dollar gives less utility than the preceding one. Under this assumption, for example, the utility of $1,000 in evaded tax would be less for a taxpayer with $100,000 of after-tax income than for a taxpayer with $10,000 of after-tax income. In addition, people's attitudes toward risk are usually presumed to depend on their incomes.

2. An exception is the model of Klepper and Nagin (1987a), which predicts that an increase in the tax rate will decrease reported income. In their model, the necessary condition for that prediction is that taxpayers perceive that their underreporting is subject to nonmonetary informal sanctions, which are independent of the tax rate.

3. Note that, since the Tax Reform Act of 1986, the incentive analyzed by Slemrod has increased, since the tax rate differential between brackets is larger than before.

4. For this proposition to hold, the costs of administering penalties must be sufficiently low, and individuals must recognize that there is a nonzero probability that the penalty will be imposed on noncompliers.

5. In discussing specific return items, the fact that audits are only one of the processes by which tax returns are examined becomes especially important. As discussed in Chapter 1, other methods include comparisons of tax return reports to information returns, to indicators of transactions in previous tax years, and to other returns (e.g., financial partners, ex-spouses). Some of these have much higher coverage and accuracy rates than personal audits, and all of them can be accomplished at lower cost per taxpayer examined.

6. A substantial fraction of audits—24 to 36 percent in 1973, according to the U.S. General Accounting Office (1976)—do not lead to a change in tax liability. Conversely, the IRS (1983f) reports that in 1976 less than $1 of every $3 in unreported income was detected, even in intensive TCMP audits. No information is available on how subsequent improvements in information reporting have affected these figures, but it would be surprising if errors did not occur at substantial rates.

7. Note that in the context of theories that invoke self-interest, the same friends and acquaintances are also sources of information and misinformation about the probability and severity of sanctions for various noncompliant acts and about compliance requirements.

8. For the low-income nonbusiness (itemized) class, VCL for the audited subjects increased by 3.4 percent (from 89.0 to 92.4), while overall VCL decreased by 3 percent (from 88.5 to 85.5). For the medium-income nonbusiness class, the comparable changes were a 0.5 percent increase for the audited subjects compared with 0.2 percent decrease overall. For the low-income business class, the figures were a 7.9 percent increase for audited subjects compared with a 5.2 percent decrease overall. (See supplementary notes to Chapter 1 for explanations of audit classes and VCL.)

9. This figure combines 48 percent who said "be more careful" with 21 percent who said "get professional help."

10. The issue may be clearer in the context of crimes against persons, for which the analogue would be to measure arrest probabilities as the ratio of arrests to population instead of arrests to offenders. The measure would be meaningful only if offenders and nonoffenders were equally likely to be arrested.

11. Note that, if perceptions of sanction probabilities are stable over time, even when subjects engage in the illegal behavior, then the cross-sectional design would give valid results. To verify that assumption, one must either measure the perceptions at multiple points in time or rely on subjects' reports of how their perceptions have changed over time. To the panel's knowledge, no surveys of taxpayer compliance have ever asked how the experience of *not* being audited after failing to report all income affected compliance in subsequent years.

12. Recall that the audit rate is not equivalent to the detection probability for noncompliance. Therefore, for example, even if audit rates are increased in response to decreasing compliance and audits detect all noncompliance, the detection probability for noncompliance will decrease if audit rates increase less than proportionally to the increase in noncompliant taxpayers.

13. An earlier analysis, Project 778, is described in an internal IRS (1978a) memorandum. Like Witte and Woodbury's analysis, Project 778 involved separate multiple regression analyses by audit class, but with slightly different explanatory variables. Using the same statistical significance test (t-statistic > 1.645 in absolute value), 9 of the 21 audit rate coefficients (7 audit classes and 3 audit rates) agreed in the two analyses.

14. For each audit class equation, explanatory variables were: the fraction of filers audited in calendar years 1967–1969, for the respective audit class and for all other classes combined; rates of civil fraud penalties in 1967 and 1969; and rates of criminal investigations, prosecutions, and sentences in 1970.

15. The elasticity is the percentage increase in VCL associated with a 1 percent increase in the audit rate. For three audit classes, the estimated elasticities were 0.0195, 0.0018, and 0.0060.

16. Over- and understatements of tax liability are treated identically in the VCL measure in the 1969 file.

17. Information reporting is a widely acknowledged indicator of visibility. Klepper

and Nagin argue that, for a return item with a small coefficient of variation, noncompliance involving a given dollar amount is easier to detect, so they use that coefficient as a measure of visibility.

18. The authors assume that expected sanction severity is less if noncompliance is more deniable through ignorance or ambiguity. They characterize an item in terms of ignorance using the fraction of reporting errors that increase tax liability and ambiguity by two indicators: the number of recent IRS revenue rulings and the need to impute financial values, as in noncash contributions. They interpret coefficients on all three measures in terms of severity.

19. Questions have been raised about the validity of future intentions as a measure of illegal behavior (see, e.g., Saltzman et al., 1982). In a recent study, Murray and Erickson (1987) report high concordance between expressions of future intentions to use marijuana and self-reports six months later of actual marijuana use. Predictors were similar for the future intentions and retrospective measures.

20. The index of social sanctions was the number among the respondent's five closest friends who had not engaged in the illegal behavior.

21. To use the return-based measure, one would measure reported taxable income or some component of it in tax years 1 and 2, as well as the number of noncompliant acquaintances just prior to the beginning of each year. If the threat of social sanctions encourages compliance, then respondents who acquired noncompliant acquaintances between the two years should report smaller average increases (or larger average decreases) in taxable income between tax years 1 and 2.

22. In their working paper, the authors do not explain either the calculation of the tax rate measure or the sources of variation in tax rate when the amount and composition of income are controlled. They do suggest that the tax rate may be a proxy for a nonlinear relationship between income and the probability of evasion as well as an incentive for noncompliance.

23. None of the reported Dubin and Wilde analyses of the 1969 data base included income as a potential determinant of compliance.

3. Expanding the Framework of Analysis

Until quite recently, taxpayer compliance research has focused almost entirely on questions considered in Chapter 2 involving self-interest, social sanctions, and social commitment. In this chapter we discuss some questions that have not been deeply explored in the context of taxpayer compliance and introduce some concepts that have been useful in studying similar questions in other contexts but have only recently been introduced in taxpayer compliance research.

Broader Perspectives on Taxpayer Compliance

CONVENTIONAL VIEWS

It should be clear from Chapter 2 that measures of taxpayer compliance are correlated with a number of factors: the risks and rewards associated with taxpayers' compliance and noncompliance, measures of taxpayers' commitments to compliance, and taxpayers' demographic characteristics. However, these factors do not provide a complete explanation of taxpayers' compliance behavior. For example, a common theme expressed by participants in Westat, Inc.'s, (1980e) focus groups is the complexity of tax laws and the uncertainty it produces for the taxpayer and for the IRS:

> The IRS still doesn't understand it, so how are we going to figure it out? You know, it's gotten to a point where the tax structure is so complicated because of exceptions for this, deductions for that (p. 27).
> I really feel that you could call [the IRS] and get three different answers if you talked to three different people on some of this kind of thing (p. 35).
> One person will tell you what my consultant says. I can't claim this thing that way. Someone else will say, well listen, my tax man does it this way. And we are talking about pretty much the same situation (p. 28).
> I just received a notice for payment that I owed them and I didn't realize that I was supposed to make out this estimated tax form. Then when they sent it to me, I was trying to figure it out. You call a friend to have him figure it out for you. And I figured, well, this is so complicated that if I fill it out wrong,

then you're in trouble of some sort. So I just paid it. Just sent it in rather than try to figure it out (p 29).

One way people try to cope with the complexity of the tax law is to develop routines and habits that they follow each year, although the fifth quotation below points out the limitation of relying on routines for some people. The kind of habits people develop are likely to influence the tax liability they report.

> I have a garbage bag that I keep all year long. Anything that is questionable, if I think it pertains to income tax, I just dump it in it. At the end of the year when I am ready to make my income tax, I pull it out and then I assess it (p. 58).
> Then come the end of the year, you spend another two or three weeks weeding through these receipts that you've kept, trying to get the appropriate ones and trying to, you know, getting tax tables and figure out how they go . . . No, I'll get a better deal if I do it this way (p. 59).
> Well, over the last couple of years, I hadn't been getting as much money back [tax refund], and every year I had to scrape that much harder and find more receipts and everything, that I can claim (p. 59).
> My once-a-year pain-in-the-ass task. It's a course in creative writing. . . . (p. 65).
> I figured I would learn how to do it [the tax form] if I did it a number of times. Each year the thing changes and shifts and the paragraphs are in different places and the whole thing is made over again. And I read the instructions about that thick. By that time, you know, it's ridiculous. Every year, I can't understand why the changes are being made constantly. There's no simplification whatsoever that I can make out. And I study it and try to figure it out every year figuring they'll stay with one set-up. They're shifting and changing and it takes a Philadelphia lawyer to do it (p. 29).

An alternative coping mechanism is to go to a tax practitioner who knows the real system, including not only deductions the taxpayer may not know about but also the reasonable amounts that can be deducted without fear of getting caught. Practitioners offer the possibilities of avoiding an unpleasant task, reducing tax liability, and reducing fear of contact with the IRS. Of course, some practitioners' clients wind up being disappointed.

> Sure, they come up with things I never would have thought of (p. 62).
> I'm shifting the liability of sorts to somebody else's shoulders and relieving me of the burden of worrying about it if they happen to audit me. Whereas, if you do it yourself, it's you and God against [the IRS] (p. 66).
> My man tells me I was allowed a certain amount. And as far as he knew he

never had anybody that they questioned if they kept it below a certain percentage or figure. But they will not allow you a thing when they're checking you if they don't want to that you can't back up with proof (p. 63).

I think any CPA knows in his mind when you tell him you made $20,000 this year, he knows what percentage in each category you are allowed to take without being chased. . . . And then when they've [the IRS auditors] grabbed your form out of the bin and they set it down, they look down to see if your percentages are within what they expect of a person who makes 20 grand. You might not have ever spent those dollars, but if your CPA is sharp, he's taken it, and knows he'll never get caught (p. 63).

I had an accountant do mine at one time because my wife thought I wasn't doing what I was supposed to do, and it ended up that it cost me $40 and he came within $5 of what I had (p. 65).

I have always filled out my returns with the exception of two years, and both CPAs made mistakes, and I had to take them back and show them their mistakes, so I always do my own taxes (p. 65).

SOCIAL SCIENCE PERSPECTIVES

These comments suggest that understanding taxpayer compliance may require attention to a broader set of factors and processes than compliance researchers have traditionally considered. This set includes the external context in which taxpaying occurs: for example, the complex and changing legal and administrative environment; the social and commercial acquaintances who may offer (mis)information about that environment or express values concerning compliance; and the tax practitioners whom taxpayers consult for help in coping with that environment. It also includes the internal processes through which individuals assimilate and act on their perceptions and values about taxpaying.

These factors and processes are the focus of social science disciplines such as political science, sociology, psychology, and economics. Because they had received so little attention in taxpayer compliance research at the time the panel began its work, we decided to commission papers by researchers in those fields to consider applications of current ideas and methods from their disciplines to the study of taxpayer compliance. The ideas in this chapter evolved from consideration of how the disciplinary orientations and methods presented in those papers might advance understanding about taxpayer compliance. Although those ideas could have been organized in any of a number of ways, the panel adopted the structure illustrated in Figure 2. The sections of this chapter keyed to Figure 2 briefly describe the relevant concepts, their applications in other contexts, and ways in which they might be useful in future taxpayer compliance research. The

FIGURE 2 Compliance Influences Needing Further Research

The Legal Context of Taxpayer Compliance
Tax Schemas: The Complexity of Attitudes and Beliefs
    Taxpayers' Decision Processes
        Findings from behavioral decision theory
        Findings from social psychology
    How People Develop Tax Schemas
        Tax careers
        Social and cultural contexts of taxpaying
            Occupations
            Social fields and networks
Tax Practitioners and Taxpayer Compliance

papers themselves, which appear separately as Volume 2, provide more extended discussions of some of the themes that are introduced in this chapter.

Before discussing the individual subjects listed in Figure 2, it is useful to point out that the broadened perspective illustrated has two general implications for future research on taxpayer compliance:

1. Differences in compliance patterns that should be expected across specific taxpayer subgroups and specific reporting requirements; and
2. The two-way nature of interactions between taxpayers and their environments.

First, research on differences in compliance patterns across specific taxpayer subgroups and compliance requirements is important because it can be expected to reveal relationships that are masked in studies using more aggregate measures. To illustrate the point, consider what may happen in national surveys in which taxpayers with relatively simple tax situations (e.g., all wages and salaries subject to withholding, all assets in a savings account on which a bank reports interest to the IRS, standard rather than itemized deductions) dominate the samples. Underreporting of taxable income by these taxpayers would be likely to be detected, and so they are likely to (honestly) report full compliance on the survey. They also may not give taxpaying as much strategic attention as taxpayers with more discretion to underreport income or to claim unwarranted deductions. In that case, their responses to questions about fear of getting caught cheating and commitment to paying taxes may be relatively uninformed and may contain a large random component, and may receive little weight in determining their actual compliance behavior. Therefore, even if low-discretion tax-payers with lower commitment might cheat in less constrained circumstances, the survey analysis might not reveal very strong relationships between compliance and either commitment or fear of detection. Studies that have controlled for differences among taxpayers' circumstances (e.g., Smith and Kinsey, 1985) or among tax return items (e.g., Klepper and Nagin, 1987a) have revealed compliance patterns that do not emerge as clearly in studies at more aggregated levels. Extensions of the more disaggregated work will require study designs that yield sufficient variation in the circumstances that allow discretion in taxpaying behavior.

Second, the two-way nature of interactions between taxpayers and their environments presents another opportunity for future compliance research. Not only does the objective environment influence taxpayers' perceptions and values, but also taxpayers may alter their environments by acting on their perceptions and values. Differences, for example, in social settings, in occupation, in sources of income, or in sources of information about taxes could be expected to systematically influence taxpayers' self-interest calculations and personal values. Research to date suggests that these, in turn, affect compliance with tax reporting requirements. But taxpayers also influence their objective situations (e.g., their social settings, their actual probabilities of being caught and penalized for noncompliance) as they associate with friends and business acquaintances who turn out to be more or less supportive of noncompliance, as they choose more or less formal occupational settings, as they seek advice about tax matters from more or less professional third parties, and perhaps as they join special-interest groups that lobby for changes in tax laws. Very little is known about this second set of relationships—the forces that lead individuals to shape their environments in these and other ways and thereby, perhaps quite unintentionally, to affect their risks and rewards for compliance and noncompliance. Analyses of these relationships require a variety of research methods and should receive high priority in future compliance research.

With these two general implications in mind, we begin the discussion of the specific factors and processes listed in Figure 2—topics that have received little attention in previous taxpayer compliance research but that have demonstrated value in other contexts. We begin by explaining some differences between tax laws and most other criminal and regulatory laws—differences that highlight the need for a broad variety of disciplinary orientations and methodological approaches. We then explore how tax-payers' perceptions and values—as embodied in a "tax schema"—may affect their behavior. Next, we consider how an individual's tax schema develops over the "tax career"—the lifetime progression of experiences that shape the relevant perceptions and values. Next we discuss the influence on decision processes of social and cultural contexts in which taxpayers live, with particular emphasis on occupations and on social networks and fields. Finally, we consider the role of tax practitioners—the professionals who prepare about half of all federal tax returns—in influencing taxpayer decision processes and compliance behavior.

The Legal Context of Taxpayer Compliance

Those concerned with understanding street crimes such as robbery and burglary are no doubt already familiar with many of the concepts that taxpayer compliance researchers have used and that were discussed in Chapter 2: deterrence, social sanctions, moral commitment, and demographic/socioeconomic patterns, for example. But it may be that compliance with tax laws can be better understood with the use of some of the concepts and approaches that researchers have applied to compliance with regulatory laws. Regulatory laws include rent control (Ball, 1960), price control (Katona, 1945; Kagan, 1978), antitrust laws (Ball and Friedman, 1965), social regulation involving health and safety issues (Bardach and Kagan, 1982; Hawkins and Thomas, 1984), affirmative action, and regulations such as traffic laws (Ross, 1961). Noncompliance with tax and regulatory laws differs from street crime in at least five important ways:

1. Noncompliance with tax and other regulatory laws is not widely considered morally reprehensible in itself but instead is declared reprehensible by the legal system because of its consequences for society. The role of social stigmatization in preventing noncompliance is therefore both more complex and less influential than in preventing street crimes.

2. Many tax and regulatory offenders are high-income people in high-status occupations, while many street crimes are more heavily concentrated among the poor.

3. Tax offenses rarely injure readily identifiable personal victims who are likely to report them; the adverse affects are spread among a large group of individuals who may not recognize the injury, and so government inspection is the primary means of detection.

4. Tax and other regulatory laws require a range of positive actions, such as filing tax returns, paying estimated taxes, and keeping records of income and certain expenditures. The technical nature of some of these

requirements leads to large numbers of minor infractions only peripherally related to regulatory or tax goals.

5. Specialized judicial and enforcement institutions such as the United States Tax Court and the Internal Revenue Service have been created to relieve criminal courts, prosecutors, and police from many of the specialized tasks imposed by tax administration.

The approach to compliance outlined in this chapter and the research suggested here and in Chapter 4 should enrich the literature on compliance with regulatory laws generally. However, some special characteristics of tax law warrant emphasis on issues that may be less important for other regulatory laws:

1. Taxpayer noncompliance is a private act not subject to public scrutiny, unlike drunken driving and other forms of regulated behavior. Current law prohibits the IRS from publicly disclosing individual tax information, and even information about civil penalties for cheating rarely becomes public.

2. The costs of complying with tax law as well as the benefits of tax evasion are for the most part readily calculated in monetary terms, unlike those for other laws, for which the value of compliance alternatives requires extra effort to calculate. Thus the deterrence calculus appears more applicable to taxpayer compliance behavior than to most other compliance arenas.

3. Income tax payment is one of the most common and costly acts of conscious support provided to the federal government by the average citizen and therefore may be more affected by the citizen's perception of the legitimacy of government than compliance with other administrative laws.

4. The complexity of tax laws imposes a considerable burden on many individuals to determine their true tax liability. The burden is made even more difficult by the constant flux in the tax laws and in the tax situations of individuals, and so inadvertent noncompliance may result from carelessness or lack of ability to understand the legal requirements.

5. For many taxpayers who earn income in ways other than wages and salaries, compliance requires frequent decisions throughout the year about whether and how to record financial transactions. These taxpayers may lack the methodical record-keeping systems that are needed to achieve full compliance.

6. As a consequence of complexity, record-keeping burden, and other factors, almost half of all tax returns are filed with the assistance of tax practitioners, whose work strongly influences compliance behavior.

Tax Schemas: The Complexity of Attitudes and Beliefs

In most of the studies reviewed in Chapter 2, the objective elements of self-interest and the subjective values related to social commitment were presumed (at least implicitly) to affect taxpaying through individuals' predictions, judgments, and evaluations. Taxpayers were presumed to make predictions about how alternative courses of action would affect their self-interest, to judge the congruence of the alternatives with their values related to commitment, and to behave in accord with these predictions and judgments. As indicated in Chapter 2, however, taxpayers' compliance behavior seems only loosely connected to the objective circumstances that should theoretically affect the relevant predictions, as well as to many attitudes—toward law, government, tax laws, and tax administration—that presumably influence the relevant values. In short, taxpayers do not comply or fail to comply as if they systematically attended to all available relevant information and to all the values that they express to interviewers in survey research.

Such apparent inconsistencies are not unique to taxpayer compliance. As explained by Lindzey and Aronson (1985, 1:142–144), they were found in a variety of contexts by social psychologists during the 1970s. In attempting to explain these departures, researchers postulated the existence of mental processes by which individuals select, restructure, categorize, store, and retrieve information about the external environment. These internal information processors have gone under a variety of names, such as *inferential sets, frames, attitudes,* and *schemas* (Stotland and Canon, 1972; Neisser, 1976).

Although there is academic controversy about the precise meaning of the term *schema,* one frequent interpretation is that it is a theory about how the world operates, which an individual has developed by generalizing across his or her experiences (Lindzey and Aronson, 1985, 1:145). For example, through experience, a child can be said to develop a *conservation schema*—an understanding that a given quantity of liquid is the same whether it is poured into a short, squat container or a tall, thin one. Later, through experience, people develop less precise schemas about entities that are more abstract or at least harder to observe directly, such as the digestive system, God, government, and taxes.

Despite the imprecision of the term *schema,* the panel found it useful for much of the discussion that follows to adopt the term *tax schema* to refer to all understandings and values that an individual holds about the federal income tax system. The tax schema defined here differs from conventional use of the term *schema* by cognitive psychologists, because it embraces values as well as information. The concept encompasses ordinary, everyday understandings and values concerning tax matters, such as those expressed in the quotations above. The characteristics of tax schemas may help to explain some apparent anomalies in taxpayer compliance behavior.

Most important, the concept can be used to draw attention to several phenomena that are not captured in studies focusing only on how particular understandings or values are related to taxpayer compliance. First, tax schemas appear to vary across taxpayers in terms of how tax matters are perceived and tax decisions are considered. For some people, the payment of taxes is a routine matter that they think little about and that does not engage important values; for such people, paying taxes is a routine obligation rather like paying tolls on the turnpike. For others, paying taxes is like avoiding getting arrested for speeding; there may be little sense of obligation, and reducing tax liability by legal or illegal means may be experienced as an amusing and exciting game. For still others, paying taxes involves a view of the state as an uncontrolled leviathan, in which case defeating the tax system amounts to a matter of moral obligation.

Second, tax schemas may vary in the accuracy of taxpayers' beliefs about objective conditions and in the logical consistency of values and attitudes. Surveys have found considerable variation in perceptions of, for example, the probability of being audited (Kinsey, 1984; Jackson and Jones,1985a). Many studies have found beliefs about tax policies to be inaccurate (Lewis, 1982a) and inconsistent (Sears and Citrin, 1982), particularly on issues of less relevance to the individual.

Of particular importance is the likelihood that a taxpayer's general values may be inconsistent with his or her values and attitudes affecting a specific behavior, such as taxpaying (Ajzen and Fishbein, 1977). That is, a general commitment to comply with community laws may not translate into a specific commitment to comply with tax laws if, for example, the tax schema strongly condemns the intrusiveness of tax administration and therefore supports tax evasion as a form of protest. In a review of empirical studies of the attitude-behavior link, Ajzen and Fishbein (1977) conclude that the links between general and more specific values and attitudes are quite loose and that the attitudes most closely related to a given behavior (e.g., filing a tax return) are the best predictors of that behavior.

Internally inconsistent beliefs and attitudes about taxes may develop because people find it hard to cope with complex tax laws. They may also develop because people are exposed to inconsistent and possibly conflicting norms of behavior in different social settings. Taxpayers may therefore develop very diverse tax schemas as they adapt to the complex and diverse legal and social context of taxpaying.

These properties of tax schemas have several implications for compliance research. First, survey measures of beliefs and attitudes must be interpreted cautiously, since, as Lewis (1982a) warns, survey questions may be interpreted and answered differently by the respondent depending on the particular aspect of the tax schema that is brought forth by the context and wording of the question.

Second, the beliefs and attitudes toward self-interest, social sanctions, and social commitment may be linked to compliance behavior in different ways for taxpayers with different kinds of schemas. For example, there may be no relation at all between perceived self-interest and compliance among habitual compliers who think about taxes only once a year, but a very strong relationship for taxpayers who are making tax-related decisions all year long. A better understanding of how tax schemas vary in a given population may help researchers compare compliance across subpopulations within which taxpaying behavior is more homogeneous (Scott and Grasmick, 1981; Kinsey and Smith, 1987b).

Third, understanding the forces that shape a taxpayer's schema may provide a logical link between the socioeconomic environment, the individual's beliefs and values, and tax behavior. Finally, since inconsistencies within tax schemas may translate into inconsistent behavior, the concept may offer a basis for studying which of a set of conflicting values and beliefs are likely to provide the basis for decisions in a complex, uncertain setting. We discuss decision processes in the next section.

TAXPAYERS' DECISION PROCESSES

Given the potential inconsistencies among attitudes and the incomplete information available to the taxpayer, the processes that determine which attitudes and information influence a particular compliance decision become particularly important. Researchers in behavioral decision theory and social psychology have found that the context or situation in which a decision is made can dramatically change the outcome. For example, individuals have been found to be consistently more willing to accept risks to avoid possible losses than to obtain possible gains (Kahneman and Tversky, 1979). This may suggest that taxpayers owing nothing at the end of the year due to sufficient withholding will be less willing to risk evasion penalties than taxpayers who end up owing money (Loftus, 1985; Kinsey and Smith, 1987b), even though their actual tax bill may be the same. These and other well-documented deviations from the assumptions that underlie standard microeconomic models of taxpayer compliance were reviewed in papers by John Carroll (Vol. 2) and Cialdini (Vol. 2).

FINDINGS FROM BEHAVIORAL DECISION THEORY. Carroll (Vol. 2) notes that many of the assumptions of microeconomic models on which deterrence theory rests have been demonstrated to be inadequate to explain the results of experiments relating to decisions made under uncertainty. If the alternative explanations that have been developed to explain these findings are relevant to compliance behavior, then small changes in the way taxpayers perceive and frame tax decisions may have unexpectedly large results. For example, at some low probability of detection, the literature suggests that people completely discount the likelihood of adverse events, such as being caught evading taxes (Kahneman and Tversky, 1979). At some slightly higher probability, however, the penalty will be taken into consideration, potentially producing an unusually large effect for a small shift in probabilities. As another example, Slovic, Fischhoff, and Lichtenstein (1981) found that reframing the risks of an auto accident from an annual to a lifetime basis affected intentions to use seat belts. Carroll (Vol. 2) notes similarly that an annual 1 percent probability of getting caught at tax evasion translates into a 50 percent chance if continued over a working lifetime of thirty-seven years—a specification that may produce a greater deterrence incentive. When combining probabilities, such as a 2 percent chance of an audit and a 50 percent chance of being fined if audited, experiments suggest that people tend to weigh the larger second-stage probability disproportionately more than the first (Carroll, Vol. 2). Thus, decisions based separately on the chance of an audit and the chance of being penalized may lead to more compliance than would be expected from the joint 1 percent probability of being fined.

The relevance and magnitude of these processes for taxpayer decisions are not known. Although consistent evidence supporting their importance has been well documented in laboratory situations, it is not known whether they are as effective in everyday situations (Carroll, Vol. 2; Cialdini, Vol. 2), in which other factors may overwhelm them.

It may be that the differences between decisions predicted by the microeconomic models (reviewed in Chapter 2) and decisions predicted by psychological models (reviewed by Carroll and Cialdini) become less important when one looks at the sequence of decisions made by a taxpayer, in which earlier mistakes are corrected in later decisions, once the mistakes are recognized. Even for single decisions, simple rules may turn out to be efficient ways of making reasonably good decisions about compliance without expending much time and effort (Johnson and Payne, 1985). As an example, Carroll (Vol. 2) cites the simple contingent process rule of Payne (1973):

  1. Assess money in pocket (if high, no cheating; if low, go to step 2);
  2. Assess probability of gain (if low, no cheating; if high, go to 3);
  3. Assess amount of gain (if low, go to 4; if high, go to 5);
  4. Assess risk of penalty (if high, no cheating; if low, go to 5);
  5. Cheat (a process with multiple planning and execution substeps).

Even when simple rules lead to roughly the outcomes predicted by microeconomic models, they may highlight different aspects of tax administration policy, such as withholding, information reporting, auditing, and penalizing taxpayers. Research on the decision processes involved when risks and alternative outcomes are not well understood may be of particular relevance to understanding compliance, given the complexity of many tax decisions and the difficulty of knowing the probabilities of being caught cheating. The tax domain provides a fascinating laboratory for studying such decision processes, particularly regarding taxpayer responses to contacts with the IRS.

FINDINGS FROM SOCIAL PSYCHOLOGY.   Cialdini (1984) has studied ways in which social influences may affect an individual's decision processes and can increase the likelihood of compliance with requests for a specific action. In Volume 2 he suggests that the consistency/commitment principle in particular may have considerable importance for understanding and altering tax compliance. Under that principle, individuals attempt to minimize inconsistencies within their schemas by changing relatively unimportant attitudes or behavior to conform with more deeply held values, by ignoring new information that contradicts cherished beliefs, and by forming commitments to attitudes supportive of preestablished behaviors. While changes in deeply held values occur relatively rarely, the links between these basic values and more specific attitudes may change more frequently. From this perspective, compliance behavior is more likely to change in response to a change in perception that makes a deeply held commitment relevant to taxpaying. For example, a regular contributor to some charitable organization may increase his or her commitment to pay taxes if presented with a strong case that tax dollars provide a critical level of support for the charity's goals and operations.

Cialdini suggests the potential practical significance of this principle for tax administrators. Rather than attempt to alter basic values or directly increase commitment to tax compliance, tax administrators could: (1) identify the values to which a particular target group is already committed that could be related to tax compliance, (2) focus attention on those values, and (3) sensitize the taxpayers to the inconsistency between tax cheating and those values (Cialdini, Vol. 2). Schwartz and Orleans (1967) found, for example, that simply asking questions that emphasized normative reasons to pay taxes increased income reporting by a small but statistically significant amount. This tax experiment, combined with evidence from research in other contexts reviewed by Cialdini, suggests that successful attempts to link taxpaying with positive values may affect compliance. Indeed, a number of researchers have suggested that taxpayer compliance might be enhanced through the use of positive incentives and appeals to conscience, based on indirect evidence from their studies (Schwartz and Orleans, 1967; Strümpel, 1966; Silberman, 1976; Dean, Keenan, and Kenney, 1980; Lewis, 1982a).

Other researchers have suggested that government appeals are unlikely to affect commitment (Grasmick and Scott, 1982) or may be counterproductive (Westat, Inc., 1980f). One problem with such appeals is that there appears to be little agreement about what constitutes a fair tax code (Eisenstein, 1961; King, 1982) that all citizens would feel duty-bound to obey. Furthermore, the tax code is amended frequently, and the amendments often provide special tax treatment for influential interest groups (J. Witte, 1985b; Reese, 1980). Despite continuing political attempts to reduce special tax treatment for various groups, particularly in the 1930s and since 1960 (King, 1982), arguments about the unfairness of the current code are likely to be a continuing and unresolved political theme that would work against conscience-based appeals to comply.

Given these negative aspects of the tax code, the consistency/commitment principle suggests that communications that link taxpaying to negative values important to the taxpayer may decrease compliance. The tendency of elected officials and the media to focus on the more problematic and intrusive aspects of tax administration, it should be noted, has the possible effect of repeatedly linking taxpayer compliance with negative values.

A given normative appeal may affect different groups quite differently. For example, an experiment by Tittle and Rowe (1973) found that appeals to normative values in order to reduce cheating in classrooms actually led to increased cheating by some students. Some have suggested that the appeals backfired by making honest students more aware that others were getting ahead of them by cheating (Grasmick and Scott, 1982; Jackson and Milliron, n.d.). In the Schwartz and Orleans (1967) experiment, there was some evidence that blue-collar workers responded more favorably to the normative appeal than did higher-income individuals, perhaps because the higher-income strata may have had more developed tax schemas that were less amenable to change. The effects of moral appeals may be transient; links that can be readily established may also decay rapidly. If effects are transient, attempts to improve compliance through education, persuasive communication, and positive appeals for compliance (Schwartz and Orleans, 1967; Vogel, 1974; Lewis, 1982a) may depend on considerable innovativeness over repeated annual campaigns. Such campaigns may set off counterresponses in the media and the public to what might be seen as manipulative appeals.

As with the experimental and conceptual work in behavioral decision theory, these and other hypotheses developed by social psychologists should be tested in the domain of taxpayer compliance. Further research and conceptual development may substantially improve understanding of the compliance and attitudinal impact of communications from media, political figures, the IRS, practitioners, and other relevant social groups.

How Tax Schemas Develop

Tax schemas are shaped by experiences that relate to taxpaying behavior as the individual progresses from early socialization within the family, to initiation into the tax system, to the annual filing of tax returns throughout life. These experiences establish the everyday routines that make up the individual's taxpaying behavior—for example, throwing tax-deductible receipts into a bag, keeping records of last year's calculations, making habitual reponses to receipt of the annual tax package. We first consider the dynamics of individual development over a tax career and then discuss the taxpayer's socioeconomic environment, particularly the occupation and social networks that influence the pertinent individual experiences.

Two research traditions appear particularly relevant to understanding the dynamics of tax schema development: the bounded rationality research introduced by Simon and the moral development research of Piaget and Kohlberg. The theory of bounded rationality, which was developed initially to explain how decision makers with limited capabilities cope with complexity (Simon, 1955; Cyert and March, 1963), has been extended through the recent development of behavioral decision theories (Carroll, 1986). The relevance of this approach for compliance research has been described by Scholz (Vol. 2) and Kinsey and Smith (1987c), who emphasize the need to understand how taxpayers cope with the complexities of the tax law. The bounded rationality tradition argues that individuals approximate rational behavior by developing decision routines and schemas that support them. That is, a taxpayer develops standardized routines or habits to deal with common tax situations and changes routines incrementally when new problems and opportunities arise. The nature of the tax situation and the problems or opportunities that arise are assumed in this approach to be critical in shaping compliance behavior.

Investigations concerned with moral development (Piaget, 1932; Kohlberg, 1976, 1984) hypothesize that moral thought develops through a sequence of invariant, nonregressive, and universal stages. Children are initially motivated exclusively by simple self-interest but gradually develop sensitivity to the norms of others and a sense of obedience to the laws of society. In the final stage, according to Kohlberg, moral reasoning based on universal principles becomes the basis for action, transcending simple obedience to laws. If, as Kohlberg notes, some people remain indefinitely at earlier stages, variation in compliance would be expected. Although we are skeptical about the invariance in the sequences of stages in Kohlberg's theory and we abstain from his normative judgment about the superiority of the final stage, he has made an important attempt to understand the development of differences in how people approach decisions, particularly in the interaction between self-interest and normative factors. For example, Kohlberg's classification of decision processes suggests that self-interest factors would be most important for taxpayers in his first stage of moral development, peer pressure and simple commitment to obey would be more important for those in his second stage, and more general attitudes toward government, society, and taxes would be more important for those in his third stage. Research to refine and test theories of moral development, and to integrate them with theories that emphasize self-interest and social commitment, could lead to a more powerful theory of compliance.

TAX CAREERS.   The concept of a tax career may provide a useful focus for studying the dynamics of tax schema development and changes. A *tax career* is simply the series of experiences through which one's tax schema and taxpaying routines are established. Studying tax careers means investigating how routines become established and how they change. The primary analytic concern is to focus on the pattern of compliance behavior throughout an individual's taxpaying lifetime and to explain it in terms of particular circumstances that either shift taxpayers between compliance and noncompliance or change their level of noncompliance. We hypothesize that characteristic careers can be identified and that these can be associated with different taxpaying environments, which are in part shaped or selected by the evolution of a particular taxpaying career.

The individual tax career concept could explain the findings discussed in Chapter 2 concerning age and compliance in terms of young, single workers becoming more enmeshed with social and economic institutions in the community as they get married, raise families, and gain success and status in their occupations. Kagan (Vol. 2), for example, notes that, even in the underground economy, successful individuals become more enmeshed with other institutions as they take on larger contracts, hire workers, seek construction loans, and so on. Greater integration with the broader economy requires different modes of operation that in turn constrain the kinds of "off the books" transactions that encourage tax cheating.

Within the formal economy, aging may be associated with expanding connections with others and growing visibility in the community. In turn, these ties may exacerbate the threat of social sanctions for noncompliance (e.g., through embarrassment of family members or loss of personal reputation) and increase taxpayers' commitments to institutions that taxes support. In support of this hypothesis, Grasmick (1985) found that the relationship between age and compliance became insignificant if commitment (guilt) was controlled for, and that perceived informal sanctions also reduced the significance of the relationship, although to a lesser extent than did commitment.

A closer look at tax commitment patterns for young people suggests that an individual's introduction into the tax system may be a critical period. In the British survey by Keenan and Dean (1980:217), for example, commitment to avoid several minor forms of illegal behavior increased between ages twenty and thirty; tax commitment, however, dropped over that age range before increasing at a rate similar to that of the other behaviors. Several studies found this drop in commitment and compliance for the second youngest category of taxpayers (Aitken and Bonneville, 1980; Yankelovich et al., 1984; Clotfelter, 1983). One might speculate that the initial exposure to the complexities of the law, the problems of filing, and relatively low-risk opportunities to cheat in irregular jobs, combined with the growing awareness of avoidance and evasion by those higher on the occupational ladder, provides a significant challenge to socialized commitment to obey laws as the tax schema develops.

The lack of longitudinal data on individual taxpayers prevents us from drawing firm conclusions in advance about how important the study of tax careers may be. There may be important developmental patterns of tax careers similar to the patterns of criminal careers. For example, noncompliance by small amounts, if undetected, may eventually grow to higher levels. Long-practicing noncompliers, in turn, may become locked into filing untruthful returns if they believe, for example, that a large increase in taxable income might prompt the IRS to scrutinize past returns. It is not known how large a percentage of the loss of revenue from noncompliance is due to evasion by long-practicing evaders and how much is due to one-time evaders taking advantage of a nonrepeating opportunity. At minimum, concern with the tax career indicates that research should be undertaken to establish the longitudinal patterns of compliance.

But perhaps more important, attention to the tax career highlights the fact that the complexity, frequency, and nature of tax problems differ substantially across taxpayer subgroups and suggests that different tax careers may lead to tax schemas and taxpaying routines with different levels of complexity and different implications for compliance.

A relevant hypothesis from the voting behavior literature—one of the most intensively researched areas of citizen belief systems—suggests that schemas develop under a principle of conservation of energy. Simplified schemas develop to minimize information storage and retrieval costs, with the complexity and logical consistency of the schema dependent on the importance or salience of the area in question for the individual and the probable marginal value of increased effort in developing beliefs and attitudes relating to the area (Sears, Huddy, and Schaffer, 1984; Brady and Sniderman, 1985; Lewis, 1982a). There is considerable evidence that most people do not engage in consistent theoretical analysis of political issues that may affect them, that the consistency of beliefs about political matters varies with political knowledge or ideological sophistication (Converse, 1975), and that attitudes toward general political symbols are better predictors of policy positions than objective information about the consequences of a policy for the individual in such diverse areas as the economy, civil rights, the Vietnam War, busing, and the energy crisis (Sears et al., 1980:680).

On policy issues that are more obviously salient, with more direct, easily calculable personal effects, however, citizens' evaluations and behavior seem to reflect a more complex schema that relies less on general political symbols (Sears et al., 1984). For example, home ownership and public-sector employment had strong effects on the voting for reductions in property tax in California (Sears and Citrin, 1982), and the parents most affected were the most opposed to the Los Angeles busing plan (Allen and Sears, 1979).

From this perspective, the logical development and consistency of tax schemas depend on the importance of discretionary tax behavior to the individual. For example, nonitemizing wage earners whose taxes are withheld have only occasional reasons to think much about taxes. Their response to survey questions about the likelihood of being audited is likely to have little basis in knowledge, and questions about attitudes about taxes are likely to tap more general attitudes and values that may in fact have little to do with their actual taxpaying behavior. If the opportunity to earn outside income arises, the temptation not to report it may lead to a different thought process: the general values of honesty and law-abidingness that may have been triggered by a hypothetical survey question may be less important than other, potentially contradictory beliefs about the responsibility of the breadwinner to support the family. Self-employed taxpayers with more options and more complex tax problems, however, are likely to have considered the matter previously and therefore to exhibit more internal consistency over a broader range of issues and more stability under the impact of new circumstances, new information, or changing attitudes on other topics.

Differences in the socialization process over a tax career may lead not only to differences in the complexity and consistency of schemas, but also to differences in orientation toward compliance. For example, the taxpayer with a history of willful evasion, like the professional shoplifter described in Carroll and Weaver (1986), may develop a repertoire of evasive skills and become alert to evasion opportunities and potential punishments. Experienced taxpayers more oriented toward compliance, like the "strong compliers" in the Yankelovich et al. survey (1984), may study changing legal obligations and implications for tax planning. Each type of taxpayer pays attention to different aspects of taxpaying, and the two types are likely to shape the environment in different ways. Although we have little reliable information on the number of chronic evaders, one survey found that 21 percent of those reporting they had ever underreported income and 30 percent reporting they had ever overstated subtractions reported having done so three or more times (Yankelovich et al., 1984:46). The habits of such repeat evaders are likely to differ from those of the self-reported one-time noncompliers that accounted for 50 percent of those underreporting income and 32 percent of those overstating subtractions. As in much of the literature on the underground economy, the proportion of repeat evaders of both types was highest in the income groups below $15,000 and above $50,000 (Yankelovich et al., 1984:87), in which the opportunities for evasion with low-visibility transactions and supporting social networks are probably greatest.

Tax law enforcers may require significantly different techniques to discourage long-term evaders than to discourage occasional noncompliers. Carroll and Weaver (1986) found, for example, that mirrors, monitors, and other devices successfully discouraged novice shoplifters but served more as a challenge to the expert who knew countertechniques to reduce risks of detection. Similarly, enforcement actions effective in preventing cheating by the less sophisticated are likely to be less effective on long-term evaders. Carroll (1986) suggests that decision routines are organized in a hierarchical fashion, with different rules governing higher-level choices, such as whether to look for evasion opportunities, and lower-level choices, such as how much to evade when a routine opportunity is encountered. One laboratory experiment on taxation did indeed find different factors to be significant in explaining the compliance choice and the amount of evasion (Friedland, Maital, and Rutenberg, 1978). Furthermore, noncompliance caused by misinformation and a lack of knowledge about tax obligations may be more easily controlled by motivational techniques to encourage diligence rather than by coercive techniques to deter evasion. This may be particularly true for small businesses and the self-employed, for whom noncompliance is widespread. Knowledge about which tax careers lead to what kinds of compliance problems would therefore improve understanding of how taxpayers are likely to respond to tax policy and enforcement changes.

The bounded rationality approach suggests that changes in taxpaying are likely to occur when reality diverges from expectations, such as when taxpayers discover unexpected opportunities to save on taxes with little risk of getting caught or recognize conflicts between their tax behavior and their commitments or perceived interests. Initiation into the routines of filing tax forms may be one of the most important events in a tax career, particularly if compliance-oriented tax habits learned as a young worker make compliance more likely as an adult. The high school educational programs about taxpaying and the tax system sponsored by the IRS presumably attempt to influence this transition, although the initial experience in filing tax returns is probably a more important influence. For example, a first-time worker whose tax is withheld from each paycheck may develop compliance-oriented habits, since the simplified 1040EZ return is easy to understand and generates positive feedback in the form of a refund. By contrast, first-time employment in a marginal job with no withholding may establish a pattern of noncompliant habits and attitudes leading to searches for jobs and situations offering more chances for evasion. If this is true, enforcement intervention to counteract negative influences during the taxpayer's formative years, whether through the threat of audits or through the aid of special taxpayer services to encourage compliant habits, may have greater impact on current and future compliance.

Events likely to draw attention to tax matters include, in addition to initiation into the labor force and taxpaying, crises and unexpected changes in employment or living situation, contacts with the IRS, changes in the tax laws, and political and media attention to tax matters. Not only do such events present administrative opportunities and challenges, but also, by providing a chance to observe people's behavior when their attention is focused on taxpaying, these events offer research opportunities. For example, the IRS directly contacts a very large number of citizens by mail and telephone in providing forms, answering inquiries, and processing returns. Direct contacts and perhaps confrontation with the large, fragmented, impersonal tax collection bureaucracy is likely to have important effects on taxpayers and on their compliance. Knowledge about the cumulative effects of such contacts on tax careers is important for understanding tax careers and as a practical matter for allocating resources among operations generating different kinds of contacts, such as taxpayer services, computer-generated mail contacts, and various kinds of audits. In Chapter 4, we use the Tax Reform Act of 1986 and various IRS programs of taxpayer contacts to illustrate research on the compliance effects of events in the tax career.

The kinds of information sources available to the taxpayer when attention is drawn to tax matters may also affect compliance (Scholz, Vol. 2). The potential range of sources includes IRS publications and taxpayer service, tax guides, legal services, occupational networks, work associates, friends, and tax preparers ranging from relatively conservative nationally franchised return preparers to extremely aggressive tax practitioners (Aitken and Bonneville, 1980). Even a basically honest taxpayer may succumb to temptation if exposed to enough information about safe evasion techniques, whereas a potentially evasive taxpayer may remain honest if his or her search for such techniques is unsuccessful. The enforcement implication is that compliance might be improved by ensuring that clarifications of particular tax situations (e.g., selling a house, moving) are easily available at the appropriate times, so that taxpayers' searches will not be extensive enough to uncover information about illegal alternatives. Similarly, evasion may be reduced if the IRS makes information about evasive techniques more difficult to obtain by discouraging unscrupulous tax practitioners and promoters of illegal tax shelters. In Chapter 4, we focus on tax practitioners to illustrate research on how compliance is affected by information sources.

In summary, research on the interrelation of tax careers, tax schemas, and compliance holds promise for increasing understanding of how a taxpayer's objective situation affects subjective beliefs, one of the least understood aspects of compliance research. Although the important stages and critical features of tax careers are too little known to be delineated with much precision, they may include: (1) early socialization to law, government, and financial matters; (2) a critical initiation period into the labor force and the tax system; and (3) a generally stable maturation period that is occasionally disrupted by such events as job changes, family changes, tax law changes, enforcement contacts with the IRS, and eventually retirement from the labor force. If characteristic careers leading to common tax schemas and behavior can be identified, then knowledge about these careers and resultant schemas will help to predict compliance behavior.

SOCIAL AND CULTURAL CONTEXTS OF TAXPAYING.   In addition to taxpayers' individual experiences, the various social and cultural contexts that affect people's interpretation of events in their lives may help to shape tax schemas. The cultural context is reflected to varying degrees in general values as well as in specific behavioral norms that are constantly expressed and reinterpreted during everyday social contacts and that may enhance or decrease compliance. Social contacts also expand an individual's experience base, providing him or her with a much richer variety of information about tax laws, enforcement, and compliance alternatives. Individuals may learn about compliance-enhancing factors, such as the greatly increased likelihood of being audited if questionable tax shelters or ambiguous deductions such as home offices are claimed. They may also become misinformed about these requirements or may learn which kinds of income can be safely omitted from their tax return. Shared understandings of what is important, what should be done, and what could be done emerge from discussions with others in the course of our daily activities. In short, the social environment both educates and motivates people in ways that are likely to be of critical importance to understanding compliance behavior.

Empirical investigations have found some differences in compliance patterns in different social and cultural contexts. At the broadest level, studies such as those of Strümpel (1969) and Schmölders (1970), which compared cultural responses to tax administration styles in different countries, suggest the importance of national cultures in understanding compliance behavior. Within the United States, there is consistent evidence that attitudes and compliance differ significantly from region to region (Yankelovich et al., 1984; Clotfelter, 1983; Westat, Inc., 1980f). Taxpayer characteristics such as occupational class, sex, education, and race have been found to affect tax schemas (Vogel, 1974; Lewis, 1982a; Kinsey, 1985) and response to different tax appeals (Schwartz and Orleans, 1967). And at the narrowest level, studies have found that individuals reporting that their friends cheat on taxes have consistently been found to be more likely to cheat themselves, suggesting either that acquaintances influence one another's compliance or that for whatever reasons, networks of acquaintances tend to share compliance norms (Westat, Inc., 1980f; Grasmick and Scott, 1982; Scott and Grasmick, 1981; Spicer and Lundstedt, 1976; Vogel, 1974).

The theory of how identity and interaction with a group affect compliance is not yet clearly articulated. For example, Vogel (1974:512) speculates from his survey findings that "group support [for noncompliance] includes the transmission of deviant norms, techniques for tax evasion, and techniques of neutralizing deviant behavior to keep up a positive self-conception." But several social groups at different levels are likely to compete for an individual's loyalty, including the immediate family, wider kinship ties, neighborhoods and local communities, small groups associated with occupation, voluntary organizations such as churches and special interest clubs, and broader, more dispersed cultural identities with regions of the country (e.g., the South), with a religion, with a country of origin, or with the United States as a nation. A cultural explanation of taxpaying behavior must recognize the dynamic relationship between taxpayers and various social groups that potentially influence them.

Even within a single social group, cohort or generational differences may lead to substantial variation among different age groups. Workers, for example, are profoundly affected throughout their lives by the circumstances under which they enter the labor force (Easterlin, 1966; Blau and Duncan, 1967; Elder, 1974, as quoted in Kidder and McEwen, Vol. 2). The difficulties of getting and keeping a job during the Great Depression in particular led newly recruited workers to avoid risky decisions in their subsequent career choices. Kidder and McEwen (Vol. 2) speculate that regional recessions and deindustrialization such as in the steel-producing region of Pennsylvania may lead workers through a succession of odd jobs and create a temporary moral climate in which nonreporting of income is condoned throughout the community because the government has failed to provide workers with economic security. They conclude that the study of cultural influences on tax compliance should determine both the repertoire of acceptable responses in a particular social grouping and the variation in particular responses for different age cohorts as triggered by different historical conditions.

Occupations. Although little is known about the levels of social interaction that influence taxpayer compliance, occupational groupings may be among the most influential on taxpayer compliance. Given the common tax problems faced by individuals with similar sources of income, it would be quite natural for employees to discuss among themselves common tax problems relating to income and job-related deductions or exemptions, and for unions, company-sponsored employee groups, and professional or trade associations to analyze and inform members about common tax problems. Furthermore, career identity and socialization in the workplace provide important sources of identity in American society (Kidder and McEwen, Vol. 2). And since compliance levels vary considerably among different occupations, as do the particular kinds of noncompliance and the enforcement techniques needed to counter them, it is likely that an understanding of how social and cultural influences work within occupational groupings will contribute substantially to a general understanding of compliance.

Tabulations from the 1979 Taxpayer Compliance Measurement Program made available to the panel suggest that compliance patterns vary markedly for specific occupational groups. On the average across all occupational groups, the average increase in taxes owed as a result of audit (according to the auditor) was $236. However, the average increase for some occupations was nearly $1,700, and others experienced an average decrease of more than $400. The smallest average changes occurred for clerical occupations, the military service, retired individuals, students, and the unemployed; withholding tends to be high for the first two groups and taxes low for the latter three. By contrast, the largest changes occurred for independent professionals (e.g., management consultants, certified public accountants, lawyers, doctors), those employed in marketing and sales, and farmers.

For different occupational groups, noncompliance occurs in quite different areas. The most noncompliant occupations generally underreport income. Farmers tend to underreport income on both schedules C and F, that is, they underreport self-employment income earned in both farming and nonfarming endeavors. Independent professionals tend to underreport Schedule E income, and those in marketing and sales tend to underreport nonwage income and overstate adjustments to income. Those working in services; skilled crafts people; and moonlighting management, professional, and skilled production workers also tend to underreport Schedule C income. Skilled crafts workers, retired people, members of the military, and students tend to overstate adjustments to income. Groups who are otherwise rather compliant, such as teachers and librarians, service workers, and laborers, tend to overstate adjustments to income.

Categorizing common perceptions about taxes that are systematically related to specific occupations might provide the basis for linking socioeconomic conditions to taxpaying behavior in a way that would not be evident from the study of individuals. For example, low visibility of the income source combined with low status of the job appear likely to generate occupation-specific schemas in which neither fear nor social commitment is likely to develop in support of compliance (Kagan, Vol. 2). But what happens to people in high-status jobs with some additional income that has low visibility? What different kinds of socially acceptable justifications for noncompliance are developed in different kinds of occupational settings? What kinds of misinformation-related noncompliance are widespread? Are taxpayers really influenced by occupational or professional groups even when the groups are dispersed, or is this influence limited to more tightly knit networks of individuals in daily contact that have developed common understandings about taxes and other matters? Considerable exploratory work would be required to determine the occupational areas in which in-depth research is most likely to contribute to an understanding of these matters.

Social networks and social fields. While occupations may provide one important focus for research, a more general research effort is also needed on the ways in which information, values, and formal and informal rules relevant to action (primarily taxpayer compliance) develop in social contexts and are communicated to the taxpayer. Two related concepts—social networks and social fields—provide foundations for approaching this research goal.

The social network is an ego-centered concept. Lines of contact can be traced from the individual to others—family, friends, coworkers, business acquaintances, and others with whom interactions may give rise to information or values that pertain to taxpaying (Bott, 1957; Mitchell, 1969). Networks provide a means of mapping the paths through which tacit understandings and values are developed and shaped. They are a part of the social order, varying considerably in their degree of formality, topics of communication, and functions served for the individuals involved.

The concept of a social field (Moore, 1973) focuses more on the ways rules are generated and understandings about compliance formed within social groupings: "Between the body politic and the individual, there are interposed various smaller organized social fields to which the individual 'belongs.' These social fields have their own customs and rules and the means of coercing or inducing compliance" (Moore, 1978:56). While social network analyses frequently focus on communications between autonomous individuals, making no assumptions that the network operates as an organized system, social field analyses are concerned with properties of the system as a whole. Both emphases—that of social networks on the individual and that of social fields on social entities—may prove to be important in understanding how social forces shape individual interpretations of the objective tax environment.

Research on social networks in other areas of legal controls has proven valuable. For example, as cited by Tyler and Lavrakas (1985:148–149, citations deleted):

> Several recent studies of crime victimization have found that in forming risk judgments citizens are influenced primarily by experiences conveyed through social networks, not by media reports of crime. Mass media campaigns to alert citizens to social risks have had limited success in altering smoking and other health-related attitudes, seat-belt use, and contraceptive use. These same behaviors have, however, been found to be influenced by social communications from friends, family, and neighbors.

Studies have linked social networks to noncompliance, particularly among business and occupational groups. Some of the first investigators of white-collar crime argued that associations of like-minded business associates provided the necessary moral support and technical know-how to encourage illegal behavior even by individuals of high status who might otherwise have been deterred by the risks of social condemnation (Sutherland, 1939; Sykes and Matza, 1957). The influence of personal contacts may override a taxpayer's initial predisposition to compliance; a study of recruitment into social movements found networks of personal contacts to be more important than predisposition in explaining student participation in political and religious movements (Snow, Zurcher, Ekland-Olson, 1980). The importance of such personal contacts for taxpayer compliance is suggested by the consistent findings in survey research that the number of friends who cheat is related to self-reported compliance.

More evidence suggests that certain networks, particularly among occupational and professional groups, may be important for taxpayer compliance. In interviews conducted by Westat, Inc., and reported by Roth and Witte (1985), the outspoken hostility against the IRS exhibited by the independent truckers interviewed exemplifies the kinds of values that, if transmitted within networks, might promote noncompliant practices. As noted earlier, once the IRS learns of a prevalent form of noncompliance in a specific local occupation (e.g., underreporting by catfish farmers in Mississippi and Arkansas; multiple refund filing by prisoners in Albany, New York; nonfiling by watermen in the Chesapeake Bay) and finds a way of finding and penalizing those who practice it, just a few exemplary prosecutions have been documented to bring dramatic increases in compliance in subsequent years (IRS, 1978b). Presumably networks within these occupations rapidly warned associates about the dangers of continued noncompliance in view of close scrutiny by the IRS.

The degree to which a network is shaped by the characteristics of an occupation involving illegal behavior was explored in one study of drug dealers (Ekland-Olsen, Lieb, and Zurcher, 1984). Participation in criminal activities intensified the association with others who were similarly inclined; as casual drug dealers became more professional, they minimized the potentially disruptive effect of arrest and jail sentencing on their social contacts by associating increasingly with individuals whose attitudes toward drug dealing and arrest made it likely that an arrest would not harm the relationship.

In some occupations, illegal strategies for tax and other matters both are commonplace and require the implicit collusion of others, such as among informal suppliers in the underground economy. Such occupations may also develop social fields that generate and transmit new ways of getting around taxes, particularly when tax strategies require complex bookkeeping arrangements and questionable tax practices provide an important percentage of profits. Common fraudulent practices in several lines of business such as retail sales are so complex, for example, that the IRS has prepared specialized manuals to provide auditors with enforcement techniques to counter them. Particularly when collusion is required for successful evasion, social fields may incorporate effective sanctioning techniques to reduce the risk of disclosure by all involved in the illicit transactions. For example, the Westat, Inc. (1980e) focus group discussions produced anecdotal evidence that newly hired waitresses are quickly warned by "old hands" to report the "right amount" of tips—reporting less might attract IRS attention to themselves, and reporting more might focus attention on the other waitresses. When simpler types of evasion are commonplace, as for housepainters paid in cash who simply do not file a return (Kagan, Vol. 2), contacts with other painters and suppliers may contribute to the development of common attitudes and favorable (mis)interpretations of tax requirements that diminish both the guilt and the fear associated with noncompliance.

While some social fields may be restricted in membership and intensively involved with taxes and tax evasion activities, most of the social fields and networks that influence tax schemas are likely to involve broader, multipurpose contacts that only incidentally deal with tax matters. For example, the networks that integrate rural migrants into marginal jobs in the city economy (Dow, 1977) interpret legal demands and instruct migrants in what to do about taxes and many other matters. Paying domestic servants in cash and not reporting their income is so well established among both employers and employees that interactions between the groups reinforce the practice (Rollins, 1985). Similarly, networks connecting construction contractors with the informal subcontractors they routinely hire appear to be an established part of the construction business, even though they rather openly support the underreporting of income by subcontractors.

For the tax administrator, it may be important to know how networks and social fields respond to the two primary enforcement strategies, coercion and cooperation. The coercive approach consists of targeting criminal investigations, audits, and other individual contacts on a particular network or its leaders to disrupt it or to increase its members' concerns with the risk associated with noncompliance. Perhaps more effective coercive programs against networks could be devised if tax authorities knew which links in troublesome networks were most vulnerable. For example, in relatively high-status networks such as those of doctors, lawyers, and other professionals, a credible threat of criminal sanctions may have the greatest impact. If tax practitioners are identified as a major source of evasive information, penalties threatening their professional ability to practice may be more effective.

In networks with dispersed leadership, extensive audits or notices within the network may perhaps be most effective. For occupations in which networks are rarely concerned with tax matters, coverage above a certain threshold may be necessary to trigger a large change in communication about tax matters that, in turn, may increase compliance levels, either by increasing fear of punishment or by correcting misinformation. For networks with fluctuating membership or continuously changing tax situations, a continued audit presence at a certain level may be more important to reduce support for evasion. However, unusually aggressive enforcement targeted on a selected occupation may trigger communication more supportive of aggressive misinterpretations and may change diffuse networks into more cohesive ones that support noncompliance.

Cooperative strategies for enforcement attempt to increase compliance through the provision of services, to engender attitudes supportive of compliance, and to consult with affected groups in developing detailed regulations. Targeting informational services toward opinion leaders might provide a multiplier effect that would increase the impact of the service. For example, the joint IRS-American Bar Association VITA program to provide assistance to low-income and elderly taxpayers could be extended to tap existing social fields, particularly among non-English-speaking populations or among taxpayers with strong regional or ethnic identities (Dow, 1977). A cooperative strategy may also attempt to increase the sense of participation in the tax system, particularly by formal groups such as trade associations and professional groups, within which tax-relevant networks are likely to exist.

Participation in developing procedures has been found to generate support for compliance in other legal arenas (Tyler, 1986; McEwen and Maiman, 1984). By consulting with opinion leaders about ambiguous interpretations of the tax code that impose the greatest problems on a particular occupation, the IRS may gain greater support for compliance within the formal organization and reduce individual incentives to seek out more evasive networks. Instead of immediately initiating a well-publicized crackdown on networks of evading doctors, for example, the IRS might be able to negotiate with formal organizations like the American Medical Association to condemn certain specific practices of questionable legality, to isolate clearly evasive networks of doctors, and to give members greater disincentive to be part of evasive networks.

These speculations about how networks and social fields may work require considerable verification before they can be of use in understanding and improving compliance. For example, how and why do social fields develop informal norms supporting or opposing tax compliance? How and why do particular networks emphasize different positive or negative communications relating to taxes? Are negative communications due to a perceived disparity for most members between government benefits and taxes owed? To perceived injustices to the group in tax treatment? To noncompliance opportunities available to the group? Answers to such questions would not only improve understanding of compliance but would also be useful to tax administrators in developing a strategy with different packages of services, methods of contact, and enforcement strategies for people involved in different social networks or fields.

These matters are sufficiently important to understanding and improving compliance to justify three phases of research. The first phase, given the lack of information currently available, would consist of exploratory investigations to identify and classify the kinds of social fields or networks most relevant to taxpaying behavior. Differences in the relative frequency of an individual's contact with the group, the range of issues important to the individual that are also of concern to the group, and the relative importance of tax matters for the group are likely to affect the impact of the group on the taxpayer's schema and behavior. In this first phase, the experience of tax administrators with knowledge of certain networks could be tapped, through interviews and examination of the files of special projects on local compliance problems involving specific occupations (IRS, 1978b). In addition, existing surveys on the information sources commonly used by taxpayers could be analyzed for occupational differences related to noncompliance. More detailed questions tracing information sources might be added to future general surveys, although such questions may not warrant a separate survey at this point. Finally, ethnographic studies and journalistic accounts of how the underground economy operates should be reviewed for data and hypotheses about the operation of networks and social fields in areas of high noncompliance (Dow, 1977; Wiegand, 1984).

The second phase would emphasize intensive studies of the more important kinds of networks or social fields, using a range of ethnographic and survey techniques to probe the functioning of networks and their impact on the individual's taxpaying behavior. Pilot projects to test the relative utility of this approach could focus on one or two occupational groups for which noncompliance is widespread and interactions supportive of noncompliance appear likely, on the basis of evidence from the first research phase. To study the effects on compliance of networks and social fields in which taxes are likely to play a small part, it may be most efficient to encourage researchers to include questions related specifically to taxes in their ongoing studies of groups.

The third phase would focus on the interactions of the IRS (and other tax administration agencies) with various networks and social fields. Field experimentation could provide more knowledge about the responsiveness of networks to various strategies; experimentation is particularly appropriate for less well-established strategies such as those based on cooperation. Small-scale evaluations, followed by adjustments to improve the techniques and targeting of the program, would improve the administrative strategy as well as increase knowledge about networks. Initial research might concentrate on establishing standardized evaluation procedures for the ongoing IRS special projects relevant to network research, particularly including enforcement initiatives aimed at narrow local problems. As knowledge of networks and social fields accumulates, field experiments could be designed to test implications for compliance that would improve the effectiveness of tax administration.

All three phases of this research entail possible risks to taxpayer's privacy, and the third phase raises concerns about the equity of tax law enforcement. Therefore, it is essential that these lines of research be designed with full attention to the principles discussed in Chapter 5 for protecting research subjects.

TAX PRACTITIONERS.   One of the most important and least understood influences on taxpayers' schemas and compliance behavior is the community of tax advisers and preparers, which we refer to collectively as tax practitioners. Unlike members of most other social networks that contribute to the context of taxpaying, tax practitioners are sought out specifically to discuss tax matters. In addition, they frequently affect the actual risks and rewards of compliance, transmit values, and affect the costs of compliance. But like members of other networks, they affect people's tax schemas by interpreting compliance requirements and offering judgments about the consequences of various actions. As a first step in understanding the influence of practitioners on compliance, it is useful to distinguish among three services that practitioners explicitly provide: return preparation, tax advice, and risk advice. A single practitioner may provide a taxpayer with any or all of these services, each of which has potentially different effects on taxpayer compliance.

In preparing returns, practitioners are expected to collect all necessary information from taxpayers and to complete returns with all required forms and schedules. A practitioner who prepares the return is expected to sign it and to act on behalf of the client within his or her interpretation of the law.

In providing tax advice, practitioners use their knowledge of the tax regulations to advise clients on favorable but legal interpretations of those regulations. A tax adviser signs the return only if he or she also prepares the return. Advisers are expected to make use of extensive knowledge of tax laws, discretion, and diligence on their clients' behalf. Advice may be provided at the time of filing, when the adviser attempts to provide the most favorable interpretations of taxpayers' transactions during the year. Or advice may be provided throughout the tax year, to help clients structure their transactions in advance so as to minimize tax liability. In either case, providing advice may include developing novel legal arguments to support a favorable interpretation of a complex regulation that may apply to a particular transaction. If these arguments are not accepted by the IRS or eventually by the court, civil penalties may be assessed even though the interpretation was made in good faith. In this way, tax advice may lead to noncompliance through disagreements between the adviser and the tax administrator over interpretations of complex regulations, as well as through a practitioner's ignorance or lack of diligence. Consultation with an adviser usually insures the taxpayer against more severe criminal fines for tax evasion.

Risk advice, the third function of tax practitioners, emphasizes knowledge of IRS administrative practices, detection probabilities, and sanctioning practices rather than knowledge of tax regulations. In providing risk advice, practitioners advise clients on such matters as what reports are least likely to be challenged, which types of income are least likely to be found in audits, or what dollar amounts are likely to be ignored by the IRS.

IRS records indicate that about 196,000 paid practitioners prepared at least twenty individual returns each in 1980 (U.S. GAO, 1983b). Table 9 reports statistics from the 1979 TCMP cycle on the numbers of returns prepared by these practitioners, by unpaid third parties, and by taxpayers themselves. It also reports the voluntary compliance level for each type of return. As the table shows, only 44 percent of all the sample returns were prepared by taxpayers themselves. The paid practitioners are a diverse group, ranging from lawyers and CPAs to self-trained preparers, some working for large, prestigious firms and others operating out of temporary storefronts or home offices. (See Smith, Stalans, and Coyne, 1987, for a useful discussion of practitioner types.) Of all returns, 22 percent were prepared by local or national tax services, whose business is almost exclu-

TABLE 9   Use of Third-Party Tax Preparers and Clients' Voluntary Compliance Level

Type of preparer	Returns (%)	Number of returns (millions)	TCMP voluntary compliance level (%)
Local tax service	12	10.5	88.4
National tax service	10	8.6	90.7
Other (paid)	7	6.7	85.0
Certified public accountant	7	6.1	89.2
Public accountant	6	5.6	89.1
Attorney/CPA	3	2.6	91.5
Attorney	1	0.9	89.6
Other (unpaid)	8	7.4	91.6
Self	44	40.2	93.8
Total	100	90.4	90.7

Source: Tabulations of 1979 TCMP Survey of Individual Returns filed, prepared by the Research Division of the IRS for the panel.

sively preparation rather than tax or risk advice. An additional 17 percent were prepared by public accountants, CPAs, or attorneys,[1] whose primary service is tax advice but who also prepare their clients' returns. Another 15 percent are prepared by "other" paid or unpaid practitioners, who vary widely in their knowledge of tax regulations and their willingness to provide risk advice in addition to tax advice and return preparation.

The fraction of taxpayers whose compliance is influenced by practitioners must be greater than Table 9 suggests, since some taxpayers hire preparers only for some years but use this advice in subsequent years, some taxpayers seek advice on particular issues or record-keeping systems but not return preparation, and some paid preparers do not sign the returns even though failure to do so is illegal. Surveys have found that 50 percent (Opinion Research Corp., 1973), 46 percent (Citicorp, 1976), and 50 percent (Aitken and Bonneville, 1980:21) of respondents claim to have used paid preparers in a specified tax year. Aitken and Bonneville report that another 2 percent used IRS preparation services, and 16 percent of respondents reported the use of unpaid third parties such as friends and relatives to prepare their taxes. Other studies have found 14–17 percent getting help from unpaid acquaintances (Crossley, 1971, cited in IRS, 1976; Citicorp, 1976). It appears likely that over 50 percent of all taxpayers are subject to current- or previous-year practitioner influence, but our inability to make a more exact estimate of the numbers involved underscores the need for the most basic descriptive research.

Because many kinds of taxpayers use preparers we can guess that they act from a broad mixture of motives. Aitken and Bonneville (1980:22) found that respondents using preparers tended to be self-employed, older, female, with less education, filing more complex and unfamiliar forms, and with under $8,000 or over $50,000 in income. Those over age 40 and those with a college education were more likely to turn to an accountant or lawyer, while those under age 21 were more likely to turn to a friend or relative. When asked why they used a preparer, 35 percent responded that the forms were too complicated and another 14 percent were afraid they would make a mistake. Only 10 percent responded that they hoped to save money, with another 9 percent saying they did not have time to complete the forms themselves (Aitken and Bonneville, 1980:24). A survey by Citicorp (1977) found a slightly higher fraction citing the forms too complicated (53 percent) and not enough time (15 percent) and a lower rate mentioning pay less in taxes (5 percent), but the general responses were similar. A number of those who worried about the complexity of forms most likely feared that they would pay too much without the help of a preparer. Differences among taxpayer responses were predictable. Self-employed taxpayers and those filing more complex forms were motivated by the complexity of the forms; individuals earning over $25,000 were more likely than those in lower income brackets to say they did not have time; and low-income individuals were more likely than upper-income ones to worry about making a mistake. The service provided by preparers thus varies considerably from aggressive lowering of taxes (usually for high-income clients) to saving time and the worries of a confrontation with the IRS.

Although Table 9 shows little variation in voluntary compliance level by preparer category, some diverse compliance effects may be masked by this aggregate statistic. And, although conjectures on this subject abound, there is a near vacuum of formal theory on the matter. Many observers believe that tax practitioners discourage underreporting of tax liability because it makes them vulnerable to sanctions by the IRS and by their professional associations. Other practitioners, who are not members of professional associations, may encourage their clients to reduce their taxes by claiming deductions they consider safe even in the absence of corresponding documentation, by tacitly ignoring "safe" amounts of income not subject to information reporting, and by pushing questionable claims just below the point at which the IRS is likely to discover and question them. Possibly some practitioners encourage underreporting of tax liability through their own carelessness; when an unfamiliar issue arises, the temptation may be to guess at the most favorable interpretation that seems arguable rather than to spend time researching the issue, particularly when the amount involved seems unlikely to trigger an audit and the client is unwilling to pay for the time required to develop a reasonable basis for the decision. There is a need to develop theories to explain practitioners' investment in training to maintain and improve their skills; their diligence; and their decisions to emphasize aggressiveness, conservatism, or accuracy in developing their reputations.

Much of the available empirical data have not been collected with guidance from theory and do not provide a clear picture at this point. For example, the Westat survey found that self-preparers were more likely to admit to cheating (Ekstrand, 1980), and Yankelovich et al. (1984) found the use of preparers to be positively related to commitment to comply (but did not report any relationship to admitted cheating). The TCMP data in Table 9 indicate that self-preparers have a slightly higher voluntary compliance rate than all categories of preparers—but the TCMP data cannot be taken as a direct measure of the compliance effect of practitioners, for two reasons. First, practitioners who provide advice but not preparation are not noted in TCMP. Second, income levels, the complexity of tax issues, and commitment may differ between those who use practitioners and those who do not. Such differences would have to be controlled by appropriate statistical techniques to get a clearer picture of the effect of preparers on compliance.

Important steps in this direction are taken in two recent papers (Klepper and Nagin, 1987b; Mazur and Nagin, 1987). Proceeding from a microeconomic model of taxpayers as maximizers of expected utility, the authors predict that use of a preparer leads to better compliance with relatively unambiguous features of the tax code but to poorer compliance with more ambiguous features, which are subject to exploitation by practitioners. In analyses of tabulated data from the 1982 TCMP Survey of Individual Filers, the authors find support for those predictions, but only within audit classes with higher income and more complex returns, i.e., returns that invoke more ambiguous features of the tax laws. They also find support in an analysis of Pennsylvania state tax data.

The IRS has viewed the main compliance problem caused by preparers to be the result of a few thousand unscrupulous operators. After 1976 legislation provided the IRS with penalties as a means to deal with incompetent and dishonest preparers, it set up several programs to cope with these problems (U.S. GAO, 1983b). The IRS began in 1977 to collect the names of practitioners who identified themselves on tax forms and used the examination program to identify preparers who had (illegally) not signed the returns they prepared. The agency also introduced a special "unscrupulous preparer" examination program at the district level, in which other returns signed by a preparer found to break the law were selected. At one time this program accounted for about 5 percent of all examinations (U.S. GAO, 1976). The U.S. GAO (1983b) study of penalties imposed on tax return preparers concluded, however, that the problem was a continuing one even five years after the penalties and enforcement powers provided in 1976. A random survey of preparers listed in IRS files estimated that 22 percent of these preparers, or 42,000, had been involved in an IRS penalty action in 1977–1980, most of which involved multiple penalties. But the GAO noted that the IRS had not developed a data collection system that would allow it to assess the effectiveness of its preparer program and penalty provisions, and that the means of detecting problem preparers have been weakened because of budget cuts in the early 1980s (U.S. GAO, 1983b:30).

Several general studies of lawyers and accountants suggest that problem practitioners may be those who lack an established place in the profession, such as membership in major professional societies (e.g., the Tax Section of the American Bar Association and the American Institute of Certified Public Accountants). Carlin's (1966) study of lawyers in New York City and Handler's (1967) study of lawyers in a Midwestern city found that lawyers with the wealthiest and most prestigious clients were less likely to take advantage of opportunities to violate professional norms, while lawyers at the lower strata of prestige in the profession were more likely to be exposed to client pressures and to violate professional norms. Loeb's dissertation (1970, cited in Renfer, 1982:28) found that CPAs were less likely to violate ethical standards when they were members of larger, more financially secure firms, were members of AICPA, and had higher-status clients. Unlike the Carlin and Handler studies, in which offenses against clients were found to be more numerous, violations against other professionals (e.g., solicitation) were more common among the CPAs in Loeb's study. Yerkes's dissertation (1975, cited in Renfer, 1982:29) found similar results for other public accountants as well, with accountants in smaller firms feeling greater pressure from clients and competition to ignore ethical standards. Broden (1977), using a mail survey of accountants and IRS agents, found that exposure to and attitudes toward ethical conflicts varied with the size and status of the firm. Based on a series of in-depth interviews, Coyne and Smith (1987) concluded that while individual practitioners' professional status does not appear to influence ethical attitudes, the status of their organizations does. They also noted practitioners' recognition of inherent conflict between their obligations to clients and IRS regulations that are intended to cause practitioners to encourage compliance.

While these studies do not directly address the question of intentional assistance in tax cheating, they do suggest that at least the size of the practice and the status of the clients are related to compliance (Renfer, 1982; Kinsey, 1986; Burrell, 1982). The drop in voluntary compliance levels in Table 9 from national (90.7 percent) to local tax services (88.4 percent) to the single practitioners and seasonal establishments included in the "other" category (85 percent) supports the hypothesis about size of establishment.

One study (Ayres, Jackson, and Hite, 1987) supports the conventional wisdom within the tax community that, among the lawyers and CPAs dealing with high-income clients, those working for the largest organizations are likely to push the most aggressive strategies of tax minimization. Even though these new interpretations usually do not constitute noncompliance, they may affect compliance in two ways. First, aggressive representation requires considerable IRS enforcement resources to prevent abusive expansion of questionable interpretations, and these resources are drawn away from efforts to encourage compliance by other taxpayers. Second, the knowledge that high-priced tax practitioners can reduce taxes for those who can afford their services may adversely affect the tax commitment of other taxpayers, justifying the widespread belief that high-income taxpayers (and corporations) do not pay their fair share of taxes. We do not know of documentation of these hypotheses, however.

In general, many topics relevant to practitioners need further study. We need to know more about important dimensions of tax practice likely to affect compliance. The impact of practitioners on compliance may be affected by professional identity (lawyer, accountant, financial planner, tax preparer), by the extent of training, certification, and professional membership, by the size of the firm, and by the nature of the clientele (income level, occupation, literacy). The impact on compliance may come not only from reducing the cost of determining accurate reporting levels, but also from increasing knowledge about possible penalties and from influencing the taxpayer's attitudes and commitment to tax compliance.

From a policy perspective, greater knowledge about the relationships between tax practitioners and taxpayer compliance could offer one of the most promising areas for improving compliance. The practitioner population is small and more easily targeted than the population of taxpayers they serve. To the extent that practitioners can be encouraged to foster compliance in their clients, enforcement resources could be concentrated on the most problematic areas. IRS could provide greater inducements to taxpayers to use appropriate private tax services and concentrate its own taxpayer services on compliance problems less suited to private practitioners. To properly consider these policies, however, more knowledge is also needed about the interaction between the IRS and the various practitioner communities. For example, would stricter control increase the number and quality of reputable tax preparers, or simply drive marginal preparers underground, where they would be even more difficult to control? Would cooperation between the IRS and professional associations to refine and promulgate codes of ethics have a positive effect on practitioners? Could self-regulation be strengthened? Should training and professional education be encouraged through greater care in certification, perhaps by devising audit strategies that would reduce the probability of audits for preparers with the best credentials and audit record? Given the variety observed in the tax practitioner community, knowledge and policy suggestions should be developed with the important distinctions in mind.

Conclusion

The concepts briefly introduced in this chapter are meant to provide a broader framework than has been used in most research on taxpayer compliance. By focusing on tax schemas, on decision processes that convert elements of the tax schema into action, and on how the environment shapes tax schemas—through careers, occupations, social networks, and practitioners—researchers can acquire knowledge about important interactions between self-interest, social sanctions, and social commitment. The research that is needed is exploratory and descriptive. It need not be centrally coordinated, and much of it is best carried out independently of the IRS and other tax authorities, for both ethical and practical reasons. The work will require several methods that have not been widely used in taxpayer compliance research to date. These include ethnographic studies of social networks or fields, laboratory studies of simulated compliance behavior in controlled situations, and intensive study of individual taxpayers to observe the mental processes by which they cope with their actual taxpaying decisions.

Notes

1. As noted by Coyne and Smith (1987), not all lawyers who prepare tax returns are tax specialists. Many of them prepare only a few returns a year and are therefore not particularly experienced as tax practitioners.

4. Extending Research on Tax Administration

The preceding chapter indicated that much exploratory and descriptive research is needed to understand how taxpaying schemas evolve, and how those schemas and taxpayers' environments shape compliance behavior. But even at this preliminary stage, recognition of the importance of those questions suggests the need to refocus applied research that is intended to improve tax administration. As a start, there is a need to examine how changes in requirements and enforcement methods affect compliance, not merely revenue recovery—a point noted by Smith and Kinsey (1985a). More broadly, there is a need to examine how compliance responds to features of the tax system that are influenced by those who write and administer tax laws.

As illustrative examples, this chapter discusses three research programs that we believe can contribute to the quality of tax administration and explore many of the questions raised in Chapter 3. These programs address three important and largely unstudied issues in taxpayer compliance: (1) taxpayers' adjustments to major changes in the tax structure, using the Tax Reform Act of 1986 as an example; (2) the relationships between tax practitioners and taxpayer compliance; and (3) taxpayers' responses to different types of contact from the tax administrator. These programs were selected with the following criteria in mind: value as input to the analysis of tax administration policy, centrality to understanding compliance behavior, the extent of current gaps in knowledge, and the likelihood of successful completion of the research. There are, however, a number of excellent research opportunities not included in these programs, and other programs deserving research attention could be developed. In particular, opportunities should be sought to conduct exploratory and descriptive research in conjunction with more applied work, when it is possible to do so without compromising either the independence of the researchers or the rights of subjects.

The research projects in each program are described only briefly to suggest the kinds of research that are possible. Many of the projects raise common problems of compliance measurement, access to data bases, and protection of research subjects. Instead of discussing these matters separately for each program, we discuss them more generally in Chapter 5. Chapter 6 discusses the administrative arrangements needed to facilitate the research.

Research on Taxpayer Responses to Policy Changes

One of the major concerns that emerged from the panel's review of taxpayer compliance research was the lack of attention to the dynamics of taxpayer responses to changes in tax laws and enforcement policies. Compliance requirements are complex, and frequent legislatively mandated changes are likely to continue. We therefore emphasize the need to understand more about the dynamics of tax schemas: how people learn about changes, how they interpret them, and how they modify their behavior. Changes in laws and administrative procedures provide natural experiments for the study of compliance. The results of those studies can form a basis for anticipating compliance responses to future changes.

Such studies need not require much more than collection and analysis of tax return data for an appropriate sample from time periods before and after the change. But their value will be greatly enhanced if they incorporate two other features whenever possible. First, if small-scale randomized experiments are used to introduce a given change in different ways to comparable samples of taxpayers, the compliance effects of the different introduction methods can be compared. Second, ethnographic research that probes the effects of the change in different taxpayer subgroups is likely to help in interpreting compliance patterns.

The next few years present particularly important opportunities to study the impact of the major changes introduced in the Tax Reform Act of 1986 (TRA86), which first affected compliance requirements for tax year 1987 and will continue to change requirements for some tax items over the following several years. The opportunity is particularly important for at least two reasons. First, the law not only changed marginal tax rates and deductions that directly affect individual taxpayers' self-interest, but it also changed characteristics of the code related to broader perceptions of fairness. Sweeping changes affecting taxpayer self-interest are not likely to occur again in the foreseeable future, and the TRA86 changes were widely and vocally endorsed by politicians and the media as enhancing fairness. The reform therefore offers an opportunity and a common framework to study the compliance effects of changes affecting both self-interest and fairness elements of the tax schema. Second, by introducing new information needs, the reform created an unusual opportunity to study the role of information in taxpayer compliance.

We therefore recommend that the research projects already being conducted on certain effects of TRA86 be broadened to analyze systematically the impact of the 1986 law on tax compliance. We recommend projects that focus on the effects of changes in: tax rates, allowable deductions, and the value of exemptions; perceptions of fairness; and information needs. Besides having intrinsic importance, such projects exemplify the research opportunities that will be created by future legal and administrative changes that affect elements of taxpayers' compliance schemas.

TAX RATES, DEDUCTIONS, AND EXEMPTIONS

Three elements of TRA86 potentially alter the self-interest compliance calculus for nearly all taxpayers: reduction of the number of tax brackets and marginal rates, increase in the value of the personal exemption, and elimination of deductions for certain types of expenditures such as consumer interest and state sales taxes. Different theories predict different compliance effects for these changes, and the actual outcome will depend on the relative strengths of these effects.

Economic models of individual decision making attend to the effects of these changes on calculations of self-interest and therefore on compliance, assuming that all the changes are perfectly visible and understandable to taxpayers. As explained in Chapter 2, in these models the predicted compliance effects of changes in marginal rates depend on assumptions about how aversion to risk is related to after-tax income and about how the IRS responds to changes in compliance patterns.

Cognitive models concerned with the information costs of decisions suggest several different possible outcomes. Taxpayers whose marginal rates were reduced have less incentive to search for new tax strategies; TRA86 may thus not result in much change in tax-related behavior. But the changes themselves call attention to taxpaying and may cause many taxpayers to review their compliance behavior, especially the minority whose taxes were raised by TRA86. Taxpayers for whom all aspects of the changes are equally salient may behave as economic models predict. Alternatively, those for whom subtle changes in marginal tax rates are less salient than the loss of customary favorite deductions may find greater incentives to seek questionable deductions and exemptions. Conversely, those for whom the larger personal exemption is more salient may behave less aggressively; if this group predominates, compliance may actually improve.

The alternative theoretical frameworks—economic and cognitive—present contradictions that can be resolved only through empirical research. A major component of this research should be a comparative analysis of the 1985 and 1988 TCMP surveys. Since passage of TRA86 was a surprise to most observers and since 1987 is the first tax year affected by the changes, anticipation of the law should not have affected the 1985 returns in any significant way. By tax year 1988, taxpayers will have had two years to familiarize themselves with the changes in provisions that affect them most directly, and so lack of information should not be abnormally important as a cause of noncompliance. Therefore, by comparing changes in compliance between 1985 and 1988 on specific return items across taxpayer subgroups that are affected in different ways by the legislation, it should be possible to test the hypotheses summarized above that emerge from economic theories of compliance. One difficulty with this approach is created by lags in TCMP processing, which would normally delay availability of the 1988 file until 1991. Another important limitation is that the 1985–1988 comparison, which would involve different samples, cannot provide information about the dynamic adjustments—learning, changes in financial status, for example—to the legal changes.

Sources of Information

TRA86 changed the compliance requirements for virtually all taxpayers. Taxpayers were therefore confronted with the problem of finding out how they were affected. Thus the tax year 1987 filing season (January–April 1988) provided a major opportunity to study how taxpayers get and use information in making their tax decisions and what influence this information has on compliance. The role of practitioners, the media, publications, tax networks, and the IRS in educating taxpayers about their changed obligations is likely to have been more open to observation during that period than at any time in the near future. It seems especially important to implement research projects to study three activities during the time of transition surrounding the new law: use of practitioners, search for information, and the role of taxpayer services provided by the IRS. Such projects will have future value even if they involve retrospective observation of the filing season for tax year 1987.

Later in this chapter, we recommend a taxpayer survey that focuses on practitioner use and the events that precipitate changes in patterns of practitioner use. That effort would be particularly valuable if it were conducted in late 1989 and its reference period spanned the 1988 and 1989 filing seasons. In that way the survey would facilitate analyses not only of how changes in practitioner use affected compliance, but also of how TRA86 affected practitioner use, both immediately and over the long term. For example, did more or fewer taxpayers make use of practitioners for tax year 1987 than previously? For which categories of taxpayers was this change most pronounced? What return items and tax law changes were most cited as problems by taxpayers who began to use a practitioner or changed to a different practitioner (i.e., did changes in practitioner use seem to reflect general confusion or the need for specific advice)? Were practitioners used only for tax year 1987 to get advice about coping with the new law, or did use continue for 1988? Were practitioner use patterns for taxpayers who stopped itemizing deductions under the new law similar to the patterns for other taxpayers? All these questions could be addressed in a 1989 taxpayer survey, and the results would provide valuable insights into the roles of practitioners during periods of future legal or administrative change.

PERCEIVED FAIRNESS AND COMPLIANCE

One of the most important claims made by political supporters of TRA86 was that the new tax law would restore the legitimacy of the tax code in taxpayers' eyes. By reducing marginal rates for many taxpayers, eliminating a number of deductions broadly perceived as loopholes, strengthening minimum tax provisions, shifting some of the tax burden to corporations, and removing many poor people from the tax rolls, political leaders claimed to have increased the fairness of the tax law. To the extent that public opinion responded in the expected direction, these changes provide an excellent opportunity to examine the relationships between attitudes and compliance—relationships that have not been completely determined by previous research but are potentially important in influencing compliance.

Two different relationships are in need of investigation, the one between the new tax law and the tax schema, and the one between any changes in schema and compliance behavior. Both relationships should be investigated with taxpayer surveys, combined if possible with 1986, 1987, and 1988 return data. We discuss these projects below.

TAXPAYER SURVEYS. To test the effect of TRA86 on tax schemas, responses to fairness questions in the most recent IRS taxpayer survey (conducted during 1987) could be compared with the responses to similar questions in the Yankelovich et al. (1984) survey. Such comparisons, of course, will be less precise to the extent that the two surveys differ in terms of sampling frame and the wording of questions. There is also no control group to enable the analyst to separate the impact of other historical events and trends from the impact of TRA86 and the publicity that surrounded it.

A second survey, conducted during 1989, could provide a basis for studying additional questions. The questionnaire should be designed to elicit a number of separate dimensions of fairness (e.g., of the law; of administrative processes; of outcomes relative to previous years, to other taxpayers, and to expectations of TRA86). Responses could be used to probe the relative importance of each dimension in affecting the taxpayer's overall judgment about the tax law change and to examine how perceptions of fairness are related to the effect of TRA86 on the taxpayer's well-being. Correlations between the self-interest and fairness responses could be used to test alternative theories noted earlier in this chapter that have contradictory implications for tax administration: under one theory, interests determine attitudes and so taxpayer attitudes can be ignored as long as interests are known; under the other, attitudes and perceptions of fairness are formed independently of interests and outcomes and may therefore have independent effects on compliance.

SURVEYS MERGED WITH RETURN DATA. If administrative mechanisms can be devised that would permit the linking of the 1987 taxpayer survey respondents' tax returns to their responses without jeopardizing their rights as research subjects and as taxpayers, then two additional lines of research could be followed. First, using their tax year 1986 returns, the actual effect of the reform on taxpayer self-interest could be measured by projecting how each return would have been changed by the new law if the taxpayer made no adjustments in economic behavior; then that measure could be used as an explanatory variable to analyze both the accuracy of perceptions of self-interest and the effect of variations in actual self-interest on attitudes about fairness.

Second, by merging the 1987 survey results with tax return information for 1987, the first year directly affected by the new tax law, 1986–1987 differences could be computed for reported income and deduction items that were not changed definitionally by the law. Subject to certain errors, these differences would provide a measure of the compliance effect of the law. This compliance measure could serve as the dependent variable in a multivariate analysis in which the survey data on perceived changes in fairness and self-interest and the projections of actual changes in self-interest appeared as explanatory variables. Analyzing the relationships of compliance to measures of fairness and of self-interest in a common data base is not only of intellectual interest, as discussed in Chapter 2, but is also of considerable practical significance in determining the compliance impact of future changes in the tax system that could alter perceptions of fairness, self-interest, or both.

IRS RESPONSES TO TAX REFORM

Most of the research we have reviewed and most of the research we propose focuses exclusively on the taxpayer and the social and political environment. Yet we have noted at several places that the taxpayer's behavior cannot be fully understood without considering the tax enforcement environment in which the taxpayer exists. It is particularly important for researchers to understand the nature of IRS actions to which taxpayers respond, including audits, letter contacts, penalties, taxpayer services, and the other actions discussed in Chapter 1. For example, different representations of audit strategy and constraints used to model IRS-taxpayer interactions result in quite different theoretical predictions about compliance outcomes (Graetz, Reinganum, and Wilde, 1986).

The major changes in the Internal Revenue Code introduced by TRA86 provide an important opportunity to study how the IRS adapts to significant statutory changes. Anecdotal evidence about new programs that are continually being developed within the IRS, combined with GAO reports on progress made (as well as needed improvements) in ongoing programs, suggests a general receptivity to change. However, the only available systematic study of responsiveness by an outside scholar (Long, 1985) found that the development of the computerized audit targeting system based on DIF scores did not make a significant difference in the pattern of audits and that shifts in the composition of the IRS work force had greater impact on audit patterns than did improved selectivity in auditing returns. Understanding organizational factors that constrain enforcement strategies and that limit the ability of the IRS to implement promising compliance-improving strategies developed through research is important for determining strategies for both reform and research.

To analyze IRS adaptive processes, several enforcement actions affected by changes in the code could be followed, and comparisons made of response time before changes are actualized. For example, TRA86 and earlier programs to terminate abusive tax shelters should release substantial resources for other uses. How long will it take to redirect these resources to different areas of emphasis, and how will the resources be redirected? Given the smaller number of taxpayers needing to file and able to itemize because of TRA86, will there be commensurate alterations in the internal allocation process to reflect the reduced workload related to these changes? To the extent that these changes vary in different parts of the country, for example, will there be shifts in the work force to compensate, or are decisions about staffing so restricted by other factors that responses to changes in compliance problems are difficult to make? By comparing the responses to a number of issues, the relative responsiveness to different issues might also be established. Analytic methods could make use of operational data on budgets, staffing, and enforcement activities to establish the pattern of change over the years before and after the change, IRS memos and documents to establish the new internal procedures begun in response to the changes, and interviews at different levels of the organization to establish the perspective of officials involved in the decision process. Academic researchers have done research requiring such access to information and personnel in many government agencies. Cooperation from the IRS in arranging access to needed documents and officials would be required.

Although there have been a number of studies about the politics of tax law changes (Manley, 1965, 1970; Reese, 1980; Hansen, 1983; J. Witte, 1985b), none of these studies has traced the implications of tax change on enforcement resources and practices (Scholz, Vol. 2). Several changes introduced in 1986 were widely expected to increase compliance. But if budgetary decision makers routinely respond to compliance-increasing legislation by reducing funding for enforcement, the net combined effect on compliance may be negative. Understanding the political environment of a tax administration agency is unlikely to help in predicting specific political outcomes—most political observers were quite surprised that TRA86 was actually passed—but knowledge of the general political constraints within which tax administrators operate is important for converting knowledge about compliance effects into agency policy. Other than the instinctive responses of experienced administrators, little is known about the difficulties a tax administration agency like the IRS would have in implementing some of the more innovative ideas that may be generated from an active program of applied research. What are the kinds of actions, for example, that the agency will not undertake because similar actions in the past have caused trouble? What factors historically have affected the budgets and the statutory authority of the IRS? What are the political consequences of using different enforcement techniques or different levels of enforcement in different congressional districts, and to what extent do these consequences limit the IRS's ability to experiment? Given the proclivity of any agency to use such limitations to justify inaction, direct knowledge of real versus imagined political constraints could be of considerable importance for tax policy makers concerned with improving compliance.

A number of studies could increase our knowledge of political constraints. On the broadest level, a historical study of budget and oversight activities of Congress and the Office of Management and Budget—particularly the kinds of activities that follow major legislative initiatives such as the 1981 and 1986 acts—should increase our understanding of the general constraints on tax enforcement in the federal political system. Studies of the determinants of different levels of enforcement actions on the district level might clarify the extent of both organizational (Long, 1985) and political constraints that reduce the ability of the IRS to shift resources according to measures and predictions of resource needs. Information about budgets, enforcement actions, and organizational resources are in the public domain, and such research would be most appropriately undertaken by outside researchers, presumably with the cooperation of the IRS. In addition, a series of case studies of successful and failed enforcement innovations within the IRS or state tax administration agencies would be useful to ascertain the specific kinds of problems that arise and the conditions necessary to overcome them. Such research would be more appropriate for the agency, perhaps in conjunction with a public administration specialist, since it would require considerable knowledge about how the agency operates.

OTHER RESEARCH OPPORTUNITIES.   Although TRA86 provides an exceptional opportunity to study the responses of both taxpayers and the IRS, changes in enforcement and in tax policies take place continually. We want to emphasize the importance, both for policy analysts within the IRS and for independent researchers, of taking advantage of these changes to learn more about how compliance is affected by changes in compliance requirements and enforcement techniques.

Opportunities for research can come from unplanned as well as planned changes. For example, the well-publicized problems the IRS encountered in processing returns and issuing refunds during the 1985 tax season were clearly not planned but could still be used to analyze a number of issues relating to the impact on compliance of people's judgments about the IRS. One hypothesis might be that those who received very late refunds on average reported less income in the following year or two than those receiving refunds at the usual time. Records detailing the mailing date of refunds could be used to select two or more groups for comparison. The importance of individual experience could be tested against the importance of group phenomena by comparing return items for early- and late-refund groups before and after the 1985 tax season in different geographic locations in which the problems of mailing refunds and the tone of the media coverage varied. If the difference between groups was consistently significant, the finding would suggest that individual experience was most important. Significantly lower compliance for both groups in areas with the worst problems or the most hostile press coverage, however, would suggest the greater influence of networks of shared experience or the media in shaping compliance behavior. And if none of the differences were significant, it would suggest either that such blunders make no measurable impact (given the rough measures of compliance available) or that the overall national impact of reporting had comparable effects everywhere. Similar quasi-experiments can be analyzed whenever programs such as introduction of the revised W-4 form during 1987 affect taxpayers differently.

The most powerful research, however, can result when planned administrative changes or new programs are designed as field experiments, in which control groups and groups experiencing different levels or varieties of treatments are used in order to compare effects on compliance. The advantage of planned experiments over analysis of existing quasi-experiments is that greater care can be taken to produce a more suitable control group (e.g., by random assignment, when possible and appropriate) and to measure a greater number of potentially confounding factors. Many innovations, such as new ways of responding to taxpayers' telephone inquiries, could be introduced in randomly selected areas rather than universally, so that compliance effects could be measured as well as administrative costs and feasibility. The results of a recent IRS project on clustering IRS districts could serve as a basis for such randomized introduction of new procedures. Other specific possibilities and problems relating to randomized experiments are discussed further in a paper prepared for the panel by Robert Boruch (Appendix B). Our emphasis here is that compliance research opportunities continually grow out of the inevitable changes in tax laws and tax administration procedures and that the IRS needs to develop a permanent capacity to measure the compliance effects of those changes.

Research on Tax Practitioners

As explained in Chapter 3, compliance by well over half of all taxpayers each year is influenced by paid tax practitioners. Despite the pervasiveness of practitioners in the taxpaying process, most research on taxpayer compliance fails to integrate practitioners into theoretical models and empirical research designs. Compliance-related research that incorporates the roles of practitioners is a recent phenomenon. Therefore, the panel recommends that research projects be undertaken on three basic questions:
  1. Why do taxpayers seek practitioners' services, and how do they choose practitioners?
  2. How do practitioners' credentials and organizational structures affect their clients' compliance?
  3. Are there common practitioner routines that encourage or discourage compliance by their clients?

A better understanding of these issues would be valuable to both administrative and scholarly perspectives. To tax administrators, practitioners offer leverage as a small and accessible group of about 200,000 that affects the compliance of at least 50 million taxpayers. Practitioners are also visible to tax administrators as they advertise their services to potential clients, and many of them can be influenced through professional associations. From a scholarly perspective, the first two questions represent natural extensions of ongoing work in economics (see, e.g., Slemrod, 1985b, Tauchen and Witte, 1986; Graetz et al., 1986; Scotchmer, Vol. 2). They also extend recent sociological work at the American Bar Foundation that involved in-person practitioner interviews (Kinsey, 1987a,b).

The recommended research programs are described in the following pages.

PATTERNS OF PRACTITIONER USE AND COMPLIANCE
Most research on taxpayers' use of practitioners has focused on the function of preparing returns rather than the functions of giving tax advice and risk advice. Much of this work has attempted either to describe the characteristics of taxpayers who use preparers' services—in such terms as

age, income, marginal tax bracket, education, and return type—or to inventory taxpayers' objectives in seeking a preparer—to get an accurate return, a lower tax liability, or a reduction in preparation time. Consequently almost nothing is known about either the events that stimulate a taxpayer to begin or end a working relationship with a practitioner, about practitioner characteristics or routines that attract clients, or about patterns of secondary practitioner use, such as the use of routines learned from practitioners in previous years.

To learn more about these patterns and events, we recommend two phases of research: a cross-sectional survey of taxpayers that focuses especially on practitioner use, followed by a longitudinal survey that collects information about shifts in taxpayers' practitioner use and certain events in the tax career that precede and follow such shifts.

CROSS-SECTIONAL SURVEY.   A cross-sectional survey of practitioner use could be accomplished either by researchers who are not affiliated or supported by the IRS or through a focused supplement to the next taxpayer survey sponsored by the IRS. In either case, it should request at least the following kinds of information: circumstances under which a taxpayer begins, changes, or ends a working relationship with a practitioner; the ways in which the taxpayer uses the practitioner's services; taxpayers' expectations about their practitioners; practitioner actions that seem to encourage or discourage compliance; and the effect of the practitioner's actions on the taxpayer's compliance and intentions about future practitioner use. In view of the preliminary state of knowledge about these issues, designers of the survey should expect to use combinations of open- and closed-ended questions. Efforts should also be made to design a sample that overrepresents taxpayers who are likely to consider using practitioners' services.

More specifically, the survey could include two lines of questions. The first would be a series of questions designed to measure the extent to which practitioner services are used in ways that are not reflected in a preparer signature on the return or in the response to a survey question: "Did you prepare your return yourself or use a preparer?" Examples include not only tax advice and risk advice, but also various secondary uses of practitioners. Secondary uses include the use of taxpaying routines suggested by a practitioner in a previous year, "cribbing" of a complex section of a relative's or financial partner's return that was prepared by a practitioner, and other less obvious uses that might emerge in responses to open-ended questions.

Tabulations of the responses would provide prevalence estimates for these kinds of practitioner use that are not currently available, for taxpayers overall and by characteristics that are known to be associated with above- or below-average compliance levels.

The second line of questions would seek information about events and motivations that have previously led respondents to decide to use a practitioner, to search for one in a particular way, to choose a particular one, to switch practitioners, or to terminate a working relationship with a practitioner. Such events might include changes in circumstances such as a divorce or a home purchase, changes in financial status, encounters with the IRS, or changes in tax laws. Motivations might include determining and satisfying compliance at least cost, structuring transactions so as to minimize tax liability, and establishing a record of attempting to ascertain compliance requirements to prevent a negligence penalty if noncompliance is eventually determined. Respondents would also be asked about their objectives and expectations at the times of such shifts, as well as their expectations about how the shifts would affect future compliance.

This cross-sectional component would be especially useful at the present time, while respondents can still recall changes in patterns of practitioner use associated with the Tax Reform Act of 1986. The data might also provide a picture of how practitioner use affected compliance during a period of transition.

LONGITUDINAL SURVEY.   The longitudinal component of this research could involve, for example, annual interviews of a sample of taxpayers about events in the tax career during the year and the consequences for their decisions to use practitioners, their methods for finding and selecting practitioners, their decisions to switch practitioners, and their decisions to do without assistance in return preparation, tax advice, and risk advice. If each wave of interviewing contained questions about compliance on the most recent return, then the data could support analyses of the effects of changes in practitioner use on self-reported compliance.[1]

Analyses of the longitudinal data would be informative about events in the lives of taxpayers, other taxpayer characteristics, and practitioner actions and other characteristics that lead to shifts in practitioner use that have consequences for compliance. They would suggest combinations of taxpayer and practitioner characteristics that encourage or discourage utilization, and they would provide information about the events and underlying motivations that lead taxpayers to establish or disrupt relationships with different types of practitioners. Techniques such as logit analysis could be used to estimate the effects of various events and practitioner routines on the odds that a taxpayer will initiate or terminate a practitioner relationship. Responses to open-ended questions on these decisions will help in interpreting the results.

PRACTITIONER STRUCTURE AND STATUS

There are a variety of frequently heard conjectures about how various types of practitioners affect their clients' compliance. Because practitioners play such a pervasive role in taxpaying, the patterns that are described in these conjectures could potentially be quite important in explaining compliance. To learn whether they describe reality, however, they must first be formulated as testable hypotheses, and then research must be designed to test those hypotheses. To the extent that the hypotheses are derived from more general theories, the empirical tests will also contribute to general knowledge about such topics as how professional advisers affect behavior, how the occupational status of professionals is related to that of their clients, and how the objectives of advisers and their clients interact in determining choices.

Many speculations about practitioners are concerned with how the objectives associated with different practitioner characteristics affect clients' compliance behavior. For example, it is sometimes said that the large national preparation services, which do not provide tax advice, have a bias against underreporting tax liability. To maintain their reputations for integrity and to avoid the costs of fulfilling pledges to accompany their clients to audits or appeals, such practitioners are said to interpret potentially ambiguous issues in conformance with anticipated IRS interpretations, perhaps to the point of overreporting tax liability. In contrast, some part-time or seasonal solo practitioners, without either the credentials of CPAs or attorneys or the reputation of the large preparation services, are sometimes said to advertise themselves with difficult-to-verify claims of inside knowledge needed to assist clients planning to evade part of their tax liability, and even to advocate modes of noncompliance they believe to be low in risk. They are also said to be haphazard in keeping abreast of tax law changes and in checking themselves for errors and are therefore thought to generate noncompliance through misinterpretations and mistakes.

Accountants and lawyers are sometimes said to affect compliance in still a different way. The vast majority of them subscribe to the ethical standards of their professional organizations, the American Institute of Certified Public Accountants and the American Bar Asociation. These standards require them not only to abide by IRS regulations (especially Treasury Circular 230), but also to represent their clients as adversaries against the government. In balancing these obligations, accountants and lawyers encourage their clients to comply with all legal requirements but interpret requirements aggressively (i.e., in favor of their clients rather than the IRS) when there is a precedent or an arguable basis for doing so. Some aggressive interpretations may be disallowed by the IRS and by courts on appeal, thus directly increasing measured noncompliance. Even when such interpretations are eventually sustained in the taxpayer's favor, analyzing and disputing them draws IRS resources away from other administrative efforts and therefore may indirectly reduce the agency's ability to improve compliance by other taxpayers. Aggressive positions that are sustained may be seen as inequitable loopholes by other taxpayers, who, it is sometimes said, may consequently feel encouraged to cheat on their own taxes.

It should be reiterated that very little evidence either supports or contradicts these speculations. Not only have the necessary tests not been performed, but even the necessary prior steps—deriving conjectures from theory or ethnography and stating them in testable form—have hardly been begun (but see Klepper and Nagin, 1987b, and Kinsey, 1987a,b). Once testable hypotheses have been formulated, at least three kinds of research will be of use in learning how practitioners' structure and status affect clients' compliance: analysis of individual-level TCMP data, organizational studies, and an "exemplary practitioner" program.

TCMP ANALYSES.   Analyses of individual-level TCMP data could be used to study how practitioner use and taxpayer characteristics interact in determining compliance. A beginning along this line of research, using tabulated data from the 1982 TCMP survey of individual filers, has been made by Klepper and Nagin (1987b) and by Mazur and Nagin (1987). For different kinds of return items, these papers report various relationships between aggregate compliance measures and the extent of practitioner use. It seems likely that these relationships also depend on characteristics of the taxpayer who files the return, but such interactions cannot be studied except with individual-level data. It seems likely that such relationships depend on the type of paid preparer (e.g., attorney, CPA, national service, solo practioner), but the current TCMP check sheets do not contain this information. In the short run, it would probably be of some use to replicate the Klepper and Nagin (1987b) and Mazur and Nagin (1987) analyses with the 1979 TCMP data, which had more detailed preparer categories. To learn about these relationships under the current law, it would be desirable to develop more detailed preparer categories for use on future TCMP check sheets, and it is necessary to analyze the check sheet data at the individual level.

ORGANIZATIONAL STUDIES.   Replications of the organizational studies of practitioners that have been conducted under the aegis of the American Bar Foundation (see, e.g., Kinsey, 1987a,b; Smith, Stalans, and Coyne, 1987) would be of great value. These studies suggest that practitioners' credentials, form, and size of organization—all self-determined characteristics—are related to their clients' financial status, the expectations of practitioners, and also to many practitioner routines that could affect compliance. Replications of these studies with larger samples and in multiple locations would provide information about the general applicability of the findings.

AN "EXEMPLARY PRACTITIONER" PROGRAM.   Since results of the American Bar Foundation studies suggest that credentials are important to practitioners and may be related to their actions that influence compliance, it would be of interest to study the effects of a credential designated by the IRS. More specifically, it would be useful to examine the effects of an IRS program designed in cooperation with the practitioners' professional societies to designate and publicize certain practitioners as exemplary in preparing returns and providing tax advice. Such an effort would presumably require an initial survey to ascertain conditions under which such a program would be acceptable to the practitioner community. If an acceptable program could be developed, then it could be field-tested in a small number of communities. Evaluation criteria would include satisfaction of the designated exemplary practitioners, as well as such direct measures as volume of business of the exemplary practitioners, compliance by their clients, and post-program compliance (similarly measured) among clients of nonexemplary preparers. The evaluation should also include a longitudinal component to track the effects on business volume of receiving and not receiving exemplary designation.

PRACTITIONER ROUTINES AND COMPLIANCE

Research on patterns of practitioner use, practitioner structure and status, and compliance is likely to identify some actions by practitioners that show promise of encouraging compliance (e.g., probes for unreported income, probes for documentation supporting claimed deductions) that do not violate practitioners' obligations to act in their clients' behalf and that are welcomed by at least some taxpayers as methods of helping them to comply. It is possible that practitioners could be encouraged by joint efforts of their professional organizations and the IRS to carry out such actions routinely as a means of fostering compliance. However, before efforts are begun to encourage such routines, it is important to verify that they do in fact encourage compliance.

The most straightforward approach to this verification, if cooperation between the IRS and the practitioners' professional associations can be obtained, is field experimentation. Suppose, for example, that one possible addition to a practitioner association code of ethics is a requirement that practitioners ask their clients, "Have you told me about *all* income you received during the year?" Through field experiments, the compliance effect of this routine could be estimated before changes in the ethical code were attempted.

A sample of participating practitioners would randomly ask or not ask the question of their clients. To measure the compliance effect, the clients' returns would be examined for changes from the preceding year in the items covered by the question. (This return-based compliance measure was first used in Schwartz and Orleans, 1967.) In the example above, clients who were asked the question should report larger income increases than do other clients if the question actually encourages compliance. The random assignment of the treatment is intended to guarantee that any compliance differences between the treatment and control groups are due to the treatment itself. However, because differences in the compliance effect of the treatment may relate to other taxpayer characteristics, rather large samples would be needed to distinguish between effects of the treatment and effects of taxpayer characteristics.

The basic design can be extended in several interesting ways. By measuring and comparing the year-to-year differences in items not covered by the questions, it would be possible to test for halo effects (i.e., improved compliance on items covered by the question may transfer to improved compliance on other items) or substitution effects (i.e., noncompliance on items not covered may be a means of escaping the practitioners' probes). In subsequent years, the returns of the treatment and control groups could be analyzed to see if being probed had any long-term effect on using a practitioner. The returns could also be examined to see if the probe produced transitory or long-term changes in compliance.

This study could later be replicated with samples of different kinds of practitioners and larger samples of taxpayers. In this way, the effectiveness of various routines could be compared across practitioner types and, with multivariate techniques, across different types of clients.

This approach has the advantage of testing the effectiveness of the new routine in advance of universal implementation, and of identifying practitioner-taxpayer combinations for which even the new routine will fail to encourage compliance. However, even with the active cooperation of professional associations, it will be difficult to maintain the integrity of the randomization.

Research on Taxpayer Contacts with the IRS

As discussed in Chapter 1, the IRS contacts a very large number of households each year for reasons other than audits and delivery of the annual tax form package, yet there has been little systematic work to understand the effect of these contacts on compliance. The contacts reach individuals by mail and telephone and also through the mass media—television, radio, newspapers, and magazines.

The IRS has introduced many innovations intended to improve the effectiveness of taxpayer contacts but until recently has not attempted to measure how these innovations affect compliance. Some of the recent innovations have been to automate mail and telephone notices of apparent discrepancies discovered through the Information Returns Program (IRP), which matches tax returns with information reports. Efforts have been made to improve the readability of tax forms and to provide simplified guides for specific tax items as well as for special groups such as small businesses, farmers, and commercial fishermen. Several other aspects of taxpayer contacts have been emphasized in the IRS Strategic Plan (IRS, 1984g). A public affairs strategy is being considered to make more extensive use of the media to communicate the IRS's mission and to appeal to the taxpayer's sense of responsibility and citizenship. Another initiative calls for a survey to determine why a significant number of taxpayers fail to respond to IRS communications (e.g., appointment letters for office audits) and what kinds of communication would be most effective in reducing nonresponse. Two other initiatives in the strategic plan would expand automated return examinations and notices to increase the sense of enforcement presence, particularly by expanding capacities in both programs to examine a taxpayer's returns for several years at once.

IRS choices of which innovations to adopt are commonly based on pilot tests, the results of which are measured in terms of administrative feasibility, program cost, and direct revenue yield. The panel believes these measures are incomplete as criteria for selecting innovations to introduce and may be seriously misleading. There are sound reasons to expect any innovation in taxpayer contacts (whether at the individual level or through the mass media) to affect taxpayer compliance, and there are often reasons to expect the compliance effect to be positive in some taxpayer subpopulations and negative in others. But since no attempts to measure the compliance effects have been completed, we have no basis for even an informed guess about their magnitudes. For any taxpayer contact program or innovation, these compliance effects may be trivial in dollar terms, or they may substantially exceed the direct revenue yields.

We believe that over time, more effective tax administration may be achievable through a more systematic approach to innovation in taxpayer contacts. We recommend an approach that involves three phases:

1. Evaluation of current practice;
2. Design and pretesting of innovations to improve problem areas; and
3. Testing promising innovations with randomized experimental designs, whenever possible, to measure both compliance effects and revenue yields.

Since the compliance effects of taxpayer contacts have never been measured, there is very little empirical basis for assessing in advance the policy importance of this recommendation. But even if there is substantial error in the IRS (1986b) estimate that all its individual taxpayer contacts together recover only 6 percent of the individual nonreporting tax gap, compliance effects may well be relatively important as a criterion for designing and selecting innovations in tax administration policy. Innovations in taxpayer contacts may initially produce little in terms of increased compliance. But findings of even small effects may be useful in refining compliance theories, which in turn may suggest more effective innovations.

The specifics of this approach for making innovations in taxpayer contacts will vary, depending on the type of contact being attempted. The first two steps—evaluating existing approaches and pretesting innovations—are somewhat different for: (1) proactive individual contacts such as letters to taxpayers, in which the IRS initiates the contact; (2) reactive individual contacts, such as responding to telephone inquiries from taxpayers; and (3) mass media contacts. In the following pages, we illustrate the approach we propose using an example of each type of contact. The examples are intended to demonstrate how the methods are used and should not be interpreted as recommendations for specific innovations. The examples we have chosen do illustrate innovations that are suggested by several of the theories discussed earlier in this chapter.

EXAMPLE 1: COMPUTER-GENERATED MAILINGS

From an administrative perspective, the recent expansions in information reports and the improvements in computer technologies to match documents with returns and to send out computer-generated letters has made these activities an important addition to traditional enforcement contacts. Given the relatively low cost per taxpayer contact and the flexibility and ability to target different letters for specific populations, this enforcement tool has attracted strong interest from senior IRS administrators, but alternative approaches have just begun to be explored. From a research perspective, the low cost of obtaining large random samples and the ease with which the intervention can be altered provide ideal conditions for field experiments to verify both the validity and the magnitude of effects associated with various hypotheses about taxpayers' schemas and compliance.

As indicated earlier in this chapter, several experiments suggest that even implicit compliance decisions may be altered either by conveying important new information to the taxpayer or by changing the context in which the information is considered and the decision is made. For example, a personal letter from the IRS, because of the high anxiety level that is likely to accompany its receipt, is likely to capture the taxpayer's attention. Personal notification of a tax deficiency due to a failure to report income that appeared on an information return can be expected to change the perception of the risk that noncompliance will be detected. But as advertising professionals have long known and the experimental literature reviewed by Cialdini (Vol. 2) and Carroll (Vol. 2) also suggests, subtle distinctions in when and how a message is presented may make a considerable difference in the impact of the message on behavior. Are threatening messages more effective when they emphasize penalties (potential interest and fines, amount of penalties collected last year), the risk of being caught (the IRS's capability to match information returns, the amount of unreported income detected last year), or when the threat is left implicit by the receipt of the letter? Are threatening messages most effective, or is some mixture of veiled threat and reference to social acceptance and civic duty more likely to induce a compliance response? How long do the effects last? Are the effects stronger or more permanent when the communication is sent as soon as possible after the return being questioned is filed, or during a following tax season when the next tax return is being filed? Or is the effect strengthened by sending a follow-up warning during the following tax season? What is the most effective treatment for those who do not respond to the communication? The answers to all these questions may be more important from a policy standpoint than the amount of revenue yielded directly through response to the letter.

The three-phase approach that we are recommending—evaluate, refine in the laboratory, and test with field experiments—could answer such questions. We illustrate the approach in terms of the Information Returns Program, an automated system that matches income reports with return information and sends letters to taxpayers when an apparent discrepancy is found. We discuss each of these phases in the sections that follow.

EVALUATION.   Since the IRP has been in effect for several years, there are a number of ways to evaluate its current effectiveness. One useful technique would be to exploit administrative differences or changes in the content or coverage of existing programs with quasi-experimental analytical techniques such as multiple regression or interrupted time-series analysis. Different message formats may well have been used in different years and in different parts of the country. If so, and if similar classes of letter recipients could be identified in each year or region, then differences in response rates to the letters and in tax liability reported the following year (as a measure of compliance) could be tentatively attributed to the different messages.

Alternatively, the fact that notices are sent at different times of the year because of internal processing lags might present another possibility for evaluation of the current program. If groups of taxpayers could be identified who are similar except that some of them received their notices during tax filing season while others received them later in the same year, differences between the groups in tax returns could be used to estimate the compliance effects of timing of the notices (see Klepper and Nagin, Vol. 2, for further discussion).

These basic evaluation designs could be strengthened in several ways: by analyzing specific line items rather than overall tax liability, by comparing outcomes across relatively homogeneous and problematic subgroups of taxpayers, and by supplementing compliance measurements with subsequent in-depth interviews that probe cognitive and emotional responses to receipt of the notices.

REFINING AND PRETESTING.   If the evaluation of current practice suggests that revisions in the notices might improve compliance, then in-depth interviews might suggest promising approaches to revision. A variety of laboratory procedures applied to small samples of taxpayers could be used at low cost in designing and pretesting the most promising revisions. Even though revisions that seem effective when isolated in laboratory settings may not be effective in the taxpayer's everyday life, the principles embodied in the revisions may be useful in designing more effective letters. For example, the results of laboratory experiments could produce tentative findings on whether a letter is more effective in generating compliance if it is more or less personal, if it specifies fines and penalties or just refers to general threats, if it looks more like a bill, a collections notification, or a personal letter.

This laboratory development effort could begin with individual and group discussions with taxpayers about the meaning and affective content of different styles of letters, move to more formalized think-aloud protocol analysis (Carroll, Vol. 2) in which individuals given hypothetical tax problems are asked to comment on how different letters affect their treatment of the problem, and finally conduct small-scale experiments to measure the impact of randomly assigned treatments (e.g., letters) on tax and attitudinal factors related to hypothetical tax problems.

EXPERIMENTAL FIELD TESTING.   Once potentially useful revisions to letters are identified, then the effort could move to the third phase: field experimentation to measure the compliance effect of the revision. Field experiments are especially simple to conduct with computer-generated letters. Once computer programs identifying taxpayers with a suspected tax deficiency are operational, a sample of such taxpayers can be divided randomly into groups that receive different form letters. Items important to the study are recorded for taxpayers in each group, including in particular amounts reported for specific return items on the preceding and following year's tax return, whether and how long before a response is received, the nature of the proposed settlement, and so on. To the extent that the experimental design and timing succeed in assigning sufficient numbers of taxpayers randomly and in preventing systematic contaminating effects, differences between groups in the year-to-year changes in return items can be attributed to the different interventions. By reserving one group as an untreated control, the absolute effect of different notices can be measured as well as the comparative effectiveness of different messages.

Since automated letters are likely to become increasingly important as an enforcement tool and since they are ideally suited for relatively inexpensive field experimentation, refinement and compliance testing could become a permanent compliance research program. A permanent program would provide a basis for occasional revisions to letters made to prevent taxpayers from becoming overly familiar with and unresponsive to particular messages. New ideas could easily be developed and tried experimentally on small populations. More refined experiments could be devised to develop and test notices tailored specifically to different populations, such as urban versus rural dwellers. Effects on attitudes could be tested by adding a survey component to a random subsample of the letters.

POSSIBLE INNOVATIONS.   Experimentation with alternative forms of letters could test hypotheses such as those outlined by Cialdini (Vol. 2) for their relevance to tax compliance behavior and to the effectiveness of ongoing programs. For example, notices of discrepancies might be more effective if they included a personalized touch such as the name of a specific IRS staff member who should receive the taxpayer's response.[2] Different combinations of appeals and threats could be developed. The theory of reciprocity (Cialdini, Vol. 2) suggests that, if the IRS establishes the impression that it is trying to be helpful, the taxpayer may reciprocate with greater diligence in checking the validity of questionable reporting strategies. Other letters could have a stronger implicit threat, such as listing the usual errors associated with transactions that the taxpayer has reported and the number of individuals penalized for each kind of error (if the numbers are likely to convey a threat rather than an opportunity). A customized letter accompanying the package of tax forms and instructions might point to specific instructions that seem pertinent to a taxpayer on the basis of the previous year's return; such a letter might enhance the reputation of the IRS as helpful and knowledgeable and at the same time reduce noncompliance due to ignorance, misinformation, or lack of diligence. Other ideas concerning both letters and the tax form itself are described in Cialdini (Vol. 2).

EXAMPLE 2: REACTIVE INDIVIDUAL TAXPAYER SERVICES
    The mailing of letters and tax forms is proactive, in the sense that the IRS initiates the contact rather than the taxpayer. Tools that are reactive, in the sense that the IRS offers a point of contact but taxpayers initiate the contacts, include responses to telephone inquiries from taxpayers and assistance provided by targeted outreach programs for special taxpayer populations (e.g., elderly or non-English-speaking taxpayers in particular neighborhoods).
    Although experimental strategies are useful for studies of both proactive and reactive interventions, the actual designs for the two types are somewhat different. The difference arises because the IRS or the researcher can select the samples for analyses of proactive interventions, but samples select

themselves for programs that involve reactive interventions. Therefore, for programs involving reactive interventions, the alternative treatments must be defined in terms of what can be controlled—the levels or characteristics of the services offered in randomly selected areas—and the effects are measured by comparing compliance measures for the different areas. We discuss two examples in the following sections: responses to telephone inquiries to IRS taxpayer services offices and special outreach programs targeted to particular taxpayer subgroups.

TELEPHONE INQUIRIES.   To assess the compliance effects of the telephone services program, a field experiment could be designed in which perhaps three pairs of IRS districts are randomly selected and assigned to provide different levels of service (perhaps measured by operators per 1,000 taxpayers). To control costs and to increase the range of options investigated, one pair might maintain its preexisting level of service, the second pair would provide a substantial increase,and the third pair an offsetting decrease. To evaluate the compliance effects of the variations, pre- and postexperiment compliance measures would be compared across the three pairs of districts. The simplest compliance measure to collect would be the year-to-year change in reported tax liability. But more refined measures would involve year-to-year changes in the particular items that are the most frequent subjects of telephone inquiries.

Besides the compliance effects, other effects could be measured as well through extensions of the analysis and the experiment. For example, comparisons by district of the fraction of returns signed by preparers could indicate the extent to which changes in ease of access to IRS telephone services cause taxpayers to switch between IRS and practitioner assistance. Comparisons of the error rates found by IRS error-checking computer programs might provide insights about the kinds of items that are not being satisfactorily handled by telephone services. Finally, to examine the effects of public information campaigns on use of the telephone service, another pair of districts could be randomly selected to receive both the increase in coverage and a media campaign announcing it. As these extensions suggest, one straightforward administrative change in taxpayer services could be evaluated in a number of ways in order to quantify its compliance effects more precisely than they have been to date.

OUTREACH PROGRAMS.   Another reactive program targets special outreach to particular taxpayer subgroups, such as neighborhoods, ethnic associations, non-English-speaking taxpayers, visually impaired taxpayers, and workers in particular plants or workplaces. The IRS has already demonstrated different approaches to conducting these programs, and systematic experimental evaluations could produce information about how the different approaches work in different networks of taxpayers. As with the telephone services, comparisons between experimental areas with special programs and control areas without them provide the basis of evaluation. The difference is that the compliance measures would be computed only for members of the targeted group in the area (e.g., those claiming an exemption for blindness, those sharing a common employer identification number). By combining this experiment with ethnographic observation of the targeted group, more detailed information about information seeking and use as well as comparisons of attitudes, interpretations, and motivations that develop in the experimental and control areas could be analyzed to understand the interaction of social networks and taxpayer service programs in providing information that is relevant to compliance.

EXAMPLE 3: MASS MEDIA CONTACTS

Contacts between taxpayers and the IRS through television, radio, newspapers, and magazines provide many potentially valuable opportunities for compliance research. Such research could also contribute directly to future public affairs campaigns of the sort that are being conducted with the aid of the Advertising Council. For example, an advertising campaign to emphasize normative duties (e.g., "tax evasion is not a victimless crime—it victimizes the good citizen") can be tested on a small scale to determine the effects on individuals. One established research technique brings subjects into the laboratory to watch the evening news, which includes specially designed items spliced into the regular broadcast. The effects of these special news items on attitudes and behavior can be examined through various survey and hypothetical-problem techniques as well as through charting the effect on actual tax returns of groups receiving different treatments.

Cialdini (Vol. 2) has outlined a research program that develops the implications of the psychological principle of commitment/consistency for a public affairs compliance program. The principle, as noted in Chapter 3, suggests emphasizing existing values and commitments of the taxpayer that are consistent with compliance. More specifically, the program would be based on three research phases:

1. Identify established norms and values within the citizenry most associated, conceptually, with taxpayer compliance. Paired-comparison

or multidimensional scaling techniques are suggested to probe these relations.

2. Focus attention on the existence of the most salient norms and values.
3. Increase the salience of these values to taxpaying behavior and sensitize taxpayers to the inconsistency between personal commitment to these norms and failure to report taxes honestly.

Cialdini suggests that a National Tax Test television program aired during the filing season might provide an effective means to accomplish the latter two goals. Since the IRS participated in seven television and four radio clinics in 1985 and has been producing instructional videocassettes for some time, this suggestion simply calls for keeping compliance effects in mind while producing such shows. One experiment demonstrated that a television quiz program designed to focus viewers on the link between their personal commitment to certain values (e.g., freedom) and their current beliefs and behaviors could produce long-term behavioral effects (Ball-Rokeach, Rokeach, and Grube, 1984, cited in Cialdini, Vol. 2); uninterrupted viewing of this single program increased the contributions to causes consistent with the values even two to three months after the program had been aired. Laboratory and field experimentation with a national tax test program, or perhaps several programs designed for different audiences, could be readily designed to test for attitudinal and compliance effects.

Of course, the success of such approaches depends on their not being seen as manipulative. Otherwise they may provoke counterreactions to what may be perceived as improper activities for a government agency. Furthermore, the possibility of adverse effects on particular subpopulations must be carefully considered in drawing experimental samples and evaluating effects, since in our pluralistic society values that appeal to one group may be anathema to others.

Finally, the importance of other methods of communication should not be overlooked simply because mass media are more immediately available. Studies of a number of programs reviewed by Tyler and Lavrakas (1985) found that public programs that stimulate communication in informal networks are more effective in changing individual behavior than programs intended to influence behavior directly. For example, mass media programs appear to be less effective than efforts by existing community organizations in altering personal beliefs about how the crime problem is connected to an individual's fears and behavior (Tyler, 1986). Nonetheless, the media campaigns accompanying state tax amnesty programs have generated considerable interest in using the media and should be evaluated for potential compliance effects. And IRS efforts to develop a more proactive public affairs program should be accompanied by research to identify potentially counterproductive campaigns.

Notes

1. Analyzing the relationship between changes in practitioner use and compliance may be a problem for which survey self-reports are the only practicable way to measure compliance. Audits to measure compliance might trigger a shift in practitioner use. Compliance measures obtained from changes in return items (see Schwartz and Orleans, 1967) would confound compliance effects with other effects that a newly engaged practitioner might have on the return. Compliance measurement is discussed in Chapter 5.
2. At least one state revenue agency uses this approach with its notices of discrepancies between state and federal income tax returns.

5. Data Needs for Taxpayer Compliance Research

In this chapter we present recommendations for improving the data that are needed for taxpayer compliance research and for protecting the rights of taxpayers on whom research data are assembled. Much of the empirical research recommended in previous chapters requires measures of compliance that are linked to measures of explanatory variables—factors that, theory or evidence suggests, may influence individuals' compliance with federal income tax laws. Examples of explanatory variables include personal values and attitudes related to compliance, expectations of the risks and rewards of compliance and noncompliance, previous experience with tax law enforcement, and elements of taxpayers' environments.

Large, complex data bases containing records of compliance measures and explanatory variables have been essential in building what knowledge exists about taxpayer compliance, and they will no doubt continue to play an important role. In this chapter we examine four types of data bases that have been widely used in compliance research to date: the Taxpayer Compliance Measurement Program, taxpayer surveys, an aggregate cross-sectional file, and experimentally generated data bases in which compliance effects are measured as changes in tax return items. Because each type has its own strengths and weaknesses, the types are complementary rather than competitive. All four should continue to be useful in future compliance research, but there are a number of ways in which their research value and their accessibility to researchers could be improved.

Summary of Compliance Research Data Recommendations

To enhance the value of these four approaches to data collection, the panel makes six recommendations:

1. To expand the research uses of TCMP, we recommend that the IRS consider modifying the TCMP check sheet to include a more detailed description of the preparer who signs the return, information on others whose advice may have affected the return, information on the taxpayer's primary and secondary occupation and industry, and information on the issues underlying changes the auditor recommends on the return.

2. To improve the timeliness of DIF development, compliance research, and analyses of the effects of legislative and administrative changes, we recommend that the IRS formally consider restructuring TCMP from a three-year cycle to an annual or a biennial cycle (with a corresponding fraction of the entire sample audited in each year) and search for ways to reduce the three- to four-year delay in file development.

3. To enhance the value of taxpayer surveys for researchers and tax administrators, we recommend that the IRS and others who undertake surveys expand their research focus—to include the relationships between values, perceptions, and compliance; to give greater emphasis to the processes, circumstances, and events in the tax career that affect the relevant values and perceptions; and to provide more resources for the replication of findings.

4. To strengthen the foundations of survey research on taxpayer compliance, we recommend a research program to improve the interpretation of self-reports of noncompliance and to ascertain whether and how the specificity and validity of those reports can be improved through the randomized response technique, innovations in questionnaire design, and repeated interviews.

5. As a possible basis for more current information about the ripple effects of IRS enforcement and administrative activity, including general deterrence, we recommend that the 1969 aggregate cross-sectional data base (Project 778) be updated and refined, if the reliability of the compliance measure can be demonstrated for a more recent year.

6. To provide a basis for stronger inferences about the compliance effects of innovations in tax administration, we recommend that the IRS and external researchers increase their use of randomized experiments in both field and laboratory settings.

Taxpayer compliance research raises very difficult questions about how to produce useful knowledge without jeopardizing taxpayer privacy, other generally accepted rights of research subjects, and the IRS mission. To deal with these matters, the panel recommends long-term cooperative efforts— involving the IRS and the broad research community—in three areas:

1. To develop and implement policies governing access by researchers to compliance research data, especially external use of sensitive IRS data;

2. To develop and implement policies to foster compliance research within the IRS that uses the most methodologically sound research techniques, including randomized experiments where needed to address problems in tax administration, while protecting research subjects from unfair burdens and risks; and

3. To formally and thoroughly consider the feasibility and desirability of arranging for the deposit of sensitive IRS data in an independent secure repository.

A standing authority on protection of research subjects should be established to interpret and monitor the policies and arrangements in light of evolving research ideas, changes in compliance requirements and forms of noncompliance, innovations in tax administration, and advances in statistical matching techniques.

Even if these recommendations are implemented, they will not eliminate certain intrinsic weaknesses in each of the four data collection approaches. The panel therefore carefully considered several more intrusive and costly measurement approaches, including audits of several previous tax returns at one time, preaudit surveys or experimental interventions with taxpayers selected for TCMP audits, and linkages of survey respondents' self-reports of noncompliance to the results of auditing their tax returns. Many efforts of this sort would no doubt yield important intellectual and administrative benefits. But they also raise extremely sensitive issues: taxpayer privacy, the balance between benefits for researchers and tax administrators and burdens on respondents, and the security of administrative data that the IRS believes it must hold confidential.

The panel believes it is feasible at this time to link survey responses to tax return and audit data without compromising either taxpayers' rights or the IRS mission, and this approach is needed for several of the illustrative projects described in Chapter 4. But we stop short of recommending specific projects that involve either multiyear audits or preaudit contacts with the TCMP sample. This is because the trade-offs between additions to knowledge and risks to subjects will differ from one project to the next and the methods available for resolving the trade-offs will improve over time. Since these contingencies cannot be precisely anticipated, the panel believes that a permanent mechanism is needed to facilitate judgments about projects involving the development of sensitive data bases in an open forum under public guidelines. Providing such a forum would be one function of the Compliance Research Advisory Group that we recommend in Chapter 6.

The next section provides a brief discussion of the characteristics of the four types of data base used in research on taxpayer compliance. Then four sections explain more fully our recommendations concerning each of the four types of data base. The remainder of the chapter discusses the issues involved in protecting research subjects when collecting data for taxpayer compliance research.

Characteristics of Data Bases Used for Compliance Research

Four types of data bases, which have been widely used in research on individual compliance with the federal income tax reporting requirements, relate compliance measures to explanatory variables; the four types require significant resources to construct.[1]

1. *The Taxpayer Compliance Measurement Program survey of individual returns filed.* TCMP cycles are conducted by the IRS, usually every three years, most recently for tax year 1985. Each recent cycle included comprehensive audits of a random sample of approximately 50,000 taxpayers. Each taxpayer's TCMP record contains line-by-line values for each return item, as reported by the taxpayer and as corrected by the auditor (see Chapter 1, Supplementary Note B). Although only federal employees and contractors have been allowed access to individual records from a complete TCMP cycle, tabulations and partial samples have been provided to researchers.[2]

2. *Taxpayer surveys.* Several taxpayer surveys (e.g., Mason, Calvin, and Faulkenberry, 1975; Aitken and Bonneville, 1980; Westat, Inc., 1980f; Yankelovich et al., 1984) using samples ranging from 500 to 2,000 respondents have recorded taxpayers' reports of failures to file or to report taxable income accurately in previous years, along with a broad range of demographic, socioeconomic, experiential, and attitudinal explanatory variables. Most of these surveys have also included reports of previous contacts with enforcement authorities. Access to these files is not specially restricted.

3. *Aggregate cross-sectional file.* Only one such file (known within the IRS as Project 778) has been constructed (for tax year 1969), and it has been analyzed by the IRS (1978a) and independent researchers (Witte and Woodbury, 1984, 1985; Dubin and Wilde, 1988; Beron, Tauchen, and Witte, 1988). For each three-digit zip code area, the file contains an

estimate of the voluntary compliance level, measures of IRS administrative and enforcement activity in preceding years, and some socioeconomic data, which have been augmented by the independent researchers (see Chapter 1, Supplementary Note B, for more detail).

4. *Experimentally generated data bases.* If a randomized experiment is conducted that involves an intervention with a treatment group and nonintervention with a control group, then the compliance effect of the intervention can be estimated by comparing tax returns before and after the intervention. Differences between the treatment and control groups in the year-to-year changes in return items can be attributed to compliance effects of the intervention if the randomization succeeds in removing all other systematic differences. To avoid releasing records of individual tax returns to researchers outside the IRS, the necessary tabulations can be provided for the treatment and control groups and for subgroups of particular interest. This approach was used by Schwartz and Orleans (1967).

Each of these types of data base has different strengths and weaknesses for taxpayer compliance research. For example, a strength of taxpayer surveys is that they can capture a broad range of explanatory variables known only to respondents; among the most important are understandings of compliance requirements, relevant values and attitudes, expectations of risks and benefits of compliance and noncompliance, and details of events and circumstances that affect taxpayers' willingness to comply and ability to conceal noncompliance. In contrast, TCMP is limited to explanatory variables that can be inferred from the tax return, aggregate cross-sectional files are limited to area descriptors that have been compiled for the same geographic units, and experimentally generated data are limited to randomized interventions as explanatory variables unless the experiment is supplemented by a survey.

An advantage of TCMP is that it readily provides compliance measures disaggregated to the level of return items. For many income components, TCMP compliance measures are considered relatively accurate. For others, however—especially those not subject to withholding or information reporting or difficult to compute, such as business and farm income and rents and royalties—auditors' oversights and misinterpretations of compliance requirements introduce substantial errors into compliance measures.

Another advantage of TCMP is that it captures noncompliance of which even the taxpayer is unaware. At best, survey self-reports of noncompliance can capture only misstatements that are recognized and remembered by respondents. Self-reports are also subject to some distortion by respondents who wish to conceal their illegal behavior from interviewers. To reduce respondents' sensitivity, survey researchers have refrained from even attempting to capture noncompliance measures at the level of specific return items.

All four methods fail in different ways to adequately support research on the determinants of taxpayer compliance. Since a taxpayer's TCMP record contains no information on previous sanctions or on sanction risk, TCMP data must be supplemented with other information to facilitate analysis of these relationships.[3] Conceptually, experiments in which legally permissible sanctions are randomly imposed on noncompliant taxpayers could produce the most clear-cut findings about how sanctions affect subsequent taxpaying behavior—but ethical and political concerns obviously restrict the use of this strategy with punitive sanctions. The aggregate cross-sectional data base that contains estimated compliance measures for the tax year 1969 also contains rates per 1,000 returns of IRS audits and criminal investigations in prior years, and these data have been used to study general deterrence or ripple effects of IRS activity on aggregate compliance levels. However, as noted in Chapter 2, the results of these analyses are extremely sensitive to the model specifications, the accuracy of the compliance measure has been questioned, and the per capita rates of IRS activity may not be appropriate estimates of the sanction risks faced by noncompliant tax-payers. Taxpayer surveys offer the best opportunity to construct the explanatory variables associated with sanction risks: perceived probabilities and severity of punishment, the sources of information on which these perceptions are based, and even the taxpayer's version of how changes in these perceptions would change later behavior. However, concerns about the accuracy of self-reports about compliance should limit one's confidence in survey-based inferences about how sanction risks affect taxpaying behavior.

In short, none of these four data collection approaches by itself is likely to produce definitive findings about how taxpayer compliance is affected by changes in the probabilities and severity of sanctions for noncompliance. Solid insights about those relationships are likely to accumulate only as future analyses of all four types of data begin to produce consistent or reconcilable results.

The preceding discussion about sanctions and compliance suggests two general points. First, all four types of data discussed here are of some value in taxpayer compliance research, and certain innovations would enhance the ability of each type to support future studies. The sections that follow suggest specific enhancements for TCMP and for taxpayer surveys, recommend exploratory work toward updating the 1969 aggregate cross-sectional file, and advocate expanded efforts to generate compliance research data bases through randomized experiments.

Second, the partially offsetting strengths and weaknesses of the four data collection approaches suggest that marriages of techniques could have enormous benefits for the understanding of compliance. For example, through a preaudit survey of TCMP respondents, one could learn about differences between auditors' and taxpayers' concepts of compliance and about the validity of self-reports as a compliance measure. A data base generated in this way would also be a powerful tool for estimating how compliance is affected by the perceptions, values, and circumstances that taxpayers report to interviewers. As another example, if subjects in a randomized experiment were surveyed and the survey responses linked to the two years of returns needed as outcome measures, then it might be possible to learn how overall compliance effects of interventions are moderated by the taxpayer characteristics collected in the surveys. In-depth ethnographic observation of taxpayers who were subject to interventions (a data source that is not a focus of this chapter) could provide even richer information about how the intervention affected behavior and about how taxpayers exchange information about experiences relevant to taxpaying.

These approaches could greatly enrich knowledge about factors related to taxpayer compliance. However, they also raise problems of protecting research subjects from undue burdens and risks, protecting the privacy of tax returns, and maintaining the security of the TCMP data base, which the IRS considers essential to its mission. Because of concern about these issues, the panel stopped short of recommending several promising research ideas that use these approaches, although there was support for each of them. Instead, in the conclusion to this chapter, the issues surrounding those approaches are explained more fully, and the panel recommends that procedures be developed and implemented for resolving them on a case-by-case basis in the future.

Enhancing Data Bases for Compliance Research

The following sections are addressed primarily to the IRS Research Division. The first two sections recommend specific changes to two ongoing programs of the IRS Research Division: TCMP and the series of taxpayer surveys. The next sections recommend that the 1969 aggregate cross-sectional file be updated if a valid compliance measure can be developed and that the IRS adopt, whenever feasible, strategies for expanded use of randomized experiments to assess the effects of innovations and administrative modifications on taxpayer compliance.

MODIFICATIONS TO TCMP

As explained in Chapter 1, the Taxpayer Compliance Measurement Program is conducted primarily to support development of a Discriminant Index Function system for selecting tax returns for audit.[4] Administratively, the large cost of a TCMP cycle ($127 million for the 1985 cycle) is justified by the improvements in audit selection efficiency made possible by the DIF system. However, as a by-product, TCMP data have also been used in compliance research, for example, to estimate the revenue gap due to noncompliance (see, e.g., IRS, 1983f) and to support creation of the 1969 cross-sectional data base. The panel believes that without adding substantially to the cost of TCMP, it is possible to make TCMP data available on a more timely basis and to increase the capacity of the data to support important lines of compliance research.

To make TCMP data available on a more timely basis for resource allocation and compliance research, the panel recommends that the IRS seriously consider the feasibility of restructuring the program from a three-year cycle to an annual or biennial one, so that one-half or one-third of the sample is audited each year. We also recommend that the IRS reexamine its procedures for administering TCMP, with a view toward reducing the delay between return filing and data base completion. These steps would substantially increase the value of TCMP to legislators and tax administrators who are concerned about how their actions affect compliance and might reduce the chances that audit resources are allocated according to obsolete DIF rules.

The panel also believes that the following three changes in the TCMP would greatly expand the research uses of TCMP data without adding significantly to program cost, taxpayer burden, or processing time. We therefore recommend that these changes be undertaken in future cycles of TCMP:

1. The TCMP check sheet should be redesigned to contain more detailed codes describing the preparers who sign returns. It should also collect information about other third parties, including tax practitioners, whose advice may affect the accuracy of the filed return.

2. The TCMP should use standard Department of Labor or Census

Bureau codes to record information about taxpayers' primary and secondary occupations and industries.

3. Agents conducting TCMP audits should record the issues underlying changes they recommend on returns, provided a useful set of explanatory codes can be developed.

These recommendations are developed in more detail in the following pages.

IMPROVING THE TIMELINESS OF TCMP. As explained in Chapter 1, TCMP data support three important objectives of tax administration and taxpayer compliance research: to develop DIF rules to select returns for audit, to measure taxpayer compliance, and to support taxpayer compliance research. The panel is concerned that data obsolescence reduces the ability of the program to support these objectives.

TCMP operates in three-year cycles, most recently for tax years 1982, 1985, and 1988. Each cycle requires three to four years after returns are filed to select the sample, complete the audits, and develop the data base. This schedule frequently has unfortunate consequences. As of this writing, for example, the most recent TCMP data available even within the IRS relate to tax year 1982. Consequently, statements here and elsewhere about compliance trends over the past six years depend on projections whose underlying assumptions cannot be tested. As another example, the 1985 TCMP cycle will be the first to reflect any compliance effects of the 1982 Tax Equity and Fiscal Responsibility Act; the data are not expected to be ready for analyses of the compliance effects of that law until 1989. Although such analyses will be of historical interest to legislators and tax administrators and will have some implications for testing theory, the timing guarantees that they will have limited practical applicability because the Tax Reform Act of 1986 has altered compliance requirements and enforcement tools substantially. For similar reasons, not even the first stage of TRA86 implementation (in tax year 1987) will be reflected in DIF-based selection rules before 1992, when the formulas can first be updated on the basis of 1988 TCMP data. The costs of audit selection errors due to the use of outdated DIF formulas in the meantime may be substantial.

To reduce the problems associated with out-of-date TCMP data, the panel believes that serious consideration should be given to permanently restructuring TCMP to annual or biennial cycles. If it is desirable to hold TCMP costs roughly constant, samples one-third or one-half the current size could be audited each year. One advantage of shorter cycles would be the ability to provide more timely estimates of compliance trends and of compliance effects of legislative and administrative changes (albeit with greater sampling error). There may also be advantages for TCMP administration, since TCMP audits would become an ongoing activity within the Examination Division, rather than a cyclical project seen as a diversion from routine activities.

It may seem to some that this approach could occasionally cause some TCMP audits to be wasted from the standpoint of DIF development. If substantial legislation were enacted between the two years of a biennial cycle, for example, the first half-sample might include taxpayers subject to laws so different from those in the second half-sample that the two should not be combined in developing a DIF rule for future use. However, in these circumstances a full sample audit at the first point in time would necessarily have produced a DIF formula that would be misleading after the legislation. Moreover, tax law changes ordinarily affect the behavior of most taxpayers so slightly that the biases from combining the samples could be ignored in many if not all audit classes. Even when the biases must be recognized, the biennial cycle expands the choices available to the IRS. Either it can continue to select returns using DIF rules developed before the legislation (as it must under current practice), or it can use the second half-sample to develop new DIF formulas. The new formulas will describe behavior under the appropriate laws, but sampling error will be larger than if the entire sample were available. The choice between the old and new DIF rules can be based on their performance in pilot tests.[5]

This recommendation involves greater changes in existing procedures than do the panel's other recommendations for improving TCMP. Its implementation should therefore be considered especially carefully before action is taken—a responsibility that might be entrusted to an ad hoc specialized working group that includes experts from inside and outside the IRS or to the Compliance Research Advisory Group that this report contemplates (see Chapter 6). The panel believes that the costs associated with this transition, although substantial, are justified both by the more current DIF selection rules and by the more timely information that would result about compliance trends and how they are affected by legislative and administrative innovations.

INFORMATION ABOUT PRACTITIONER USE.   As indicated in previous chapters, understanding the relationships between practitioner use and compliance should receive a high priority in future research. TCMP identifies only practitioners who prepare and therefore sign returns and provides less detail about the type of preparer now than in tax year 1979. In that cycle, the TCMP classified third-party preparers into thirteen categories. Beginning with the 1982 cycle, TCMP check sheets record only whether a paid preparer signed the return, and there are no plans to record more detail in future cycles.

Differences in compliance across the thirteen categories of preparers were reported in Table 9 (Chapter 3). Plausible explanations of these differences are suggested by Klepper and Nagin (1987b) and in Chapter 3. Moreover, preliminary findings by Klepper and Nagin (1987b) suggest that different types of preparers adjusted quite differently to recent changes in the Pennsylvania state tax laws. Thus it should be especially revealing to be able to compare compliance by clients of different types of preparers following enactment of the Tax Reform Act of 1986. While it is clear that more detail is needed, it is not necessarily true that the 1979 classification system is best. That system may not tap the most pertinent preparer attributes or may require information that many taxpayers will be unable to provide accurately to the TCMP auditors. Therefore, the panel recommends that the IRS—in consultation with the Compliance Research Advisory Group or an ad hoc working group that includes researchers and tax practitioners—develop a more detailed preparer classification scheme for future TCMP check sheets. It would also be desirable for this group to participate in pretesting and monitoring future use of this scheme.

This step alone will not support analyses of how practitioners who do not prepare returns affect compliance through the advice they provide about the meaning of the tax law and about possible outcomes of various strategies for maximizing after-tax income. Therefore, along with developing a more detailed classification system for preparers, the IRS should consider how categories of advisers might also be recorded on the TCMP check sheet. One feasible approach may be to ask whether anyone (other than a preparer who signed the return) provided specific advice or information that was used in preparing the return and, if so, to determine and code the status of that party.

DATA ON TAXPAYER OCCUPATION AND INDUSTRY. As indicated in previous chapters, there are many reasons to expect taxpayers' compliance to depend in part on their sources of income. The visibility of income to the IRS is affected by how income is earned and by various characteristics of those with whom a taxpayer does business (see Kagan, Vol. 2, for a discussion of these issues). Business associates, friends, and neighbors may also encourage or discourage compliance. Not only do they send normative messages, but they also provide information (or misinformation) about compliance requirements and the likely practical consequences of compliance and non-compliance. We have, however, little systematic knowledge about the influence of such factors. The panel recommends that the IRS facilitate quantitative research into such issues by recording more information on TCMP check sheets about taxpayers' occupations and industries.

Currently TCMP examiners code principal occupation, as reported on the return and as corrected, into three-digit IRS categories for all taxpayers and record industry for farms and small businesses indicated on Schedule F or C. At least three modifications to these procedures seem worth considering. First, to facilitate comparisons with data from other resources, the IRS should consider replacing its coding schemes for occupation and industry with standard Department of Labor or Census Bureau coding schemes.

Second, with respect to occupation, it would be useful to probe all TCMP respondents for secondary income-producing activities in addition to their principal occupations. These activities are less likely than principal occupations to be subject to withholding or information reporting and may therefore be more likely than principal occupations to be involved in noncompliance. Although some noncompliant taxpayers would no doubt conceal their secondary income sources, collecting and recording information about them during the TCMP audit would facilitate testing some hypotheses about the relationships between secondary occupations and compliance for a broader segment of taxpayers.

Third, to enhance the ability of TCMP to support research on the compliance effects of income visibility and occupational associates, it would be useful to record the taxpayer's nature of business or employer's industry. This is already coded directly for taxpayers who file Schedule C or F. To provide comparable information for other taxpayers, it would be useful to record the industries of their primary employers. This recommendation is motivated by the fact that knowledge of both the industry and occupation may be needed to understand compliance. Workers in some industries or occupations may have different attitudes toward risk than others. Even when motivations are identical, tax environments may differ in ways that affect the probability that noncompliance would be detected. Salespeople in retail stores, for example, may be less able to successfully claim unwarranted business expense adjustments than are salespeople who travel to customers' offices; similarly, free-lance writers and editors are likely to receive income in less visible ways and to face different compliance obligations (e.g., maintaining records of business expenses and filing quarterly estimated tax returns) than those employed by large organizations. Thus, from the standpoints of income visibility and of complexity, both the occupation and the industry are key parts of the taxpayer's environment.

Detailed recommendations about how to code and verify such information would best be made either by the Compliance Research Advisory Group or an ad hoc group representing the relevant units within IRS, the taxpayer compliance research community, and economists and statisticians who produce and use occupational data in other contexts. This group could also design pretests of the system and monitor its use in future TCMP cycles.

RECORDING ISSUES IN RETURN ITEM CHANGES.   In TCMP data, a recommended change—the difference between the values of a return item as reported by the taxpayer and as recommended by the auditor—may occur for many reasons, only some of which reflect noncompliance. Some changes stem from disputes over unsettled legal issues or from misclassifications of income that do not affect tax liability at all. Even when noncompliance occurs it may result from careless record keeping, good-faith but rejected interpretations of close legal questions, intentional fraud, or other causes. As noted by Kidder and McEwen (Vol. 2), these different forms of potential noncompliance occur through different taxpaying processes and are likely to be explained by different theories. TCMP's usefulness for testing these theories would be greatly enhanced if recorded changes were supplemented by a brief statement of the reasons for them. In turn, this knowledge could alert legislators and tax administrators to features of legislation, regulations, instructions, and forms that may be contributing to noncompliance.

The panel recommends that the IRS develop and test TCMP procedures to record auditors' reasons for changes to return items. Ideally the taxpayer's justification for the initial return item would also be recorded if it could be collected. To facilitate both recording and later analysis a scheme for coding the taxpayer's and auditor's positions, perhaps the scheme already developed by the IRS general counsel, should be used. While total coverage of TCMP audits is desirable, a sample approach might be a more feasible way to start. Recommendations about these and other details are best made by the Compliance Research Advisory Group or an ad hoc group that represents IRS, taxpayer, tax practitioner, and research perspectives. Such a group could then be involved in testing the system, revising it if needed, and monitoring its use in future TCMP cycles.

IMPROVING TAXPAYER SURVEYS

As explained in Chapter 2, samples of the taxpaying population have been surveyed about taxpaying many times over the past fifteen years. Some of the surveys were commissioned by the IRS (e.g., Aitken and Bonneville, 1980; Westat, Inc., 1980f; Yankelovich et al., 1984), and others have been conducted by scholars independently of the IRS (e.g., Grasmick and Bryjak, 1980; Mason and Calvin, 1977, 1984). One common purpose of most of these surveys has been to study empirical relationships between self-reports of noncompliance and various personal characteristics and attitudes. This line of research can be expected to continue in the future.

In general, when statistically significant relationships have been reported, they correspond with expectations based on theory and common sense. For example, compared with other respondents, those who admit previous noncompliance tend to express less fear that noncompliance will be detected, less moral commitment to taxpaying, less support of government, and less fear of social disapproval.

Many methodological problems with this work (discussed in Chapter 2 and in Klepper and Nagin, Vol. 2) stem from the possibility that probes about previous illegal behavior are threatening to respondents, who are likely to refuse to answer or to distort their answers. According to several psychological theories, survey respondents are also likely to report attitudes and perspectives that are consistent with their reported behavior. And like surveys generally, these are subject to lapses of respondents' memories. These problems preclude confident and precise statements about the magnitudes of the relationships between self-reports and reported attitudes and perceptions. Until progress is made on these methodological problems, taxpayer surveys seem unlikely to yield more definitive statements about these relationships.

Therefore, rather than simply collecting and analyzing additional survey data of the kind accumulated in the past, the panel recommends research that emphasizes:

1. Understanding the processes, circumstances, and events in people's taxpaying careers that account for variations in relevant perceptions and attitudes and in compliance behavior; and
2. Interpreting self-reports of noncompliance and assessing and improving their specificity and validity.

These issues are explained in more detail below.

UNDERSTANDING TAXPAYING CAREERS AND COMPLIANCE.   The panel urges survey researchers to address questions about the processes, circumstances, and events that help shape risk perceptions and other attitudes related to tax compliance. The kinds of questions that should be explored cover a wide range of issues. For example, we need to know more about how taxpayers form their perceptions of what the tax law requires, what the consequences are of different ways of structuring and reporting financial transactions, and what the taxpaying practices of friends and acquaintances are like. Researchers should also try to learn how taxpayers interpret such information and adapt it to their own circumstances (e.g., the visibility of their income sources, their expenditure patterns, and the nature of their financial transactions) and how they use this information in managing their own taxpaying. Little is known about how people attempt to satisfy complex, burdensome requirements—when they seek assistance, what shortcuts they take, and when they give up. There are theories of how compliant or noncompliant values are acquired and changed but little empirical confirmation. Childhood socialization experiences with withholding and refunds as teenagers or young adults, discussions with friends or business acquaintances, reactions to experiences with the IRS, and interaction with advisers or return preparers may all play a role in inculcating relevant values. We also know little about the events that cause taxpayers to question their tax-related assumptions, practices, and values. Are reexaminations prompted by changes in personal or financial circumstances, by events that trigger comparisons to others' behavior or circumstances, by news about taxes or the IRS, or by advice from other taxpayers, practitioners, or the IRS?

Survey methods are useful for studying such processes in large samples. Detailed information about pertinent circumstances, events, and taxpayer actions are extremely unlikely to be recorded in any administrative data bases. Respondents should be less sensitive to questions about these matters than to questions about previous noncompliance. Although surveys rarely capture the richness of detail of ethnographic studies and so cannot substitute for them, they are more feasible to carry out within short time frames with sizable samples from multiple populations.

Compared with previous surveys, the studies we recommend here would place more emphasis on explaining taxpayers' (mis)understandings of compliance requirements, (mis)perceptions of risks and benefits of failing to satisfy those requirements, and moral evaluations of specific noncompliant actions. They would seek more information on a variety of topics: sources of income (e.g., to assess its visibility); types of expenditures (e.g., to ascertain characteristics of specific adjustments and deductions that may affect perceived audit risks); amount of wealth (e.g., to ascertain financial ability to participate in tax shelters); childhood experiences related to obeying rules and seeking risks; early experiences with tax withholding, filing, and refunds; significant recent changes in income levels and sources and other aspects of financial status; experiences with taking shortcuts in taxpaying and other compliance contexts; contacts and disputes with the IRS and the lessons learned from them; sources of information about compliance requirements and their sensitivity to changes in the tax law; events that lead respondents to reassess what they know or to seek new information about taxpaying requirements and practices; and events that affect taxpayers' opinions about the legitimacy or efficiency of government.

These surveys should probably not strive for representative samples of the general population but rather should overrepresent groups of special interest, such as workers in occupations that are especially conducive to noncompliance or that present special taxpaying problems. Panel studies, that is, reinterviews of the same people over time, may be useful in exploring the stability of perceptions and attitudes and in identifying causal relationships. In particular, since some sample members will experience IRS contacts in the normal course of events, successful longitudinal designs will permit researchers to distinguish the effects of contact with the IRS on perceptions of the risks associated with noncompliance (Paternoster et al., 1982a) and on attitudes concerning the legitimacy of the IRS.

IMPROVING SURVEY-BASED COMPLIANCE MEASURES.   Valid survey-based measures could offer a valuable complement to audit-based measures in compliance research. But existing survey-based measures are subject to question on grounds of validity and lack of specificity. The panel therefore recommends a research program to improve the validity and specificity of survey-based measures of compliance and noncompliance. This program should include pilot tests using specific probes about the nature of previous noncompliance; it should experiment with the randomized response technique for asking sensitive questions; and it should study how self-reports of noncompliance are affected by repeated interviewing. Comparisons between self-report and audit-based measures of individuals would be desirable if taxpayer privacy can be protected. The results of such a program would provide useful guidance on the appropriate use of survey techniques in future compliance research.

Need for the program. Survey-based compliance measures offer a potentially valuable complement to measures based on audits. They can be linked to a broad range of explanatory variables without raising the privacy concerns associated with tax returns and audit results. They may provide better information than audits on unreported income not subject to withholding or information reporting. They may identify instances in which revenue agents' errors during audits lead to unfounded records of noncompliance. Since repeated interviews are less likely than repeated audits to change taxpayer compliance behavior, survey-based measures are likely to be more useful for studying compliance responses over time to changes in circumstances and for studying the direction of causality between noncompliance and perceived detection risk.

Surveys are likely, however, to miss various forms of noncompliance that audits capture. Surveys cannot capture errors of which respondents are unaware or instances of noncompliance that they have forgotten. Special questions may be needed to elicit reports of incidents the respondent defines as differences of opinion with the IRS rather than instances of noncompliance. Perhaps most important, taxpayers may distort reports of their taxpaying behavior because they do not want to admit to illegal activity or because they desire to report behavior that is consistent with reported attitudes.

Survey-based noncompliance measures have to date been much less specific than audit-based measures, about both the nature of identified noncompliance and when it occurred, probably because researchers expect respondents to feel less threatened by vague questions. Instead of probing for details that might offer more insight into taxpaying behavior, surveys have probed only for the general form of noncompliance practiced (e.g., underreporting income, overclaiming deductions, or failing to file). In addition, survey researchers have nearly always asked about instances of noncompliance over a long period (e.g., "ever" or "within the past five years") rather than in a specific year.

The potential errors and vagueness in survey-based compliance measurement have had at least four undesirable effects. First, they have created possibilities for misinterpretations of the data. For example, even though the attitudes captured by measures of moral commitment or fear of punishment may not limit evasion but simply make people reluctant to admit to it, survey data suggest that these factors discourage evasion.

Second, because probes for noncompliance are usually vague about amounts of tax liability involved, it is usually impossible to restrict the analysis to instances involving large amounts of tax liability. Indeed to reduce respondent sensitivity and secure a large enough pool of admitted evaders for multivariate analysis, probes for noncompliance usually include the phrase "even by a small amount." Therefore, analysts must lump to-gether trivial incidents with substantial ones, even though large and small misreports may have quite different causes as well as consequences for the tax gap.

Third, the vagueness of survey questions has limited the kinds of ques-tions they can address. For example, without information about the nature of reported noncompliance (e.g., the source of unreported income), it is difficult to test directly hypotheses about the compliance effects of income visibility or changes in taxpayers' family circumstances. The long reference periods for survey questions about noncompliance have also precluded studies of some important matters that involve sequences of events—for example, the extent to which perceptions of low detection risk are an effect rather than a cause of noncompliance.

Fourth, vague or lengthy time frames also make it difficult to compare compliance patterns in survey data with compliance patterns in audit data, which have clear one-year reference periods because they concern particular returns. Not surprisingly (as reported in Chapter 1), when comparable survey and audit data do exist, there are substantial discrepancies in preva-lence estimates for noncompliance. In the one study that matched survey- and audit-based measures for a sample of individuals, the correlation was essentially nil (Hessing, Elffers, and Weigel, 1986).

Despite the problems that have characterized most surveys of tax compliance, surveys are potentially a valuable tool in understanding com-pliance, and the panel recommends concerted efforts to improve survey-based measures of compliance and to study their relationships to audit-based measures. We have not attempted to specify a complete program to refine survey-based compliance measures, but three developmental efforts, each involving pilot tests of different questionnaire designs and interview approaches, should be components of any such program:

1. Experimentation with randomized response techniques for probing respondents about previous noncompliance;
2. Experimentation with questions that are more specific with respect to amounts, types of income, and expenditures; and
3. Experimentation with repeated interviews of subjects about com-pliance and related tax matters.

These developmental efforts all aim at learning how response rates and results are affected by different approaches to framing questions, by differ-ent approaches to informing subjects about the research they are asked to participate in, and by different levels of respondent burden. They also promise improvements in data quality, which will permit a better understanding of the relationships between survey-based and audit-based measures of compliance, a relationship that has never been systematically studied in this country.[6] The three developmental efforts are described more fully in the following paragraphs. While these three programs certainly do not exhaust the list of useful methodological studies that should be undertaken, they would provide valuable information for assessing the most appropriate roles for survey techniques in future taxpayer compliance research.

Randomized response technique. Two special survey techniques—the locked box and the randomized response—are in common use to reduce sensitivity to potentially incriminating (or embarrassing) questions.[7] Of these the randomized response technique seems more promising for taxpayer compliance research, because randomized responses can be used in multivariate analyses and because compliance statistics obtained in this way in one pilot test (Aitken and Bonneville, 1980) could be reconciled with TCMP statistics. Further testing is needed, however, before the technique can be firmly recommended.

In one version of the randomized response technique, the interviewer presents the respondent both the sensitive question (e.g., "Did you fail to report all your tip income on last year's tax return?") and a nonsensitive alternative for which the answers have a known probability distribution (e.g., "Were you born in December?" for which the distribution is 1/12 "Yes" and 11/12 "No"). The respondent is then instructed to use a randomizing technique such as flipping a coin to select which question to answer. Although no one can tell which respondents admitted to noncompliance, the fraction of any subsample that did so can be estimated.

The randomized response technique has several properties that make it potentially useful in survey research on taxpayer compliance. Respondents are expected to be more truthful because they feel protected by the randomization, and this expectation was supported in one study (Aitken and Bonneville, 1980; but see Habib, 1980). The randomized response technique can be used with questions that require numerical rather than yes/no answers. Randomized responses also can be used as dependent variables in multivariate analyses (Fox and Tracy, 1986). Finally, because the technique creates no records in which reports of illegal behavior are linked to specific individuals, it reduces the need for administrative confidentiality safeguards on the survey file as well as more general concerns about putting research subjects at risk. In fact, a presidentially appointed Privacy Protection Study

Commission (1977) recommended use of the technique to protect respondents' privacy. The major drawback of the technique is that it increases the sample size needed to achieve a given precision level.

Because the randomized response technique has potential research value, the panel encourages further testing of the technique in surveys of self-reported noncompliance with tax laws. These tests should involve samples from a variety of taxpayer subpopulations, should test alternative randomizing techniques in field conditions, should explore how response bias and precision are affected by changing the selection probability and content of the nonsensitive alternative, and should compare the results of randomized response surveys with surveys that directly seek reports of sensitive behavior.

More specific questions. As we have already noted, most surveys that ask about noncompliance do not follow up with specific questions about types of unreported income (e.g., "How did you receive the income that didn't get reported?") or unjustified deductions (e.g., "What kind of deduction was it?"). The concern is that asking such questions will reduce respondent candor or lead respondents to refuse to be interviewed further. However, no study has tested the extent to which increased specificity provokes these responses. Because additional specificity would allow researchers to address important questions that cannot be investigated with only global measures of noncompliance, the panel recommends pilot testing more specific probes, using explicit open- and closed-ended questions as well as the randomized response technique.

Repeated interviews. As noted in Chapters 2 and 3, little is known about changes in individuals' taxpaying behavior over time or about the tax compliance effects of changes in family and financial circumstances, contacts with the IRS, or experiences with practitioners and other information sources. We also do not know whether taxpayers' perceptions of the risk and severity of sanctions for noncompliance change markedly over time and, if they change, how the changed perceptions relate to compliance behavior. Retrospective measures of such changes can in principle be obtained by asking people how their views have changed over the past few years. But since current perceptions can color recollections, the validity of retrospective measures is always suspect. Nothing is known specifically about the effects of repeated interviewing on compliance itself or on response to questions about compliance. The best approach to these matters is a panel study that involves interviewing the same respondents several times and linking changes in attitudes and behavior across surveys. To learn about these effects, the panel recommends a pilot test of compliance surveys that reinterview the same respondents at several points in time. If the multiwave interview process does not contaminate the results, the potential payoff in knowledge could be great.

UPDATING THE AGGREGATE CROSS-SECTIONAL FILE

The panel commends the IRS for making available the aggregate cross-sectional data base (Project 778) it constructed for tax year 1969. We recommend that this data base be updated and refined if the reliability of the compliance measure can be demonstrated for a more recent year. This data base is described in some detail in Chapter 1, Supplementary Note B.

To summarize, for each three-digit zip code area, the compliance measure in the file is an estimate of the voluntary compliance level—the fraction of true tax liability that is reported on returns for tax year 1969 as they were filed. Explanatory variables include rates per 1,000 returns of IRS enforcement activity (e.g., audits, criminal fraud investigations, collection notices for past due accounts) and of sanction imposition (e.g., civil fraud penalties and criminal fraud convictions) in previous years. Other explanatory variables include measures of economic activity related to taxpaying (e.g., unemployment rates, percentage employed in manufacturing and therefore subject to withholding), demographic characteristics (e.g., region, percentage nonwhite, percentage over age sixty-five), and socioeconomic conditions (e.g., percentage of high school graduates, average income, divorce rates, household mobility).[8]

Analyses of the file (by Witte and Woodbury, 1984, 1985; Dubin and Wilde, 1988; Beron, Tauchen, and Witte, 1988) and their results were discussed in Chapter 2. A common question addressed by these analyses has been the general effects of IRS activities on compliance by all taxpayers in a geographic area: this includes both the specific effects on the taxpayers who are contacted and the ripple effects on taxpayers who are not contacted.

For IRS administrators, the general compliance effects of IRS activities represent an important but understudied issue. IRS analysts regularly use internal data to measure the revenue recovery effects of IRS functions, and surveys can be designed to study the specific deterrence effects of IRS contacts on future compliance by the contacted taxpayers. But the general effects, including ripple effects of taxpayer contacts, have been studied by only a few researchers—largely because of the lack of recent data.[9] Some knowledgeable observers believe that the ripple effects may be far larger than the revenue recovery and specific deterrence effects.

Updating the 1969 data base and making certain adjustments could advance research on general effects in several important ways. Because compliance behavior is likely to have changed substantially since 1969, a more current assessment would be valuable. There are both cultural and structural reasons for expecting substantial changes in compliance behavior since 1969. Federal tax revenue is not currently being used to support an unpopular war; society seems to offer less support for opposing government institutions and more support for pursuing financial self-interest; and the visibility of income has changed as the structure of occupations has changed and records have been computerized. In addition, new IRS administrative techniques have been introduced, the applications of others have changed, and tax avoidance penalties have been strengthened. For example, audit coverage has dropped substantially since 1969, while the fraction of information returns matched to tax returns has increased.

An updated aggregate cross-sectional file could support analyses of compliance under these new conditions if the reliability of the compliance measure can be shown. Because information reporting has broadened substantially since 1969, an updated data base could contain a compliance measure that captured unreported income more fully. The file should also be augmented with additional data on IRS resource allocations and activity levels; with such data, researchers could specify more adequate compliance models.

The value of the updated data is critically dependent on the validity of the compliance measure, which was calculated with the procedure described in Chapter 1, Supplementary Note B. Therefore, before undertaking development of the complete file, that procedure should be validated by comparison of the calculated measure with a TCMP compliance measure for the same year, and revised if necessary. Therefore, the updated file would have to correspond to the year of a recent TCMP cycle—1982, 1985, or 1988.[10] The choice should probably consider currency of the data and relevance to the existing tax administration environment, delays until the updated file could be prepared, proximity to a year when the Census Bureau collects the relevant demographic and socioeconomic data, and the stability of the tax system.

A more disaggregated file—perhaps at the five-digit rather than three-digit zip code level—would permit analyses of more homogeneous units. It might, however, force the deletion of explanatory variables not available at that level. In deciding how to redesign the data base, the IRS would find it helpful to consult regularly with researchers interested in analyzing the new data base and with statisticians in the agencies that produce data on potentially includable explanatory variables, as well as with the Compliance Research Advisory Group proposed in Chapter 6.

EXPERIMENTALLY GENERATED DATA BASES

The panel recommends that the IRS and external researchers collaborate to expand the use of field and laboratory experiments to analyze the compliance effects of innovations in tax administration.

Empirical analyses of preexisting data are guided more or less closely by models of behavior, as indicated in Chapter 2. Such models hypothesize that compliance is determined by a set of explicitly listed explanatory variables on which data are available, plus a large number of unobserved small causes. Instead of incorporating the unobserved causes explicitly into the model, the analyst assumes that their combined effects may be represented as a random disturbance term. Analyses based on such models are often quite sensitive to choices about what variables to include explicitly and which to treat as random disturbances. These problems are illustrated in quantitative analyses across the range of social science research, including that on taxpayer compliance (see, e.g., Dubin and Wilde, 1986, 1987a,b, 1988; Beron et al., 1988). With preexisting data bases, it is often difficult to test for the effects of such choices and to revise them if necessary. As a result, erroneous inferences may be made about the causes of compliance.

However, if a researcher can control a crucial variable, the more powerful randomized experimental design may be used. An example of a controllable variable is IRS notices to taxpayers, which can be altered according to a plan.[11] In a randomized experiment, subjects are randomly assigned either to receive an experimental treatment or to be placed in a control group, and the outcomes are compared between the experimental and control groups. If the experiment is properly designed and carried out, differences in outcomes between the two groups can be attributed to the treatment because the randomization eliminated other systematic differences between them.

As tax administration policy evolves, questions inevitably arise that can be effectively addressed only by using randomized experiments. Nevertheless, the technique has been used only rarely in field settings—that is, with actual taxpayers with real tax obligations. Schwartz and Orleans (1967) used the technique to assess the relative effects of appeals to morality and reminders of sanctions on taxpaying, and the IRS used it to study how alternative procedures and notices affected collections from past due accounts (Perng, 1985). The experimental technique has been more widely used in laboratory settings, which have involved simulations of taxpaying (see, e.g., Friedland et al., 1973, 1978; Friedland, 1982; Spicer and Becker, 1980; Webley and Halstead, 1985).

FIELD EXPERIMENTS.   Despite their power to measure effects of interventions, field experiments have been underused in taxpayer compliance research for a variety of reasons. Carrying out the randomization, providing different treatments to the experimental and control samples, and collecting the outcome measures all impose administrative burdens and opportunity costs on the IRS.[12] Moreover, since an experiment explicitly involves differential treatment of similar taxpayers, the law limits what can be done. Even when there is no legal impediment to experimentation, if one treatment is more burdensome or intrusive than another, valid equity concerns arise and the disparity increases the difficulty of maintaining political support for the experiment.[13]

The IRS can participate in valuable experiments in two important ways. In some instances, as in the case of Schwartz and Orleans (1967), researchers unconnected with the IRS and not specifically motivated by its agenda may be able to carry out the randomization and interventions themselves, but they require IRS data to measure the compliance effects. If the research is well designed and addresses important underlying questions, IRS cooperation in providing data or computing outcome measures could make an important contribution to the understanding of taxpayer compliance behavior and perhaps indirectly to tax administration.

In other instances, a problem in tax administration, such as how to collect past due accounts most efficiently, may motivate the IRS to initiate an experiment for which the analysis is done either internally or by an external researcher on a contract basis. Because preliminary experiments may produce strong predictions about the compliance effects of full-scale policy innovations, they should play a more important role than they now do in IRS policy development. If experiments are used to test innovations that are strongly supported by theory, they can simultaneously contribute to knowledge about compliance.

Some fruitful areas for experimentation were suggested in Chapter 4. Others involve the functions of tax administration (noted by Klepper and Nagin, Vol. 2):

1. Providing the means for taxpayers to comply—for example, through simplified forms and instructions, information packages, and other taxpayer assistance;

2. Expanding agency capacity to process returns—for example, through alternative staff training programs, computerization of processing functions, and improved office procedures; and

3. Bringing noncompliant taxpayers into compliance—for example, through direct contacts or widely disseminated messages intended to encourage compliance or discourage noncompliance.

By ascertaining how to perform these functions more effectively, programs of experiments—to test new ways of using administrative tools, to test further refinements suggested by the early results, and to replicate tests with different subpopulations of taxpayers—could benefit both the IRS and taxpayers who wish to abide by the law. By sharing with independent researchers the data bases that such programs create, the IRS could help them to resolve ongoing debates, contributing to a deeper understanding of taxpayer compliance.

Designing and carrying out field experiments is never a simple matter. In all fields, attention must be directed to reducing public resistance to the experiment, maintaining the integrity of the randomization when there are policy pressures to violate it, informing research subjects in a candid but nonthreatening way, delivering uniform experimental and control treatments, and observing postexperiment outcomes long enough to distinguish long-lasting from transitory effects. Moreover, unanticipated problems usually arise during the course of such experiments, often involving staff turnover, pressures to override the randomization procedure in exceptional cases, and unexpected barriers to implementation that result in a smaller yield of analyzable cases than expected. Because inappropriate choices in response to such problems can easily invalidate the results of field experiments, involvement of an experienced researcher throughout the project is essential to project success. These problems are discussed more fully by Boruch (Appendix B).

A problem that is unique to experimental research on taxpayer compliance is how to measure the compliance effect of the intervention. The two most obvious methods are likely to have quite different implications for public and political resistance to the experiment. The first, audit-based method is to audit the subjects after the intervention and use the audit results as outcome measures. When audits are comprehensive, as in TCMP, they are generally considered to provide adequate outcome measures for many return items. However, not only are such audits costly to the IRS and burdensome to taxpayers, but they also place the experimental subjects in special jeopardy, since the IRS currently interprets existing law to require collection of tax deficiencies discovered in audits, whatever the purpose of the audits. For these reasons, there is a danger that both internal and public support for experiments may be diminished if audits are used to measure outcomes.

The second, "return-based" method, which was used by Schwartz and Orleans (1967), is to use the average year-to-year change in one or more return items as reported by taxpayers in the experimental and control groups—a measure that requires only tabulations from IRS files created during normal return processing. The measure is based on the idea that taxpayers' reports may be partitioned into two components—the true value of the item plus a noncompliance component. Between two tax years, changes in the true values should be the same on average for the experimental and the control group. Therefore, any difference between the groups in the year-to-year changes is attributable to compliance effects of the intervention. The major advantages of this measure are that it is unobtrusive to subjects and inexpensive and straightforward to compute from existing IRS data.

The measure may, however, confound compliance with other effects. For example, unlike audit-based measures such as TCMP, the return-based measure confounds decreases in income underreporting and increases in income overreporting as measures of improved compliance. If the intervention causes changes in the true values of return items (e.g., if a reminder about sanctions for noncompliance causes a taxpayer to change to an occupation in which wages are lower but less visible to the IRS), then the return-based measure will confound these changes with compliance effects. Finally, if other events that occur near the time of the intervention (e.g., a change in the tax rate structure) affect both compliance and financial behavior, the measure will confound those two effects. Under most circumstances, these measurement problems will not pose serious threats to the analysis, and changes in return items will provide a fairly good if somewhat imprecise measure of the compliance effects of experimental interventions.

LABORATORY EXPERIMENTS.   Laboratory experiments differ from field experiments in that they study behavior under carefully controlled rather than actual conditions.[14] For example, laboratory subjects might be asked to play a game in which they are paid relatively small sums of "income" and must make decisions about how much of it to report to a simulated tax authority. The experimental manipulation is to present the subjects randomly with different conditions (e.g., tax rates, risks that underreporting will be detected, and penalties for underreporting) that have been hypothesized to affect compliance. Since the experimenter knows the subjects' assigned incomes and experimental conditions, their payments can be analyzed to test how the different conditions affect compliance.

For some questions about how compliance is affected by changes in the tax environment, laboratory experiments offer certain advantages over field experiments or nonexperimental methods. They can examine the compliance implications of conditions, such as interactions between tax rates and penalty rates, which cannot be created in the real world. Other issues that could theoretically be studied in field settings, such as the compliance effects of variations in detection probability, are far more amenable to study in laboratory settings. Finally, there is less concern about the privacy of subjects in a laboratory setting, because no records of illegal behavior are created and because the data need not be linked to administrative data.

Despite these potential advantages, laboratory experiments have been used only occasionally in the context of taxpayer compliance—primarily by independent researchers to study the compliance effects of interactions between detection probabilities and penalties (see, for example, Friedland et al., 1978; Thibaut et al., 1974) and by the IRS to study the effectiveness of simplified forms in reducing error rates. One reason for the small number of laboratory experiments to date has been doubts about the ability to generalize experimental findings from the laboratory to taxpaying in the real world.

These doubts arise from two conditions. First, the experimental setting and procedures differ from those faced by actual taxpayers. The rules are simpler, subjects can focus their attention on the task at hand, social stigma is generally not a factor, and rewards and penalties are smaller. Often the subjects have been university students with little taxpaying experience. It has also been conjectured that, compared with actual taxpaying, the game-like setting may encourage subjects to give more weight to optimizing strategies and less to ethical inhibitions against cheating (Webley and Halstead, 1985). Second, because of the difficulty of assembling experimental subjects from distant locations, experimental samples have usually been more homogeneous than the U.S. population. Therefore, relationships found significant in laboratory manipulations may be so insignificant in normal taxpaying situations as to be uninteresting and possibly misleading (Cialdini, Vol. 2).

Even accepting these limitations, laboratory experiments may be useful for investigating a number of questions related to taxpayer compliance. For example, laboratory experiments can generate data on how alternative forms and instructions affect rates of errors in understanding and following directions. They can be used to investigate how different presentations (e.g., pamphlets or audiovisual material) affect perceptions of fairness. They can be used in the taxpaying context, as they have been in other contexts, to learn how subjects seek and use information about risks and probabilities to make decisions under uncertainty.

Considering the discussions of field and laboratory experiments together, it seems clear that neither setting is universally preferable and that the two strategies can complement each other. Programs can begin with small-scale laboratory trials to suggest promising innovations. The robustness of these findings can then be tested through replications that involve different measurement techniques and variations of procedures. Once a finding has demonstrated robustness, its policy significance can be investigated through replications with samples that represent the relevant taxpaying populations.

Protecting Research Subjects and Compliance Research Data

While the research and data collection efforts recommended in this and preceding chapters should be of value to researchers and tax administrators alike, they are subject to certain difficulties. Three considerations constrain both the IRS and the external research community in taxpayer compliance research: (1) protecting the confidentiality of tax returns and, more generally, taxpayer privacy; (2) protecting IRS internal information from uses that could compromise the agency's ability to administer the tax system; and (3) protecting compliance research subjects from unfair burdens and risks.

The panel does not believe that any of the research or data-base development efforts recommended in this report would compromise these objectives to any significant degree, nor did we find any examples of published compliance research that has done so. The panel strongly believes that promising research initiatives should not be stifled because of technically possible harms that are almost certain not to be realized. Nevertheless, where the potential for harm exists, the needs of the IRS and of human subjects must play an important role in the design of research. Most external researchers are already subject to procedures in their universities or private research institutions that are intended to protect research subjects, but there is a need to inform the institutional review boards (IRBs) that administer those procedures about special considerations related to data from tax returns and taxpayer audits. And analogous procedures are needed both to guide the IRS in deciding what cooperation to offer external researchers and to facilitate important internal research using designs that protect research subjects.

Therefore, the panel recommends long-term cooperative efforts—involving the IRS and the broad research community—in three areas:

1. To develop and implement policies governing access by researchers to compliance research data, especially external use of sensitive IRS data;
2. To develop and implement policies to foster compliance research within the IRS that uses the most methodologically sound research techniques, including randomized experiments where needed to address problems in tax administration, while protecting research subjects from unfair burdens and risks; and
3. To formally and thoroughly consider the feasibility and desirability of arranging for the deposit of sensitive IRS data in an independent repository.

A standing authority on protection of research subjects should be established to interpret and monitor the policies and arrangements in light of evolving research ideas, changes in compliance requirements and forms of noncompliance, innovations in tax administration, and advances in statistical matching techniques.

A small group representing all the relevant interests and expertise would be an appropriate standing authority. Initially, such a group would perform functions analogous to those of the Census Bureau's Micro-Data Utilization Review Board, which processes external requests to use the agency's data. Eventually, if support grows for internal projects that raise more difficult questions of taxpayer protection (e.g., field experiments as recommended by the panel, multiyear audits for research purposes, projects in which audit records are linked to survey records), this group would come to perform the functions that institutional review boards now perform for most external researchers and some research sponsors—ensuring that research designs meet generally accepted standards for protecting human subjects.

Facilitating research access to data while protecting individual privacy is exceedingly difficult. A joint panel of the National Research Council and the Social Science Research Council has been formed to develop recommendations on this subject. The following sections explain in more detail the considerations involved in developing procedures for access to taxpayer compliance research data and for facilitating promising IRS research in ways that protect research subjects.

DEVELOPING PROCEDURES FOR DATA ACCESS

The Research and Statistics of Income Divisions of the IRS have supported external use of IRS data in three ways:

1. Archiving and documenting public-use files, such as the samples of tax returns for the national and state tax revenue models and the taxpayer survey by Yankelovich et al. (1984);
2. Providing existing files (e.g., the 1969 aggregate cross-sectional data base) and custom files (e.g., tabulations of TCMP data) to researchers who request them; and
3. Performing tabulations of confidential files under instructions from outside researchers (including this panel).

IRS responses to requests for external use are not always predictable. Some requests for data access are rejected, and others are supported. Although the panel has not systematically reviewed IRS procedures for responding to data access requests, three considerations seem to be weighed. First, there is a statutory requirement that disclosed information not "be associated with, or otherwise identify directly or indirectly, a particular taxpayer" (26 U.S.C. 6103). Second, the agency has a desire to prevent analyses of internal information (including, most prominently, TCMP data) that could help taxpayers evade taxes by informing them how enforcement decisions are made. Third, decisions on requests for access to data reflect the recognition that some proposed compliance research has potential value to tax administration that may be enhanced through the scientific processes of replication and cumulation, but that decisions to support external research with IRS resources (e.g., to prepare and document files, to interpret data, and to answer questions about recording procedures) must consider the costs and benefits to the agency.

Each of these considerations is important in the panel's view, but each is open to a wide range of interpretations. The lack of public guidelines governing IRS responses to external requests for support may have unnecessarily discouraged researchers from undertaking projects that could contribute both to scientific knowledge and to tax administration effectiveness, or even from entering the taxpayer compliance field at all.

Therefore, the IRS, alone or perhaps jointly with the National Science Foundation, should support a project for the development of administrative guidelines for access to data for taxpayer compliance research. Such a project should be broadly conceived, involving persons with diverse perspectives on the privacy issue and a wide range of expertise and experience with sensitive data both inside and outside the IRS. It should deal with access to and linkages among not only IRS data bases but also data from surveys, whether sponsored by the IRS or not, internal records of enforcement activity, and related informational sources such as results from ethnographic research. The development of guidelines should be treated as the beginning of a long-term process, because modifications will be needed as new data bases are designed and technologies evolve for accomplishing and preventing record matches. Modifications should continue to be planned by a diverse group that includes knowledgeable persons from within and outside the IRS and the compliance research community.

The proposed project would have several important benefits. First, the mere existence of public guidelines should encourage new researchers to enter the taxpayer compliance field. Second, such guidelines could reduce the burden on the IRS of formulating ad hoc responses to the requests it receives. Third, if properly structured, the guidelines could foster advances in the methodologies used in compliance research; advance the scientific processes of cumulation, reanalysis, and replication; and increase the cost-effectiveness of IRS efforts to support external research by reducing the duplication of its efforts in creating and documenting custom files, performing analyses, and educating external researchers about internal procedures.

The following paragraphs suggest some principles that must be considered in developing guidelines for data access.

SHARING RESEARCH DATA.   Sharing research data is essential to scientific progress in any field, including taxpayer compliance (Fienberg, Martin, and Straf, 1985). Reanalysis of existing data, which is of course less costly than the collection of new data for original analysis, can resolve important disputes of interpretation, uncover errors, inform policy makers of options not noted in original analyses, and improve techniques for measurement and data collection.

Guidelines for data access could be designed to encourage data sharing in several ways. They might provide that whenever possible, public-use versions of raw data files be deposited in archives that are accessible to the research community within a reasonable period of time. That is likely to be feasible, for example, with taxpayer surveys after identifiers have been removed, and it has been done for years by the IRS Statistics of Income Division with tax return samples.

Similar guidelines could be developed for special-purpose aggregated files that are created for external researchers when the raw data are considered too sensitive to be released. The guidelines could provide that the IRS deposit such files in an archive after a reasonable period of time. To foster data sharing and to ensure that their resources benefit the entire community, many research sponsors impose such requirements on their grantees. (For example, the National Institute of Justice requires its grantees to make public-use files available at the expiration of a grant.) For similar purposes, the IRS could negotiate analogous agreements with researchers whom it supports by creating special files. Such agreements should allow time for the researcher to complete the work for which the file was requested.

If public-use files are to be of value, of course, they must be accompanied by documentation and interpretation. Established data archives usually have fairly demanding documentation requirements, which are burdensome in the case of complex files such as those housed in the IRS. However, once the IRS has taken the one-time step of documentation, archive staff members inform themselves about the data set sufficiently to handle questions of routine interpretation, thus relieving other IRS staff of this burden, except when adequate interpretation requires knowledge of IRS administrative or recording practices.

PROTECTING TAXPAYER PRIVACY.   The best protections for taxpayer privacy are ethical investigators, strong penalties against those who misuse data, and the recognition that in most cases there are no substantial incentives for linking particular taxpayers to particular return information. If these factors cannot be relied on, then protecting taxpayer privacy could be extremely difficult. Even when obvious identifiers are removed from individual records, the identities of individuals can sometimes be deduced from information in the file. Possibilities for such deductive disclosure are heightened for individuals with unusual characteristics that are reflected in their records.

A variety of disclosure-limiting techniques are frequently used to reduce the probability of deductive disclosure. Instead of releasing individual records, some agencies release only data tabulations in which even the smallest cells include a minimum number of people. Data on continuous variables such as income may be recoded into intervals or rounded off. Random disturbances may be added to data items, or segments of records may be swapped across similar subjects. A single synthetic record may be created from three actual records, with synthetic values created from three-record means or a value selected at random from one of the three records. For a data file that is very large, the probability of deductive disclosure can be reduced by releasing only a small, randomly selected sample from the file. These and other techniques are described in detail in many sources (see, e.g., Privacy Protection Study Commission, 1977; Federal Committee on Statistical Methodology, 1978; Pearson, 1986.)

These techniques have two limitations. First, although they substantially reduce the risk of deductive disclosure, tests and simulations have demonstrated that they cannot eliminate that risk entirely. Second, some of them alter the systematic and random relationships between variables that exist in the raw data. Because of such alterations of the covariance structure, standard analytical techniques may lead to erroneous conclusions, and it may not always be possible to modify the techniques appropriately. For these reasons, federal agencies and others concerned with this issue have begun to adopt a standard of acceptable disclosure risk, rather than of zero disclosure risk, and to prescribe stringent penalties for misuse of data (Pearson, 1986). The panel supports this reorientation and believes that disclosure-limiting techniques will always need to be supplemented by administrative arrangements that facilitate worthwhile research and also protect both the privacy of taxpayers and the security of IRS enforcement techniques.

PROTECTING IRS ENFORCEMENT SECURITY. While privacy protection problems can arise with any set of records related to individuals, the use of some IRS data bases is constrained by another possibility—that by analyzing the data, an unscrupulous person could learn about IRS enforcement procedures and use the information to evade taxes or to help others do so. Probably the most widely known example of this kind of data base is TCMP, which is used to develop discriminant index functions that are used to select tax returns for audit. At least one academic researcher has sought research access to TCMP data through litigation (*Long* v. *Internal Revenue Service,* 1984). The IRS resisted the effort on the grounds that reanalysis of the data could jeopardize the secrecy of the DIFs, which it considers vital to tax administration. The courts recently granted Long access to portions of the 1969, 1971, and 1973 TCMP data bases that had not been used for DIF development.

Exact duplication of current DIF-based rules through reanalysis of the Long data is impossible, since the data were never used in DIF development. In addition, the DIF formulas have been revised several times since any 1969–1973 TCMP data were used in DIF development. However, a more general problem exists with respect to research access to future cycles of TCMP data and to any future data bases that might contain tax items and noncompliance measures for individuals. Exact duplication of DIF even by reanalyzing TCMP data that have been used to develop them is perhaps unlikely, but the public release of a data base that permits analysis of correlations between tax return items and noncompliance measures could certainly increase the likelihood that an analyst could acquire additional knowledge about IRS selection rules based on those same correlations. Guidelines for data access should therefore recognize the difficulty for the IRS of releasing TCMP or any other data that could be misused to make tax evasion easier, even as they recognize the value of up-to-date TCMP data for independent research, for example, on the compliance implications of recent changes in tax law.

AN INDEPENDENT DATA CENTER.   One possibility for coping with a number of problems posed by sensitive data is the establishment of a designated data center located outside the IRS that would have contractual authority to take custody of sensitive data files. Such files might include IRS records, records of survey responses that might be self-incriminating, or identifying information needed to relocate subjects for reinterviews in a longitudinal survey. It could regulate the use of such files by negotiating contracts with subsequent users and by performing especially sensitive computer operations itself. Examples of such sensitive operations might include analyses of raw TCMP data, analyses requiring merges of survey and IRS records relating to a common sample, and the creation of longitudinal data files for specific individuals—a procedure that requires access to personal identifiers. Such a center might be used to carry out comparisons between survey- and audit-based compliance measures, as recommended earlier in this chapter.

For files with complex problems of confidentiality or interpretation (e.g., a survey that involved self-reports of noncompliance linked to administrative records), such a center could facilitate secondary data use by other researchers—including those within IRS—without unduly burdening the original user.

By assuming some of the responsibility for administering access to data, the center could increase the number of researchers able to use sensitive data under appropriate restrictions while reducing disruptive demands on IRS Research Division staff. It might also assume responsibility for providing IRS-generated public-access data tapes and answering general inquiries about their contents, again shifting the more routine burdens of data access away from the IRS research staff. An independent, prestigious center could provide a legitimate arena for deciding on appropriate confidentiality restrictions for novel research situations—a desirable alternative to avoiding the possibility of such situations by undertaking only safe research projects.

Protecting Subjects of Research Initiated by the IRS

Since most external researchers are subject to institutional review boards in their home institutions, the IRS, by cooperating on projects that have been approved by an IRB, is unlikely to jeopardize the research subjects. There is, however, no comparable formal mechanism for protecting subjects of research initiated by the IRS.

The panel recommends that the IRS develop guidelines for protecting the subjects of its research. Not only can such guidelines reduce risks to research subjects, but also, if the guidelines are developed in a way that builds a broad consensus, their existence should also help preclude unwarranted objections to ethically and methodologically sound research.

A useful starting point for thinking about such guidelines is the widely accepted human subjects protection regulation adopted by the U.S. Department of Health and Human Services (45 CFR Subtitle A, Section 35.10, Part 46). Although this particular regulation may not be entirely appropriate to guide taxpayer compliance research, it is the departure point for model legislation being developed by the Interagency Human Subjects Coordinating Committee, to which seventeen federal agencies voluntarily subscribe. Because the HHS regulation covers virtually all areas of ethical concern, it is reassuring to note that its adoption by the IRS would have precluded no taxpayer compliance research projects of which we are aware.

The HHS regulation exempts many kinds of research from review, reflecting a presumption that certain kinds of research cannot possibly jeopardize the subjects. One exempt category is studies of subjects required only to follow routine administrative procedures. In the tax administration context, this category would seem to exempt the Accounts Receivable Treatment Study carried out by Perng (1986) as well as future studies involving variations in procedures for computerized notices, return examinations, and the like.

Another exempt category includes surveys that do not request information on sensitive or illegal behavior, such as previous noncompliance. Even a taxpayer survey that probed for self-reported noncompliance could be exempt if the self-reports were recorded so as to be either equivocal (as in randomized response questions) or not linkable to an individual (as in locked-box techniques).

Another exempt category is studies involving confidential documents, if the documents are recorded so as to preclude linkage to individuals. Under the HHS regulation, the Schwartz and Orleans (1967) study would have been exempt, because only tabulations were involved, not individual tax returns. Future studies that use the same basic approach would be exempt, even if separate tabulations were produced for subsamples.

Under the HHS criteria, projects in nonexempt categories can be approved if their designs adhere to certain principles. The first, privacy and confidentiality, has already been discussed. The second, minimized risk, means that the research design must employ the least risky procedures consistent with sound practice and that, whenever appropriate, it should use procedures that are already being performed on the subjects for other purposes. In the context of taxpayer compliance, if valid compliance measures can be obtained from changes in year-to-year return items for example, then the minimized risk principle would call for using that measure instead of research audits—a decision that might well be supported on other grounds as well.

The third principle, reasonable risks to benefits, requires that the research risks (or burdens) to subjects be reasonable when compared with foreseeable benefits. As interpreted by the Federal Judicial Center (1981:7), this principle should discourage burdensome research intended to produce knowledge only for its own sake. Some would dispute this interpretation, because basic research, even when it lacks obvious applications, can enhance the knowledge base in a way that has valuable widespread consequences in the long run. Much of the government's investment in the National Science Foundation is, for example, based on the latter expectation. Even when the research is likely to produce immediate and important benefits to society, some would advocate that subjects be rewarded by specific benefits. Sometimes such benefits will be inherent—for example, in a field test of alternative tax forms in which all the forms are simpler than existing forms, the subjects benefit from reduced preparation time. When direct benefits to the subjects are not intrinsic, a common practice is to compensate them with payment.

The fourth principle, equitable selection of subjects, precludes the arbitrary selection of preidentified individuals as research subjects. It is consistent with sampling plans that assign selection probabilities to all members of a population rather than including or excluding certain members from the sample on a priori grounds. In taxpayer compliance research, some sampling plans (e.g., selecting a group of people who have the same employer or snowball sampling, in which subjects are nominated by acquaintances) might be questioned because they are seen as inequitable selection methods.

The equitable selection principle is consistent with the use of randomized experiments for studying the compliance effects of innovations in tax administration before they are introduced universally. Randomization is designed to provide equal opportunities to receive a treatment, and lotteries with equal selection probabilities are traditionally accepted in American society as a fair method of allocating scarce resources. When a policy shows promise of reducing taxpayer noncompliance but there is doubt about its effectiveness, randomized experiments seem not only ethically permissible but even preferable to the alternatives as a means of testing the effectiveness of the new policy.[15] While there has been no definitive resolution of legal questions about governmental administrative experiments that impose costs or confer benefits on individuals, Boruch (Appendix B) and Diamond (1986) cite federal court decisions (*Aguayo* v. *Richardson*, 1973; *Massachusetts Board of Retirement* v. *Murgla*, 1976) that have permitted such experiments, even when fundamental rights (i.e., to vote, to travel across state lines, and to exercise freedom of speech) are involved.

Although randomized experiments seem generally acceptable as a research procedure, it is clear that on ethical grounds not all conceivable experiments should be permitted. For example, regarding the related issue of punishing criminals, Morris (1966) has written that, although experimentation is generally permissible, punishments administered under experiments should not be seen as more severe than existing practice. Diamond (1986:673) would extend Morris's principles to preclude experiments that introduce greater variability in outcomes than occurs under present practice through the exercise of professional judgment and discretion. These principles are not universally accepted, and there have been experiments involving arrest, incarceration, and other severe punishments. In the context of tax administration, they would appear to prohibit subjecting samples of taxpayers to procedures that could never be universally and publicly implemented because of citizens' objections.

The fifth principle, informed consent, requires that a researcher obtain potential subjects' consent before involving them in certain kinds of research and, in obtaining that consent, inform subjects about the nature of the study. This principle is difficult to apply because there are questions about how much information should be presented in what ways to ensure truly informed consent, and because some research, particularly research that seeks to ascertain subjects' voluntary response to particular procedures, can be invalidated by providing subjects with honest information about what the research is designed to test.

The consequences of such principles for the validity of the research can be substantial. If receiving information about potential risks of participation causes large numbers of potential subjects to refuse participation, then the generalizability of the experimental results is seriously reduced. Even if potential subjects agree to participate after being informed of the risks, their behavior in an experiment could be distorted by the knowledge that they are being observed (the so-called Hawthorne effect) or that the intervention is temporary.

Because the informed consent requirement can pose difficult problems, a safety valve is generally needed. For example, under the HHS regulations, the requirement can be waived if the research could not be carried out without the waiver, and if the research neither imposes more than minimal (i.e., everyday) risks on subjects nor adversely affects their rights and welfare.

The sixth principle is the noncoercion of subjects. In taxpayer compliance research sponsored by the IRS, the appearance of coercion could arise if potential subjects thought their refusal to participate would invite special attention to their tax returns. To avoid this possibility, procedures are needed to conceal from the IRS all information about potential subjects' refusal to participate in the research. Such procedures might have to involve data-processing centers outside the IRS that could guarantee immunity from subpoenas, as is the case with research sponsored by the National Institute of Justice.

As this discussion indicates, the IRS could undertake a wide range of worthwhile taxpayer compliance research projects without undermining a strong commitment to the protection of research subjects of the kind that other federal agencies have espoused. In fact, adoption of strong procedures for the protection of research subjects could be expected to legitimize certain types of research, such as randomized experiments. It should also be clear that no procedures can anticipate all questions that might arise in protecting research subjects and that a permanent structure to administer the procedures is essential.

Notes

1. Other data bases discussed in Chapter 2 are not considered in this chapter: state-level data from the Annual Report of the Commissioner of Internal Revenue (Dubin et al., 1987a), Roper (1978) opinion surveys, several surveys of practitioners (e.g., Ayres et al., 1987; Kinsey, 1987b), and data generated by laboratory experiments (e.g., Friedland et al., 1973).

2. Long and Schwartz (1987) have analyzed data from partial samples of the 1969, 1971, and 1973 TCMP cycles.

3. In an unpublished paper, Long and Schwartz (1987) analyzed compliance statistics for the 1969 and 1971 TCMP samples, which included some taxpayers in common, to study the effect of the first audit on compliance two years later. In another unpublished paper, Klepper and Nagin (1987a) created variables that described return items in terms of variables (e.g., traceability, tangibility, and ambiguity) thought to affect sanction risk and analyzed the relationships between these variables and compliance measures.

4. Strictly speaking, this section is concerned with Phase III of TCMP, the program component concerned with individual filers of tax returns. Other TCMP phases are concerned with such groups as nonfilers, corporations, tax-exempt organizations, and so forth.

5. Whether the old or new formulas perform best in particular circumstances, comparative analyses of the two half-samples would be useful in studying taxpayers' compliance adjustments to the new law.

6. The most informative method of studying this relationship is to link self-reports with audit results for individuals in a sample. However, this approach is not feasible if the survey data are obtained with randomized response (because the technique does not create a record that unambiguously indicates whether or not a respondent reported noncompliance) and may be objectionable on other grounds (e.g., concern that postsurvey audits cause subjects to lodge complaints of taxpayer harassment). Even if one-to-one linkages cannot be made, aggregate analysis can still tell us a good deal about the relationship between audit and survey measures of noncompliance.

7. The locked-box technique allows the respondent to answer the sensitive question on a slip of paper and drop the paper through a slot into a locked container along with others' responses. Since the paper contains no identifiers, it cannot be linked to the respondent. The randomized response technique was first proposed by Warner (1965), and properties of the original technique and of subsequent enhancements are described in Fox and Tracy (1986), on which much of the following discussion is based.

8. Actually, for each area, compliance measures and audit rates are reported separately for each of the seven IRS audit classes used in 1969; other variables are reported for the area as a whole. Separate analyses can therefore be carried out for each audit class.

9. Dubin et al. (1987a) have analyzed both the revenue recovery effects and the general effects of audits using a 1977–1985 time series of aggregate data assembled from Annual Reports of the Commissioner of Internal Revenue.

10. Note that the TCMP sample is too small to support direct construction of a cross-sectional file aggregated to the three-digit zip code. A procedure that uses information from more than 50,000 returns is needed.

11. Experiments cannot be used to study the effects of such taxpayer characteristics as age, which cannot be assigned by an experimenter. In addition, if the law introduces a new requirement or procedure for all taxpayers simultaneously, its effects cannot be studied with a randomized experiment.

12. The results of an experiment may be invalidated if either the experimental or control treatment is varied across subjects. This restriction against tailoring special treatments to meet the characteristics of individual subjects may reduce the efficiency of tax administration; if so, the reduced efficiency is an opportunity cost of the experiment.

13. There is considerable experimental research that involves disparate use of legal sanctions, such as sentencing or parole decisions, and measurements of the effect on compliance with laws. Perhaps the most common view is that the differential treatment of experimental subjects is ethically permissible if the experimental group receives more favorable treatment than they would receive under the status quo. However, some acclaimed experiments, such as the Minneapolis spouse abuse experiment (Sherman and Berk, 1984), have accorded subjects harsher treatment than they would have otherwise received.

14. In this discussion, the term *laboratory experiments* refers to experiments that involve simulated rather than actual taxpaying, whether they take place in physical laboratories or elsewhere. Microcomputers have extended the ability to perform simulations in locations that are more convenient to respondents; doing so should decrease refusal rates and facilitate access to respondents that more fully represent typical taxpayers.

15. As noted by Diamond (1986:672), the alternatives are: (1) to implement an untried policy universally; (2) to implement no policy, making no effort to reduce the burden that noncompliant taxpayers place on compliant ones; and (3) to selectively implement the policy, an approach that is methodologically inferior and raises issues of equal protection.

6. Getting Started:
What Needs to be Done

A primary theme of this report is that the base of knowledge about individual taxpayers' compliance with income tax reporting requirements is small compared with the importance of the phenomenon. There is little scientific evidence on which to base policies to encourage compliance, and there are few mechanisms in place for systematically accumulating more. The research recommended in previous chapters addresses a minimal set of needs. Other compliance problems, such as tax collection and corporate noncompliance, would no doubt benefit from efforts on a similar scale. The particular research recommendations the panel makes are less important, however, than the broader-based need we see for long-term research efforts to understand compliance. These efforts should include a larger community of independent scholars, private foundations, and government institutions. And they should be structured to balance the need for sustained attention to researchable questions against the need for flexibility in the face of new developments in research and in tax administration.

The kinds of cumulative research programs illustrated in previous chapters are hampered by the limited sources of funding for research, the difficulties and special problems that independent researchers face in gaining access to IRS data sources, the complexities and technical difficulties of understanding the tax system and the sources of data for compliance research, the limited incentives for the multidisciplinary efforts necessary to analyze complex behavior, and the lack of a critical mass of researchers concentrating on a sufficiently focused range of issues to make significant progress.

The understanding of taxpayer compliance can best be advanced through the involvement of an intellectually exciting community of researchers that extends across the tax professions and the social sciences. Such a community has already begun to form, and its growth can best be encouraged by a diverse array of organizations—including private foundations, federal research sponsors, and the tax policy community, in addition to the Internal Revenue Service.

The IRS has already played a major role in launching the compliance research enterprise, but it needs to do more to enhance the research potential of its data bases and to facilitate their expanded use for research, to integrate research and evaluation more fully into its policy deliberations, and to strengthen the infrastructure that supports the independent external research community. To assist the IRS in these efforts and to provide a structure for sustained communication with the research community, we recommend that it establish and regularly convene a Compliance Research Advisory Group. Such a group could bring external experts in taxpayer compliance research together with agency administrators to regularly review research priorities and to revise them as conditions change. Consideration should also be given to the possible need for new organizational arrangements to strengthen and broaden the compliance research community—such as a center for compliance research, a consortium of sponsors supporting a range of activities, or a looser federation of cooperating institutions.

The remainder of this chapter explains more fully: (1) the need for a broadened research community; (2) the roles of organizations other than the IRS in fostering taxpayer compliance research; (3) ways in which the IRS can continue to support needed research with the help of a Compliance Research Advisory Group; and (4) possible new organizational arrangements.

Broadening the Research Community

From our review of existing academic studies of tax compliance, we are disturbed by the isolation of different study traditions and the lack of familiarity with the tax system reflected in much of the previous research. Research initiated by tax administration agencies tends to consist largely of scattered studies with little attempt to build on previous findings. As in all fields of science, the interaction of alternative theoretical perspectives and empirical research methods, the questioning of assumptions, and the awareness of relevant research findings are needed to build compliance knowledge. To develop cumulative scientific knowledge about tax compliance, the active research community must extend beyond the administrative agencies to include the tax professions and the social sciences.

One of the advantages of involving independent researchers is that they are less constrained than are researchers in federal and state taxing authorities by the need for immediate policy relevance and may therefore be more likely to question current agency policies and practices. University researchers also work in a more appropriate setting for exploratory, hypothesis-generating research that raises questions and requires techniques not readily promoted within a mission-oriented agency. But even (and perhaps especially) in academic settings, the disciplinary boundaries of individual researchers need to be crossed frequently by critics with other professional, administrative, and disciplinary perspectives, particularly because of the complexity of the tax system and resultant compliance behavior.

For independent researchers, the incentives to pursue theoretical or empirical interests in the context of taxpayer compliance stem from the breadth of intellectual issues the subject raises. Tax practitioners, policy analysts, and administrators have interest in the practical and ethical consequences of citizens' efforts to minimize the taxes they pay. Social scientists are beginning to use the rich laboratory of tax compliance behavior to test theories and apply methods developed in various disciplines. The excitement in these communities about taxpayer compliance research is reflected in recent increases in the numbers of journal articles being published, formally and informally established university-based centers for research on taxes and compliance, panels on taxpayer compliance being organized at academic conferences, and research projects currently being funded. Both state and federal innovations in tax administration and broader access to administrative data are providing new opportunities to test competing theories about human behavior in a setting of considerable practical importance. With larger funding and broader institutional backing, the climate would allow for challenging debates within academic and professional disciplines, foster growth in taxpayer compliance research, which has sometimes lagged behind state-of-the-art disciplinary research, and encourage the kind of cross-fertilization between disciplines that generates creativity and intellectual breakthroughs.

If federal and state tax agencies were part of a broad network of compliance scholars, they could tap specialized research skills located in basic research institutions at minimal cost for consultation, peer review, or sponsored research. Even when the agencies possess all requisite research skills, an independent research community can perform the scientific tasks of broadening their perspectives and challenging their research priorities, assumptions, and methods, thereby increasing the credibility of the findings. Finally, even the most carefully designed single project executed by highly qualified researchers is unlikely by itself to make a substantial contribution to the current state of compliance knowledge. The resources of tax authorities alone are unlikely to generate the large number of studies, some inevitably unsuccessful, that is required to make significant progress on such matters as the ripple and long-term effects of enforcement, the compliance effects of social sanctions, and the paths through which tax practitioners affect compliance.

Significant problems impede the potential growth of the nascent research community. Data have been exceedingly difficult for researchers to obtain and interpret correctly. Information is difficult to obtain about important aspects of the enforcement process. Academic disciplines provide little incentive for applied research and accord such research low visibility. Start-up costs for new researchers to learn the complexities of the tax system and research data bases are formidable in light of the current low level of research funding and lack of certainty of future funding. A broad base of financial and institutional support is needed to extend the important work that has already begun.

Broadening Institutional Support for Research

The Internal Revenue Service has played an important role in launching the taxpayer compliance research enterprise, but maintaining that enterprise requires a broader base of support. Private foundations, other government agencies, and the tax policy community can all make important financial and other contributions to broaden the research community and to support the research needed to advance knowledge about taxpayer compliance.

PRIVATE FOUNDATIONS
Why should private foundations be interested in supporting compliance research? To begin with, doing so could help solve an important national problem. The noncompliance revenue gap is a large percentage of the federal deficit, and the techniques for recovering lost revenue are costly to tax administrators and burdensome to taxpayers. As indicated in Chapter 2, insights that may improve the efficiency and reduce the burden of tax administration have already emerged from relatively inexpensive theoretical, ethnographic, and small-sample survey research that does not require

IRS data or financial support. Far more could be done with additional resources.

Although the IRS clearly has a substantial stake in taxpayer compliance research, as a mission-oriented agency its role in fostering compliance research is inherently limited, for reasons that extend beyond budget limitations. Mission agencies inevitably and correctly give highest priority to projects in direct support of policy and administrative concerns, which shift frequently. Cumulative research, in contrast, requires longer-term commitments of resources to more speculative projects that may initially yield little information with direct policy significance. Furthermore, mission agencies find it difficult to support research that can be expected to challenge conventional agency wisdom or to create new problems for the agency. Even (and perhaps especially) when research results turn out to support agency beliefs or policy, their credibility may be undermined by agency sponsorship. Some worthwhile research projects, especially those that require researchers to gain subjects' confidence in order to learn details about their illegal behavior, become more difficult to carry out and more questionable on ethical grounds if they are sponsored by an enforcement agency. For all these reasons, the health of the taxpayer compliance research enterprise depends critically on a diversity of sponsorship.

Funding from a variety of sponsors would overcome several problems. Additional sources of funding increase the likelihood of attracting the critical mass of scholars needed for sustained intellectual progress in the area. Sponsors differ in the research subjects and methodologies they are willing to support and in the time horizons they envision for expected results. Private foundations in particular are able to provide long-term support for potentially important research of little immediate relevance to the IRS, as well as for ethnographic and survey projects for which IRS sponsorship could heighten subjects' sensitivities and perhaps distort their responses. A broad base of support might attract some university scholars with needed research skills who might be reluctant to become dependent on IRS support, and it would prevent the potential domination of compliance research by a small group of researchers favored by one institution.

Several of the research suggestions made in this report seem especially appropriate for support by private foundations. Exploratory research on how interactions between taxpayers and their environments affect compliance depends critically on subjects' candor in describing illegal behavior in detail; considerations of both feasibility and research ethics suggest that nongovernmental sponsorship is likely to be most appropriate. Research that involves linking self-reports of compliance behavior to IRS records (e.g., research on the relationships between self-report and audit-based compliance measures) requires special procedures to protect the self-reports from IRS access and to prevent unauthorized access to the subjects' tax return and audit data. Mentioning private sponsorship may well reduce subjects' concerns about the researcher's ability to protect the self-reports from IRS inspection.

For research involving tax practitioners, the good auspices that accompany sponsorship by certain organizations may encourage respondents' cooperation. Researchers sponsored by the American Bar Association and by the Arthur Young and Peat Marwick foundations, for example, have had notable success in obtaining practitioners' participation as research subjects; as long as researchers' independence could be ensured, such organizations would be natural sponsors (or cosponsors) of the research on practitioners recommended in Chapter 4. Research on IRS administrative adjustments to the Tax Reform Act of 1986 is probably most appropriately sponsored by one or more nongovernmental organizations. Finally, sponsors concerned with the progress of basic social science are natural sources of support for some of the microeconomic and econometric research recommended in Chapter 2, to advance knowledge about issues that lie beyond the day-to-day concerns of tax administrators but may eventually produce insights useful to them.

Several activities aimed at the broader objective of strengthening the compliance research community are likely to work best if they are cosponsored by organizations commonly identified with a diverse array of interests—tax policy, tax administration, tax practitioners, citizen-taxpayers, and support of the social sciences. This is especially true of efforts to enhance communication, such as newsletters, special compliance-related issues of relevant journals, workshops, and conferences. It also applies to research programs in which a balance of alternative perspectives is important, such as dissertation support, postdoctoral fellowships, and unsolicited grant programs. Private organizations should play a significant role in strengthening the research community, even though substantial support is provided by governmental sources, including the IRS.

FEDERAL RESEARCH SPONSORS
Several government agencies that are not responsible for tax administration are potential sources of financial support for research on taxpayer compliance. One is the National Institute of Justice (NIJ), the research arm

of the Department of Justice, which administers research grants to individual scholars. Its legislative mandate includes developing information on the causes and correlates of crime, developing new methods for reducing crime, and making recommendations to federal, state, and local units of government for improving their systems of criminal justice. Although the larger share of its efforts are concerned with laws that are enforced by state and local authorities, it has occasionally sponsored research on the measurement of noncompliance and the enforcement of federal income tax laws (see, e.g., Long, 1980b).

Of the research recommended in this report, two categories would fall clearly within the NIJ mandate: data reanalyses and experiments intended to measure the compliance effects of variation in the certainty and severity of sanctions, and ethnographic studies of how perceptions of certainty and severity are formed (National Institute of Justice, 1986). NIJ is also a natural source of support for research on sanctioning processes for noncompliant taxpayers.

A second federal program that has become an increasingly active sponsor of taxpayer compliance research in recent years is the Law and Social Sciences Program of the National Science Foundation (NSF). This program sponsors basic research on such questions as how laws and sanctions affect individual behavior and societal structure and how laws are created by legislators, enforced by executive authorities, and interpreted by courts. The program has already funded about a dozen taxpayer compliance research projects, with part of the cost underwritten by the IRS Research Division. It could support taxpayer compliance research that contributes to any of a variety of research traditions, including:
- Deterrence theory;
- Cultural and developmental influences on individual compliance with rules;
- Complex decisions made under risk and uncertainty;
- Relationships between laws, perceptions of equity, and compliance;
- Learning complex rules in natural environments;
- Integrating environmental influences into models of individual compliance.

Of the research recommended in this report, most of the efforts cited above for support by private foundations would also find a natural home within the NSF program. In addition, jointly with other NSF programs, the Law and Social Sciences Program is well placed to sponsor more methodologically oriented research that is unlikely to attract private support. Examples of such research that are recommended in this report include:

- Refining econometric models of compliance to capture enforcement practices, measurement errors, and random events more realistically;
- Testing the sensitivity of econometric results to alternative model specifications;
- Applying game theory and information economics to questions about taxpayer compliance;
- Examining and refining techniques for surveying respondents about their illegal behavior and measuring correlations between their self-reports and other factors; and
- Refining and evaluating methodologies for protecting the privacy of subjects of public-use data sets that contain information about illegal behavior.

NSF funds could also sponsor discussions of alternative administrative structures for providing research access to data on private or illegal behavior without unduly compromising subjects' privacy or the security of enforcement systems. The IRS TCMP data files are a particularly interesting example. But many of the issues involved extend to other data that are potentially usable in research on other forms of illegal behavior, for example, police arrest and investigative records, offenders' self-reports of crimes, and delinquents' school and juvenile court records.

Both the National Institute of Justice and the Law and Social Sciences Program of the National Science Foundation foster research that extends across the boundaries of traditional academic disciplines. By encouraging scholarly exchanges and collaborations across multiple disciplines, they can help to broaden the foundation on which future scholars with other relevant specialties can build without excessive start-up costs. Interactions that bring intellectual traditions together in novel ways could enhance the understanding of taxpayer compliance beyond what more isolated research can accomplish. And, by encouraging the application of an innovative theory or technique to compliance issues, cross-disciplinary exchanges can enhance the diffusion of intellectual innovations beyond traditional professional boundaries.

THE TAX POLICY COMMUNITY

As authors of tax legislation and overseers of tax administration, Congress and the executive branch must share primary responsibility for ensuring that administrative and policy decisions are based on an adequate understanding of taxpayer compliance behavior. Three institutions concerned with taxes—the General Accounting Office (GAO), the Office of Tax Analysis (OTA) within the Treasury Department, and the Joint Committee on Taxation of the U.S. Congress—have shown some interest in compliance research, although their primary mandates lie in other areas. While financial support for compliance research lies outside these organizations' spheres of interest, they can provide valuable encouragement for the IRS in its efforts to support external research and to integrate the findings into policy-making procedures.

The GAO, in its role of supporting congressional oversight of the IRS, routinely produces analyses of particular IRS enforcement procedures. These studies are valuable to the compliance research community, since the GAO has access to sensitive enforcement data, including case files and internal memos, that outside researchers have greater difficulty in obtaining. The GAO's independent status enhances the credibility of its studies as a source of information about tax administration procedures. The GAO has consistently supported the need for more compliance research at the IRS (U.S. GAO, 1979b, 1982, 1984) and could set an example by bringing compliance concerns more directly into the design of its research projects.

The Office of Tax Analysis and the Joint Committee on Taxation have primary responsibility for estimating the revenue effects of prospective changes in tax laws. Traditionally, their estimates have incorporated the revenue yield of IRS activities but have ignored compliance effects. The resulting errors may be important because the noncompliance revenue gap is large and compliance is affected by how taxable income and allowable deductions are defined. For these reasons, these agencies and other organizations that make such projections should begin to support the research needed to incorporate compliance effects into their projections. In addition to forecasting effects of tax policy changes, these agencies have begun to provide estimated revenue effects for policy options attempting to recover revenue lost through noncompliance. Their continued reliance on the IRS to develop data and methods for such estimation may be most efficient, given their range of other responsibilities, provided that outside experts are available to them to critique the data sources and methods being used from an independent scholarly perspective.

Finally, as links between the IRS and the Congress and other executive agencies, these three agencies are in a position to broaden the consensus needed to encourage the IRS to undertake three kinds of activities that have been politically difficult for it to sustain, in part because the benefits are speculative and long-term:

- Randomized experimentation to ascertain the compliance effects of its innovations;
- Long-range compliance research within the IRS that does not directly support management decisions; and
- Financial and nonfinancial support of independent research on taxpayer compliance carried out in universities and other independent research centers.

Strengthening IRS Support for Research

The Research Division of the Internal Revenue Service can be expected to remain the principal catalyst for research on individual taxpayer compliance. We strongly recommend that the IRS continue to foster the development and use of compliance research by: (1) enhancing the research potential of IRS data bases, especially TCMP, (2) facilitating external research use of IRS data bases, (3) integrating research and evaluation more fully into tax administration policy making, and (4) strengthening the external compliance research community. To provide a permanent structure for the communication associated with these efforts and for advising the Research Division, we recommend that the IRS create a Compliance Research Advisory Group of experts in tax practice and taxpayer compliance research.

Although several IRS divisions carry out research and sponsor research activities, the center for coordinating most taxpayer compliance research is the IRS Research Division. As described in Chapter 1, the Research Division employs a staff of about sixty professionals and controls an annual budget of just over $4 million for purchasing equipment, supplies, and services under the general heading of research and development. However, the lion's share of individual compliance research and measurement, $127 million in direct and opportunity costs, is devoted to each cycle of the TCMP Survey of Individual Filers, which is a key data set for compliance research. As indicated in Chapter 1, investment in long-range compliance research activities—sponsored research and liaison with the research community—is less than 2 percent of the cost of TCMP and internal management studies.

Even with this limited investment, the IRS Research Division has played a critical role in creating a taxpayer compliance research community. It has sponsored conferences that have attracted scholars from many disciplines, provided certain kinds of data to outside researchers, publicized internal research on compliance, and supported compliance research grants through the National Science Foundation.

Nevertheless, the panel believes that the IRS is substantially underinvesting in support of long-range compliance research compared with its other activities. Greater support of taxpayer compliance research offers one route—albeit a slow and uncertain one—for the IRS toward insights that can be used to reduce the noncompliance tax gap. Specific recommendations of ways in which the IRS can support taxpayer compliance research are described below.

ENHANCING THE RESEARCH POTENTIAL OF IRS DATA BASES

In Chapter 4 we described ways to improve the research potential of IRS data bases. First, the recommendations concerning TCMP enhancements—additional information on practitioner use and taxpayer occupation and industry and changing the three-year cycle to a one-year cycle with smaller samples—would increase the research and operational value of that data base. Second, it is important to reorient taxpayer surveys sponsored by the IRS away from remeasuring cross-sectional correlations between compliance and attitudes and perceptions toward more intensive investigation of the processes by which taxpayers form their attitudes toward commitment and their perceptions of the risks and benefits of compliance and noncompliance. Third, planning efforts should begin for possible updating of the 1969 aggregate cross-sectional file (Project 778) with a new file containing measures of compliance, IRS administrative activity, and theoretically relevant socioeconomic characteristics.

In planning how to carry out these data base enhancement and development efforts, representatives of the statistical and social science communities should work with representatives of all the affected IRS program units.

FACILITATING RESEARCH USE OF IRS DATA

By helping external researchers to use its rich internal administrative data, the IRS can leverage its resources. External use represents an exchange of internal expertise, programming, and documentation efforts for analytical work by researchers located elsewhere.

Two steps will encourage this beneficial exchange. First, as explained in Chapter 5, by developing public-use guidelines and convening a standing authority with internal and external members to review requests under the guidelines and to recommend changes in them as the need arises, two goals are advanced: encouraging reasonable requests and protecting the privacy of taxpayers and the security of information that must be kept confidential for enforcement purposes.

Second, additional resources should be provided for the IRS Research Division to continue and expand its technical efforts to support outside researchers' use of IRS data bases. For some kinds of data, creating and archiving public-use files can be an effective way to foster the scientific processes of criticism and replication and to stimulate the widest possible use. For public-use files, additional resources could support improved file documentation and more IRS staff time to respond to the inevitable inquiries about the interpretation and use of data fields. Timely, informed responses to such inquiries are essential to prevent misinterpretations.

When raw data are considered too sensitive for public-use files, aggregation or other special techniques described in Chapter 5 can sometimes be used to create less sensitive files that are suitable for particular research purposes. Computer and programming resources should be increased for creating and documenting such files when feasible and for carrying out special analyses of the sensitive data according to the external researcher's instructions when no special-purpose file is releasable. All these efforts represent exchanges of IRS resources for analytical work by external researchers.

INTEGRATING RESEARCH AND EVALUATION INTO POLICY MAKING

The panel recommends three ways in which the IRS could integrate compliance research and evaluation more fully into tax administration policy making, and it believes that such integration would be healthy for both tax administration and the research enterprise. First, the agency could adopt a general strategy of using what seem to be the inevitable changes in tax laws as opportunities to learn about taxpayers' responses to such changes. Such a strategy would require ongoing consultation with research methodologists to design quasi-experimental studies of the effects of legal changes, coordination across IRS program units to capture the necessary data, and an active effort to disseminate findings within the IRS for use in policy analysis. An example of this strategy is developed in Chapter 4 with reference to the Tax Reform Act of 1986.

Second, the IRS could initiate a policy analysis program of evaluation-innovation-refinement of various internal procedures, in which compliance effects as well as revenue recovery are used as criteria of success. Such a program involves the use of quasi-experimental analyses to identify problems with existing practices, and the introduction of remedial interventions using the principles of randomized experimentation, in order to provide the strongest possible evidence about their effects on compliance. The results of such an experiment would then suggest refinements, if needed, in the innovation. The discussion in Chapter 4 pointed to IRS contacts with taxpayers as examples of procedures for which this approach could be used. The strategy recommended there could also be extended to many other IRS operations.

Third, the IRS could make more direct use of researchers' insights by focusing portions of its annual research conferences on specific policy questions (as the Treasury Department did in its 1986 conference on tax amnesty) or by adding members to its advisory groups. Such expanded involvement would be healthy for both tax administration and compliance research, providing an opportunity for conventional agency wisdom to be challenged by diverse perspectives and researchers' assumptions and theories to be tested against administrative realities.

All three of these strategies should have the short-term effect of improving the knowledge base for tax administration policy making and, as the benefits of that become recognized, the long-term effect of enhancing agency-wide support for compliance research.

EXPANDING SUPPORT OF INDEPENDENT COMPLIANCE RESEARCH

This discussion has described many ways in which the IRS already supports compliance research. There are several ways in which compliance research with more distant and more speculative payoffs could be supported at a fairly small cost. First, a number of innovative arrangements involving personnel could enhance the agency's contact with the wider research community: temporary appointments (perhaps through internships or Intergovernmental Personnel Agreements, IPAs) of external researchers to the IRS, with time split between regular Research Division activities and undirected research that requires access to sensitive data; released time for Research Division staff to pursue undirected research with a view toward academic publication; and support (through programming support and released staff time) of collaboration between researchers on the IRS staff and researchers located elsewhere.

Second, in addition to specific projects, there is a need for financial support of the organizational and information-sharing infrastructure of a broad-based compliance research community. Examples include catalogues and abstracts of relevant internal and external research and a newsletter concerning ongoing compliance research activities.

Third, both multidisciplinary and single-discipline scientific conferences are also important elements of the infrastructure for compliance research. Even though many disciplinary perspectives can contribute to the understanding of taxpayer compliance and multidisciplinary conferences have already demonstrated great value, more focused scientific conferences also perform important functions. They provide forums for resolving ongoing controversies, for identifying new applications of existing findings, and for exchanging views on research findings and methods.

A PROPOSED COMPLIANCE RESEARCH ADVISORY GROUP

The IRS will continue to play a central role in tax compliance research because of its expertise, access to data, and need to understand and respond to compliance problems. Many of the initiatives recommended above are intended to permanently strengthen communication between the agency and the research community. To provide a structure for this ongoing communication, to advise the IRS on compliance research, and to create channels for scholarly contacts with the IRS, we recommend the establishment of a Compliance Research Advisory Group.

To maintain a broad liaison with the relevant research community, the advisory group should be composed of distinguished researchers and practitioners from several social science disciplines and tax professions. A rotating membership with staggered terms would provide some continuity but protect against stagnation. To nurture the independent status required to function as a liaison with the scientific community, the IRS would find it useful to offer the advisory group latitude in setting its own agenda and selecting new members. To ensure a close working relationship with the IRS, the advisory group could include the associate and assistant commissioners who oversee research and planning as well as the directors of the research and planning divisions, perhaps as ex-officio members; staff support functions could be provided by the IRS. Resources for the advisory group to hire consultants on occasion would be desirable.

The advisory group could assist the IRS in implementing at least four of the recommendations made in this report:
1. Identifying administrative research opportunities;
2. Advising on changes in compliance research priorities;
3. Enhancing research use; and
4. Routinizing communication with and nonfinancial support of the compliance research community.

IDENTIFYING ADMINISTRATIVE RESEARCH OPPORTUNITIES. As noted earlier, natural variation in the levels and nature of IRS activities provides opportunities to evaluate the effects of those activities on taxpayer compliance. The introduction of administrative innovations using randomized experimental designs could also provide an opportunity to test the effects of the innovations on taxpayer compliance. The resulting improved estimates of compliance effects associated with administrative alternatives would inform administrative choices, which must now be based on the more narrow criterion of direct revenue recovery. The Compliance Research Advisory Group could advise in the development of in-house capabilities for routinizing the design and implementation of studies of the compliance effects associated with administrative procedures.

RECOMMENDING AND MONITORING COMPLIANCE RESEARCH PRIORITIES. The research recommendations the panel makes in this report reflect the philosophy that a number of research approaches need to be focused on a limited number of high-priority research questions. These recommendations reflect priorities that we believe to be important and promising at the present time. However, setting and revising long-term research priorities is an ongoing process that requires consultation and consensus among researchers, operational and research units within the IRS, and tax policy makers. This process is needed to sustain research programs in the priority areas, to identify lines of research that are not bearing fruit, and to ensure the continuing relevance of the priority areas to enforcement and tax policy decisions made under changing conditions. Our suggested agenda could serve as a starting point for this consultation process, and the advisory group could provide routine reviews by knowledgeable scientific advisers.

ENHANCING RESEARCH USE. The Compliance Research Advisory Group could also help to promote the use of research results in policy analysis and development. Policy-focused analysis to apply research findings must take place close enough to the line management problems of the tax agency to incorporate an understanding of what policy alternatives and organizational modifications are feasible and desirable. At the same time, policy-focused analysis must be insulated enough from the agency's customs and internal political situations to encompass broad issues affecting the agency, to maintain creativity, and to develop ideas that may challenge ongoing routines. The Compliance Research Advisory Group, if established, could work with the IRS in creating these conditions.

COMMUNICATING WITH THE RESEARCH COMMUNITY. The Compliance Research Advisory Group would provide a natural bridge between outside researchers and the IRS. In order to capitalize on existing skills in the broad research community, the IRS could make use of the advisory group to identify researchers with particular specialized skills. The advisory group could also assist with peer review to provide inputs from several scientific perspectives as research is planned.

The advisory group could also provide ongoing assistance with several outreach functions already mentioned: planning workshops to deal with specific high-priority issues, institutionalizing a broad range of techniques for supporting outside research, disseminating research findings, and broadening institutional support for taxpayer compliance research.

Of all the liaison functions the advisory group could perform, none would be more valuable than assisting the IRS in developing, using, and revising (as needed) procedures for research use of IRS data. As indicated in Chapter 5, decisions on this subject are both technically complex and ethically sensitive. A broad-based advisory group could be invaluable in helping the IRS to develop and implement procedures that are both effective and widely accepted.

Considering Organizational Initiatives

In this chapter we have suggested a number of activities that would help to support an active research community, including:

- Establishing a broad base of private and public financial sponsorship for compliance research;
- Coordinating efforts to define research priorities;
- Encouraging sequential, multidisciplinary research efforts on focal problems;
- Working with IRS and existing data centers to expand research access to data;
- Establishing guidelines for the protection of taxpayers as subjects of compliance research;
- Enhancing communication within the research community through a newsletter, special compliance issues in relevant journals, workshops, and conferences; and
- Promoting young scholars through dissertation support, postdoctoral fellowships, research internship programs at the IRS, and IPA programs.

An open question is whether these activities would be advanced by some new organization, such as a Center for Tax Compliance Research. Other possibilities include a consortium of supporting institutions jointly funding a range of projects and research centers and a looser federation of institutions supporting coordinated projects. Such an organization could provide an institutional focus for these activities. However, sustained attention would be needed to ensure that any new organization served to complement and expand the efforts of individual researchers, existing tax research centers, and established data centers rather than to dominate taxpayer compliance research, institutionalize particular perspectives, or reduce the resources available for work by individual scholars.

Of the models considered in a National Academy of Sciences report on science and technology centers (National Academy of Sciences, 1987), the "center without walls" model may be most appropriate. Like grant-giving foundations, such a center might consist primarily of a governing board of sponsors, a prestigious research advisory board representing a variety of academic disciplines and professional perspectives, and a small executive office. It might develop a core of active researchers at different locations who communicate frequently through electronic mail and workshops. This structure could draw on research talents scattered throughout the country while avoiding much of the overhead and costly recruitment of researchers usually associated with traditional research institutions that conduct in-house projects. Avoiding concentration of effort and talent at a single institution that could gain undue influence over research funding or tax policy, this model may also reduce unnecessary duplication of activities and investment at several institutions.

Other models might also be appropriate, however, depending on the opportunities and sources of funding that are available for various purposes. A small center could be formed specifically around data made available from the IRS and state agencies, since access to these data is both essential for making progress in compliance research and problematic for outside researchers. A center staffed with data experts could considerably enhance knowledge of available data, interpretation of data items, and development of data access procedures.

The IRS and the NSF could jointly take a leading role in organizing one or more meetings to consider the feasibility of these or other new institutional arrangements for the support activities listed above. If such a meeting is held, the list of invitees should be very broad, including interested researchers, representatives of existing tax research centers in universities and state governments, members of public interest groups, and potential sponsors of research related to tax policy and tax administration. Such a meeting would provide a forum for considering whether new organizational structures are needed to advance compliance research and, if so, how to assemble the necessary resources without jeopardizing compliance research itself. The level of success of outreach activities to attract governmental and private support and interested researchers will itself help to determine how support of compliance research activities will be provided in the future.

References and Bibliography

Advisory Commission on Intergovernment Relations
    1984   Changing Public Attitudes on Governments and Taxes: A Commission Survey (1974–83). Washington, D.C.: Advisory Commission on Intergovernment Relations

Advisory Committee on Experimentation in the Law
    1981   *Experimentation in the Law*. Report of the Federal Judicial Center Advisory Committee on Experimentation in the Law. Washington, D.C.: U.S. Government Printing Office.

Aitken, S.S., and Bonneville, L.
    1980   A General Taxpayer Opinion Survey. Prepared for Office of Planning and Research, Internal Revenue Service, March 1980, by CSR Inc., Washington, D.C. (Contract No. TIR-79-2)

Ajzen, I., and Fishbein, M.
    1977   Attitude-behavior relations: a theoretical analysis and review of empirical research. *Psychological Bulletin* 84(5):888–918.
    1980   *Understanding Attitudes and Predicting Social Behavior*. Englewood Cliffs, N.J.: Prentice-Hall.

Akerlof, G.A., and Dickens, W.T.
    1982   The economic consequences of cognitive dissonance. *American Economic Review* 72(3):307–319.

Alden, J.
    1981   Holding two jobs: an examination of "moonlighting." Pp. 43–57 in J.S. Henry, ed., *Can I Have It In Cash?* London: Astragal Books.

Alexander, C., and Feinstein, J.
    1986   A Microeconometric Analysis of Income Tax Evasion. Unpublished paper, Massachusetts Institute of Technology.

Allen, H.M., and Sears, D.O.
    1979   Against them or for me: community impact evaluations. Pp. 171–175 in L. Datta and R. Perloff, eds., *Improving Evaluations*. Beverly Hills, Calif.: Sage Publications.

Allingham, M.G., and Sandmo, A.
    1972   Income tax evasion: a theoretical analysis. *Journal of Public Economics* 1:323–338.

Almond, G., and Verba, S.
    1963   *The Civic Culture*. Princeton, N.J.: Princeton University Press.

American Bar Association
   1987   Commission on Taxpayer Compliance Report and Recommendations.
          Tax Management Educational Institute. July 1987. American Bar Associa-
          tion, Washington, D.C.
American Institute of Certified Public Accountants
   1983   *Underreported Taxable Income: The Problem and Possible Solutions.* Wash-
          ington, D.C.: Federal Taxation Division, AICPA.
Andersen, P.
   1977   Tax evasion and the labor supply. *Scandinavian Journal of Economics*
          79:375–383.
Antonovsky, A., and Anson, O.
   1976   Factors related to preventive health behaviors. In J. W. Cullen et al., eds.,
          Cancer: The Behavioral Dimensions. Washington, D.C.: National Cancer
          Institute.
Ashenfelter, O., and Smith, R.S.
   1979   Compliance with the minimum wage laws. *Journal of Political Economy*
          87:333–359.
Ayres, F.L., Jackson, B., and Hite, P.
   1987   Factors Related to Tax Return Positions Recommended by Professional
          Tax Preparers in Ambiguous Situations. Unpublished paper, University
          of Oklahoma.
Balachandran, K.R., and Schaefer, M.E.
   1980   Optimal diversification among classes for auditing income tax returns.
          Public Finance 35(2):250–258.
Ball, H.V.
   1960   Social structure and rent-control violations. *American Journal of Sociology*
          65:598–604.
Ball, H., and Friedman, L.
   1965   The use of criminal sanctions in the enforcement of economic regulations.
          Stanford Law Review 17:197.
Balter, H.G.
   1983   *Tax Fraud and Evasion,* 5th Ed. Boston: Warren, Gorham & Lamont.
Bardach, E., and Kagan, R.A.
   1982   *Going by the Book: The Problem of Regulatory Unreasonableness.* Philadel-
          phia: Temple University Press. A Twentieth Century Fund Report.
Becker, G.S.
   1967   Crime and punishment: an economic approach. *Journal of Political Econ-
          omy* 78(2):526–536.
Becker, G.S., and Stigler, G.J.
   1974   Law enforcement, malfeasance, and compensation of enforcers. *Journal of
          Legal Studies* 3:1–18.
Benjamini, Y., and Maital, S.
   1985   Optimal tax evasion and optimal tax evasion policy: behavioral aspects.
          Pp. 245–264 in W. Gaertner and A. Wenig, eds., *The Economics of the
          Shadow Economy.* New York: Springer-Verlag.

Bentham, J.
    1948   *Principles of Morals and Legislation*. New York: Hafner.
Beron, K., Tauchen, H.V., and Witte, A.D.
    1988   A Structural Equation Model for Tax Compliance and Auditing. Working Paper No. 2556, National Bureau of Economic Research, Cambridge, Mass.
Black, J.S., Stern, P.C., and Elworth, J.T.
    1985   Personal and contextual influences on household energy adaptations. *Journal of Applied Psychology* 70:3–21.
Blau, P., and Duncan, O.D.
    1967   *The American Occupational Structure*. New York: John Wiley & Sons.
Blumstein, A.
    1983   Models for structuring taxpayer compliance. Pp. 159–172 in P. Sawicki, ed., *Income Tax Compliance: A Report of the ABA Section on Taxation, Invitational Conference on Income Tax Compliance*. Washington, D.C.: American Bar Association.
Blumstein, A., Cohen, J., and Nagin, D., eds.
    1978   *Deterrence and Incapacitation: Estimating the Effects of Criminal Sanctions on Crime Rates*. Panel on Research on Deterrent and Incapacitative Effects, National Research Council. Washington, D.C.: National Academy of Sciences.
Boorman, S.A.
    1979   A Dictionary of Compliance Factors. Unpublished manuscript. Draft #4, May 15, 1979. Internal Revenue Service, U.S. Department of the Treasury, Washington, D.C.
Boruch, R.F.
    1976   On common contentions about randomized field experiments. Pp. 158–194 in G.V. Glass, ed., *Evaluation Studies Review Annual, 3*. Beverly Hills, Calif.: Sage Publications.
Boruch, R.F., and Cecil, J.S.
    1979   On record linkage and the need for identifiers in research. Pp. 30–58 (Chapter 5) in *Assuring the Confidentiality of Social Research Data*. Philadelphia: University of Pennsylvania Press.
Bott, E.
    1957   *The Family and Social Network*. London: Tavistock.
Bowles, C.
    1971   *Promises to Keep*. New York: Harper and Row.
Bracewell-Milnes, B.
    1979   *Tax Avoidance and Evasion: The Individual and Society*. London: Panopticum Press.
Brady, H.E., and Sniderman, P.M.
    1985   Attitude attribution: a group basis for political reasoning. *American Political Science Review* 79(4):1061–1078.
Brandon, R.B., Rowe, J., and Stanton, T.H.
    1976   *Tax Politics*. New York: Pantheon Books.

Break, G.F.
  1984 Avenues to tax reform: perils and possibilities. *National Tax Journal* 37(1):1–8.

Broden, B.C.
  1977 Ethics in Tax Practice. Unpublished D.B.A. dissertation, University of Maryland.

Brown, C.V., Levin, E.J., Rosa, P.J., and Ulph, D.T.
  1984 Tax evasion and avoidance on earned income: some survey evidence. *Fiscal Studies* 5(3):1–22.

Brown, D.W.
  1974 Cognitive development and willingness to comply with the law. *American Journal of Political Science* 18(3):583–594.

Buchanan, J.M.
  1984 The ethical limits of taxation. *Scandinavian Journal of Economics* 86(2):102–114.

Bureau of Economic Analysis
  1981 *National Income and Product Accounts of the United States, 1929–76 Statistical Tables*. Washington, D.C.: U.S. Department of Commerce.

Burrell, S.
  1982 Legal malpractice of the tax attorney. *The Tax Executive* 34:259–277.

Cahalan, M., and Ekstrand, L.E.
  n.d. Incidence and Correlates of a White Collar Offense: A Pilot Survey of Tax Noncompliance. Unpublished paper, Westat, Inc., Rockville, Md.
  1980 *Who Are the Tax Cheaters and Why Do They Cheat?* Rockville, Md.: Westat, Inc.

Campbell, D.T., and Stanley, J.S.
  1966 *Quasi-Experimentation: Design and Analysis Issues for Field Settings.* Skokie, Ill.: Rand McNally.

Carlin, J.E.
  1966 *Lawyers' Ethics: A Survey of the New York City Bar*. New York: Russell Sage Foundation.

Carroll, J.S.
  1980 Analyzing decision behavior: the magician's audience. Pp. 69–76 in T. S. Walsten, ed., *Cognitive Processes in Choice and Decision Behavior*. Hillsdale, N.J.: Lawrence Erlbaum Associates.
  1986 Decisions About Taxpaying Careers. Paper presented in the Tax Compliance Panel of the Law and Society Association Meeting, Chicago, June 1, 1986.

Carroll, J.S., and Weaver, F.M.
  1986 Shoplifters' perceptions of crime opportunities: a process-tracing study. In D. Cornish and R. Clarke, eds., *The Reasoning Criminal*. New York: Springer-Verlag.

Carson, C.S.
   1984   The underground economy: an introduction. *Survey of Current Business* 64(May):21–37; 64(July):106–118.

Causey, D.Y.
   1985   *The Tax Practitioner: Legal and Ethical Rights and Responsibilities.* Mississippi State, Miss.: Accountant's Press.

Christiansen, V.
   1980   Two comments on tax evasion. *Journal of Public Economics* 13:389–393.

Cialdini, R.B.
   1980   Full cycle social psychology. *Applied Social Psychology Annual* 1:21–47.
   1988   *Influence: Science and Practice.* Second edition. Chicago: Scott, Foresman and Company.

Cialdini, R.B., and Ascani, K.
   1976   Test of a concession procedure for inducing verbal, behavioral, and further compliance with a request to give blood. *Journal of Applied Psychology* 61(3):295–300.

Citicorp
   1976   1976 Survey of Taxpayers and Tax Return Filing. Public opinion survey, CITICORP, New York.

Citrin, J.
   1979   Do people want something for nothing: public opinion on taxes and government spending. *National Tax Journal* 32(2)(Supplement): 113–129.

Clotfelter, C.T.
   1983   Tax evasion and tax rates: an analysis of individual returns. *Review of Economics and Statistics* 65(3):363–373.

Cnossen, S., ed.
   1983   *Comparative Tax Studies—Essays in Honor of Richard Goode.* New York: North-Holland.

Cohen, J., and Tonry, M.H.
   1983   Sentencing reforms and their impacts. Pp. 305–459 in A. Blumstein, J. Cohen, S. E. Martin, and M. H. Tonry, eds., *Research on Sentencing: The Search for Reform,* Vol. 2. Panel on Sentencing Research, National Research Council. Washington, D.C.: National Academy Press.

Converse, P.E.
   1975   Public opinion and voting behavior. In R. Greenstein and N. Polsby, eds., *Handbook of Political Science,* Vol. 4. Reading, Mass.: Addison-Wesley.

Cooter, R.
   1984   Prices and sanctions. *Columbia Law Review* 84:1523–1560.

Cordes, J.J., and Galper, H.
   1985   Tax Shelter Activity: Lessons from Twenty Years of Evidence. Paper prepared for National Tax Association—Tax Institute of America Summer Symposium, Arlington Va., May 20–21, 1985.

270   Bibliography

Corporate Management Tax Conference
  1982   *Income Tax Enforcement, Compliance, and Administration*. Proceedings of
         the Corporate Management Tax Conference, Canadian Tax Foundation,
         Toronto, Ont., June 17–18; Vancouver, B.C., Oct. 5–6, 1982.

Cowell, F.A.
  1985a Public policy and tax evasion: some problems. Pp. 273–284 in W. Ga-
         ertner and A. Wenig, eds., *The Economics of the Shadow Economy*. New
         York: Springer-Verlag.
  1985b Tax evasion with labor income. *Journal of Public Economics* 26(1):
         19–34.
  1985c The economic analysis of tax evasion. *Bulletin of Economic Research*
         37(3):163–193.

Cox, D.
  1984   Raising revenue in the underground economy. *National Tax Journal*
         37:283–288.

Coyne, M.L., and Smith, K.W.
  1987   Between Scylla and Charybdis: A Conceptual Framework of the Incen-
         tives and Constraints of Tax Practice. Unpublished paper available from
         American Bar Foundation, Chicago.

Cross, R., and Shaw, G.K.
  1981   The evasion-avoidance choice: a suggested approach. *National Tax Jour-
         nal* 34:489–491.
  1982   On the economics of tax aversion. *Public Finance* 37:36–47.

Cyert, R.M., and March, J.G.
  1963   *A Behavioral Theory of the Firm*. Englewood Cliffs, N.J.: Prentice-Hall.

Dalenius, T.
  1985   Privacy and Confidentiality in Censuses and Surveys. Paper presented at
         the Conference on Access to Public Data, Social Science Research Coun-
         cil, Washington, D.C., November 21–22, 1985.

Darnell, A.T., and Gallaher, H.E.
  1985   Taxes and Government: Changes in Public Opinion from Roosevelt to
         Reagan. American Bar Foundation Taxpayer Compliance Project Work-
         ing Paper 84-3. American Bar Association, Washington, D.C., August
         1985.

Davidson, G.
  1985   Encouraging Taxpayers to Pay Taxes (And Feel Good About It): A Study
         of Ways to Increase Voluntary Compliance in Massachusetts. Policy Ana-
         lytic Exercise, Kennedy School of Government and the Massachusetts
         Department of Revenue, April 15, 1985.

Dean, P., Keenan, T., and Kenney, F.
  1980   Taxpayers' attitudes to income tax evasion: An empirical study. *British
         Tax Review* 1:28–44.

Deane, K.D.
1981   Tax evasion, criminality and sentencing the tax offender. *British Journal of Criminology* 21(1):47–57.

De Grazia, R.
1980   Clandestine employment: a problem in our times. *International Labour Review* 119:544–583.

Demers, D.K., and Lundman, R.J.
1987   Perceptual deterrence research: some additional evidence for designing studies. *Journal of Quantitative Criminology* 3:185–194.

Diamond, S.
1986   Methods for the empirical study of law. In L. Lipson and S. Wheeler, eds., *Law and the Social Sciences*. New York: Russell Sage Foundation.

Ditton, J., and Brown, R.
1981   Why don't they revolt? 'Invisible income' as a neglected dimension of Runciman's relative deprivation thesis. *British Journal of Sociology* 32(4):521–530.

Diver, C.S.
1983   The optimal precision of administrative rules. *Yale Law Journal* 93(1):65–109.

Dornstein, M.
1976   Compliance with legal and bureaucratic rules: the case of self-employed taxpayers in Israel. *Human Relations* 29(11):1019–1034.

Dow, L.M., Jr.
1977   High weeds in Detroit: the irregular economy among networks of Appalachian migrants. *Urban Anthropology* 6:111–128.

Dubin, J.A., Graetz, M.J., and Wilde, L.L.
1987a   Are we a nation of tax cheaters? New econometric evidence on tax compliance. *American Economic Review* 77(2):240–245.
1987b   The effect of tax and audit rates on compliance with the federal income tax, 1977–85. Social Science Working Paper 638. California Institute of Technology, Pasadena, April, 1987
1987c   Penny-wise and pound-foolish: new estimates of the impact of audits on revenue. *Tax Notes* 35(8):787–791.

Dubin, J.A., and Wilde, L.L.
1986   An empirical analysis of federal income tax auditing and compliance. Social Science Working Paper. California Institute of Technology, Pasadena, October, 1986.
1987a   An empirical analysis of federal income tax auditing and compliance. Social Science Working Paper. California Institute of Technology, Pasadena, October 1986, revised February 1987.
1987b   An empirical analysis of federal income tax auditing and compliance. Social Science Working Paper. California Institute of Technology, Pasadena, October 1986, revised November 1987.

1988   An empirical analysis of federal income tax auditing and compliance. *National Tax Journal* 16(1):61–74.

Easterlin, R.

1966   Economic-demographic interactions among long swings in economic growth. *American Economic Review* 56(5):1063–1104.

Easton, D.

1965   *A Systems Analysis of Political Life*. New York: John Wiley & Sons.

Egger, R.L., Jr.

1982   Compliance from the viewpoint of the Internal Revenue Service. Pp. 279–286 in Income Tax Enforcement, Compliance, and Administration. Proceedings of the Corporate Management Tax Conference, Canadian Tax Foundation, Toronto, Ont., June 17–18, and Vancouver, B.C., October 5–6, 1982.

Ehrlich, I.

1973   Participation in illegitimate activities: a theoretical and empirical investigation. *Journal of Political Economy* 81(3):521–565.

1975   Deterrence: evidence and inference. *Yale Law Journal* 85(2):209–227.

Eisenstein, L.

1961   *The Ideologies of Taxation*. New York: Roland Press.

Ekland-Olsen, S., Lieb, J., and Zurcher, L.

1984   The paradoxical impact of criminal sanctions: some microstructural findings. *Law and Society* 18(2):159–178.

Ekstrand, L.E.

1980   *Factors Affecting Compliance: Focus Group and Survey Results*. Rockville, Md.: Westat, Inc.

Elder, G.

1974   *Children of the Great Depression*. Chicago: University of Chicago Press.

Evans, L.

1976   Federal Tax Reform Efforts: Their Ideological Context and Potential for Success. Ph.D. dissertation, Department of Sociology, Boston College.

1978   Obstacles to federal tax reform: an exploratory inquiry into the fiscal attitudes of a small group of tax payers. *American Journal of Economics and Sociology* 37(1):71–86.

Farioletti, M.

1973   Tax administration funding and fiscal policy. *National Tax Journal* 24(1):1–18.

Farris, J.D.

1979   Criminal and civil tax fraud. *Criminal Justice Journal* 3(1):25–150.

Federal Committee on Statistical Methodology

1978   *Report on Statistical Disclosure and Disclosure-Avoidance Techniques*. Statistical Policy Working Paper 2, May, 1978. Subcommittee on Disclosure-Avoidance Techniques, Office of Federal Statistical Policy and Standards. Washington, D.C.: U.S. Department of Commerce.

Feeley, M.M.
  1970   Coercion and compliance: a new look at an old problem. Chapter 2 in S. Krislov et al., eds., *Compliance and the Law*. Beverly Hills, Calif.: Sage Publications.

Feest, J.
  1967   Compliance with legal regulation: observations of stop sign behavior. *Law and Society Review* 2:447–461.

Feffer, G.A., Timbie, R.E., Weiner, A.J., and Ernst, M.L.
  1983   Proposals to deter and detect the underground cash economy. Pp. 293–316 in P. Sawicki, ed., *Income Tax Compliance: A Report of the ABA Section on Taxation, Invitational Conference on Income Tax Compliance*. Washington, D.C.: American Bar Association.

Feige, E.L.
  1979   How big is the irregular economy? *Challenge* 22(Nov–Dec):5–13.
  1980   A New Perspective on a Macroeconomic Phenomenon. Unpublished manuscript, University of Wisconsin.
  1985   The meaning of the "underground economy" and the full compliance deficit. Pp. 19–36 in W. Gaertner and A. Wenig, eds., *The Economics of the Shadow Economy*. New York: Springer-Verlag.

Feldman, J., and Kay, J.A.
  1981   Tax Avoidance. Pp. 320–333 in P. Burrows and C.G. Veljanovski, eds., *The Economic Approach to Law*. London: Butterworth.

Fellegi, I.P., and Sunter, A.B.
  1969   A theory of record linkage. *Journal of the American Statistical Association* 64:1183–1210.

Ferman, L.A., and Berndt, L.E.
  1981   The irregular economy. Pp. 26–42 in J.S. Henry, ed., *Can I Have It In Cash?* London: Astragal Books.

Festinger, L.
  1957   *A Theory of Cognitive Dissonance*. Stanford, Calif.: Stanford University Press.

Fhaner, G., and Hare, M.
  1973   Seat belts: factors influencing their use. *Accident Analysis and Prevention* 5:27–43.

Fienberg, S.E., Martin, M.E., and Straf, M.L., eds.
  1985   *Sharing Research Data*. Committee on National Statistics. Washington, D.C.: National Academy Press.

Fincham, F.D., and Jaspers, J.
  1983   A subjective probability approach to responsibility attribution. *British Journal of Social Psychology* 22:145–162.

Fishburn, G.
  1979   On how to keep tax payers honest (or almost so). *Economic Record* 55:267–270.

Fisher, F.M., and Nagin, D.
    1978 On the feasibility of identifying the crime function in a simultaneous model of crime rates and sanction levels. In A. Blumstein, J. Cohen, and D. Nagin, eds., *Deterrence and Incapacitation: Estimating the Effects of Criminal Sanctions on Crime Rates.* National Research Council. Washington, D.C.: National Academy of Sciences.

Fisher, V.L.
    1985 Recent innovations in state tax compliance programs. *National Tax Journal* 38(3):365–371.

Fox, J.A., and Tracy, P.E.
    1980 The randomized response approach: applicability to criminal justice research and evaluation. *Evaluation Review* 4(5):601–622.
    1986 *Randomized Response: A Method for Sensitive Surveys.* Beverly Hills, Calif.: Sage Publications.

Frank, M., and Dekeyser-Meulders, D.
    1977 A tax discrepancy coefficient resulting from tax evasion or tax expenditures. *Journal of Public Economics* 8:67–78.

Fratanduono, R.J.
    1986 Trends in voluntary compliance of taxpayers filing individual tax returns. In IRS Research Division, *Trend Analyses and Related Statistics: 1986 Update* (Document 6011). Washington, D.C.: U.S. Department of the Treasury.

Friedland, N.
    1982 A note on tax evasion as a function of the quality of information about the magnitude and credibility of threatened fines: some preliminary research. *Journal of Applied Psychology* February:54–59.

Friedland, N., Maital, S., and Rutenberg, A.
    1978 A simulation study of income tax evasion. *Journal of Public Economics* 10:107–116.

Friedland, N., Thibaut, J., and Walker, L.
    1973 Some determinants of the violation of rules. *Journal of Applied Social Psychology* 3:103–118.

Friedman, L.M., and Macaulay, S.
    1977 *Law and the Behavioral Sciences.* New York: Bobbs-Merrill Company, Inc.

Furnham, A.
    1983 The Protestant work ethic, human values, and attitudes towards taxation. *Journal of Economic Psychology* 3:113–128.

Gaertner, W., and Wenig, A., eds.
    1985 *The Economics of the Shadow Economy.* New York: Springer-Verlag.

Geis, G., and R. Meier, eds.
    1977 *White Collar Crime.* Rev. ed. New York: Free Press.

Gibbs, J.P.
    1968 On crime, punishment, and deterrence. *Southwestern Social Science Quarterly* 49(March):157–162.

Gijsel, P.D.
  1985   A microeconomic analysis of black labour demand and supply. Pp. 218–226 in W. Gaertner and A. Wenig, eds., *The Economics of the Shadow Economy*. New York: Springer-Verlag.

Glatzer, W., and Berger, R.
  1985   Household composition, social networks and household production. Pp. 330–351 in W. Gaertner and A. Wenig, eds., *The Economics of the Shadow Economy*. New York: Springer-Verlag.

Gordon, R.A.
  1983   Evasion and avoidance of U.S. taxation through foreign transactions—some issues. Pp. 339–350 in P. Sawicki, ed., *Income Tax Compliance: A Report of the ABA Section on Taxation, Invitational Conference on Income Tax Compliance*. Washington, D.C.: American Bar Association.

Graetz, M.J., Reinganum, J.F., and Wilde, L.L.
  1984   An Equilibrium Model of Tax Compliance with a Bayesian Auditor and Some "Honest" Taxpayers. Unpublished paper, Yale Law School.
  1986   The tax compliance game: toward an interactive theory of law enforcement. *Journal of Law, Economics and Organization* 2(1):1–32.

Graetz, M.J., and Wilde, L.L.
  1985   The economics of tax compliance: fact and fantasy. *National Tax Journal* 38(3):355–364.

Grasmick, H.G.
  1985   The Application of a Generalized Theory of Deterrence to Income Tax Evasion. Unpublished paper, Department of Sociology, University of Oklahoma, June 1985.
  1986   The Measurement of Tax Compliance. Report prepared for symposium on taxpayer compliance sponsored by the Committee on Research on Law Enforcement and the Administration of Justice, Panel on Research on Taxpayer Compliance Behavior, January 17, 1986.

Grasmick, H.G., and Bryjak, G.J.
  1980   The deterrent effect of perceived severity of punishment. *Social Forces* 62(2):471–491.

Grasmick, H.G., Finley, N., and Glaser, D.
  1984   Labor force participation, sex-role attitudes, and female crime. *Social Science Quarterly* 65:703–718.

Grasmick, H.G., and Green, D.E.
  1980   Legal punishment, social disapproval and internalization of inhibitors of illegal behavior. *Journal of Criminal Law and Criminology* 71(3): 325–335.
  1981   Deterrence and the morally committed. *The Sociological Quarterly* 22: 1–14.

Grasmick, H.G., Jacobs, D., and McCollom, C.B.
  1983   Social class and social control: an application of deterrence theory. *Social Forces* 62(2):359–374.

Grasmick, H.G., and Scott, W.J.
　　1982　Tax evasion and mechanisms of social control: a comparison with grand and petty theft. *Journal of Economic Psychology* 2:213–230.

Green, J., and Laffont, J.J.
　　1986　Competition on Many Fronts: A Stackelberg Signalling Equilibrium. Discussion Paper Number 1250, Department of Economics, Harvard University.

Greenberg, J.
　　1984　Avoiding tax avoidance: a (repeated) game-theoretic approach. *Journal of Economic Theory* 32:1–13.

Groenland, E.A.G., and van Veldhoven, G.M.
　　1983　Tax evasion behavior—a psychological framework. *Journal of Economic Psychology* 3:129–144.

Groves, H.M.
　　1958　Empirical studies of income tax compliance. *National Tax Journal* 11(December):291–301.
　　1959　Income-tax administration. *National Tax Journal* 12(1):37–53.

Gutmann, P.M.
　　1977　The subterranean economy. *Journal of Financial Analysis* Nov/Dec:26.

Habib, M.G.H.
　　1980　*A Comparison of Direct Elicitation and Random Response Techniques for Measuring Level of Income Tax Evasion.* Corvallis, Ore.: Survey Research Center, Oregon State University.

Handler, J.R.
　　1967　*The Lawyer and His Community—The Practicing Bar in a Middle-Sized City.* Milwaukee: University of Wisconsin Press.

Hansen, S.B.
　　1983　*The Politics of Taxation: Revenue Without Representation.* Praeger Special Studies/Praeger Scientific. New York: Praeger Publishers.

Hansson, I.
　　1985　Tax evasion and government policy. Pp. 285–299 in W. Gaertner and A. Wenig, eds., *The Economics of the Shadow Economy.* New York: Springer-Verlag.

Havemann, J.
　　1983　Political fight over withholding of interest matched by war of numbers. *National Journal* 15:648–649.

Hawkins, K., and Thomas, J.M., eds.
　　1984　*Enforcing Regulation.* Boston: Kluwer-Nijhoff Publishing.

Haws, R.J.
　　1983　A brief history of American resistance to taxation. Pp. 113–132 in P. Sawicki, ed., *Income Tax Compliance: A Report of the ABA Section on Taxation, Invitational Conference on Income Tax Compliance.* Washington, D.C.: American Bar Association.

Heinz, J., and Laumann, E.
  1978   The legal profession: client interests, professional roles, and social hierar-
         chies. *Michigan Law Review* 76:1111–1117.

Henry, J.S.
  1975   The Currency Connection. Unpublished manuscript available from au-
         thor, McKinsey and Co., New York.
  1976   Calling in the big bills. *Washington Monthly* 8(May):27.
  1983   Noncompliance with U.S. tax law—evidence on size, growth, and com-
         position. Pp. 15–112 in P. Sawicki, ed., *Income Tax Compliance: A Report of
         the ABA Section on Taxation, Invitational Conference on Income Tax Com-
         pliance*. Washington, D.C.: American Bar Association.

Henszey, B.N., and Roadarmel, R.L.
  1981   A comparative analysis of state individual income tax enforcement proce-
         dures. *National Tax Journal* 34:207–216.

Herschel, F.J.
  1978   Tax evasion and its measurement in developing countries. *Public Finance*
         33(3):232–268.

Hessing, D.J., Elffers, H., and Weigel, R.H.
  1986   Self-Report Versus Behavior: An Examination of the Correlates of Tax
         Evasion. Unpublished paper, Erasmus University, Rotterdam.

Hoeflich, M.H.
  1983   Of reason, gamesmanship, and taxes: a jurisprudential and games theoret-
         ical approach to the problem of voluntary compliance. *American Journal of
         Tax Policy* 2(Spring):9–88.

Holland, D.M., and Oldman, O.
  1984   A review of selected recent research on measuring income tax base eva-
         sion, including lessons to be drawn from the data from measuring and
         controlling income tax evasion. *The Challenge of Tax Administration Until
         the End of the 20th Century: Technical Papers and Reports of 15th General
         Assembly of the Inter-American Center of Tax Administrators (CIAT),
         Mexico City, June 29–July 3, 1981*. 35:146–166. Amsterdam: International
         Bureau of Fiscal Documentation.

Hotaling, A.W., and Arnold, D.F.
  1981   The underground economy. *Massachusetts CPA Review* May–June:
         8–14.

Hyde, A.
  1983   The concept of legitimation in the sociology of law. *Wisconsin Law Re-
         view*: 379–426.

ICF Incorporated
  1985   *Summary of Public Attitude Survey Findings*. Prepared for the Research
         Division, Internal Revenue Service, U.S. Department of the Treasury.
         Washington, D.C.: ICF Incorporated.

Internal Revenue Service

1968 *Report on Role of Sanctions in Tax Compliance*. Office of Assistant Commissioner (Planning, Finance and Research), Internal Revenue Service. Washington, D.C.: U.S. Department of the Treasury.

1973 Measuring the Deterrent Effect of an Audit. Internal memorandum, Project 777. Office of Assistant Commissioner (Planning, Finance and Research), Internal Revenue Service, U.S. Department of the Treasury.

1974 *Taxpayer Compliance Measurement Program [TCMP] Phase III. Cycle 5. User's Manual*. Research Division, Internal Revenue Service. Washington, D.C.: U.S. Department of the Treasury.

1975a *Annual Report 1975*. Commissioner of Internal Revenue, Internal Revenue Service, U.S. Department of the Treasury. Washington, D.C.: U.S. Government Printing Office.

1975b Effect of a Prior Year TCMP Audit. September 1975. Office of Assistant Commissioner (Planning, Finance and Research), Internal Revenue Service, U.S. Department of the Treasury.

1976 Comments on CITICORP 1976 Survey of Taxpayers and Tax Return Filing. Internal memorandum dated May 20, 1976, from Chief, Statistical Research Staff, Internal Revenue Service, to R. Renoud, Internal Revenue Service, U.S. Department of the Treasury.

1977a *Annual Report 1977*. Commissioner of Internal Revenue, Internal Revenue Service, U.S. Department of the Treasury. Washington, D.C.: U.S. Government Printing Office.

1977b Master File Non-Master File IDRS System Codes Booklet. Document 6209. Internal Revenue Service, U.S. Department of the Treasury.

1977c Package X: Informational Copies of Federal Income Tax Forms. Internal Revenue Service, U.S. Department of the Treasury.

1977d *Taxpayer Compliance Measurement Program [TCMP] Handbook*. Office of Assistant Commissioner (Planning and Research), Internal Revenue Service. Washington, D.C.: U.S. Department of the Treasury.

1978a Background Memo on Project 778 Regression Model: Some Pertinent In-House Data on Factors Affecting Compliance. Internal memorandum dated August 24, 1978. Internal Revenue Service, U.S. Department of the Treasury.

1978b   Criminal Investigation Planning Model Study. Interim report. Criminal Investigation Division, Internal Revenue Service, U.S. Department of the Treasury.

1978c   Final Report of the Tax Package Questionnaire Survey. Prepared by Tax Package Questionnaire Committee, Internal Revenue Service, U.S. Department of the Treasury.

1978d   IRS Work Statement [Compliance Studies Review]. Request for proposal from the Internal Revenue Service, U.S. Department of the Treasury.

1978e   National Register of Active Decision Information Projects: Studies, Tests, and Research Projects being conducted by the U.S. Internal Revenue Service. Document 6426. Internal Revenue Service, U.S. Department of the Treasury.

1978f   The Collection Division Organization. Brochure assembled from Internal Revenue Manual MT1100-221, pp. 1100-15 to 1100-178. Internal Revenue Service, U.S. Department of the Treasury.

1978g   United States Historical Data 1975–78. Form M-6370. Internal Rvenue Service, U.S. Department of the Treasury.

1979a   Calendar Year Projections 1979–1990. Number of Returns To Be Filed. Internal document. Statistics Division, Internal Revenue Service, U.S. Department of the Treasury.

1979b   *Estimates of Income Unreported on Individual Income Tax Returns.* Publication 1104(9-79), Internal Revenue Service. Washington, D.C.: U.S. Department of the Treasury.

1979c   *Taxpayer Compliance Measurement Program [TCMP] Phase III. Cycle 7. User's Manual.* Research Division, Internal Revenue Service. Washington, D.C.: U.S. Department of the Treasury.

1980   Requests for Proposal: Development of a Survey to Determine Unreported Income of Informal Suppliers (RFP: IRS 80-105). Contract and Procurement Branch, Internal Revenue Service, U.S. Department of the Treasury.

1981a   Case Selection Criteria and Resources Planning Procedures. Report of the SEP/GEP Task Force. Criminal Investigation Division, Internal Revenue Service, U.S. Department of the Treasury.

1981b   Collections Task Force, 1979–1981. Collection of documents supplied by Internal Revenue Service, U.S. Department of the Treasury.

1981c   *Study of the Information Returns Program (IRP) TY 1975 and 1976.* Office of Assistant Commissioner (Planning and Research), Internal Revenue Service, Washington, D.C.: U.S. Department of the Treasury.

1982a   *Annual Report 1982.* Commissioner and Chief Counsel, Internal Revenue Service, U.S. Department of the Treasury. Washington, D.C.: U.S. Government Printing Office.

1982b   Effect of a Prior Year TCMP Audit (Second Panel). January 1982. Office of Assistant Commissioner (Planning, Finance and Research), Internal Revenue Service, U.S Department of the Treasury.

1982c   *Information Reporting on Bearer Obligations.* Research Division, Office of Planning, Finance and Research, Internal Revenue Service, Washington, D.C.: U.S. Department of the Treasury.

1982d   Memorandum on Clotfelter paper dated November 5 from Chief, Compliance Estimates Group to Director, Research Division, Internal Revenue Service, U.S. Department of the Treasury.

1982e   *Report on Bearer Obligation Interest Compliance.* Research Division, Office of Planning, Finance and Research, Internal Revenue Service. Washington, D.C.: U.S. Department of the Treasury.

1982f   Requests for proposal: discriminant function formulas for 12 examination classes of individual income tax returns (RFP: IRS 82–89). Contract and Procurement Branch, Internal Revenue Service, U.S. Department of the Treasury.

1982g   *Simplification of Information Returns.* Research Division, Office of Planning, Finance and Research, Internal Revenue Service. Washington, D.C.: U.S. Department of the Treasury.

1982h   State Income Tax Refund Project Report (DATC). February 1982. Internal Revenue Service, U.S. Department of the Treasury.

1982i   Taxpayer Compliance Measurement Program [TCMP] Report, Table 10, Phase III, Cycle 7. Office of Assistant Commissioner (Planning, Finance and Research), Internal Revenue Service, U.S. Department of the Treasury.

1983a   *Annual Report 1983.* Commissioner and Chief Counsel, Internal Revenue Service, U.S. Department of the Treasury. Washington, D.C.: U.S. Government Printing Office.

1983b   *Energy Credit and Limitations Project of The Deferred Adverse Tax Consequences Program* (DATC). December 1983. Internal Revenue Service. Washington, D.C.: U.S. Department of the Treasury.

1983c   Environmental Scan: Demographic, Public Attitude, and Federal Tax Compliance Projections. Advisory Report prepared by Assistant Commissioner (Planning, Finance and Research), Internal Revenue Service, U.S. Department of the Treasury.

1983d   *Final Report of the Delinquent Form 1099-MISC Follow-up Study.* Internal Revenue Service. Washington, D.C.: U.S. Department of the Treasury.

1983e   *Form 1099 NEC Compliance Study.* Office of Assistant Commissioner (Planning, Finance and Research), Internal Revenue Service. Washington, D.C.: U.S. Department of the Treasury.

1983f   *Income Tax Compliance Research: Estimates for 1973–1981.* Office of Assistant Commissioner (Planning, Finance and Research), Internal Revenue Service. Washington, D.C.: U.S. Department of the Treasury.

1983g   *Research Strategies Volume I: Summary.* Conference on Tax Administration. Office of Assistant Commissioner (Planning, Finance and Research), Internal Revenue Service. Washington, D.C.: U.S. Department of the Treasury.

1983h   *Research Strategies Volume II: Proceedings.* Conference on Tax Administration. Office of Assistant Commissioner (Planning, Finance and Research), Internal Revenue Service. Washington, D.C.: U.S. Department of the Treasury.

1983i   Stock Sales Disclosed by Dividend Cessations Test of the Deferred Adverse Tax Consequences Program (DATC). June 1983. Internal Revenue Service, U.S. Department of the Treasury.

1983j   Taxpayer Compliance Measurement Program [TCMP] Report, Table C, Phase III, Cycle 7. Office of Assistant Commissioner (Planning, Finance and Research), Internal Revenue Service, U.S. Department of the Treasury.

1984a   *Annual Report 1984.* Commissioner of Internal Revenue. Internal Revenue Service, U.S. Department of the Treasury. Washington, D.C.: U.S. Government Printing Office.

1984b   ASTA Pretest Report for Non-Cash Unsupported Charitable Contributions. June 1984. Internal Revenue Service, U.S. Department of the Treasury.

1984c   ASTA Pretest Report on Government Grant Offsets of Residential Energy Credits. September 1984. Internal Revenue Service, U.S. Department of the Treasury.

1984d   Combined Annual Wage Reporting Reconciliation Study (Phase II) Tax Year 1978. January 1984. Internal Revenue Service, U.S. Department of the Treasury.

1984e   Description of Active Research Projects. October 1984. Internal document prepared by the Office of Assistant Commissioner (Planning, Finance and Research), Internal Revenue Service, U.S. Department of the Treasury.

1984f   DIF Research Study: Benefits of Second Stage DIF Development are Substantial. Study prepared by D. Wilt for the Director, Planning, Finance and Research, Internal Revenue Service, U.S. Department of the Treasury.

1984g   Internal Revenue Service Strategic Plan. Document 6941. Internal Revenue Service, U.S. Department of the Treasury.

1984h   Package X: Informational Copies of Federal Income Tax Forms. Internal Revenue Service, U.S. Department of the Treasury.

1984i   Pre-Test Study Report: Activities Not Engaged in For Profit Study (DATC). July 1984. Internal Revenue Service, U.S. Department of the Treasury.

1984j   Pre-Test Study Report: Alimony Not Reported as Income Study (ASTA). July 1984. Internal Revenue Service, U.S. Department of the Treasury.

1984k   Recapture of Accelerated/Accrued Deductions on HUD Involved Housing Study of the Deferred Adverse Tax Consequences Program (DATC). June 1984. Internal Revenue Service, U.S. Department of the Treasury.

1984l   *Statistical Use of Administrative Records: Recent Research and Present Prospects. Volume 1.* Compiled and edited by B. Kilss and W. Alvey, Statistics of Income Division, Internal Revenue Service. Washington, D.C.: U.S. Department of the Treasury.

1984m   *Statistical Uses of Administrative Records: Recent Research and Present Prospects, Volume 2.* Compiled and edited by B. Kilss and W. Alvey, Statistics of Income Division, Internal Revenue Service. Washington, D.C.: U.S. Department of the Treasury.

1984n   *Taxpayer Compliance Measurement Program [TCMP] Handbook.* Office of Assistant Commissioner (Planning, Finance and Research), Internal Revenue Service. Document 6457. Washington, D.C.: U.S. Department of the Treasury.

1985a   *Annual Report 1985.* Commissioner of Internal Revenue. Internal Revenue Service, U.S. Department of the Treasury. Washington, D.C.: U.S. Government Printing Office.

1985b   *Conference on Tax Administration Research. Volume I. Summary.* January 1985. Office of Assistant Commissioner (Planning, Finance and Research), Internal Revenue Service. Washington, D.C.: U.S. Department of the Treasury.

1985c   *Conference on Tax Administration Research. Volume II. Proceedings.* January 1985. Office of Assistant Commissioner (Planning, Finance and Research), Internal Revenue Service. Washington, D.C.: U.S. Department of the Treasury.

1985d   Description of Active Research Projects. Office of Assistant Commissioner (Planning, Finance and Research), Internal Revenue Service, U.S. Department of the Treasury.

1985e   Flowcharts of IRS pipeline, and auditing of tax returns. Photocopies received from Internal Revenue Service Conference, January 1985. Internal Revenue Service, U.S. Department of the Treasury.

1985f   IRS Function Summaries: A Descriptive Summary of IRS Operations. Paper from the IRS Conference, Washington, D.C., January 1985. Internal Revenue Service, U.S. Department of the Treasury.

1985g   Master File Tape Record Sample Manual. Abridged version of data base procedure manual. Internal Revenue Service, U.S. Department of the Treasury.

1985h   Research Agenda. Unpublished list of research prepared by Office of Assistant Commissioner (Planning, Finance and Research), Internal Revenue Service, U.S. Department of the Treasury.

1985i   Statistics of Income Bulletin 4(3).

1985j   *Trend Analyses and Related Statistics.* Document 6011 (Revised 2-85), Internal Revenue Service. Washington, D.C.: U.S. Department of the Treasury.

1985k   Work Statement: Survey of Tax Practitioners. Internal memorandum from Office of Assistant Commissioner (Planning, Finance and Research), Internal Revenue Service, U.S. Department of the Treasury.

1986a   Net Tax Gap Briefing. Internal Revenue Service, U.S. Department of the Treasury.

1986b   Trend Analyses and Related Statistics: United States, Districts, Regions and Service Centers. 1986 Update. Office of Assistant Commissioner (Planning, Finance and Research), Internal Revenue Service, U.S. Department of the Treasury.

1987   *Annual Report 1987.* Commissioner of Internal Revenue. Internal Revenue Service, U.S. Department of the Treasury. Washington, D.C.: U.S. Government Printing Office.

1988   *Income Tax Compliance Research: Gross Tax Gap Estimates and Projections for 1973–1992.* Research Division pub. no. 7285 (3-88). Washington, D.C.: U.S. Department of the Treasury.

Isachsen, A.J., Samuelsen, S.O., and Strøm, S.
1985   The behaviour of tax evaders. In W. Gaertner and A. Wenig, eds., *The Economics of the Shadow Economy.* New York: Springer-Verlag.

Isachsen, A.J., and Strøm, S.
1980   The hidden economy: the labor market and tax evasion. *Scandinavian Journal of Economics* 82(2):304–311.

Jackson, B.R., and Jones, S.M.
1985a   Salience of tax evasion penalties versus detection risk. *Journal of the American Taxation Association* Spring:7–17.

1985b   Stemming income tax evasion. *Journal of Accountancy* (January): 76–78.

Jackson, B.R., and Milliron, V.C.
1987   Research on the Practitioner's Role in the Compliance Process: State of the Art. Unpublished paper, University of Colorado and The Pennsylvania State University.

n.d.   Tax Compliance Research: Findings, Problems, and Prospects. Unpublished paper, University of Colorado.

Jackson, I.A.
1984   Putting the Private-Public Partnership to the Test of Practice. Paper prepared for the 1984 Research Conference, Association for Public Policy Analysis and Management, October 18, 1984.

1985   *Voluntary Compliance: The $564 Million Story.* Boston: Massachusetts Department of Revenue.

Johnson, F.J., and Payne, J.W.
1985   Effort and accuracy in choice. *Management Sciences* 31:395–414.

Jones, J.F.A., ed.
   1974   *Tax Havens and Measures against Tax Evasion and Avoidance in the EEC.*
         London: Associated Business Programmes.
Kagan, R.A.
   1978   *Regulatory Justice: Implementing a Wage-Price Freeze.* New York: Russell
         Sage Foundation.
Kahneman, D.A., Slovic, P., and Tversky, A., eds.
   1982   *Judgment Under Uncertainty: Heuristics and Biases.* Cambridge: Cam-
         bridge University Press.
Kahneman, D.A., and Tversky, A.
   1979   Prospect theory: an analysis of decision under risk. *Econometrica*
         47(2):263–291.
   1984   Choices, values, and frames. *American Psychologist* 39(4):341–350.
Kaplan, S.E., and Reckers, P.M.J.
   1985   A study of tax evasion judgments. *National Tax Journal* 38(1):97–102.
Karchmer, C.L.
   1985   Money laundering and the organized underworld. Pp. 37–48 in H.E.
         Alexander and G.E. Caiden, eds., *The Politics and Economics of Organized
         Crime.* Lexington, Mass.: Lexington Books.
Katona, G.
   1945   *Price Control and Business.* Bloomington, Ind.: Principia Press.
Kay, J.A.
   1979   The economics of tax avoidance. *British Tax Review* 354–365.
Keenan, A., and Dean, P.N.
   1980   Moral evaluation of tax evasion. *Social Policy and Administration* 14:209–
         220.
Kenadjian, B.
   1982   The direct approach to measuring the underground economy in the
         United States: IRS estimates of unreported income. Pp. 93–101 in V.
         Tanzi, ed., *The Underground Economy in the United States and Abroad.*
         Lexington, Mass.: D.C. Heath and Company.
Kilss, B., Scheuren, F., and Aziz, F.
   1973   1973 CPS-IRS-SSA Exact Match File Codebook, Part I—Code Counts
         and Tape Layout. Report No. 8. Office of Research and Statistics, Social
         Security Administration, U.S. Department of Health, Education and
         Welfare.
King, R.F.
   1982   From redistribution to hegemonic logic: the transformation of American
         tax politics, 1894–1963. *Politics and Society* 12:1–52.
Kinsey, K.A.
   1984   Survey Data on Tax Compliance: A Compendium and Review. American
         Bar Foundation Tax Compliance Working Paper 84-1, December 1984.
         American Bar Foundation, Chicago.

1986   Advocacy and Perception: The Structure of Tax Practice. Paper presented at annual meeting of the Law and Society Association, Chicago, June 1, 1986.

1987   Theories and models of tax evasion. *Criminal Justice Abstracts* 18:403. Revision of American Bar Foundation Tax Compliance Working Paper 84-2, December 1984. American Bar Foundation, Chicago.

1987a   Advocacy and Perception: The Structure of Tax Practice. American Bar Foundation Working Paper. American Bar Association, Washington, D.C.

1987b   The Social Dynamics of Tax Encounters: Perspectives of Practitioners and Officials. American Bar Foundation. Presented at the IRS Research Conference on the Role of the Tax Practitioner in the Tax System. American Bar Association, Washington, D.C., November 1987.

Kinsey, K.A., and Smith, K.W.

1987a   Income Tax Cheating: Opportunities and Preferences. American Bar Foundation Tax Compliance Working Paper 87-1. American Bar Foundation, Chicago.

1987b   Understanding taxpaying behavior: a conceptual framework with implications for research. *Law and Society Review* 21(4):639–663.

Klepper, S., and Nagin, D.

1987a   The Anatomy of Tax Evasion. Unpublished paper, Department of Statistics and School of Urban and Public Affairs, Carnegie-Mellon University.

1987b   The Role of Tax Practitioners in Tax Compliance. Unpublished paper, Department of Statistics and School of Urban and Public Affairs, Carnegie-Mellon University.

Klovland, J.T.

1984   Tax evasion and the demand for currency in Norway and Sweden. *Scandinavian Journal of Economics* 86:423–439.

Kohlberg, L.

1976   Moral stages and moralization: the cognitive-developmental approach. In T. Lickons, ed., *Moral Development and Behavior*. New York: Holt, Rinehart, and Winston.

1984   *Essays on Moral Development, Vol. 2: The Psychology of Moral Development: The Nature and Validity of Moral Stages*. New York: Harper and Row.

Kolm, S.

1973   A note on optimum tax evasion. *Journal of Public Economics* 2:265–270.

Koskela, E.

1983a   A note on progression, penalty schemes and tax evasion. *Journal of Public Economics* 22:127–133.

1983b   On the shape of tax schedule, the probability of detection and the penalty schemes as deterrents to tax evasion. *Public Finance* 38:70–80.

Krislov, S., Boyum, K.O., Clark, J.N., and Shaefer, R.C., eds.
1972   *Compliance and the Law.* Beverly Hills, Calif.: Sage Publications.

Kurtz, J., and Pechman, J.A.
1982   Tax fraud hyperbole. *New York Times,* July 12, p. 15.

Kuttner, R.
1980   *Revolt of the Haves: Tax Rebellions and Hard Times.* New York: Simon & Schuster.

Ladd, H.F., and Wilson, J.B.
1982   Why voters support tax limitations: evidence from Massachusetts' Proposition 2-1/2. *National Tax Journal* 35(2):121–143.

Lansberger, M., and Meilijson, E.
1982   Incentive generating state dependent penalty system. *Journal of Public Economics* 19:333–352.

Lattimore, P.K., and Witte, A.D.
1985   Models of decision making under uncertainty: the criminal choice. In D.B. Cornish and R.V. Clarke, eds., *The Reasoning Criminal: Rational Choice Perspectives on Offending.* New York: Springer-Verlag.

Leamer, E.E.
1983a   Let's take the con out of econometrics. *American Economic Review* 73(1):31–43.
1983b   Model choice and specification analysis. In Z. Griliches and M. Intriligator, eds., *Handbook of Econometrics.* Amsterdam: North-Holland.

Lewis, A.
1979   An empirical assessment of tax mentality. *Public Finance* 34(2): 245–257.
1982a   *The Psychology of Taxation.* New York: St. Martin's Press.
1982b   The social psychology of taxation. *British Journal of Social Psychology* 21:151–158.

Lindblom, C.E.
1961   Decision-making in taxation and expenditures. *Public Finances: Needs, Sources and Utilization.* National Bureau of Economic Research. Princeton, N.J.: Princeton University Press.

Lindzey, G., and Aronson, E.
1985   *Handbook of Social Psychology,* 3rd Edition. New York: Random House.

Loftus, E.F.
1985   To file, perchance to cheat. *Psychology Today* (April):35–39.

Long v. Internal Revenue Service
1984   WD Wash Cause Number 75-228S, 596 F.2d 362 (9th Cir. 1979), certiorari denied, 446 U.S. 917 (1980), and 742 F.2d 1173 (9th Cir. 1984).

Long, S.B.

   1980a   *The Internal Revenue Service: Measuring Tax Offenses and Enforcement Response.* Document DOJ-1980-11. National Institute of Justice. Washington, D.C.: U.S. Department of Justice.

   1980b   Measuring White Collar Crime: The Use of the "Random Investigation" Method for Estimating Tax Offenses. Paper presented at the 1980 annual meeting of the American Society for Criminology, San Francisco, Calif., November 5–8, 1980.

   1981   Social control in the civil law: the case of income tax enforcement. Pp. 185–214 in H.L. Ross, ed., *Law and Deviance.* Beverly Hills, Calif.: Sage Publications.

   1985   The Impact of Information on Law Enforcement. Paper presented at the annual meeting of the Law and Society Association, San Diego, Calif., June 7, 1985.

Long, S.B., and Schwartz, R.D.

   1987   The Impact of IRS Audits on Taxpayer Compliance: A Field Experiment in Specific Deterrence. Paper presented at the annual meeting of the Law and Society Association, Washington, D.C., June 1987.

Long, S.B., and Swingen, J.A.

   1985   An Approach to the Measurement of Tax Law Complexity. Unpublished paper, Center for Tax Studies, School of Management, Syracuse University.

Lowery, D., and Sigelman, L.

   1981   Understanding the tax revolt: eight explanations. *American Political Science Review* 75(4):963–974.

Machina, M.J.

   1987   Choice under uncertainty: problems solved and unsolved. *Journal of Economic Perspectives* 1(1):121–154.

Madeo, S., Shepanski, A., and Uecker, W.C.

   1985   Modeling Judgment of Taxpayer Compliance. Unpublished paper, University of Iowa.

Malanga, F.

   1986   The relationship between IRS enforcement and tax yield. *National Tax Journal* 39:333–338.

Manley, J.F.

   1965   The House Committee on Ways and Means: conflict management in a congressional committee. *American Political Science Review* 59(December):927–939.

   1970   *The Politics of Finance: The House Committee on Ways and Means.* Boston: Little, Brown & Co.

Mansfield, H.K.
  1983   The role of sanctions in taxpayer compliance. Pp. 217–234 in P. Sawicki, ed., *Income Tax Compliance: A Report of the ABA Section on Taxation, Invitational Conference on Income Tax Compliance.* Washington, D.C.: American Bar Association.

March, J.G., and Simon, H.A.
  1958   *Organizations.* New York: John Wiley & Sons.

Marrelli, M.
  1984   On indirect tax evasion. *Journal of Public Economics* 25:181–196.

Mason, R.
  1985   Discussion of "Deterrence, Duty, and Diligence: Extending the Theory of Tax Compliance." Survey Research Center, Oregon State University. Paper presented at the 75th Annual Conference on Taxation sponsored by the National Tax Association—Tax Institute of America, Denver, Colo., October 14, 1985.

Mason, R., and Calvin, L.D.
  1977   *A Model of Admitted Income Tax Evasion.* Corvallis: Survey Research Center, Oregon State University.
  1978   A study of admitted income tax evasion. *Law and Society Review* 13(Fall):73–89.
  1984   Public confidence and admitted tax evasion. *National Tax Journal* 37:489–496.

Mason, R., Calvin, L.D., and Faulkenberry, G.D.
  1975   *Knowledge Evasion and Public Support for Oregon's Tax System.* Corvallis: Survey Research Center, Oregon State University.

Mason, R., and Lowry, H.
  1981   *An Estimate of Income Tax Evasion in Oregon.* Corvallis: Survey Research Center, Oregon State University.

Mazur, M., and Nagin, D.
  1987   Tax Preparers and Tax Compliance: A Theoretical and Empirical Analysis. Unpublished paper, School of Urban and Public Affairs, Carnegie-Mellon University.

McBarnet, D.
  1984   Law and capital: the role of legal form and legal actors. *International Journal of the Sociology of Law* 12:231–238.

McCaleb, T.S.
  1976   Tax evasion and the differential taxation of labor and capital income. *Public Finance* 31(2):287–294.

McCrohan, K.F.
  1982   The use of survey research to estimate trends in non-compliance with federal income taxes. *Journal of Economic Psychology* 2:231–240.

McCrohan, K.F., and Pearl, R.B.
  1983 Tipping Practices of American Households: Consumer Based Estimates for 1979. Paper presented at the annual meeting of the American Statistical Association, Toronto, Canada, August 15–18, 1983.
McDaniel, P.R.
  1983 The effect of tax preferences on income tax compliance. Pp. 259–274 in P. Sawicki, ed., *Income Tax Compliance: A Report of the ABA Section on Taxation, Invitational Conference on Income Tax Compliance*. Washington, D.C.: American Bar Association.
McEwen, C.A., and Maiman, R.J.
  1984 Mediation in small claims courts: achieving compliance through consent. *Law and Society Review* 18(1):11–49.
McGraw, K.M.
  1985 Subjective probabilities and moral judgement. *Journal of Experimental Social Psychology* 21:501–518.
Mendelsohn, H., O'Keefe, G.J., Lin, J., Spetnagel, H.T., Vengler, C., Wilson, D., Wirth, M.O., and Nash, K.
  1981 Public Communications and the Prevention of Crime. Paper presented at the meeting of the Midwestern Association of Public Opinion Research, Chicago.
Milliron, V.C.
  1984 A behavioral study of the meaning and influence of tax complexity. *Journal of Accounting Research* 23:794–816.
  1985 An analysis of the relationship between tax equity and tax complexity. *Journal of Accounting Research* 23:794–816.
Minarik, J.J.
  1985 *Making Tax Choices*. Baltimore: Urban Institute Press.
Minor, W.W.
  1978 Deterrence research: problems of theory and method. In J.A. Cramer, ed., *Preventing Crime*. Beverly Hills, Calif.: Sage Publications.
  1981 Techniques of neutralization: a reconceptualization and empirical examination. *Journal of Research in Crime and Delinquency*. 18:294–319.
Mintz, J.H.
  1985 Guess who Uncle Sam wants now: an analysis of the tax advisor aiding and abetting penalty. *Taxes* 63(3)(March):221–237.
Mitchell, J.C.
  1969 The concept and use of social network. In J.C. Mitchell, ed., *Social Networks in Urban Situations*. Manchester: Manchester University Press.
Molefsky, B.
  1982 America's underground economy. Pp. 47–67 in V. Tanzi, ed., *The Underground Economy in the United States and Abroad*. Lexington, Mass.: D.C. Heath and Company.
Moore, M.H.
  1983 On the office of taxpayer and the social process of taxpaying. Pp. 275–292 in P. Sawicki, ed., *Income Tax Compliance: A Report of the ABA Section on*

Taxation, Invitational Conference on Income Tax Compliance. Washington, D.C.: American Bar Association.

Moore, S.F.

1973   Law and social change: the semi-autonomous social field as an appropriate subject of study. *Law and Society Review* 1:719–746.

1978   *Law as Process: An Anthropological Approach.* New York: Methuen.

Mork, K.A.

1975   Income tax evasion: some empirical evidence. *Public Finance* 1:70–76.

Morris, N.

1966   Impediments to penal reform. *University of Chicago Law Review* 33: 627–656.

Murphy, J.H.

1959   Selecting income tax returns for audit. *National Tax Journal* 12: 232–238.

Murray, G.F., and Erickson, P.G.

1987   Cross-sectional versus longitudinal research: an empirical comparison of projected and subsequent criminality. *Social Science Research* 16: 107–118.

Nacev, L.

1986   A bibliography of the literature on tax policy. *Tax Notes* 30(10):1019–1086.

National Academy of Sciences

1987   *Science and Technology Centers: Principles and Guidelines.* Panel on Science and Technology Centers. Washington, D.C.: National Academy Press.

National Institute of Justice

1986   *Research Program Plan Fiscal Year 1987.* NCJ-102667. Washington, D.C.: U.S. Department of Justice.

National Research Council

1984   *Cognitive Aspects of Survey Methodology: Building a Bridge Between Disciplines.* Report of the Advanced Research Seminar on Cognitive Aspects of Survey Methodology, Committee on National Statistics, Commission on Behavioral and Social Sciences and Education. Washington, D.C.: National Academy Press.

Nayak, P.B.

1978   Optimal income tax evasion and regressive taxes. *Public Finance* 33(3):358– 366.

Neisser, U.

1976   *Cognition and Reality: Principles and Implications of Cognitive Psychology.* San Francisco: Freeman.

Neumann, J. von, and Morgenstern, O.

1947   *Theory of Games and Economic Behavior,* 2nd ed., Princeton, N.J.: Princeton University Press.

Oldman, O., and Woods, L.

1983   Would a value-added system relieve tax compliance problems? Pp. 317–338 in P. Sawicki, ed., *Income Tax Compliance: A Report of the ABA Section on*

Taxation, Invitational Conference on Income Tax Compliance. Washington, D.C.: American Bar Association.

O'Neill, D.M.

1983   *Growth of the Underground Economy, 1950–1981: Some Evidence from the Current Population Survey.* Joint Economic Committee, U.S. Congress, December 9, 1983. Washington, D.C.: U.S. Government Printing Office.

Opinion Research Corporation

1973   The Federal Income Tax: Reform vs. Simplification. A nationwide public opinion survey conducted for H&R Block. Opinion Research Corp., Princeton, N.J.

Organization for Economic Cooperation and Development

1980   Tax Evasion and Avoidance. A Report by the OECD Committee on Fiscal Affairs. Document 20.391, Organization for Economic Cooperation and Development, Paris.

1985   Trends in International Taxation. A report by the OECD Committee on Fiscal Affairs. Organization for Economic Cooperation and Development, Paris.

Parker, J., and Grasmick, H.G.

1979   Linking actual and perceived certainty of punishment: an exploratory study of an untested proposition in deterrence theory. *Criminology* 17(3):366–379.

Parker, R.P.

1984   Improved adjustments for misreporting of tax return information used to estimate the national income and product accounts, 1977. *Survey of Current Business* 64(June):17–25.

Paternoster, R.

1987   The deterrent effect of the perceived certainty and severity of punishment: a review of the evidence and issues. *Justice Quarterly* 4(2): 101–146.

Paternoster, R., Saltzman, L.E., Chiricos, T.G., and Waldo, G.P.

1982   Perceived risk and deterrence: methodological artifacts in perceptual deterrence research. *Journal of Criminal Law and Criminology* 73:1238–1258.

Paternoster, R., Saltzman, L.E., Waldo, G.P., and Chiricos, T.G.

1982   Causal ordering in deterrence research: an examination of the perceptions-behavior relationship. Pp. 55–70 in J. Hagan, ed., *Deterrence Reconsidered: Methodological Innovations.* Volume 28, Sage Research Progress Series in Criminology. Beverly Hills, Calif.: Sage Publications.

Payne, J.W.

1973   Alternative approaches to decision-making under risk: moments versus risk dimensions. *Psychological Bulletin* 80:439–453.

1980   Information processing theory: some concepts and methods applied to decision research. Pp. 95–115 in T.S. Walsten, ed., *Cognitive Processes in*

Choice and Decision Behavior. Hillsdale, N.J.: Lawrence Erlbaum Associates.

Peacock, A.T., and Shaw, G.K.
1982   Tax evasion and tax revenue loss, *Public Finance* 32:333–342.

Pearl, R.B., and McCrohan, K.F.
1984   Estimates of tip income in eating places. *Statistics of Income Bulletin* (Internal Revenue Service) 3(3)(Winter 1983–84):49–53.

Pearson, R.W.
1986   Research Access to Publicly Collected Data. Report based on a conference, November 21–22, 1985 and submitted to the Measurement Methods and Data Improvement Program of the National Science Foundation, Committee on the Survey of Income and Program Participation, Social Science Research Council, New York.

Pechman, J.A.
1983a   *Federal Tax Policy.* Studies of Government Finance, Second Series, 4th Edition. Washington, D.C.: Brookings Institution.
1983b   Anatomy of the U.S. individual income tax. Pp. 61–84 in S. Cnossen, ed., *Comparative Tax Studies: Essays in Honor of Richard Goode.* New York: North-Holland Publishing Company.

Pechman, J.A., ed.
1985   *A Citizen's Guide to the New Tax Reforms.* Totowa, N.J.: Rowman & Allanheed.

Pencavel, J.H.
1979   A note on income tax evasion, labor supply, and nonlinear tax schedules. *Journal of Public Economics* 12:115–124.

Perng, S.S.
1985   Accounts receivable treatments study. Pp. 55–62 in R.F. Boruch and W. Wothke, eds., *Randomization and Field Experimentation: New Directions for Program Evaluation.* San Francisco: Jossey-Bass.

Persson, M., and Wissen, P.
1984   Redistributional effects of tax evasion. *Scandinavian Journal of Economics* 86:131–149.

Piaget, J.
1932   *The Moral Judgment of the Child.* Trans. 1965 by M. Gabain. New York: Free Press.

Polinsky, M., and Shavell, S.
1979   The optimal trade-off between the probability and magnitude of fines. *American Economic Review* 69:880–891.

Porcano, T.M.
1984   Distributive justice and tax policy. *Accounting Review* 59(4):619–636.

Porter, R.D., and Bayer, A.S.
1984   A monetary perspective on underground economic activity in the United States. *Federal Reserve Bulletin* 70(3):177–190.

Poterba, J.M.
1987   Tax evasion and capital gains legislation. *American Economic Review* 77(2):234–239.

Privacy Protection Study Commission
   1977a   *The Citizen as Taxpayer.* Report of the Privacy Protection Study Commission, Appendix 2. Washington, D.C.: U.S. Government Printing Office.
   1977b   *The Privacy Act of 1974: An Assessment.* Report of the Privacy Protection Study Commission, Appendix 4. Washington, D.C.: U.S. Government Printing Office.

Quester, A.
   1979   Women's behavior and the tax code. *Social Science Quarterly* 59(4): 665–680.

Reese, T.J.
   1980   *The Politics of Tax Reform.* Westport, Conn.: Quorum Books.

Reid, J.D., Jr.
   1979   Tax revolts in historical perspective. *National Tax Journal* 32(2)(Supplement):67–74.

Reinganum, J.F., and Wilde, L.L.
   1985a   Equilibrium Verification and Report Policies in a Model of Tax Compliance. Unpublished paper, California Institute of Technology.
   1985b   Income tax compliance in a principal-agent framework. *Journal of Public Economics* 26(1985):1–18.

Renfer, K.E.M.
   1982   The Impact of Professional Ethics on Decision Making in Tax Practice: An Examination of Strategies and Tradeoffs. Unpublished Ph.D. dissertation, Department of Business Administration, University of Michigan.

Richards, P., and Tittle, C.
   1981   Gender and perceived chances of arrest. *Social Forces* 59(4):1182–1199.

Richupan, S.
   1984   Measuring tax evasion. *Finance Development* 21(4):38–40.

Rickard, J.A., Russell, A.M., and Howroyd, T.D.
   1982   A tax evasion model with allowance for retroactive penalties. *Economic Record* 58:379–385.

Ricketts, M.
   1984   On the simple macroeconomics of tax evasion. *Public Finance* 39:420.

Riecken, H.W., and Boruch, R.F.
   1974   *Social Experimentation: A Method for Planning and Evaluating Social Intervention.* Orlando, Fla.: Academic Press.

Roberts, S.I., Friedman, W.H., Ginsburg, M.D., Louthan, C.T., Lubick, D.C., Young, M., and Zeitlin, G.E.
   1972   A report on complexity and the income tax. *Tax Law Review* 27: 325–376.

Robertson, L.S.
   1975   The great seat-belt campaign flop. *Journal of Communication* 26: 41–45.

Robertson, L.S., Kelley, A.B., O'Neill, B., Wixon, C.W., Eiswirth, R.S., and Haddon, W.
 1974   A controlled study of the effects of television messages on safety belt use. *American Journal of Public Health* 64:1071–1080.
Rollins, J.
 1985   *Between Women: Domestics and Their Employers*. Philadelphia: Temple University Press.
Roper Organization, Inc.
 1978– *Roper Reports*. Series of bulletins (incomplete) beginning December 1978. New York: The Roper Organization, Inc.
Ross, L.
 1961   Traffic law violations: a folk crime. *Social Problems* 8:231–241.
Roth, J.A., and Ekstrand, L.E.
 1979   *Targeting Tax Law Enforcement: Some Preliminary Qualitative Results*. Rockville, Md.: Westat, Inc.
Roth, J.A., and Witte, A.D.
 1985   Understanding Taxpayer Compliance: Major Factors and Perspectives. Unpublished paper, National Research Council, Washington, D.C.
Rudick, H.J.
 1940   The problem of personal income tax avoidance. *Law & Contemporary Problems* 7:243–265.
Saltzman, L.E., Paternoster, R., Waldo, G.P., and Chiricos, T.G.
 1982   Deterrent and experiential effects: the problem of causal order in perceptual deterrence research. *Journal of Research on Crime and Delinquency* 19:172–189.
Sandmo, A.
 1981   Income tax evasion, labor supply, and the equity-efficiency tradeoff. *Journal of Public Economics* 16(December):265–288.
Sawicki, P.
 1983a A summary of what can be learned from the experience of other countries with income tax compliance problems. From a paper presented by N. Boidman. Pp. 149–158 in P. Sawicki, ed., *Income Tax Compliance: A Report of the ABA Section on Taxation, Invitational Conference on Income Tax Compliance*. Washington, D.C.: American Bar Association.
 1983b (ed.) *Income Tax Compliance: A Report of the ABA Section on Taxation, Invitational Conference on Income Tax Compliance*. Washington, D.C.: American Bar Association.
Schlicht, E.
 1985   The shadow economy and morals: a note. Pp. 265–271 in W. Gaertner and A. Wenig, eds., *The Economics of the Shadow Economy*. New York: Springer-Verlag.
Schmidt, P., and Sickles, R.C.
 1984   Production frontiers and panel data. *Journal of Business and Economic Statistics* 2:367–374.

Schmölders, G.
   1970   Survey research in public finance—a behavioral approach to fiscal theory. *Public Finance* 25:300–306.
Schoemaker, P.J.H.
   1982   The expected utility model: its variants, purposes, evidence and limitations. *Journal of Economic Literature* 20:529–563.
Scholz, J.T.
   1984   Cooperation, deterrence, and the ecology of regulatory enforcement. *Law and Society Review* 18:179–224.
Schwartz, R.D.
   1961   Field experimentation in sociolegal research. *Journal of Legal Education* 13:401–410.
Schwartz, R.D., and Orleans, S.
   1967   On legal sanctions. *University of Chicago Law Review* 34:274–300.
Schwartz, S.H.
   1977   Normative influences on altruism. In L. Berkowitz, ed., *Advances in Experimental Social Psychology,* Vol. 10. New York: Academic Press.
Scott, W.J., and Grasmick, H.G.
   1981   Deterrence and income tax cheating: testing interaction hypotheses in utilitarian theories. *Journal of Applied Behavioral Science* 17:395–408.
Sears, D.O., and Citrin, J.
   1982   *Tax Revolt: Something for Nothing in California.* Cambridge, Mass.: Harvard University Press.
Sears, D.O., Huddy, L., and Schaffer, L.G.
   1984   Schemas and Symbolic Politics: The Cases of Racial and Gender Equality. Unpublished paper, University of California, Los Angeles.
Sears, D.O., Lau, R.R., Tyler, T.R., and Allen, H.M.
   1980   Self interest vs. symbolic politics in policy attitudes and presidential voting. *American Political Science Review* 74:670–684.
Sheppard, L.A.
   1985   Unpopular spending: IRS budget and tax administration. *Tax Notes* 28(8):821–825.
Sherman, L.W., and Berk, R.A.
   1984   The specific deterrent effects of arrest for domestic assault. *American Sociological Review* 49:261–272.
Shishko, R., and Rostker, B.
   1976   The economics of multiple job holding. *American Economic Review* 66:298–308.
Siegel and Gale
   1983   Final Report: Tax Forms Simplification Study. Unpublished report to the Internal Revenue Service Research Division. Siegel and Gale, Washington, D.C.

Silberman, M.
  1976   Toward a theory of criminal deterrence. *American Sociological Review* 41:442–461.

Simon, C.P., and Witte, A.D.
  1980   The underground economy: estimates of GNP, structure and trends. In Joint Economic Committee, *Government Regulation: Achieving Social and Economic Balance,* Vol. 5. Washington, D.C.: U.S. Government Printing Office.
  1981   The Underground Economy: What Is It and What Should We Do? Unpublished paper, March 1981, The Osprey Company, Tallahassee, Fla.
  1982   *Beating the System: The Underground Economy.* Boston: Auburn House.

Simon, H.A.
  1945   *Administrative Behavior.* New York: Free Press.
  1955   A behavior model of rational choice. *Quarterly Journal of Economics* 59:99–118.

Skogan, W.G., and Maxfield, M.G.
  1981   *Coping with Crime.* Beverly Hills, Calif.: Sage Publications.

Slemrod, J.
  1985a   An empirical test for tax evasion. *Review of Economics and Statistics* 67(2):232–238.
  1985b   The Return to Tax Simplification: An Econometric Analysis. National Bureau of Economic Research Working Paper No. 1756, Cambridge, Mass.

Slovic, P., Fischhoff, B., and Lichtenstein, S.
  1981   Accident probabilities and seat belt usage: a psychological perspective. *Accident Analysis and Prevention* 10:281–285.

Slovic, P., and Lichtenstein, S.
  1971   Comparison of Bayesian and regression approaches to the study of information processing in judgment. *Organizational Behavior and Human Performance* 6:649–744.

Smith, K.W.
  1985   Line by Line TCMP Distributions. Unpublished paper, American Bar Foundation, Chicago.
  1986   Compliance, Noncompliance, and Aggressive Avoidance. Unpublished note, American Bar Foundation, Chicago, November 1986
  1987   Quality Service by the Internal Revenue Service and Compliance: A Structural Equation Model. Unpublished paper, American Bar Foundation, Chicago, July 1986.

Smith, K.W., and Kinsey, K.A.
  1985a   Cooperation and control: strategies and tactics for tax administration. *Tax Administration Review* 1:13–29.

1985b   Understanding Taxpaying Behavior: A Theoretical Statement and Research Agenda Developed for a Proposal to NSF for a Third Oregon Survey. American Bar Foundation Taxpayer Compliance Project Working Paper 85-1. American Bar Association, Washington, D.C., March 1985.

Smith, K.W., Stalans, L.J., and Coyne, M.L.
1987   A Taxonomy of Paid Preparers for Individual Tax Returns: A Preliminary Analysis of the Tax Practitioner Survey. Unpublished paper, American Bar Foundation, Chicago.

Snow, D.A., Zurcher, L.A., Jr., and Ekland-Olson, S.
1980   Social networks and social movements: a microstructural approach to differential recruitment. *American Sociological Review* 45(Oct.): 787–801.

Song, Y.-D., and Yarborough, T.
1978   Tax ethics and taxpayer attitudes: a survey. *Public Administration Review* 38(Sept/Oct):442–452.

Spicer, M.W.
1974   A Behavioral Model of Income Tax Evasion. Unpublished Ph.D. dissertation, Ohio State University.
1986   Civilization at a discount: the problem of tax evasion. *National Tax Journal* 39(1):13–20.

Spicer, M.W., and Becker, L.A.
1980   Fiscal inequity and tax evasion: an experimental approach. *National Tax Journal* 33(2):171–175.

Spicer, M.W., and Hero, R.E.
1985   Tax evasion and heuristics: a research note. *Journal of Public Economics* 26:263–267.

Spicer, M.W., and Lundstedt, S.B.
1976   Understanding tax evasion. *Public Finance* 31(2):295–305.

Spicer, M.W., and Thomas, J.E.
1982   Audit probabilities and the tax evasion decision: an experimental approach. *Journal of Economic Psychology* 2:241–245.

Sproule, R., Komus, D., and Tsang, E.
1980   Optimal tax evasion: Risk-neutral behavior under a negative income tax. *Public Finance* 35(2):309–317.

Srinivasan, T.N.
1973   Tax evasion: a model. *Journal of Public Economics* 2:339–346.

Stern, P.C., and Oskamp, S.
1987   Managing scarce environmental resources. Pp. 1043–1086 in D. Stokols and I. Altman, eds., *Handbook of Environmental Psychology*, Vol. 2. New York: John Wiley & Sons.

Steuerle, C.E.
1986   *Who Should Pay for Collecting Taxes? Financing the IRS.* Washington, D.C.: American Enterprise Institute for Public Policy Research.

Stopforth, D.
   1985   Sowing some of the seeds of the present anti-evasion system. *British Tax Review* 1:28.
Stotland, E., and Canon, L.K.
   1972   *Social Psychology: A Cognitive Approach.* Philadelphia: Saunders.
Strümpel, B.
   1969   The contribution of survey research to public finance. Pp. 13–38 in A.T. Peacock, ed., *Quantitative Analysis in Public Finance.* New York: Praeger.
Strümpel, G.
   1966   The disguised tax burden compliance costs of German businessmen and professionals. *National Tax Journal* 19(1):70–77.
Sudman, S., and Bradburn, N.M.
   1982   *Asking Questions.* San Francisco: Jossey-Bass.
Surrey, S.S.
   1957   The Congress and the tax lobbyist: how special tax provisions get enacted. *Harvard Law Review* 70(May):1145–1182.
   1969   Complexity and the Internal Revenue Code: the problem of the management of tax detail. *Law and Contemporary Problems* 1969:673–710.
Sutherland, E.
   1939   *Principles of Criminology.* New York: Lippincott.
Sykes, G., and Matza, D.
   1957   Techniques of neutralization: a theory of delinquency. *American Sociological Review* 22:664–670.
Tanzi, V.
   1980   The underground economy in the United States: estimates and implications. *Banca Nazionale Del Lavoro Q. Rev.* 33:427–428.
   1982   (ed.)*The Underground Economy in the United States and Abroad.* Lexington, Mass.: D.C. Heath and Company.
Tapp, J.L., and Levine, F.J.L.
   1970   Persuasion to virtue: a preliminary statement. Chapter 9 in S. Krislov et al., eds., *Compliance and the Law.* Beverly Hills, Calif.: Sage Publications.
Tauchen, H., and Witte, A.D.
   1986   Economic models of how audit policies affect voluntary tax compliance. In *Proceedings of the Seventy-Eighth Conference of the National Tax Association—Tax Institute of America.* Columbus, Oh.: National Tax Association.
Thibaut, J., Friedland, N., and Walker, L.
   1974   Compliance with rules: some social determinants. *Journal of Personality and Social Psychology* 30:792–801.
Thurman, Q.C., St. John, C., and Riggs, L.
   1984   Neutralization and tax evasion: how effective would a moral appeal be in improving compliance to tax law? *Law and Policy* 6:309–327.
Tittle, C.R.
   1969   Crime rates and legal sanctions. *Social Problems* 16(Spring):409–423.

1980   *Sanctions and Social Deviance: The Question of Deterrence*. New York: Praeger.

1985   Can social science answer questions about deterrence for policy use? Pp. 265–295 in R. L. Shotland and M.M. Mark, eds., *Social Science and Social Policy*. Beverly Hills, Calif.: Sage Publications.

Tittle, C.R., and Logan, C.H.

1973   Sanctions and deviance: evidence and remaining questions. *Law and Society Review* 7:371–392.

Tittle, C.R., and Rowe, A.R.

1973   Moral appeal, sanction threat, and deviance: an experimental test. *Social Problems* 20:488–498.

Tracy, P.E., and Fox, J.A

1981   The validity of randomized response for sensitive measurements. *American Sociological Review* 46(April):187–200.

Turner, C.F., and Martin, E. , eds.

1984   *Surveying Subjective Phenomena*. Committee on National Statistics, National Research Council. New York: Russell Sage Foundation.

Tversky, A., and Kahneman, D.

1973   Availability: a heuristic for judging frequency and probability. *Cognitive Psychology* 5:207–232.

1974   Judgment under uncertainty: heuristics and biases. *Science* 185:1124–1131.

1981   The framing of decisions and the psychology of choice. *Science* 211(30):453–458.

Tyler, T.R.

1978   Drawing Inferences from Experiences: The Effect of Crime Victimization Experiences Upon Crime-Related Attitudes and Behaviors. Unpublished dissertation, University of California, Los Angeles.

1980   The impact of directly and indirectly experienced events: the origin of crime-related judgments and behavior. *Journal of Personality and Social Psychology* 39:13–28.

1986   Justice, Legitimacy and Compliance. Paper presented at the annual meeting of the Law and Society Association, May 29, 1986, Chicago. Departments of Psychology and Political Science, Northwestern University.

Tyler, T.R., and Lavrakas, P.J.

1985   Cognitions leading to personal and political behaviors: the case of crime. Pp. 141–156 in S. Kraus and R.M. Perloff, eds., *Mass Media and Political Thought: An Information-Processing Approach*. Beverly Hills, Calif.: Sage Publications.

Udry, R.J., Clark, L.T., Chase, C.L., and Levy, M.

1972   Can mass media advertising increase contraceptive use? *Family Planning Perspectives* 4:37–44.

U.S. Congress
  1982a *Background on Classification of Employees and Independent Contractors for Tax Purposes and Description of S. 2369.* Joint Committee on Taxation, U.S. Congress, April 23, 1982. Washington, D.C.: U.S. Government Printing Office.
  1982b *Background on Federal Income Tax Compliance and Description of S. 2198 (Taxpayer Compliance Improvement Act of 1982).* Joint Committee on Taxation, U.S. Congress, March 19, 1982. Washington, D.C.: U.S. Government Printing Office.
  1983a *Background on Federal Income Tax Compliance.* Joint Committee on Taxation, U.S. Congress, June 21, 1983. Washington, D.C.: U.S. Government Printing Office.
  1983b *Description of Issue Areas Relating to Efforts to Reduce Taxpayer Burdens.* Joint Committee on Taxation, U.S. Congress, May 18, 1983. Washington, D.C.: U.S. Government Printing Office.
  1983c *Growth of the Underground Economy, 1950–1981: Some Evidence from the Current Population Survey.* Joint Economic Committee, U.S. Congress, December 9, 1983. Washington, D.C.: U.S. Government Printing Office.
  1984   *Tax Avoidance, Tax Equity, and Tax Revenues: The Impact of Marginal Income Tax Rate Changes in the United States, 1954–82.* Joint Economic Committee, U.S. Congress, October 26, 1984. Washington, D.C.: U.S. Government Printing Office.
  1985a *Analysis of Proposals Relating to Comprehensive Tax Reform.* Joint Committee on Taxation, U.S. Congress, February 26, 1985. Washington, D.C.: U.S. Government Printing Office.
  1985b *Recordkeeping Requirements for Automobiles and Other Property.* Joint Committee on Taxation, U.S. Congress, March 4, 1985. Washington, D.C.: U.S. Government Printing Office.
  1985c *Tax Reform Proposals: Compliance and Tax Administration.* Joint Committee on Taxation, U.S. Congress, July 30, 1985. Washington, D.C.: U.S. Government Printing Office.

U.S. Department of the Treasury
  1970   *Report of the Audit Review Committee.* Washington, D.C.: U.S. Department of the Treasury. June 1970.

U.S. General Accounting Office
  1976   *How the Internal Revenue Service Selects Individual Income Tax Returns for Audit.* Report to the Joint Committee on Internal Revenue Taxation, Congress of the United States, November 5, 1976. Washington, D.C.: U.S. General Accounting Office.
  1978   *Further Simplification of Income Tax Forms and Instruction is Needed and Possible.* Washington, D.C.: U.S. General Accounting Office.

1979a   *IRS' Audits of Individual Taxpayers and Its Audit Quality Control System Need to be Better.* August 15, 1979. Washington, D.C.: U.S. General Accounting Office.

1979b   *Who's Not Filing Income Tax Returns? IRS Needs Betters Ways to Find Them and Collect Their Taxes.* Report to Congress, July 11, 1979, GGD-79-69. Washington, D.C.: U.S. General Accounting Office.

1981a   *Illegal Tax Protesters Threaten Tax System.* Report to Congress, July 8, 1981. Washington, D.C.: U.S. General Accounting Office.

1981b   *Using the Exact Match File for Estimates and Characteristics of Persons Reporting and Not Reporting Social Security Self-Employment Earnings.* Report to the Chairman, Subcommittee on Oversight, Committee on Ways and Means, U.S. House of Representatives. July 22, 1981. Washington, D.C.: U.S. General Accounting Office.

1982   *Further Research into Noncompliance is Needed to Reduce Growing Tax Losses.* Report to Congress. Washington, D.C.: U.S. General Accounting Office.

1983a   *Computer Technology at IRS: Present and Planned.* Study by the Staff of the General Accounting Office. Washington, D.C.: U.S. General Accounting Office.

1983b   *IRS' Administration of Penalties Imposed on Tax Return Preparers.* Report to the Joint Committee on Taxation, January 6, 1983. Washington, D.C.: U.S. General Accounting Office.

1983c   *Legislative Change Needed to Enable IRS to Assess Taxes Voluntarily Reported by Taxpayers in Bankruptcy.* GAO/GGD-83-47. Washington, D.C.: U.S. General Accounting Office.

1983d   *With Better Management Information, IRS Could Further Improve Its Efforts Against Abusive Tax Shelters.* Report to Congress, August 25, 1983. Washington, D.C.: U.S. General Accounting Office.

1984   *Need to Better Assess Consequences Before Reducing Taxpayer Assistance.* Report to Congress, April 5, 1984. Washington, D.C.: U.S. General Accounting Office.

1987a   *Tax Administration: Accessibility, Timeliness, and Accuracy of IRS' Telephone Assistance Program.* Report to the Chairman, Subcommittee on Commerce, Consumer and Monetary Affairs, Committee on Government Operations, House of Representatives GAO/GGD-88-17. Washington, D.C.: U.S. General Accounting Office.

1987b   *Tax Administration: IRS Can Improve on the Success of Its Problem Resolution Program.* Report to Congressional Requesters. GAO/GGD-88-12. Washington, D.C.: U.S. General Accounting Office.

1988   *Tax Administration: IRS' Tax Gap Studies.* Washington, D.C.: U.S. General Accounting Office.

Van de Braak, H.

1983   Taxation and tax resistance. *Journal of Economic Psychology* 3:95–111.

Vitez, T.G.
  1983   Information reporting and withholding as stimulants of voluntary compliance. Pp. 191–216 in P. Sawicki, ed., *Income Tax Compliance: A Report of the ABA Section on Taxation, Invitational Conference on Income Tax Compliance*. Washington, D.C.: American Bar Association.
Vogel, J.
  1974   Taxation and public opinion in Sweden: an interpretation of recent survey data. *National Tax Journal* 27(December):499–513.
Waerneryd, K.E.
  1980   Psychological reactions to the tax system. *Skandinaviska Enskilda Banken Quarterly Review* 3–4:75–84.
Waerneryd, K.E., and Walerud, B.
  1982   Taxes and economic behavior—some interview data on tax evasion in Sweden. *Journal of Economic Psychology* 2:187–211.
Waldo, G.P., and Chiricos, T.G.
  1972   Perceived penal sanction and self-reported criminality: a neglected approach to deterrence research. *Social Problems* 19:525–540.
Wallschutzky, I.
  1984   Possible causes of tax evasion. *Journal of Economic Psychology* 2:187–211.
Warner, K.E.
  1977   The effects of anti-smoking campaigns on cigarette consumption. *American Journal of Public Health* 67:645–650.
Warner, S.L.
  1965   Randomized response: a survey technique for eliminating evasive answer bias. *Journal of the American Statistical Association* 60:63–69.
Washington Statistical Society
  1985   Abstracts and Selected Background Papers for the Workshop on Exact Matching Methodologies. Collection prepared for the Workshop on Exact Matching Methodologies, sponsored by the Washington Statistical Society and the Federal Committee on Statistical Methodology, Arlington, Va., May 9–10, 1985.
Watson, H.
  1985   Tax evasion and labor markets. *Journal of Public Economics* 27 (1985):231–246.
Weber, J.W.
  1979   Criminal prosecutions for income tax evasion. *Journal of Criminal Law & Criminology* 70(3):355–359.
Webley, P., and Halstead, S.
  1985   Tax evasion on the micro: significant simulations or expedient experiments? *Journal of Interdisciplinary Economics* 1:87–100.
Wedick, J.L., Jr.
  1983   Looking for a needle in a haystack—how the IRS selects returns for an audit. *The Tax Adviser* (November):673–675.

Weigel, R.H., Hessing, D.J., and Elffers, H.
  n.d.   Tax Evasion Research: A Critical Appraisal and Theoretical Model.
          Unpublished paper, Erasmus University, Rotterdam.

Weiss, L.
  1976   The desirability of cheating incentives and randomness in the optimal
          income tax. *Journal of Political Economy* 84(6):1343–1352.

Wertz, K.
  1979   Allocation by and output of a tax administering agency. *National Tax
          Journal* 32:143–157.

Westat, Inc.
  1979   Review and Analysis of the Literature: Working Paper. Prepared for the
          Internal Revenue Service by Westat, Inc., Rockville, Md.
  1980a   A Procedure for Estimating Taxpayer Response to Changes in IRS
          Audit Coverage. Prepared for the Internal Revenue Service, March 21,
          1980, by Westat, Inc., Rockville, Md.
  1980b   *A Research Design for the Study of Individual Income Tax Compliance.*
          Study for the Internal Revenue Service, J. Roth, Project Director. Rock-
          ville, Md.: Westat, Inc.
  1980c   *A Research Design for the Study of Individual Income Tax Compliance.
          Appendix A: Survey Instrument and Training Materials for a Procedure for
          Estimating Taxpayer Response to Changes in IRS Audit Coverage.* Study for
          the Internal Revenue Service, J. Roth, Project Director. Rockville, Md.:
          Westat, Inc.
  1980d   *Executive Summary: Individual Income Tax Compliance Factors Study.*
          Study for the Internal Revenue Service, J. Roth, Project Director. Rock-
          ville, Md.: Westat, Inc.
  1980e   Individual Income Tax Compliance Factors Study Qualitative Research
          Results. Prepared for the Internal Revenue Service, February 4, 1980, by
          Westat, Inc., Rockville, Md.
  1980f   Self-Reported Tax Compliance: A Pilot Survey Report. Prepared for the
          Internal Revenue Service, March 21, 1980, by Westat, Inc., Rockville,
          Md.

Wiegand, R.B.
  1984   Dimensions of the Shadow Economy. Unpublished Ph.D. dissertation,
          Department of Sociology, Vanderbilt University.

Williams, W.E.
  1983   Strengthening IRS examination and collection processes by administra-
          tive changes in staffing, training, deployment and technology. Pp. 235–258
          in P. Sawicki, ed., *Income Tax Compliance: A Report of the ABA Section on
          Taxation, Invitational Conference on Income Tax Compliance.* Washington,
          D.C.: American Bar Association.

Witte, A.D.
  1984   Unrecorded Economic Activity: A Survey and Some Suggestions. Un-
          published paper, Department of Economics, University of North Caro-
          lina, August 1984.
  1986   Tax Evasion. Paper presented to the Arthur Young Professors' Round-
          table. Arthur Young & Co., Washington, D.C.
  1987a   The nature and extent of unrecorded activity: a survey concentrating on
          recent U.S. research. In Sergio Alessandrini and Bruno Dallago, eds.,
          *The Unofficial Economy: Consequences and Perspectives in Different Economic
          Systems.* London: Gower Publishing.
  1987b   The underground economy in the U.S. and Western Europe: estimates
          of size and trends, and suggestions for research. In Richard W. Lind-
          hold, ed., *The Income Tax Debacle.* New York: Praeger.

Witte, A.D., and Woodbury, D.F.
  1982   Factors Affecting Voluntary Compliance with Federal Individual Income
          Tax Laws. Unpublished paper, University of North Carolina, March 1982.
  1983   What we know about the factors affecting compliance with the tax laws.
          Pp. 133–148 in P. Sawicki, ed., *Income Tax Compliance: A Report of the ABA
          Section on Taxation, Invitational Conference on Income Tax Compliance.*
          Washington, D.C.: American Bar Association.
  1984   A Test of an Economic Model of Tax Compliance. Unpublished paper,
          Wellesley College, September 1984.
  1985   The effect of tax laws and tax administration on tax compliance: the case of
          the U.S. individual income tax. *National Tax Journal* 38(1):1–14.

Witte, J.
  1985a   Democratic procedures and tax policy. Pp. 134–152 in J.A. Pechman, ed.,
          A Citizen's Guide to the New Tax Reforms: Fair Tax, Flat Tax, Simple Tax.
          Totowa, N.J.: Rowman & Allanheld.
  1985b   *The Politics and Development of the Tax Laws.* Madison: University of
          Wisconsin Press.

Wolff, E.N.
  1985   The disappearance of domestic servants and the underground economy.
          Pp. 316–329 in W. Gaertner and A. Wenig, eds., *The Economics of the
          Shadow Economy.* New York: Springer-Verlag.

Wolfgang, M.E., Figlio, R.M., Tracy, P.E., and Singer, S.I.
  1985   *The National Survey of Crime Severity.* Bureau of Justice Statistics. Wash-
          ington, D.C.: U.S. Department of Justice.

Wrong, D.
  1961   The oversocialized conception of man in modern sociology. *American
          Sociological Review* 26(April):183–193.

Yankelovich, Skelly, and White, Inc.
　1984　Taxpayer Attitudes Study: Final Report. Public opinion survey prepared for the Public Affairs Division, Internal Revenue service, December 1984 by Yankelovich, Skelly, and White, Inc., New York.
Yitzhaki, S.
　1974　A note on income tax evasion: a theoretical analysis. *Journal of Public Economics* 3:201–202.
Zimring, F., and Hawkins, G.
　1971　The legal threat as an instrument of social change. *Journal of Social Issues* 27:33.

Peter Schmidt

Appendix A: Statistical Issues in Modeling Taxpayer Compliance

In this appendix I discuss various statistical issues in the analysis of taxpayer compliance. I do so under the assumption that primary interest is not in estimating the overall level of compliance, but rather in estimating the effects of various demographic or policy-related variables on the level of compliance. As an example, Clotfelter (1983) has estimated the effect of individual (demographic) variables and of the marginal tax rate on the level of tax evasion. The statistical issues that might arise in such analyses are the subject this appendix. This should be made clear at the outset, since such issues are rather different from the statistical issues that would likely arise in the course of estimating the overall level of compliance.

Basically three types of data might be used for the estimation of models of tax compliance. First, there are data on individuals (that is, data from individual tax returns) from the IRS's Tax Compliance Measurement Program (TCMP), obtained by the IRS from rigorous audits of a stratified random sample of individual tax returns. These data are currently not available to the general research community, though the IRS has permitted some researchers (e.g., Clotfelter) access to them. Second, aggregated versions of some TCMP data are available. For example, the TCMP data for 1969 and 1979 are available, aggregated to the three-digit zip code level, along with demographic data (including data on demographic variables not found on the tax return) aggregated on the same level. Third, data from some surveys of individuals are available.

It is clear that different statistical issues will arise with different types of data. For example, a different model would almost surely be used to analyze individual TCMP data than would be used to analyze randomized response survey data.

Department of Economics, Michigan State University.

In this appendix I focus on statistical issues that would arise in the analysis of individual-level TCMP data and other similar individual-level quantitative data. I discuss aggregated data and survey data only in passing. While it may be unusual to concentrate on issues that would arise chiefly in the analysis of data that the IRS does not make generally available, one justification is that the IRS decision whether to release such data may depend on what its likely uses would be.

The plan of the appendix is as follows. In the first section I discuss the relevance of stochastic frontier models for the analysis of audit-based tax changes (or changes in taxable income, deductions, etc.). Stochastic frontier models have a one-sided error component and may be of use to the extent that fraud is one-sided (for example, one might presume that no one deliberately overreports his or her tax liability). I consider the standard frontier model as used in production theory and several obvious modifications. In the next section I discuss the problem of clustering at zero. For many individuals, the TCMP audit does not change the amount of tax due, and so the tax change is zero. This is a very serious statistical problem, and the standard techniques used to handle it in other contexts are not entirely satisfactory. I discuss these techniques and suggest some complicated alternatives. In the next section I discuss the potential advantages of panel data, that is, data with more than one year's observation per individual. I also comment on some practical issues in the construction of such data. Finally, the appendix ends with a section giving my conclusions.

Stochastic Frontier Models

The standard textbook definition of a production function is that it gives the maximum possible output that can be produced, as a function of the quantities of a specified set of inputs into the production process. Thus the production function defines a frontier that cannot be exceeded by the observed outputs. The frontier can be deterministic or stochastic, but in either case the deviations of the observed outputs from the frontier must be one-sided (nonpositive). This one-sidedness has an apparent counterpart in statistical models of taxpayer compliance, if we assume that deliberate noncompliance is also one-sided. That is, we assume that individuals may understate their tax liability, but that no one deliberately overstates his or her tax liability. Of course, this assumption can be questioned. Some individuals may indeed overreport their tax liability, either to reduce the chance of being audited, or even just to avoid the work of filling out complicated forms. It is not apparent how widespread such behavior might be; however, the applicability of stochastic frontier models hinges on its being empirically unimportant.

In this section I comment on some aspects of the applicability of stochastic frontier models to the question of taxpayer compliance. More specifically, the potential application that I have in mind is to TCMP data (or other similar audit-based data), for which the dependent variable is the dollar change in some line of the tax return. For example, the dependent variable could be the difference between after-audit and before-audit tax paid.

A SURVEY OF STOCHASTIC FRONTIER MODELS

I now present a brief summary of the stochastic frontier model and some comments on its applicability to compliance research. In order to improve readability, the discussion is in terms of a potential tax compliance application rather than in terms of production functions. Thus suppose specifically that we have TCMP audit data on a sample of N individuals (or, more precisely, individual returns) and that the dependent variable is the difference between the after-audit tax and the before-audit tax.

The stochastic frontier model of Aigner, Lovell, and Schmidt (1977) is of the form

$$(1) \qquad y_i = X_i'\beta + v_i + u_i, \qquad i = 1,. . .,N.$$

Here i indexes individuals, and y_i is the dependent variable (audit-induced tax change) for person i. The $K \times 1$ vector X_i contains the explanatory variables for person i; presumably these would be demographic variables and possibly other entries on the tax return. The vector β contains the regression coefficients to be estimated. We assume that the v_i are independently and identically distributed as $N(0,\sigma_v^2)$, and that $u_i \geq 0$ with the u_i independently and identically distributed according to some specific one-sided distribution (e.g., exponential, half-normal, gamma). Finally, we assume that v_i and u_i are independent of each other and of the explanatory variables (X_i). We observe y_i and X_i, $i = 1,. . .,N$, but not β, v_i, or u_i.

In the present context the interpretation of the errors would be that v_i represents accidental noncompliance, measurement errors, and other statistical noise, whereas u_i represents deliberate noncompliance. The normality of the statistical noise (v_i) is a more or less standard assumption in a regression model. The nonnegativity of the deliberate noncompliance error (u_i) reflects the assumption that deliberate understatements of tax liability are nonpositive, so that they lead to nonnegative changes in tax owed when discovered in the audit.

I should mention in passing that in the usual production function applications of frontier models, $u_i \leq 0$, since it represents the shortfall of output from the frontier. However, the conversion to the case in which $u_i \geq 0$ requires only obvious sign changes.

Clearly the combined error $(v_i + u_i)$ will be positive more often than negative, and this seems sensible since most audit tax changes are positive (see, e.g., Clotfelter, 1983, Appendix). However, a potentially serious problem is that zero may be a common value of the dependent variable, since for many returns the audit may not change the tax owed. This is discussed in some detail in the section on clustering at zero and is ignored for now.

I note in passing that the fact that audit-induced tax changes are mostly positive does not imply that the error terms in a regression model for such tax changes should be mostly positive. In a regression model such as equation (1) we need to distinguish the marginal distribution of y from the conditional distribution of y given X. The distribution of the error terms reflects the conditional distribution of y given X, while observable facts about the dependent variable y represent its marginal distribution. If y_i is usually positive, this may just be because $X_i'\beta$ is usually positive. Nevertheless, I believe that the inclusion of a one-sided error component in equation (1) is reasonable, in the present context, because even the portion of the audit-induced tax change that is unexplained by the model may include deliberate noncompliance, which I presume to be one-sided.

The usual method of estimating the model in equation (1) is by maximum likelihood. Suppose that v_i and u_i have density functions, $f(v_i)$ and $g(u_i)$ respectively, where $f(v_i)$ is the density of $N(0,\sigma_v^2)$ and $g(u_i)$ is the density of whatever distribution we assume for u_i. Define $\epsilon_i = v_i + u_i$. Its density is

(2) $$h(\varepsilon_i) = \int_0^\infty f(\varepsilon_i - u_i)g(u_i)du_i = \int_{-\infty}^\infty f(v_i)g(\varepsilon_i - v_i)dv_i$$

and the likelihood of the sample $y_1, \ldots, y_N$ is

(3) $$L = \prod_{i=1}^N h(y_i - X_i'\beta).$$

This can be maximized with respect to the parameters (β and the parameters of the error distributions) to yield the maximum likelihood estimates.

By standard statistical theory, the maximum likelihood estimates are consistent, asymptotically efficient, and asymptotically normal; that is, they have good statistical properties when the sample size (N) is large. Since the TCMP files are indeed large, reliance on asymptotic properties of the estimates seems justified.

For commonly assumed distributions for u_i, the integral in equation (2) is tractable, and the density $h(\epsilon_i)$ can be expressed in an explicit form. For example, Aigner, Lovell, and Schmidt (1977) give the density for the cases in which u_i is respectively exponential or half-normal, while Stevenson (1980) gives the density for the case in which u_i is truncated normal (a normal random variable with arbitrary mean and variance, truncated from below at zero). However, even in these cases an explicit solution for the maximum likelihood estimates has not been worked out. Rather the likelihood function of equation (3) must be maximized numerically (by iterative or numerical search methods) to obtain the estimates. The need for such complicated computations is sometimes an obstacle to the use of stochastic frontier models.

An alternative method of estimation is corrected ordinary least squares (corrected OLS). Let $E(u_i) = \mu > 0$, and suppose that X_i contains an intercept (constant term). Then it is easy to see that OLS provides a consistent estimate for all elements of β except the intercept, whereas the estimated intercept provides a consistent estimate of the actual intercept plus μ. If we can obtain a consistent estimate of μ, say $\hat{\mu}$, then a consistent estimate of the (actual) intercept is obtained as the estimated intercept minus $\hat{\mu}$. Thus the corrected ordinary least squares estimate is the same as the ordinary least squares estimate for all of the regression coefficients except the intercept, which is corrected by subtracting $\hat{\mu}$. Given an assumed distribution for u_i, a consistent estimate $\hat{\mu}$ for $E(u_i) = \mu$ can be obtained from the moments of the OLS residuals. If $v_i \sim N(0,\sigma_v^2)$ and u_i contains one parameter, the solution will generally depend on the second and third moments of the OLS residuals. (As an example, see Olson, Schmidt, and Waldman, 1980:69, for an explicit solution in the case of half-normal u_i.)

An advantage of estimation by OLS (or corrected OLS) is that the consistency of the estimates of elements of β (other than the intercept) does not hinge on the correctness of the assumed distribution for u_i. However, for large sample sizes the maximum likelihood estimates should be more efficient than the OLS estimates. The relative efficiency of maximum likelihood and corrected OLS has been investigated by Olson et al. (1980), for the case in which u_i is half-normal. They calculate and compare the asymptotic variances of the estimates and also compare the finite-sample properties of the estimates in a Monte Carlo experiment. Perhaps surprisingly, they find the efficiency difference between maximum likelihood and corrected OLS to be very small, both in finite samples and asymptotically. So, at least for one commonly assumed distribution for u_i, there appears to be little reason to go to the bother of calculating the maximum likelihood estimates.

Having estimated the parameters of the model in one way or another, it is sometimes of interest to attempt to measure the error components, v_i and u_i, separately. If $\hat{\beta}$ is a consistent estimate of β, the residual $y_i - X_i'\hat{\beta}$ can be regarded as a consistent estimate of $v_i + u_i$ (in the sense that the probability limit of $(y_i - X_i\hat{\beta}) - (v_i + u_i)$ is zero, as $N \to \infty$), and the problem is to decompose this into separate estimates of v_i and u_i. Jondrow et al. (1982) point out that the information about u_i in $(v_i + u_i)$ is summarized by the conditional distribution of u_i given $(v_i + u_i)$, and they calculate this conditional distribution for the normal/half-normal case. The expectation of this distribution is shown by Waldman (1984) to have certain desirable properties as a point estimate of u_i.

In the context of frontier production functions, u_i is a measure of the firm's technical efficiency, and a desire to estimate firm-level efficiencies is often the motivation for considering stochastic (or deterministic) frontier models. In the present context, u_i is a measure of deliberate noncompliance. More precisely, since u_i has been assumed independent of X_i, it is a measure of the portion of deliberate noncompliance not explained by X_i. Since the interesting questions in compliance research have to do with the effects of explanatory variables on noncompliance, the estimation of u_i would not seem to be of much interest in the present context.

A BIVARIATE STOCHASTIC FRONTIER MODEL

In this subsection I consider a possible extension of the stochastic frontier model, which involves moving from a univariate (single-equation) to a bivariate (two-equation) or multivariate (many-equation) setting. For example, an individual may understate his or her tax liability by understating taxable income or by overstating deductions, and we might wish to estimate separate relationships for the audit-based change in taxable income and for the change in allowable deductions. However, there are likely to be efficiency gains in jointly estimating these two relationships, since in doing so one can exploit the correlation of the error terms across equations. Such a correlation seems plausible, since individuals who are more likely to underreport income are probably also more likely to overreport deductions.

We therefore consider a two-equation model:

(4)
$$\begin{aligned} y_{1i} &= X_{1i}' + \beta_1 + v_{1i} + u_{1i} \\ y_{2i} &= X_{2i}' + \beta_2 + v_{2i} - u_{2i} \end{aligned}, \quad i = 1, \ldots, N.$$

Here, for individual i, y_{1i} = audit-induced change in taxable income and y_{2i} = audit-induced change in allowable deductions. Each equation separately is of the same form as equation (1), and we make the same assumptions as we did following equation (1). In particular, the vs are normally distributed noise and the us are nonnegative, with some specified distribution. Note however that u_{2i} is subtracted (rather than added) in the second equation since deductions tend to be reduced in the audit.

As a matter of notation, let $\epsilon_{1i} = v_{1i} + u_{1i}$ and $\epsilon_{2i} = v_{2i} - u_{2i}$ be the error terms in equation (4). In the present context these will have unusual distributions. Apart from this complication, however, equation (4) is just a bivariate regression model, or a set of seemingly unrelated regressions, in econometric jargon. From the usual textbook treatments (e.g., Kmenta, 1971, Ch. 12, or Schmidt, 1976, Sec. 2.5) we can note the following facts about such a model. First, OLS applied to each equation separately yields unbiased and consistent estimates of β_1 and β_2. Second, joint estimation of the two equations by generalized least squares yields estimates of β_1 and β_2 that are consistent and that are asymptotically at least as efficient as the OLS estimates. Third, the joint estimates are in fact asymptotically more efficient than OLS, except when ϵ_{1i} and ϵ_{2i} are uncorrelated or when $X_{1i} = X_{2i}$ for all i.

In the present context, OLS or generalized least squares will not estimate the intercept consistently; recall the discussion of corrected ordinary least squares in the last section. Except for this minor qualification, however, the three statements of the preceding paragraph remain true, since they do not depend on the normality of the errors. As noted above, correlation between ϵ_{1i} and ϵ_{2i} seems likely in the income/deductions example, so that the potential for efficiency gains from joint estimation exists. However, the other condition for such efficiency gains is that $X_{1i} \neq X_{2i}$, that is, the sets of explanatory variables in the equations for the changes in taxable income and in allowable deductions must be different. It seems to me that we should expect considerable overlap between these sets of explanatory variables, so that the potential gain from joint estimation of these two equations may be limited. However, this is clearly a question to be resolved empirically.

From the standpoint of the frontiers literature, a more interesting question is whether we can improve the efficiency of the estimates by imposing particular distributional assumptions for the vs and us in equation (4). To answer this question, we need to make plausible assumptions about these distributions. In the single equation case (1), we assumed v_i to be normal, u_i to have a particular one-sided distribution (e.g., half-normal), and v_i and u_i to be independent. In the present case (4), it is natural to assume that (v_{1i}, v_{2i}) are bivariate normal with mean zero and arbitrary variances and covariance. By analogy to the single equation case, it is also natural to assume that (v_{1i}, v_{2i}) is independent of (u_{1i}, u_{2i}). What remains is to find a reasonable distribution for (u_{1i}, u_{2i}).

The bivariate case has not been treated in the existing frontiers literature, so there is no precedent to follow in the choice of a one-sided bivariate distribution. However, a possibility that nicely generalizes the half-normal assumption in the univariate case is the bivariate half-normal distribution given by Johnson and Kotz (1972:123). This has the density

$$f(u_1, u_2) = 2[\pi \sigma_1 \sigma_2 (1 - \rho^2)^{1/2}]^{-1} \cosh \left(\frac{\rho u_1 u_2}{(1 - \rho^2) \sigma_1 \sigma_2} \right)$$

(5)

$$\cdot \exp \left(-\frac{(u_1/\sigma_1)^2 + (u_2/\sigma_2)^2}{2(1 - \rho^2)} \right),$$

where $u_1 \geq 0$ and $u_2 \geq 0$. Here cosh is the hyperbolic cosine function: $\cosh(x) = \frac{1}{2}(e^x + e^{-x})$. The marginal distribution of u_1 is half-normal; u_1 is distributed as the absolute value of $N(0, \sigma_1^2)$. Similarly u_2 is half-normal. The conditional distribution of u_2 given u_1 is folded normal, the distribution of the absolute value of $N(|\rho| u_1, 1 - \rho^2)$. This implies

(6) $$E(u_2 | u_1) = |\rho| u_1 + 2 \, \Phi \, [\rho u_1 / (1 - \rho^2)^{1/2}],$$

where Φ is the standard normal cumulative distribution function.

If we let the (bivariate normal) density of (v_1, v_2) be $g(v_1, v_2)$, we can make the transformation $\epsilon_1 = v_1 + u_1$, $\epsilon_2 = v_2 - u_2$ to obtain the density of (ϵ_1, ϵ_2) as

$$h(\epsilon_1, \epsilon_2) = \int_{-\infty}^{\infty} \int_{-\infty}^{\infty} g(v_1, v_2) f(\epsilon_1 - v_1, v_2 - \epsilon_2) dv_1 dv_2$$

(7)

$$= \int_0^{\infty} \int_0^{\infty} g(\epsilon_1 - u_1, \epsilon_2 + u_2) f(u_1, u_2) du_1 du_2.$$

This yields a likelihood function

$$(8) \qquad L = \prod_{i=1}^{N} h(y_{1i} - X_{1i}' \beta_1, y_{2i} - X_{2i}' \beta_2),$$

which is a direct generalization of equation (3) above. It could be maximized numerically to obtain the maximum likelihood estimates (MLEs) of β_1, β_2, and the parameters in the distributions of v and u.

I have not attempted the integrals in equation (7), but I believe that they are tractable, in the sense that they can be reduced to a closed-form expression times the bivariate normal cumulative distribution function. A more fundamental concern is whether this approach is likely to be fruitful. Its costs are clear. First, it will lead to very cumbersome and costly calculations. Second, the consistency of the MLEs will (presumably) hinge on the correctness of the distributional assumptions. The gain to be had from incurring these costs is less clear. First, the MLEs will be asymptotically at least as efficient as the generalized least squares estimates. The extent of this efficiency gain is unknown, and is probably worth investigating, but it was small in the univariate case. Second, if we are interested in extracting an estimate of u_1 (and/or u_2), we can use $E(u_1|\epsilon_1,\epsilon_2)$, which should have less variability than the estimate from the univariate model, $E(|u_1|\epsilon_1)$. However, while this possibly may be of some importance in the efficiency measurement exercise that motivates the production frontier literature, it is perhaps not of importance in the tax compliance setting.

It is difficult to give a conclusion to this subsection without seeing some empirical results. I would like to see a bivariate system such as equation (4) estimated, both by generalized least squares and by the MLE (using the likelihood (8), for example). My suspicion is that the MLEs will not be worth the bother, while joint estimation by generalized least squares will probably be worthwhile.

Two Asymmetric Errors

We return now to the univariate model (1), with the dependent variable being the audit-induced tax change. The two-part error term contains a symmetric error v and a nonnegative error u, with the motivation that u represents deliberate noncompliance while v represents accidental noncompliance as well as general statistical noise.

A possible criticism of this error specification is that accidental noncompliance is not distributed symmetrically. For example, it is well known that even mathematical errors and other apparent mistakes tend to be predominantly in the taxpayer's favor. This could lead to a model in which v has an asymmetric distribution rather than a normal (symmetric) distribution. If we are willing to specify a particular form for the distribution of v, a likelihood function may be constructed as in equations (2) and (3), and the model may be estimated by maximum likelihood. This should be feasible, though I have some doubts as to how well we can expect to separate v from u in such a model.

Even apart from questions of feasibility, however, I am not impressed by the usefulness of such an approach. The fact that mathematical errors or other mistakes are predominantly in the taxpayer's favor can simply be taken as evidence that some of them are deliberate. While this is an arguable point, certainly in terms of fitting the data the question of whether a mistake was deliberate is not a very fruitful one to argue. The dependent variable (tax change under audit) has a skewed distribution, and the component $u \geq 0$ is a statistical accommodation to that empirical fact. While it is nicely motivated by the distinction between accidental and deliberate noncompliance, one need not accept the distinction to decide (on the basis of data) whether the model is empirically useful and reasonable.

Remarks

In this section I have given a survey of the stochastic frontier model and discussed some possible extensions of the model that might be relevant for tax compliance research. This was done from the perspective of a possible application in which the dependent variable is the tax change induced by a TCMP audit. Such changes reflect at least in part the discovery of deliberate noncompliance. Thus the stochastic frontier model, which contains a positive error component, seems attractive.

I have reached fairly pessimistic conclusions concerning the direct applicability of this model, however. The strongest motivation for the frontier model in the production function context—namely, measurement of inefficiency in individual firms—does not appear to be applicable in the tax compliance context. The main parameters of interest can be estimated consistently by ordinary least squares, without making such strong assumptions about the properties of the error terms as are required for maximum likelihood estimation of the stochastic frontier model. Furthermore, the efficiency gains obtained by making these assumptions are small.

However, these conclusions depend strongly on the simplicity of the model. The linear regression model with a well-behaved additive error, as we have so far considered, cannot account for an important empirical feature of the dependent variable, namely its clustering at zero. As I discuss in the next section, a successful accommodation of this feature of the data will necessarily hinge on the correctness of the distributional assumptions for certain error terms. Thus a more complicated version of the stochastic frontier model may yet be plausible and useful.

Clustering at Zero

In the last section we considered models in which the dependent variable is the tax change induced by a TCMP audit. However, we ignored an important feature of the data, namely, that this variable is often exactly equal to zero, since many audits do not change the tax owed. Such a variable may be said to be clustered at zero. Clearly other potential audit-based dependent variables (e.g., change in taxable income or change in deductions) will also be clustered at zero.

In this section I discuss the serious statistical problems that clustering at zero causes. I survey some standard statistical models designed to handle this problem and suggest some modifications of these models. Finally, because one reason for clustering at zero is measurement error (i.e., there is additional tax owed but the audit does not reveal it), I also discuss measurement error and the extent to which it can be incorporated into these models.

STATISTICAL IMPLICATIONS OF CLUSTERING
Consider a linear regression model

$$(9) \qquad y_i = X_i'\beta + \epsilon_i, \qquad i = 1, \ldots, N,$$

with the notation basically the same as in equation (1). That is, for individual i, y_i is the audit-induced tax change, X_i is a vector of explanatory variables, and ϵ_i is an error term. Such a model is often estimated by ordinary least squares (OLS), and the OLS estimates have many desirable properties if the errors (ϵ_i) in turn satisfy certain assumptions. In particular, if the errors are independently and identically distributed (iid) and independent of the explanatory variables (X_i), then the OLS estimates are unbiased and consistent, regardless of the actual distribution of the errors.

Now suppose that the dependent variable is often exactly equal to zero. Such a dependent variable cannot be represented by a linear model such as (9), with iid errors that are independent of the explanatory variables. To see this, note that $y_i = 0$ is equivalent to $\epsilon_i = -X_i'\beta$. Therefore the distribution of y_i has nonzero mass at $y_i = 0$ if the distribution of ϵ_i has nonzero mass at $\epsilon_i = -X_i'\beta$. Since this point varies over observations, the distribution of ϵ must vary over observations; the ϵ_i cannot be identically distributed. Worse yet, the distribution of ϵ_i depends on X_i, since the point at which it has nonzero mass is $-X_i'\beta$. Therefore we should expect ϵ_i and X_i to be correlated. This implies that the OLS estimates will be biased and inconsistent, and that inferences based on them will be invalid. Thus application of OLS to a model in which the dependent variable is clustered at zero (or elsewhere) is not advisable.

An obvious question that this raises is whether we can simply discard the observations for which $y = 0$ and estimate the model by OLS applied to the nonzero observations. This is actually a fairly complicated question. Its answer hinges on whether, conditional on $\epsilon_i \neq -X_i'\beta$, the ϵ_i are iid and independent of X_i. If so, OLS is justified. If not, OLS will be in general be biased and inconsistent, and we have an example of what Heckman (1976, 1979) termed *sample selection bias*.

To be able to say whether sample selection bias would be present in an analysis of the nonzero observations only, we need to make additional assumptions. Essentially, we need to expand the model to account for the occurrence of $\epsilon_i = -X_i'\beta$ with nonzero probability. This is discussed in some detail in the next subsection. For now I simply note the following, at an intuitive level. An audit reveals no tax change either because of a measurement error in the audit outcome (there should have been a tax change, but the auditor did not discover it) or because there was no tax change to be found (in which case we presume, or hope, that measurement error does not occur). If for the moment we assume away the second possibility, the question is simply whether returns without such measurement errors tend on average to have different ϵs than returns with such measurement errors. In my opinion the answer must be yes, since on average returns with higher ϵs have more tax change to be discovered, and this must imply a lower probability of its being undiscovered. If this is so, we should expect sample selection bias to be present if we attempt a simple analysis of the data with the no-change observations deleted.

EXISTING MODELS FOR CLUSTERING

In this subsection I discuss briefly three existing models to handle clustering of the dependent variable. A less brief treatment can be found in Schmidt and Witte (1984, Chapter 4), while an encyclopedic source is Maddala (1983).

The first model is the so-called Tobit model, which dates back to Tobin (1958). Consider a regression model,

$$\text{(10)} \qquad\qquad y_i^* = X_i'\beta + \epsilon_i, \qquad i = 1,\ldots, N$$

where the ϵ_i are iid $N(0,\sigma^2)$. However, y_i^* is unobserved and instead we observe

$$\text{(11)} \qquad\qquad y_i = \max(0, y_i^*) = \begin{cases} y_i^* & \text{if } y_i^* > 0, \\ 0 & \text{if } y_i^* \le 0. \end{cases}$$

(We also observe X_i for all i.) The Tobit model is also referred to as a censored normal regression model, because the distribution of y^* given X is normal and because the observable y corresponds in statistical terminology to a censoring of the unobservable y^* at zero.

Clearly $y_i \ge 0$, and $y_i = 0$ with nonzero probability. Thus the model is often applied in cases in which the dependent variable of interest is non-negative and zero is a common value. Clotfelter (1983) has used the Tobit model to analyze the determinants of the audit-induced change in adjusted gross income in a sample of 1969 TCMP audits. Similarly, Westat, Inc. (1980) analyzed the revenue yields of a sample of 1973 TCMP audits of business returns greater than $30,000.

The Tobit model is usually estimated by maximum likelihood. This requires a numerical maximization of the likelihood function, but such a maximization is not unduly hard because the likelihood function is reasonably easy to evaluate and because it is known to have only one local maximum. The maximum likelihood estimates are consistent and asymptotically efficient, so long of course as the model is correctly specified. However, the consistency of the MLEs hinges on the correctness of the normality assumption for the errors. Alternative estimators have been developed recently that are less efficient than the MLEs when the normality assumption is correct, but that remain consistent under alternative distributions of the errors, so long as the errors remain iid. Examples are Powell (1984, 1986), Manski (1985), and Fernandez (1986). In my opinion such robust estimators may be very worthwhile in the present context. There may be good reason to expect skewness in the error distribution (as discussed in detail in the previous section), so that it is unattractive to depend strongly on the correctness of an assumption of normality.

A considerable disadvantage of the Tobit model in the present context is that the audit-induced changes in tax owed (or adjusted gross income, or other line item) are in fact not one-sided. Positive and zero changes predominate, but there are negative changes as well; the Tobit model cannot well accommodate this feature of the data. Thus Clotfelter (1983) is forced to set negative changes in adjusted gross income equal to zero. Similarly Westat, Inc. (1980) reports that they "limit the dependent variable to nonnegative values," which I find ambiguous. (It could mean that negative values are set to zero, or it could mean that such observations are discarded, and neither option is attractive.) Presumably overstatements of tax liability represent mistakes on the part of the taxpayer, but it is not appropriate to trim such statistical noise from one tail of the distribution without somehow trimming it from the other tail as well. It is more appropriate to simply regard negative values of the dependent variable as an indication that the Tobit model is incorrect.

A second possible model is the two-part Tobit model of Cragg (1971). This is a generalization of the Tobit model, in the following sense. In the Tobit model one set of parameters (β, σ^2) determines both the probability that $y = 0$ and the form of the distribution of the positive values of y. In Cragg's model there are two separate sets of parameters to determine these two features of the distribution of y. Thus the probability that $y_i = 0$ is specified as

$$(12) \qquad\qquad P(y_i = 0) = \Phi(-X_i'\beta_1)$$

where Φ is the standard normal cdf; this is just a probit specification. Second, the density of y_i, conditional on X_i and on $y_i > 0$, is assumed to be $N(X_i'\beta_2, \sigma^2)$, truncated from below at zero. Thus the positive values of y follow a truncated normal distribution. If $\beta_1 = \beta_2 / \sigma$, Cragg's model reduces to the Tobit model.

In the present context Cragg's model suffers from the same defect as the Tobit model, namely an inability to accommodate negative values of the dependent variable. This could be handled by considering some other distribution than truncated normal for the nonzero y_i. However, a more fundamental problem is that the model focuses on the distribution of the observations conditional on their being nonzero. This is precisely the distribution one analyzes if the observations that equal zero are discarded, and in the present context it is probably not the distribution of interest. In my opinion Cragg's model is a reasonable one when clustering at zero is real, in the sense that the actual change in tax due is zero, but it is not reasonable when clustering at zero is the result of failure of the audit to discover a nonzero change in tax due. In the latter case the distribution of discovered changes should be expected to be different from the distribution of undiscovered changes, and conditioning on observability of a tax change distorts the distribution to be estimated.

The third model to be discussed here is the sample selection model of Heckman (1976, 1979). This is a two-equation model of the form:

(13A) $$y_{i1} = X_i'\beta_1 + \epsilon_{i1},$$

(13B) $$y_{i2} = X_i'\beta_2 + \epsilon_{i2},$$

where the pairs of errors $(\epsilon_{i1}, \epsilon_{i2})$ are iid as bivariate normal. We observe X_i and y_{i2} for all observations, but we observe y_{i1} only for observations such that $y_{i2} > 0$.

The classic example in economics is the determination of wage rates for women. Here the second equation in (13) is a probit equation explaining whether a woman works ($y_{i2} > 0$) or does not work ($y_{i2} \leq 0$). The dependent variable (y_{i1}) of the first equation is the woman's wage, and this is observed only if she works. However, it is crucial to observe that the variable y_{i1} is assumed to be meaningful for all observations, whether or not it is observed. Thus y_{i1} is interpreted as the potential wage that the individual would earn if she chose to work, and the point of the model is to be able to estimate the effect of explanatory variables on the potential wage, without incurring the bias that may result by using only the observations on individuals that work.

As a matter of notation, let $\sigma_{12} = \text{Cov}(\epsilon_{i1}, \epsilon_{i2})$. Then OLS of y_{i1} on X_i, using only the observations for which y_{i1} is observed, will be unbiased if $\sigma_{12} = 0$; in this case the rule governing observability is independent of the process generating the observed y_{i1}. However, if $\sigma_{12} \neq 0$, OLS will generally be biased, and we call this phenomenon sample selection bias. One way to see the problem is that the regression function over all potential observation is

(14) $$E(y_{i1}|X_i) = X_i'\beta_1$$

while the regression function over observations such that y_{i1} is observed is

(15) $$E(y_{i1}|X_i, y_{i2} > 0) = X_i'\beta + \frac{\sigma_{12}}{\sqrt{\sigma_{22}}}\lambda_i.$$

In (15), $\sigma_{22} = \text{var}(\epsilon_{i2})$, $\lambda_i = \phi_i/(1 - \Phi_i)$, and ϕ_i and Φ_i are respectively the standard normal density and cdf, evaluated at $-X_i'\beta_2/\sqrt{\sigma_{22}}$. Unless

$\sigma_{12} = 0$, equations (14) and (15) are different and OLS applied only to the complete observations will not give unbiased estimates of β_1.

The model (13) may be estimated by MLE or by a simpler two-step method. In either case the consistency of the estimates hinges on the correctness of the assumption of bivariate normality of the errors. Alternative distributional assumptions are possible, but consistency will then in turn hinge on these assumptions. That is, no distribution-free estimation procedure currently exists for this model.

The sample selection model (13) may be applied to the present problem (analysis of determinants of the audit-induced tax change) in a fairly straightforward way, if we assume that a tax change of zero corresponds to nonobservability of the dependent variable. That is, we assume $y_{i1} = 0$ if $y_{i2} \leq 0$; otherwise y_{i1} is determined according to (13A). How sensible this is seems to me to depend on whether there is real clustering at zero or whether all observed clustering is just measurement error. The model as just described does not accommodate real clustering (i.e., actual change in tax due equals zero) very well, since equation (13A) is assumed meaningful for all observations and will not generate a cluster at zero. It does handle well the case in which all observations of zero are measurement error, in the sense of failure of the audit to discover the true change in tax due.

In the present context, I would expect $\sigma_{12} > 0$, since larger ϵ_{i1} mean more tax change to be discovered and thus a lower probability of observing $y_{i1} = 0$ (i.e., a higher probability of $y_{i2} > 0$). Thus I believe that an analysis of only the observations with nonzero tax changes will indeed suffer from sample selection bias, and some model similar in spirit to that in equation (13) may be needed to avoid this bias. I discuss possible modifications of the model in (13) in the next subsection.

A final point to note is that, of the three models discussed so far, only the sample selection model is consistent with nonzero observations that are both positive and negative. This is another advantage of the sample selection model, in the present context. While audit-induced tax changes are usually positive, they can be negative, and the Tobit model cannot handle this possibility reasonably.

Extensions of Existing Models

In this subsection I suggest some modifications of the models presented in the last subsection. These modifications will attempt to address particular issues that have already been discussed, such as measurement error and possible skewness of the errors in the compliance relationship. In particular I try to address three important questions. First, can we accommodate the stochastic frontier error structure discussed in the previous section? Second, what kinds of measurement error can we handle? Third, can we distinguish real clustering of tax changes at zero from clustering caused by measurement error?

In order to address these questions I discuss four possible models. The following notation is useful. Let us distinguish three (possibly different) tax amounts: T_{REP}, the tax reported on the return as being due; T_{AUD}, the tax due as of the end of the audit, and T_{TRUE}, the true tax due. The first two are observable, while the third is not. We then define

$$y_1{}^* = T_{TRUE} - T_{REP},$$

(16) $$y_1 = T_{AUD} - T_{REP},$$

$$A = T_{AUD} - T_{TRUE}.$$

Note that $y_1{}^*$ measures compliance, so that its determination is of interest. However, $y_1{}^*$ is unobservable. We observe y_1, the audit-induced tax change. Clearly $y_1 = y_1{}^* + A$, where A is the measurement error (of tax due) in the audit. We also note that y_1 will be clustered at zero, and that y_1 may equal zero either because $y_1{}^* = 0$ (in which case we assume $A = 0$) or because of measurement error, that is, $A = -y_1{}^*$. In the last subsection it was argued that it is reasonable to condition on $y_1{}^* \neq 0$, but in the presence of measurement error it is not reasonable to condition on $y_1 \neq 0$.

The first and simplest model to be considered is a modification of the sample selection model (13) to accommodate the stochastic frontier error structure. For now, we assume that there is no real clustering at zero. We also assume that there is no measurement error, except that some nonzero changes in tax due are undiscovered in the audit. (Thus $y_1 = y_1{}^*$ or $y_1 = 0$, and $y_1 = 0$ is the result of measurement error.) Then the model (13) can be modified slightly:

(17A) $$y_{i1} = X_i'\beta_1 + v_{i1} + u_i,$$

(17B) $$y_{i2} = X_i'\beta_2 + v_{i2},$$

As in equation (13), we assume (v_{i1}, v_{i2}) iid as bivariate normal. As in equation (1), we assume $u_i \geq 0$ to represent deliberate noncompliance, and a particular distribution (such as half-normal) is assumed for u_i. Furthermore u_i is assumed independent of (v_{i1}, v_{i2}). The independence of u_i and v_{i2} is a very unattractive assumption, since higher deliberate noncompliance should increase the probability of detection, but at present I don't know of a reasonable way to relax this assumption. As in equation (13), we observe

$y_{i1} = 0$ when $y_{i2} \geq 0$, and we observe y_{i1} as in (17A) when $y_{i2} > 0$. We do not observe y_{i2} itself, but from the value of y_{i1} we observe whether $y_{i2} \leq 0$ or $y_{i2} > 0$.

The second model to be considered is the same as (17) except that y_{i1} is added as an explanatory variable in the y_{i2} equation. This yields

$$(18A) \qquad y_{i1} = X_i'\beta_1 + v_{i1} + u_{i1},$$

$$(18B) \qquad y_{i2} = X_i'\beta_2 + \gamma y_{i1} + v_{i2}.$$

This seems reasonable to me because the higher the level of noncompliance (y_{i1}), the more likely it is to be discovered (i.e., the higher should be y_{i2}). Thus I would expect $\gamma > 0$. This is a simultaneous equation model of the type commonly considered in econometrics. In the usual textbook case, equation (18B) would be underidentified without further assumptions. Possible identifying restrictions would be that one or more elements of β_2 equal zero (i.e., some variable or variables that affect compliance do not affect the probability of detection of noncompliance), or the independence of the errors in (18B) from those in (18A). However, the presence of u_i in (18A) makes the model identified even without such restrictions.

The above two models show that we can handle the skewness of the error distribution caused by deliberate noncompliance in a straightforward manner. We now turn to the consideration of measurement error. In the above models, noncompliance is either undetected, or it is detected exactly, which is unreasonable since noncompliance may be detected but with error. In the third model, we relax this assumption by allowing additive measurement error. Thus we have

$$(19A) \qquad y_{i1}^* = X_i'\beta_1 + v_{i1} + u_i,$$

$$(19B) \qquad y_{i2} = X_i'\beta_2 + \gamma y_{i1}^* + v_{i2},$$

$$(19C) \qquad y_{i1} = \begin{cases} 0 & \text{if } y_{i2} \leq 0, \\ y_{i1}^* + A_i & \text{if } y_{i2} > 0. \end{cases}$$

Alternatively, we can rewrite (19C) as just $y_{i1} = y_{i1}^* + A_i$, where $A_i = -y_{i1}^*$ when $y_{i2} \leq 0$. Clearly, A_i is interpreted as the measurement error component of y_{i1}, just as in equation (16).

We make the same assumptions about the distribution of v_{i1}, v_{i2}, and u_i as above, and also as above we assume that only y_{i1} and X_i are observable. However, we still need to make assumptions about the measurement error

A_i. I will assume that the A_i are iid according to some specified distribution (e.g., normal), and that A_i is independent of $(X_i, v_{i1}, v_{i2}, u_i)$. Independence is a rather unpalatable assumption here, since measurement error should on average be larger when noncompliance is larger, but again a reasonable way to relax this assumption is not clear. I am not sure what a reasonable distribution for A_i would be, but normality is certainly unreasonable, since $A_i \leq 0$ must be much more common than $A_i > 0$. I would probably assume $A_i \leq 0$ and therefore assume a one-sided error distribution for it. As with the one-sided error u_i, there is frankly not much guidance for its choice.

It is not clear whether this model is identified, in the sense that we can hope to distinguish the measurement error A_i from the other errors (v_{i1}, v_{i2}, u_i). If A_i were normal, we could not do so since A_i would be indistinguishable from v_{i1}. However, if A_i has a distribution unlike those of the other errors, its distribution is probably identified. In any case, the parameters of interest (β_1, and secondarily β_2) remain identified even with measurement error on y_{i1}^*.

It is also worth noting explicitly that measurement error on X_i is far more serious than measurement error on y_{i1}^*. It can be handled only by making assumptions even less realistic than those made so far (e.g., known variance of the measurement error). This may be a serious problem if some of the explanatory variables are other line items on the return for which noncompliance is also likely.

The final and most complicated model I consider is designed to allow real clustering of tax changes at zero, as well as measurement error. It is a combination of Cragg's model and our modification of Heckman's sample selection model. It is of the form

(20A) $$y_{i0} = X_i'\beta_0 + v_{i0},$$

(20B) $$y_{i1}^* = X_i'\beta_1 + v_{i1} + u_i,$$

(20C) $$y_{i2} = X_i'\beta_2 + \gamma y_{i1}^* + v_{i2},$$

(20D) $$y_{i1} = \begin{cases} 0 & \text{if } y_{i2} \leq 0 \text{ or } y_{i0} \leq 0, \\ y_{i1}^* + A_i & \text{if } y_{i2} > 0 \text{ and } y_{i0} > 0. \end{cases}$$

We make the same assumptions as above, and in addition assume v_{i0} to be iid as standard normal and to be independent of $(v_{i1}, v_{i2}, u_i, A_i)$. We observe only y_{i1} and X_i.

Equation (20A) accounts for real clustering. The intended interpretation is that $y_{i1}* = 0$ (and $y_{i1} = 0$) if $y_{i0} \leq 0$. The probability of this event is $\Phi(-X_i'\beta_0)$, which is consistent with equation (12) in our discussion of Cragg's model. The interpretation of (20B) is that it gives the distribution of y_{i1}^* conditional on $y_{i1}^* \neq 0$ ($y_{i0} > 0$). Its interpretation as a conditional distribution justifies the assumed independence of (v_{i1}, u_i) and v_{i0}. As before, equation (20C) is interpreted as determining the probability that $y_{i1} = 0$ when $y_{i1}^* \neq 0$ (i.e., because of measurement error). Finally, (20D) governs measurement error in the observations of the nonzero observed tax changes.

Amazingly enough, I believe that this model is identified. That is, we can indeed separate real clustering at zero from clustering due to measurement error. To see how the model accomplishes this, note that

$$(21) \qquad\qquad P(y_{i1} = 0) = P(y_{i2} \leq 0 \text{ or } y_{i0} \leq 0)$$

$$= 1 - P(y_{i2} > 0 \text{ and } y_{i0} > 0)$$

$$= 1 - P(y_{i2} > 0)P(y_{i0} > 0),$$

using independence of v_{i0} from the other errors. Given that $P(y_{i1} = 0)$, $P(y_{i2} > 0)$ and $P(y_{i0} > 0)$ all depend on X_i, the model imposes enough structure on the way they change with X_i to identify β_0 and β_2 separately. (It could not do so, obviously, if $P(y_{i2} > 0)$ and $P(y_{i0} > 0)$ were constant over i.) A similar model with a similar conclusion is given by Poirier (1980). As in the Poirier model, however, identification is accomplished by having assumed specific distributions for the errors, specific (linear) functional forms for the deterministic portions of equation (20), and independence of virtually all error terms. This is unfortunate, but should have been expected. Some tax changes are observed to be zero, and basically without further information we are supposed to determine whether this is because the true tax change is zero or because a true nonzero tax change has not been detected. Such a distinction is unlikely to be made without paying a high price in terms of assumptions required.

Estimation of any of the models of this subsection will require the numerical maximization of a likelihood function. Especially for the more complicated models, this is likely to involve rather difficult and extensive computations. Furthermore, the consistency of the MLEs will depend on the correctness of the specification of the model (including the distributional assumptions for the errors), and this is unfortunate in view of the long list of assumptions underlying these models.

REMARKS

The models required to handle clustering of the dependent variable (audit-induced tax change) at zero are complicated. This is unfortunate because such clustering is inconsistent with the assumptions of simpler models, such as the linear regression model, and because it is not legitimate (except under implausible assumptions) to simply delete observations for which the dependent variable is zero. However, it is possible (under admittedly strong assumptions) to devise models that account for clustering, which include an accommodation of measurement error, and indeed which can separate clustering due to measurement error from genuine clustering of the dependent variable.

Given the difficulties caused by clustering, it may seem attractive to use data that are not clustered. For example, the 1969 and 1979 TCMP data are available, aggregated to the three-digit zip code level, along with other relevant demographic data at the same level. (Such aggregation is obviously one way in which the IRS may avoid confidentiality problems in a public-use version of the data.) I will presume that these data are the averages of the corresponding individual data, with the average taken over individuals in the TCMP file who reside in the three-digit zip code area. These data are presumably not clustered at zero, since, for example, it would be unlikely that no one in the TCMP file for a given three-digit area had a nonzero tax change. Thus it is tempting to analyze them with a simple model like the regression model. Now, it is obvious that if a linear regression model is appropriate at the individual level, it will be appropriate at the aggregate level; averaging over observations preserves linearity of the model. However, as argued above, clustering at zero in the individual data implies that a linear regression model is inappropriate at the individual level. That being the case, there is really no good justification for a linear regression model at the aggregate level. I do not at this point have a better alternative to suggest, but perhaps one can be found.

A final remark is that my pessimistic conclusions at the end of the previous section concerning the usefulness of stochastic frontier models do not apply to the more complicated models of this section. In these more complicated models the consistency of one's estimates hinges on the correctness of the distributional assumptions (which is not so in a linear regression model). If the stochastic frontier error structure seems reasonable in the compliance equation, as it does to me, it should be used.

Panel Data

By panel data I mean data on each of N individuals for T time periods (years, in the present context). This is stronger than assuming a cross-section of size N for each of T years, since in panel data the same individuals are followed over time.

For data derived from TCMP audits, it is clear that the panel length T would have to be very short. Repeated auditing of an individual, year after year, seems sure to change his or her behavior, so that observations past the first few for any individual would be of questionable use. (Of course, if we have panel data we can test whether auditing an individual affects his or her behavior, and the desire to conduct such a test is one possible motivation for collecting panel data.) This retesting bias could be a serious problem even in a very short panel (e.g., $T = 3$). However, a short panel free of retesting bias could presumably be constructed by simultaneously auditing the returns of the three most recent tax years, for example, for a set of N individuals. The maximum possible length of such a panel would be determined by the statute of limitations for tax audits.

Alternatively, we could analyze cross-sections for each of T years, where T could be as large as the number of years that TCMP audits have been done, if we do not require that the same individuals be in each cross-section. We could even match up individual characteristics so that each cross-section contains individuals with (more or less) the same values for potential explanatory variables. Thus an important question to be answered is for what purposes is it necessary to follow the same individuals over time.

The existing literature on panel data discusses three motivations for its use: (1) to increase efficiency of estimation by using more observations; (2) to control for potential biases caused by unobserved individual characteristics; and (3) to study the dynamics of the process being analyzed. I discuss these three possibilities in turn.

INCREASED EFFICIENCY OF ESTIMATION

One possible motivation for the use of panel data is to increase the efficiency of estimation. At the simplest level, the sample size may be increased by using more than one cross-section, thus leading to more efficient estimation than would be possible with a single cross-section. For example, if we were interested in estimating a production function using annual data at the state level, we might worry that the fifty observations in a single year's data would not be enough to yield precise estimates. However, if we had twenty years' data on each of the fifty states our sample size would be 1,000, and we would expect better results with 1,000 observations than with 50.

This argument may not be very compelling with TCMP data, because the sample size in a single year's data is already very large. It may perhaps be relevant in aggregated versions of the TCMP data.

A more subtle reason why panel data may increase the efficiency of estimation is that some explanatory variables may vary insufficiently in the cross-sectional dimension but more in the time-series dimension (or conversely). The classic example in economics is a budget study that attempts to explain individual consumption patterns as a function of prices and income. Income varies considerably in a cross-section of individuals, but prices do not. (There is some regional variation in prices, but not much.) Therefore a cross-sectional study may estimate the effect of income on consumption precisely, but not the effects of prices on consumption. Conversely, prices vary over time but income varies less over time than over cross-sections (especially after the change in nominal income due just to changes in the general price level is removed). Therefore a time-series study may estimate the effects of prices on consumption precisely, but it may do a poor job of estimating the effect of income changes. An obvious solution is to use panel data so that both cross-sectional and temporal variation in explanatory variables may be exploited.

Similar cases may exist in the present context. For example, it is clear in the TCMP cross-section that compliance levels are lower for younger taxpayers than for older taxpayers (e.g., Clotfelter 1983, Table 2). It is not clear whether this is an effect of age or of generation, and the distinction is very important in terms of its implications for future compliance levels. If it is an effect of age, we would expect the noncompliant younger generation to become compliant as it gets older, and the general level of compliance should not change much. However, if the noncompliant younger generation is fundamentally different from the older generation (because attitudes toward the IRS have changed over time, for example), it may remain noncompliant as it ages, and the general level of compliance will fall as the last remaining compliant generation dies off. Because age and generation do not vary independently in the cross-section, this distinction cannot be made in a simple cross-section. However, generation is constant over time while age changes, so we can get evidence about this distinction by pooling cross-sections taken at different points in time.

Given the practical difficulties in obtaining panel TCMP data, it is very important to note that nothing in the above discussion requires that the same individuals be followed over time. For example, to separate age and generation effects we need to pool cross-sections over time, but we do not really need panel data. In certain contexts (e.g., budget studies) it is cheaper to collect panel data than to collect independent cross-sections in different time periods, since the effort put into the selection and location of individuals need not be repeated every year. In the case of TCMP data, however, the retesting bias problem is potentially very severe, and I would not expect any panel data set to be long enough (cover a large enough number of years) to be satisfactory. A series of cross-sections taken at different points in time, with some care to ensure comparability of data definitions and sampling schemes, would be more feasible and more useful in increasing the efficiency of estimation.

Controlling Bias Due to Unobservables

Another motivation for using panel data is that it may enable elimination from the model of bias caused by the omission of unobservable individual characteristics. The classic example in economics is the estimation of a production function for a cross-section of farms. Suppose that for each farm we observe output and several inputs, such as labor, capital, acreage, and fertilizer. Suppose we do not observe soil quality. Clearly soil quality affects output, so it is implicitly part of the error term in the regression model (production function) we estimate. It is also clear that soil quality and input usage should be correlated; for example, a farmer may use less fertilizer on good soil than on poor soil. Thus a regression of output on inputs, not correcting for differences in soil quality across farms, will yield biased estimates. For example, the coefficient of fertilizer will presumably be biased toward zero, since we do not take into account that fertilizer is applied disproportionately to poor soil.

This potential bias may be avoided, without observing soil quality, if we have panel data and if we are willing to assume that the effect of soil quality on output is time-invariant. That is, we assume a model of the form

$$(22) \qquad y_{it} = X_{it}'\beta + \alpha_i + \epsilon_{it}, \qquad i = 1,. . .,N, \quad t = 1,. . .,T,$$

where $i = 1,. . ., N$ indexes farms; $t = 1,. . .,T$ indexes time periods (years); y is output and X is a vector of inputs (probably measured in logarithms, in this example); α_i is the intercept for farm i; and ϵ is a nicely behaved error term that is independent of α and X. Thus each farm has the same slope coefficients (β) but a different intercept (α_i). If the effect of soil quality on output is additive and time-invariant, it is absorbed into the farm-specific intercept. We can obtain unbiased estimates of β by estimating equation (22) by least squares, treating the α_i as parameters. This can be done by using dummy (indicator) variables for the individual farms. It is equivalent to least squares of y on X after transforming the data to deviations from individual-farm means, that is, regression of $(y_{it} - \bar{y}_i)$ on $(X_{it} - \bar{X}_i)$. Clearly the idea is that differences in soil quality (or any other time-invariant variables) disappear when we transform to deviations from individual means.

A second example, taken from the field of labor economics, concerns estimations of the effects on an individual's wage rate of characteristics such as age, race, sex, education, and occupation. If individuals differ in ability, which affects the wage and which is correlated (we hope) with education, then a regression of wage on individual characteristics will yield a biased estimate of the coefficient of education. A regression using data in deviations from individual means will yield unbiased results if the effect of ability on wage is time-invariant.

In the present context, it is possible to imagine that individuals differ in an unobservable characteristic that I will call honesty, which affects compliance behavior. If honesty is correlated with the explanatory variables in the compliance relationship, then the results from the analysis of a single cross-section will be biased. This bias can be avoided in panel data so long as honesty is time-invariant.

Under the assumptions we have made, equation (22) would be called a fixed-effects model since the individual effects α_i are treated as fixed parameters. The transformation to deviations from individual means is called the "within" transformation, since it corresponds to the within-class variation in an analysis of covariance. Least squares after the within transformation is often called the "within" estimator. In fact, it is just the usual analysis of covariance estimator.

A disadvantage of this fixed-effects treatment is that one cannot use time-invariant explanatory variables, since they vanish under the within transformation. Many demographic variables (e.g., race, sex) are time-invariant. To be able to estimate the effects of time-invariant regressors, it is necessary to be willing to assume (on an a priori basis) that some of the regressors are uncorrelated with the individual effects. A detailed discussion of this issue is beyond my scope here, but briefly the number of regressors assumed uncorrelated with the individual effects must be at least as large as the number of time-invariant regressors. For more details, see Hausman and Taylor (1981).

In order to eliminate the bias due to time-invariant unobservables, we do not need a long panel. We only need (at least) two observations per individual.

The above discussion has considered the case of a linear regression model. In more complicated models, such as the models suggested above to handle clustering, unobservables cannot be handled in such a straightforward manner. In particular, if we let the intercept in one or more of our equations vary over individuals in an unrestricted fashion, the maximum likelihood estimates of the slope coefficients are not necessarily consistent. This is a reflection of an incidental parameters problem; as the sample size increases, when more individuals are sampled, the number of parameters also rises. This does not cause any notable problems in the linear regression model, but it may in more complicated models. For a statement of the problem and solutions for some specific models, see Chamberlain (1980, 1984, 1985).

Consideration of Dynamics

A third possible reason for using panel data is to study the dynamics of the compliance process. At the simplest level, we may be curious as to whether there is correlation over time, at the individual level. That is, does noncompliance at some point in time raise the likelihood of noncompliance in the future? To give a statistical answer to this question clearly requires that each individual be observed at two or more points in time.

With panel data we can indeed hope to determine whether noncompliance is correlated over time. We can also make some more subtle but fundamental distinctions about the reasons for such correlation. Suppose for example that we sample a number of individuals in two different years, year 1 and year 2. It is straightforward to separate the sample into the groups that were compliant and noncompliant in year 1 and to compare the compliance rates of these groups in year 2. I presume that the compliance rate in year 2 would be higher for the group that was compliant in year 1 than it would be for the group that was noncompliant in year 1. In that sense there would obviously be correlation over time. But it is important to realize that there are (at least) two very different possible reasons for such correlation.

One possible reason is that, at the individual level, being noncompliant in year 1 has an effect on compliance behavior in year 2. Perhaps if I cheat on my taxes in year 1, I discover how easy it is to do so and, having learned that it is easy, I do it again in year 2. Note that this a genuine effect on individual behavior and it corresponds to correlation in behavior over time even if we condition on an exhaustive list of individual characteristics.

A second possible reason is simply that individuals who have characteristics that make them more likely to cheat in year 1 will have more or less the same characteristics in year 2. If honesty is genetic, for example, people with honest genes will tend to cheat in neither year, while people with dishonest genes will tend to cheat in both years. This will generate correlation of observed outcomes (noncompliance) over time, but in this case there is no correlation over time in the distribution of compliance conditional on an exhaustive list of individual characteristics (including some, like genes, that are surely unobservable).

The first possibility is called state dependence, because the state (compliance or noncompliance) occupied in year 1 influences the state occupied in year 2 for any individual. The second possibility is called heterogeneity, for obvious reasons. Given heterogeneity, the individual's state in year 1 helps to predict his or her state in year 2 only because it conveys information about the individual's characteristics.

The distinction between state dependence and heterogeneity occurs in many different kinds of models. It is an important distinction because policies designed to prevent loss of virginity are potentially valuable under state dependence but much less useful under heterogeneity. Given panel data, we can hope to distinguish between these two phenomena. The statistical techniques that are necessary depend on the model used, but a good general treatment is provided in Chamberlain (1984, 1985). The usual treatments assume a short panel of many individuals, which is exactly the kind of panel that may be feasible in the present context.

Issues of Data Collection and Sample Design

As discussed earlier, construction of a long TCMP panel data set is problematic because of the problem of retesting bias. A short panel could be constructed by simultaneously auditing the returns for several different years for a given individual. A short panel is obviously less informative than a longer panel would be, but it is sufficient to let us control for potential biases caused by time-invariant heterogeneity. A short panel may also be sufficient for studying the dynamics of the compliance process; presumably its sufficiency depends in part on how long the lags in the process are.

In terms of increasing the efficiency of estimation, I argued earlier that a series of cross-sections (not sampling the same individuals repeatedly) may be sufficient. By sampling different individuals we can hope for a longer data series without retesting bias. We cannot eliminate the bias due to heterogeneity nor study the dynamics of the compliance process with such data, however.

An apparent possibility is to construct an artificial panel by sampling an individual in period 1, sampling a different individual with identical demographic characteristics in period 2, and so on. I don't see much point in such an artificial panel, however. Insistence on carrying the same demographic characteristics through time limits the variability of the explanatory variables and is thus not recommended from the point of view of efficiency of estimation. And from the point of view of controlling bias or studying dynamics, an artificial panel is useless.

REMARKS

In my opinion, it would be very worthwhile for the IRS to collect a short TCMP panel data set by simultaneously auditing several years' returns for a set of individuals. It would also be very worthwhile for them to construct a longer series of TCMP cross-sections, in which different individuals are represented over time but some care is taken to ensure comparability of data definitions and sampling strategies over time. Many interesting questions (only a few of which have been discussed in this section) could be answered using these data sets and could not be answered with any single cross-section.

Concluding Remarks

In this appendix I have discussed a number of statistical issues that arise in the analysis of individual TCMP data or other similar individual-level quantitative data. Much of the discussion is also relevant to the analysis of aggregated versions of the TCMP data. Little of it, however, is relevant to an analysis of survey data, chiefly because in surveys the interesting compliance questions tend to yield data that is qualitative (e.g., a "yes" or "no" answer) rather than quantitative (e.g., an audit-induced tax change).

Another difficulty with survey data is that, because the honesty of answers to sensitive questions is doubtful, unusual sampling schemes may be employed, and these lead to unusual statistical issues. As an extreme example, in the "locked-box" technique, an individual's answer to a sensitive compliance question ("Did you stretch the truth a little in order to pay fewer taxes for 1978?") is placed in a locked box. Anonymity is assumed because the answers to demographic questions are kept separate.

This sampling scheme unfortunately makes it impossible to estimate the effects of demographic variables on compliance, although the average level of compliance may be estimated. Another example is the so-called random-ized response sampling scheme, in which the individual answers either the sensitive compliance question or an innocuous question, according to the outcome of a coin toss or similar simple random outcome. Here the response may be kept together with demographic data on the individual, since there is no way to know which question the individual answered. A statistical methodology exists for estimating the average level of compliance from randomized response data (see, e.g., Tracy and Fox, 1981), but surprisingly enough no methodology apparently exists for estimating the effects of explanatory variables on the level of compliance. (That is, we can estimate a proportion but cannot do the equivalent of a regression.) I believe that such a methodology could be developed. To the extent that we believe that the randomized response scheme elicits honest responses, development of this methodology would seem to be an important task.

One issue that was discussed in some detail is the statistical implication of the assumption that tax fraud is one-sided. (We presume that no one deliberately overstates his or her tax liability.) This implies that certain data, such as audit-induced tax changes, should be skewed in a predictable direction. I discussed a particular model, the stochastic frontier model, whose error structure can accommodate such one-sided errors. However, such an accommodation of one-sidedness is largely unnecessary in simple models like the regression model. In more complicated models, its accom-modation is more important (assuming that one-sidedness exists in the process generating the data) but also more complicated.

A second issue that was discussed is the clustering of observed tax changes at zero. This has profound statistical implications, since its occur-rence is inconsistent with simple models like the regression model. An important corollary is that simple models are inappropriate even for aggre-gated data sets in which clustering no longer appears. I discussed the advantages and disadvantages of standard statistical techniques to handle clustering and proposed some complicated extensions of these models. I conclude that we can handle clustering at zero, and that we can even distinguish alternative sources of it, but only under very strong assump-tions.

The third issue that this appendix has discussed is the construction and use of panel data. Here my conclusions are more optimistic. While perhaps only a short panel data set (i.e., one covering only a few years per individ-ual) may feasibly be constructed, such a data set will enable researchers to answer a variety of questions that cannot be answered from a single cross-section or even from a series of independent cross-sections. Furthermore, for other questions for which a long panel is important, a series of independent cross-sections may suffice. Thus I am able to recommend some specific, feasible data collection strategies and to indicate the advantages which the new data would offer.

I conclude by noting that I personally do not feel that the research community can be expected to make much progress in understanding the determinants of taxpayer compliance without having access to the TCMP data. To convince the IRS to release these data, it is necessary to find ways to ensure the confidentiality of individuals' identities. I presume that this is not an insuperable problem. But it is also necessary to explain the uses to which the data might be put, and the questions they might help answer. I hope this discussion is a useful part of this task.

References

Aigner, D.J., Lovell, C.A.K., and Schmidt, P.
  1977   Formulation and estimation of stochastic frontier production function models. *Journal of Econometrics* 6:21–37.

Chamberlain, G.
  1980   Analysis of covariance with qualitative data. *Review of Economic Studies* 27:225–238.
  1984   Heterogeneity, omitted variable bias and duration dependence. Chapter 1 in J. Heckman and B. Singer, eds., *Longitudinal Analysis of Labor Market Data*. Cambridge: Cambridge University Press.
  1985   Panel data. Chapter 22 in Z. Griliches and M. Intriligator, eds., *Handbook of Econometrics*, Vol. II. New York: North Holland.
Clotfelter, C.T.
  1983   Tax evasion and tax rates: An analysis of individual returns. *Review of Economics and Statistics* 65(3):363–373.
Cragg, J.G.
  1971.   Some statistical models for limited dependent variables with application to the demand for durable goods. *Econometrica* 39:829–844.

Fernandez, L.
  1986   Non-parametric maximum likelihood of censored regression models. *Journal of Econometrics* 32:35–58.

Hausman, J.A., and Taylor, W.
  1981   Panel data and unobservable individual effects. *Econometrica* 49:1377–1398.

Heckman, J.J.
  1976   The common structure of statistical models of truncation, sample se-
         lection and limited dependent variables and a simple estimator for such
         models. *Annals of Economic and Social Measurement* 5:475–495.
  1979   Sample selection bias as a specification error. *Econometrica* 47:153–162.

Johnson, N.L., and Kotz, S.
  1972   *Distribution in Statistics: Continuous Multivariate Distributions.* New York:
         John Wiley & Sons.

Jondrow, J., Lovell, C.A.K., Materov, I.S., and Schmidt, P.
  1982   On the estimation of technical inefficiency in the stochastic frontier pro-
         duction function model. *Journal of Econometrics* 23:269–274.

Kmenta, J.
  1971   *Elements of Econometrics.* New York: Macmillan.

Maddala, G.S.
  1983   *Limited-Dependent and Qualitative Variables in Econometrics.* Cambridge:
         Cambridge University Press.

Manski, C.F.
  1985   Semiparametric analysis of discrete response: asymptotic properties of the
         maximum score estimator. *Journal of Econometrics* 27:313–333.

Olson, J.A., Schmidt, P., and Waldman, D.A.
  1980   A Monte Carlo study of estimators of stochastic frontier production
         functions. *Journal of Econometrics* 13:67–82.

Poirier, D.J.
  1980   Partial observability in bivariate probit models. *Journal of Econometrics*
         12:209–217.

Powell, J.L.
  1984   Least absolute deviations estimation for the censored regression model.
         Journal of Econometrics 25:303–326.
  1986   Symmetrically trimmed least squares estimation for Tobit models. *Eco-
         nometrica* 54:1435–1460.

Schmidt, P.
  1976   *Econometrics.* New York: Marcel Dekker.

Schmidt, P., and Sickles, R.C.
  1984   Production frontiers and panel data. *Journal of Business and Economic
         Statistics* 2:367–374.

Schmidt, P., and Witte, A.D.
  1984   *An Economic Analysis of Crime and Justice: Theory, Methods and Appli-
         cations.* New York: Academic Press.

Stevenson, R.E.
  1980   Likelihood functions for generalized stochastic frontier estimation. *Jour-
         nal of Econometrics* 13:57–66.

Tobin, J.
  1958   Estimation of relationships for limited dependent variables. *Econometrica*
         26:24–36.

Tracy, P.E., and Fox, J.A.

1981   The randomized response approach to criminological surveys. Chapter 3 in J.A. Fox, ed., *Methods in Quantitative Criminology.* New York: Academic Press.

Waldman, D.M.

1984   Properties of technical efficiency estimators in the stochastic frontier model. *Journal of Econometrics* 25:353–364.

Westat, Inc.

1980   A Procedure for Estimating Taxpayer Response to Changes in IRS Audit Coverage. Paper prepared for the Internal Revenue Service, March 1980, by Westat, Inc., Rockville, Md.

Robert F. Boruch

Appendix B: Experimental and Quasi-Experimental Designs in Taxpayer Compliance Research

To tax and to please, no more [than] to love and be wise, is not given to men

Edmund Burke, *On American Taxation,* 1774

This appendix considers the use of randomized field experiments and certain quasi-experimental designs to assess tax compliance projects. The presumption is that readers are acquainted with the general idea of randomized field tests of social and institutional programs. It begins with a brief introductory treatment of the topic, followed by a section illustrating randomized tests in tax administration contexts.

The third section focuses on feasibility of randomized tests in the tax compliance arena. The criteria for judgments about feasibility are taken from the outline of issues developed by Riecken et al. (1974) to aid in resolving the problems engendered by experimentation. They include legal and ethical issues, scientific and statistical matters, political and institutional questions, and managerial requirements.

The fourth and fifth sections consider issues involved in both experimental and quasi-experimental design. The issues are general but they demand tailored approaches in the tax administration arena. These issues include: the choice of units of analysis, estimating the reactive effects of field experiments, choosing the number of sites, understanding generalizability of the

Departments of Psychology and Statistics, Northwestern University. Comments by Jeff Roth, Jan Kmenta, Al Reiss, and Richard Schwartz helped greatly to improve this paper. An earlier version was presented at the Symposium on Taxpayer Compliance Research, Padre Island, Texas, January 15–17, 1986. Background research on the topic has been supported by the National Science Foundation.

field test, and understanding how to couple experiments to quasi-experimental and survey research on compliance.

Randomized Field Experiments

Definition and Illustration

By "randomized field experiment" here is meant a situation in which individuals (or organizations) are randomly assigned to one of two or more regimens to understand the relative effectiveness of the regimens. The technology permits a probabilistic statement to be made about the results.

For example, a sample of IRS offices might be used to understand which of two procedures reduces the cost of processing certain kinds of returns. Half the sample of offices is assigned to one regimen and half to a second regimen, perhaps the conventional (control) approach. The offices are monitored over time to determine which procedure yields the largest cost reduction without an appreciable decrease in the quality of the service provided.

The main object of such an experiment is to obtain an unbiased, relatively unequivocal estimate of the relative effectiveness of the two procedures. "Relatively unequivocal" here means avoiding the problem of competing explanations—for example, that some extraneous variables, rather than the new procedure, produced the effects observed. Estimating the effects of these variables is difficult, often impossible, in normal social contexts. "Unbiased" means producing a fair estimate of the difference between the regimens.

Technically, the simplest randomized test procedure depends on the use of a regression model with one explanatory variable that is controlled and a second explanatory, the error, that is uncorrelated with the controlled variable by virtue of the randomization. The absence of correlation is crucial to making interpretable estimates of parameters in the model. See, for instance, any good text in experimental design or econometrics.

Background

A major stress on using randomized field experiments to plan and evaluate social programs began in the late 1960s and early 1970s in the United States. The main scientific justification for the emphasis was development of better, less biased, less ambiguous estimates of the effects of social programs.

The second, related justification depended heavily on political context. For instance, the Social Science Research Council's (SSRC) Committee on Social Experimentation, the President's Science Advisory Committee under the Nixon administration, the National Research Council, the Brookings Institution, and others contributed to the effort to understand how better evidence could be introduced into policy debates about effectiveness of new programs (see Riecken et al., 1974, for an early review). The individuals who contributed to the early efforts (see Riecken et al., 1974) include economists such as Joe Newhouse, Alice Rivlin, and Harold Watts; methodologists-social scientists such as Donald Campbell, Frederick Mosteller, William Kruskal, and Peter Rossi; and social scientists such as Henry Riecken. The newer contributors are acknowledged in the citations here.

The SSRC work led to Riecken and others' (1974) state-of-the-art monograph, *Social Experimentation*. It treated managerial, political, institutional, ethical, legal, and scientific problems engendered by trying to do good, controlled tests of government initiatives.

Since 1974 a variety of new research monographs and general texts on the topic have been produced for various disciplines. The Federal Judicial Center's (1983) *Experimentation and the Law*, for instance, dedicates serious attention to ethical aspects of randomized tests of new court procedures. Ferber and Hirsch (1982) and Fienberg, Singer, and Tanur (1985) are remarkable for their coverage of experiments to develop better evidence about economic projects, programs, and policy. Recently created journals, such as *Controlled Clinical Trials* in medicine and health services and *Evaluation Review* contain material that is relevant to controlled experiments in the social sector.

Randomized Experiments and Compliance-Related Research

Randomized experiments designed to understand how to improve tax administration have indeed been run. They are discussed briefly here partly to illustrate and partly to identify distinctive features of the work.

Randomized experiments eliciting information about sensitive topics have also been run in related areas, notably law enforcement and civil and criminal justice. They have been used in education as well. Examples are discussed, partly to capitalize on others' experience. For good bibliographies in these and related areas see Matt (1988), Dennis (1988) and Boruch, McSweeny, and Soderstrom (1978).

TAX COMPLIANCE

THE ACCOUNTS RECEIVABLE TREATMENTS STUDY.   The IRS's Accounts
Receivable Treatments Study, described by Perng (1985), involves tests of five
experimental methods for collecting the balance due from individual delinquent accounts. In the conventional (control) approach to collection, four
standard notices are sent to delinquents with five weeks between the first and
second notices, and with three weeks, four weeks, and four weeks between
subsequent waves (5–3–4–4).

The five new methods were variations on this basic approach. For instance,
in the first variation, an installment offer was included in the third notice. The
second variation included an installment offer and extended the time between second and third notices to fifteen weeks. Two other variations
involved telephone calls (three of them) between mailed notices. Over
46,000 delinquent individuals were involved in the study, excluding control group members.

Randomization was accomplished by using the ending digits of Social
Security numbers. This process is interesting in that social security numbers
provide an audit trail that is viewed as legitimate by the courts; the process is
legally witnessed at the IRS, for example. It is described in the IRS's *Compliance Measurement Handbook*.

The first lesson of the study is, of course, that the IRS has indeed run a
randomized field experiment on collection methods. The administrative procedures tested might be regarded as innocuous. Still, it is a beginning and an
important one. The second lesson is that special provisions for legally witnessed randomization must be used, as in draft lotteries, gaming lotteries, and
so on. It is not clear that there is a need for "auditable" random numbers in
other areas. Third, no unusual managerial control or political institutional
problems seem to have been encountered.

LEGAL SANCTIONS AND CONSCIENCE.   The Schwartz and Orleans (1967)
experiment is something of a classic. The object was to determine whether two
survey interview processes could affect subsequent taxpayer behavior. One of
the processes posed survey questions that stress the taxpayer's moral obligations to comply with law. A second process stressed the legal sanctions
engendered by failure to comply. A third (placebo) group was asked general
survey questions on political and civic issues with emphasis on tax policy; this
group constituted the control condition. Interviews were conducted a month
before individuals filed their tax returns.

Both threat of sanction and appeal to conscience appear to work in the
sense of increasing reported income. But sample sizes were small: 89–92 in
the three main groups.

The first interesting feature of the work is that the experiment was run by university scholars with IRS cooperation. Such collaboration, and other examples of it in the studies discussed below, is remarkable; other enforcement/investigatory agencies do not find collaboration desirable or feasible. Second, the potential privacy problems were resolved simply. IRS provided the researchers with only marginal distributions for the experimental groups. No records on identifiable individuals were disclosed. Third, the experiment produced interesting, potentially important results. This raises the question whether the Schwartz-Orleans experiment should be and can be replicated with larger samples, perhaps paying more attention to theory, to understand whether and how the findings bear on specific tax policy regulation or law.

METHODS FOR ESTIMATING NONCOMPLIANCE IN SURVEYS.   Aitken and Bonneville's (1980) General Taxpayer Opinion Survey includes an informative randomized trial. The trial was designed to understand which of several alternative methods of questioning people about tax cheating led to more accurate estimates of the incidence of cheating; it was sponsored by the IRS Office of Planning and Research. It is compatible with concerns expressed by Witte (1987), among others, that more accurate approaches are needed to gauge nonfiling and evasive income reporting.

The three methods that were tested were:

- randomized response to questions about cheating;
- locked-box approach to questions; and
- indirect questions, e.g., comments on approaches to cheating.

Over 4,800 individuals were assigned randomly to one of the three groups.

The randomized response methods essentially involve the respondents' injecting a response with probabilistic error so that the interviewer cannot tell what the true state of the individual is, but statistical analysis can adjust for the controlled error in large samples (see the section on feasibility below). The locked-box approach generally requires the respondent to seal a response and place it in a locked box or mail box in the presence of the interviewer.

The results were promising for the randomized response relative to the locked-box method. Perceived anonymity was higher and admission of tax cheating was consistently higher.

The first implication of this work is that such randomized tests of alternative methods of estimating cheating are feasible. This extends a fine tradition of methodological work by the U.S. Census Bureau, the National Center for Health Statistics, and others. Second, the randomized response worked well in this instance. The method does not always work, however (see the review in

Boruch and Cecil, 1979). The implication is that field tests need to be done to understand when and why it works.

LONG RANGE TAX FORMS SIMPLIFICATION STUDY.   The Long Range Tax Forms Simplification Study (IRS, 1983) focused on two kinds of alternatives to the conventional 1040A. The first, 1040S-Customized, was tailored to each of four statuses of taxpayers, as they identified themselves in a previous year. The second, 1040S-Consolidated, could be used by a 1040A filer of any filing status.

Both alternatives were developed under laboratory conditions prior to field testing. Both involved a consortium approach to redesign, e.g., simplifying language; changing format from two columns to one; increasing use of color, worksheets, and illustrations; and providing tax hints.

Each alternative was assigned to 14,000 taxpayers, and a control of 28,000 taxpayers was constructed. The experiment, executed in Georgia, appears to have involved randomized assignment. (The ambiguity in the report is noteworthy; see Betsey Hollister, and Papageorgiou, 1985, on similar ambiguity in youth employment experiments). The work was based on a stratified random sample design constructed so as to ensure that each treatment replicate was as similar as possible to the Atlanta population of taxpayers.

Use of the alternative forms was voluntary. That is, subjects could use the assigned alternative or the conventional forms. Similarly, responding to a follow-up questionnaire was voluntary.

Results of analyzing the returned forms suggest that fewer arithmetic errors were engendered by the 1040S-Consolidated relative to the 1040A (6 percent versus 8 percent) and fewer errors by separate line item (12 versus 15). Taxpayers liked the new forms better by two to one. The 1040S-Customized, however, fared badly, engendering higher error rates (8 percent versus 6 percent) than the consolidated forms.

This work is remarkable in several respects. It demonstrated that a laboratory approach plus field testing, with an independent consortium of private contractors, can be productive. It illustrates the feasibility of testing forms in formal experiments. It is a nice example of redesign features and the use of field test results to construct subsequent alternative 1040EZ and the 1040 with instructions.

The work is instructive for illustrating two problems of randomized experiments. The response rate to the questionnaire (10 percent) is low by conventional standards. Moreover, there are small but noteworthy differences in response rates across treatment categories: 10.7 percent for the 1040S-Consolidated, 10.2 percent for the 1040S-Customized, and 7.6

percent for the 1040A. What adds credibility to an otherwise suspicious sample is the lab results ("consistent" with these).

The second problem concerns the rate at which individuals choose to complete the alternative forms they are assigned (instead of choosing the conventional 1040A or 1040): 32 percent for the 1040S-Consolidated and 30 percent for the 1040S-Customized. This is a lower bound in the sense that the 1040S-Consolidated, for instance, is an alternative only to the 1040A. Taking this into account boosts the choice rate to 36 percent (3,707/6,608). This low choice rate is attributable partly to the fact that many respondents had their forms prepared by tax practitioners, and over 85 percent of these used the 1040A instead of the experimental forms. No analysis of analytic biases engendered by the rate is given in the report.

COMPLIANCE RELATED EXPERIMENTS

POLICE PROCEDURES. In the Minneapolis Domestic Violence experiment, the object was to understand how police should handle calls on domestic violence cases (Sherman and Berk, 1984). Within certain limits set by police, cases (calls to a home) were randomly assigned to three different methods of handling: arrest, mandatory mediation, or immediate temporary separation. The main object was to determine which of these regimens produced the lowest level of subsequent domestic violence in households.

The integrity of the experiment was sustained by the randomization. That is, families involved in cases in each group were equivalent on account of the random assignment. Competing explanations common in earlier nonrandomized studies could be ruled out. Such competing explanations included differential police preferences for one or another way to handle the violence complaint. The experiment helped to inform a fifteen-year debate on handling such cases and is likely to be repeated in other cities to ensure the generalizability of the findings.

ADMINISTRATIVE LAW: TELECONFERENCING. Most administrative appeals hearings for unemployment insurance and welfare are conducted face-to-face. However, travel distance, workload of hearing officers, schedules, and so on, are often impediments. Distance is a special problem in the Western states. One could argue that telephone hearings are a viable alternative in that they can result in more timely appeals and reduced costs.

Experiments by Corsi and Hurley (1979a,b) and Corsi (1983) were designed to compare the efficacy of hearings conducted over the telephone compared with those conducted in person. The experiment was conducted statewide in New Mexico during the late 1970s.

Individuals were randomly assigned to telephone versus in-person hearings. The legality of the random assignment strategy was examined in detail, based on court decisions (e.g., on opportunity to cross-examine, on due process), state statutes on conduct of hearings, and so on. The Legal Aid Society, the relevant attorneys, and others were involved in the examination and the actual design of the study. Special provision was made for exceptional claimant cases.

The experiment is remarkable in being the first conscientious attempt to understand the effectiveness of telephone versus in-person hearings. It is remarkable for its illustration of the feasibility of such a test in a complex, potentially controversial, and certainly sensitive environment. It is pertinent to compliance experiments in each respect.

OTHER RANDOMIZED EXPERIMENTS.   The bibliography to this appendix lists experiments conducted in other relatively sensitive areas. Rossi, Berk, and Lenihan (1980), for instance, report on statewide experiments in Texas and Georgia to determine whether post-prison financial support reduces recidivism. Randomized field tests in the courts are described by Goldman (1977, 1985) for pretrial hearings and Lind (1985) for assessing court-annexed arbitration, mediation in appellate courts, and others. Juvenile programs including restitution have been examined in randomized experiments by, among others, Lipsey, Cordray, and Berger (1981) and Severy and Whitaker (1982). Earlier work is listed in a bibliography by Boruch, McSweeny, and Soderstrom (1978). More recent reports can be found routinely in journals such as *Evaluation Review, New Directions for Program Evaluation,* and *Program Planning and Evaluation.*

Feasibility: Issues and Criteria

The scientific justification for randomized assignment, of course, lies in generating a less equivocal, unbiased estimate of the relative effects of a compliance program, an estimate that is coupled to a formal statement about one's certainty of the results. Such a justification is important in the sense of determining when an experiment is appropriate. When framed persuasively, it may also enhance feasibility.

Four broad categories of feasibility issues are considered in this section, including the experiment's justification:
- Legal and ethical issues;
- Scientific issues;

- Political and institutional issues; and
- Managerial issues.

These categories comport with those in Riecken et al. (1974).

LEGAL AND ETHICAL ISSUES

RANDOMIZATION.   Two themes are important. First, there is a need to distinguish between legal problems engendered by randomization and the difficulties of judging moral correctness of activities. Little can be gained by combining the two, and at worst, it may confuse matters. Randomizing at the individual level, for instance, may be legal. But the act may be unethical in the sense that it engenders great discomfort for certain respondents or in the sense that responses cannot be protected from uses that harm the respondent. For illustrations and analysis by an able legal scholar, see Breger (1983).

The second theme is that there are multiple approaches to resolving legal and ethical problems in randomized experiments. Each has some costs and benefits. The approaches considered below include legal and technical approaches to resolving problems in two areas: randomization and privacy. The last part of this section concerns institutional review boards, a useful administrative device for ensuring that community values are represented in any assessment of the ethical propriety of a social experiment. See Boruch and Cecil (1983) for more on the multiple solutions theme.

LAW AND RANDOMIZATION.   The IRS's administrative authority for conducting experiments, Congress's role in specifying statutes that encourage tax experiments, and the courts' interpretation of each are especially important. The following brief review is based on Breger (1983) and on the Federal Judicial Center (1983); these papers should be consulted for legal citations.

In general, the administrative authority for conducting experimental tests of federal projects stems from the enabling statutes of the various federal agencies. The statutes may be specific, as in the case of law that directs the U.S. Department of Housing and Urban Development to undertake housing allowance experiments. Or the law may be general, as in the case of statutory provisions that an agency head may waive compliance with other statutes for purposes of experimentation or demonstration projects, as, for example, the waiver authority of the secretary of the U.S. Department of Health and Human Services that permits social experimentation, within limits.

Administrative authority to test alternative ways to increase compliance has, of course, been exercised by the Internal Revenue Service. The Long Range Tax Forms Simplification Study (IRS, 1983) included two major alternative tax form packages. The development effort also considered a simplification, a third form suggested by discussion with the IRS commissioner, that led to the 1040EZ. A noteworthy statutory provision, Section 155 of Public Law 95-600, provided explicit authority to the IRS for contracting the job of redesigning forms.

Federal authority for randomized field tests of social intervention programs has been challenged in the courts on at least two occasions. The courts have interpreted the authority broadly, rejecting the challenges to experiments in *Aguayo* v. *Richardson* and *California Welfare Rights Organization (CWRO)* v. *Richardson*.

It is worth remembering more generally that the legal history of experimentation—experimentation being defined broadly—is compatible with a variety of court decisions. In the *Truax* v. *Corrigan* decision of 1914, for example, Justice Holmes rendered a dissenting opinion that "there is nothing I more deprecate than the use of the Fourteenth Amendment beyond the absolute compulsion of its words to prevent the making of social experiments . . . in the insulated chambers of the several states, even though the experiments may seem futile or even noxious to me and to those whose judgment I most respect." A similar spirit is reflected in comments by Justice Brandeis in *New York State Ice* v. *Liebmann*.

The use of a safety-valve category in randomized tests has been a device to ensure that unfairly harsh or severe burdens are not imposed on certain individuals (or institutions) as a consequence of the experiment. That is, providing for special exceptions to randomization can reconcile institutional responsibility to take action on the basis of special needs or conditions of the individual in law, medicine, and elsewhere with the need for fair assessments of innovative practices. The categories to be excepted should be specified beforehand; e.g., the Sherman-Berk police experiments recognized the need to provide for police discretion in handling particularly violent domestic battles. Of course, providing ambiguous or large exception categories can undermine experiments; e.g., judges may overuse exceptions in a court experiment (Conner, 1977).

TECHNICAL DESIGN APPROACHES AND RANDOMIZATION.   There are a variety of strategies for tailoring experimental designs so as to avoid legal and ethical problems. They are as relevant to compliance experiments as they are to research in other areas.

One obvious tactic is to ensure that the number of individuals (or other entities) exposed to potentially burdensome treatments is kept to a minimum by choosing the appropriate sample size with statistical advice and by coordinating efforts to avoid unnecessary redundancy in risk-laden studies. The technology for minimizing the number of questions that must be asked and minimizing sample size under a variety of constraints is adaptable from sample design technology developed to reduce costs without appreciably reducing precision in research.

Second, testing components of programs rather than full programs, for example, is often warranted on management grounds, since full-blown tests are expensive and may not be worth the effort, as well as on ethical or legal grounds. The Perng (1985) experiments, for example, focus on letters as a device for encouraging compliance, rather than the broad range of communication devices available to the IRS. Similarly, variations in program intensity may be compared to skirt the ethical problem of testing a program against a no-program control condition.

Third, one may alter the units of randomization and analysis, randomizing institutions when that process is legal and ethical and randomization of individuals is not. This approach puts stress on directly estimating a new program's impact on institutions. Experiments that use as the unit IRS offices, or special groups within each office, will at times be more feasible than experiments that randomize individuals.

Graduated introduction or withdrawal of benefits whose effect is not clear can be tailored to designs that capitalize on the stagewise character of the process. These are discussed below in the special context of compliance work.

PRIVACY. Private information is defined here as information that, if disclosed, would bring harm to the individual. The term *confidential* refers to the state of the information, notably the fact that it is not disclosed or should not be disclosed. These definitions, adopted from suggestions by Albert J. Reiss, Jr., improve on earlier ones (Boruch and Cecil, 1979). The approaches described below ensure that private information once collected will remain confidential. Some methods also protect privacy in the sense that not even the researcher knows the true status of the research participant.

The functional distinction between research information and administrative information is often critical to law, regulations, and development of privacy protection methods. Administrative information is defined as information used in making judgments and decisions about specific identifiable individuals. Research information uses individuals' identification only as a tracking device. It is not material to the conclusions, usually statistical, drawn about the group to which identifiable individuals happen to belong. This distinction can become blurred for compliance research. Indeed, the conduct of legitimate social research by an enforcement agency such as the IRS (or state tax bureau) itself presents some interesting ethical problems. They are discussed briefly below.

The first major theme of the discussion is that there are multiple solutions to protecting privacy or confidentiality of individual responses in compliance research. The classes reviewed here are procedural, statistical, and statutory solutions. The second theme is that the risk of forced or accidental disclosure of sensitive information is very low. Fewer than a dozen subpoenas have ever been issued; few cases of accidental disclosure have ever been discovered. This implies that a sensible balance must be found between the cost of privacy protection and (usually weak) threats to privacy. The material is adapted from Boruch and Cecil (1979) and elsewhere.

PROCEDURAL APPROACHES TO PROTECTING PRIVACY.   These are nontechnical approaches to assuring confidentiality or privacy. In mail surveys, for example, anonymous responses and alias responses (when the study is longitudinal) are not uncommon approaches. Inquiry that is indirect may be made through brokerage agencies, an archive or the Census Bureau, for example, to obtain data without necessarily obtaining identification, for both cross-sectional and longitudinal studies. Insulated data bank approaches may be used to link records from different archives without breaching privacy rules governing each archive.

The strategies are imperfect to the extent that deductive disclosure is possible and the procedures are burdensome and time-consuming. Deductive disclosure seems critical to compliance research and the work by Schueren (1985) among others should be explored. At times, the more important cost is degraded quality of research, since it may be difficult or impossible to assay the validity of the sampling and the quality of the response.

STATISTICAL APPROACHES TO PROTECTING PRIVACY.   Over the past ten years, a variety of clever statistical devices have been developed to obtain information from identifiable responses in direct surveys without degrading either privacy or quality of research. One such approach has in fact been tested by the IRS in field studies of opinion about tax cheating (Aitken and Bonneville, 1980).

A simple variation involves presenting two questions to a respondent, one sensitive (e.g., Did you avoid paying legitimate taxes last year?) and an innocuous one (e.g., Did you give to a charity last year?) that is independent of the first. The respondent is asked to choose one or the other based on the roll of a die and to answer it without disclosing which question is being answered. The respondents might be instructed to address the first question if a 1 appears on the thrown die, for instance, and to address the second question if a 2 or 3, etc., appears. The interviewer receives only yes or no responses and does not know which question was answered. Given two large samples in which the odds of answering each question differ, and the odds of answering each question are known, the statistician can legitimately estimate the fraction who avoided paying legitimate taxes. Yet privacy is protected in the sense that no unambiguous sensitive information is disclosed.

Such devices amount to having the respondent inject his or her response with random error so that the interviewer cannot link a response with a specific question or state of the individual. Tested in the United States and abroad, the methods have considerable promise and appear to work well often but not always. The methods have failed, for instance, in that at times they produce negative estimates of the incidence of the trait of interest. Part of the problem appears to be that some respondents view a "no" as the safest possible response, that is, they do not conform to instructions despite the logical guarantee that sensitive information remains private. The failure to conform and the kinds of formats and questions that increase willingness to abide by instructions need a good deal more research.

Even when the methods work well, the direct costs of their use increase in complexity of analysis and in required sample size. They are useless with small samples and with clinical inquiries. The implications of the new work in this area for compliance research need to be examined.

STATUTORY APPROACHES TO PRIVACY PROTECTION. Statutory approaches refer to laws that state that identifiable information collected for research purposes cannot be used for judicial, administrative, legislative, or other purposes against the individual. The level of protection available varies by statute. In some cases, identification and information are protected; in others, only identifiers are protected.

Statutes have been created to protect respondents in federally supported research on criminal justice, mental health, and drug and alcohol abuse. A few court cases have helped to clarify the limits of their protection. The laws apply to data on individuals, not institutions, and this may limit their usefulness in compliance research, for example, on small businesses.

The statutes most pertinent to compliance research include:

- Public Health Services Act, P.L. 93-282, Par. 303;
- Crime Control Act of 1973, P.L. 93-83, Par. 524(a); and
- Drug Abuse Office and Treatment Act, P.L. 92-255, Par. 408,

and there are others. To illustrate, Section 524(a) of the Crime Control Act says that persons receiving federal research grants or contracts under the Act shall not reveal research information identifiable to any person for any purpose other than that for which it was collected. Copies of such information shall be immune from legal process, and shall not, without respondent consent, be admitted as evidence or other purpose in judicial or administrative proceedings.

Evaluations of the statutes are given in Nelson and Hedrick (1983). There appears to be no focused investigation of the extent to which such statutes are applicable to tax administration research. However, the statutes are broad enough and sufficiently well tested in the courts to warrant attention in this context. In particular, they may help to elicit more candid reporting in research on nonreporting and dishonest reporting by reducing the respondents' concerns about the research and to encourage the cautious researcher to enter tax compliance research by ensuring that he or she can adhere to promises of confidentiality.

INSTITUTIONAL REVIEW BOARDS: GENERAL PROTECTION. An institutional review board (IRB) is a group formally convened to review the ethical propriety of research on human subjects carried out at an institution. In biomedical and behavioral research, for example, IRBs are required by federal regulation (45 CFR 46) to oversee the rights and welfare of individuals involved in such research, risks and potential benefits of the work, and appropriateness of methods used. The regulations require diversity in committee composition; e.g., no committee or quorum of a committee can consist of employees of the institution or of members of a single professional organization.

The regulations generally recognize lower risks typically accruing to social research in contrast to medical research. Expedited review processes are possible for the former and for innocuous varieties of the latter (e.g. cuticle samples). The performance of IRBs has been assessed intensively since 1974 by a variety of organizations. Regulations have been changed during that period by the Department of Health and Human Services and the Food and Drug Administration among others to strengthen protection and reduce unnecessary constraints on the research (see Levine, 1981, for example).

The legitimacy of IRBs has been reinforced partly by the federal courts. In *Crane* v. *Mathews*, for instance, the court ruled that an experiment involving medical insurance copayment plans did indeed involve human subjects at risk and required that the research be assessed by an IRB. In doing so, the court ruled against a 1976 position taken by the Department of Health, Education, and Welfare (Breger, 1983). More recent rulings have further clarified the IRB role.

The IRB approach to ensuring propriety of experiments is relevant to tax compliance research for several reasons. First, the IRBs are designed to cover the propriety of research on human subjects. Tax compliance research, including experimental tests of compliance programs, does involve research on human subjects. Analogous research, such as the negative income tax experiments, insurance copayment experiments, and administrative hearings experiments have been routinely assessed by IRBs in the interest of protecting subjects' rights.

Second, IRBs are empowered to review a great deal of work that is at least as sensitive as tax compliance research. This includes medical experimentation, of course, and social experimentation on topics such as medical insurance copayments, prison sentences and police methods, white collar crime and deception in surveys, divorce and reconciliation, and so on.

Third, IRB performance has since the 1970s been clarified well by federal agencies, examined often and found appropriate by independent groups, and improved with respect to quality of review. Tax compliance research can capitalize on this administrative experience.

Fourth, the IRB reviews of social experiments of the sort the IRS might run, in contrast to medical experiments, have been made much more efficient over the past few years. These improvements have taken the form of exemptions, expedited review procedures, and waivers of informed consent requirements for certain classes of studies. It is likely, for example, that waivers would be relevant for relatively innocuous administrative experiments involving, say, different letters sent to delinquent taxpayers. The experiments that put subjects at plausible risk but with plausible benefits to society are most likely to be legitimate subjects for IRB attention.

Information about institutional review boards appears frequently in publications such as *IRB*, issued by the Hastings Center's Institute of Society, Ethics and the Life Sciences (360 Broadway, Hastings-on-

Hudson, NY 10706). Recent developments in the federal sector provide an opportunity for the IRS to explore the use of IRBs and ethics regulations in its own work. In particular, the Interagency Human Subjects Coordinating Committee consists of about seventeen federal agencies dedicated to developing a model policy for human subjects research. The committee is chaired by Charles McCarthy of the National Institute of Health's Office for Protection from Research Risks. Joan Porter, Special Assistant to McCarthy, was kind enough to provide information about the committee and an updated copy of the regulations regarding human subjects research.

The committee's draft model policy is similar in many respects to the regulations, but it has not been formally approved by all the agencies contributing to it. Definitions of research, human subjects, and other concepts in both model policy and current regulations are as pertinent to the IRS's contracted research as to other federal agencies' work.

It is in the interest of agencies such as the IRS to learn about the interagency committee. It is clearly in IRS's interest to consider adoption of existing regulations or model policy in order to ensure the ethical propriety of its own work regardless of whether the work involves randomized field tests. It is also in the IRS's interest to learn about the committee insofar as exemptions justifiably remove some research from IRB review.

SCIENTIFIC ISSUES

A variety of scholarly review papers in various disciplines display no essential disagreement about the scientific merit of randomized tests in principle. This includes Farrington (1983) on criminal justice, Rossi and Freeman (1981) on health services research, and Ferber and Hirsch (1982) and others on employment and training experiments.

Differences do appear among the disciplines in scholarly debate about the extent to which alternative methods produce equally persuasive evidence. In particular: Do other statistical methods produce as accurate an estimate of project effect as a randomized experiment? That is, what do we know from empirical comparisons? The question is as relevant to tax compliance research as it is to other areas.

EMPIRICAL COMPARISONS OF RANDOMIZED AND NONRANDOMIZED TESTS. The idea of comparing outcomes of a randomized experiment to results achieved in nonrandomized trials is not new. To clarify arguments with Gosset in the 1930s, for example, Fisher appears to have tried such a comparison in experiments on wheat (Box, 1978:269) and in reanalyzing

Darwin's data on stock fertilization. In the first case, results of the experiment differ from those of the quasi-experiment. In the second, they do not.

Similar comparisons have been undertaken by medical researchers. Randomized trials on the Salk vaccine, for example, gave estimates of the vaccine's effect that differed from estimates based on nonrandomized quasi-experiments (Meier, 1972). The debate over when randomized tests are appropriate in medicine is not new, in the U.S. at least (Freund, 1968; Gray, 1975). What remains to be done in the medical arena includes increasing capacity and willingness to do experiments, if we may judge from the Institute of Medicine's (1985) report on postmarketing surveillance for drugs and other technologies.

The tradition of evaluating employment and training programs has been based on econometric models and survey data. That is, in the absence of a randomized trial, one posits an explicit statistical model on which to base estimates of program effect. It is relevant to compliance research in that similar models and estimation techniques are often used to analyze survey data on compliance.

That conventional econometric models are often wrong seems clear from recent work by Fraker and Maynard (1984; but see Heckman et al., 1987). In particular, a broad array of such models produced results that differed widely from randomized field tests of programs on similar populations for youth. The results did not, however, differ appreciably for samples of welfare-supported women with children. The important lesson here, as in the Salk trials and in other cases (Boruch, 1976), is that one cannot be sure beforehand that a nonrandomized design will produce the same results as a randomized set-up.

The same lesson can be drawn from studies of groups of program evaluations. Gordon and Morse (1975), for example, found remarkably different estimates of social program effects when the evaluation design was taken into account. Glass and Smith (see Light and Pillemer, 1984) found differences in tests of the effect of class size on students' learning, when the quality of experimental design was taken into account. In a fascinating series of papers on medical experiments and quasi-experiments, Chalmers and his colleagues find analogous differences. Little recent evidence of a similar sort, however, appears to have been generated in criminal justice, law enforcement, or compliance research.

The randomization procedure avoids the need for elaborate statistical models whose assumptions, though explicit, are often untestable. The battle between modelers and randomizers began in 1935 between Fisher and Neyman (Box, 1978:265). It continues insofar as modelers are willing to trust their model and cannot invent (or imagine) experiments that help to test that trust. It continues insofar as the experimentalists distrust the models, plump for experiments, and do not have the resources to conduct the experiments that test the models. The implications of all this for compliance research and tax administration research more generally are that:

1. One cannot predict well that an experiment will produce the same result as a quasi-experiment;
2. Empirical comparisons are desirable to understand when the different methods are likely to converge; and
3. Calibration experiments are likely to be a useful device for gauging the appropriateness of nonrandomized trials.

"Calibration experiments" here mean set-ups in which economical methods for nonrandomized tests are run side by side in various contexts with randomized tests in order to estimate the biases engendered by the former and to use these estimates in other similar contexts that do not permit randomization.

POLITICAL AND INSTITUTIONAL ISSUES

A policy experiment is, as Riecken and others (1974) observe, a political act. It often demands recognition of political and institutional realities, including the need to negotiate with a variety of stakeholders.

The Internal Revenue Service is positioned well to avoid political and institutional problems insofar as it confines attention to testing important low-visibility administrative innovations. The Accounts Receivable Experiment and the randomized response experiments described earlier illustrate the genre. Tests of more visible innovations are likely to be a good deal more controversial, and as important. Learning to cope with predictable problems seems sensible.

Consider, for example, the use of telephone hearings instead of in-person hearings on administrative appeals. The early discussions leading to Corsi's (1983) administrative law experiment concerned whether due process in welfare appeals cases was indeed met through telephone hearings instead of the more conventional in-person hearings, whether administrative agencies had authority to use the innovative telephone approach, and whether random assignment was really necessary to compare telephone with in-person hearings. The negotiations involved a half-dozen government agencies, assorted public administrators, and lawyers; discussions gradually clarified concerns of these stakeholders.

Sherman and Berk (1984) focused on the law enforcement decision chain in the Minneapolis experiment. The sponsoring agency's concerns about ethical issues were handled partly through discussion of the sparse evidence concerning police effectiveness in handling domestic violence. The objections of interest groups, such as the American Civil Liberties Union and women's rights groups, had to be met with evidence and argument, too. Mayoral support in two administrations had to be developed and sustained. Meetings and retreats with beat cops and their supervisors appear to have been frequent and effective in handling their concerns.

The Work/Welfare Demonstration (Gueron, 1985) also demanded considerable negotiation and planning, partly because eight state governments were involved. The Manpower Development Research Corporation's negotiative work appears to have been productive by capitalizing on local expertise to nail down details, introduce good ideas, and ensure realism.

PUBLIC ATTITUDES ABOUT RANDOMIZATION. Certain attitudes can be regarded as indicators of social ethics. For instance, do individuals involved in experiments find randomized assignment objectionable or demeaning? What do we know about attitudes, preferences, and opinions or about the accuracy of information on which the opinions are based? In fact, we know little—but evidence is accumulating.

Laboratory studies on attitudes, for instance, are just beginning. In Australia, J. M. Innes has executed small studies to understand how individuals view random assignment to new family therapy programs when various justifications for such assignment are stressed to the eligible families: scientific need for evidence on the program's effect, the equity of randomization when resources are scarce, and the possible negative effects of innovative treatment. The results suggest that the appeals to scientific or equity arguments do not appreciably affect a favorable attitude toward randomization but that the possibility of negative program effects on participants does.

Studies by Hillis and Wortman (1976) in the United States on medical experiments suggest that randomization is indeed viewed in a more favorable light when scientific merit of the experiment is emphasized and that it is viewed in a less favorable light than are alternatives when resources are scarce. Subsequent work by Boruch, Dennis, and Greer (1988) and Boruch and Cecil (1983) laid out problems and alternative solutions in experiments that engender ethical or professional issues.

EXPERIMENTS IN EXPANSIONIST AND REDUCTIONIST PUBLIC POLICIES. The 1960s and 1970s were expansionist in the sense that the U.S. government provided increasing services to the disadvantaged. The Great Society ideas were often innovative. When there was opportunity to innovate, there was also opportunity to experiment formally, to assess the consequences of the innovation. And in fact, major economic experiments were undertaken during this period.

This interest in assessment is a fine scientific rationale for experiments. It may also serve the scholar-bureaucrat well. The rationale does not appear to be sufficient early in an expansionist period, however. Rather, the demand for evidence from the conservative camp appears to have led to demands for better evidence. For the cautious legislator, evidence from field experiments appears to have played a role in deciding whether and how to support or oppose legislation.

During a conservative regime there is more likely to be interest in learning more about the effectiveness of new variations on existing programs and new approaches to cost reductions, law enforcement, and compliance-related programs. Some of the pressure to present evidence is likely then to come from the opposition party. Here, too, randomized experiments are a natural vehicle for obtaining relevant evidence.

MANAGERIAL ISSUES

"Capacity" here means access to competent staff, resources such as money and time, the control that is needed and can be exercised to experiment, and the tolerability or tractability of constraints on the randomization process.

Staff. No good experiments are mounted without an able cadre that has *some* assurance of sustained support. In the United States, the resources expended on program evaluation generally have led to private, for-profit, and not-for-profit organizations' developing the requisite skills. These organizations engage in a competitive bidding process to provide the human resources necessary to plan and execute the field experiment. Some are specialized.

The Manpower Development Research Corporation (Gueron, 1985) and Mathematica Policy Research (Hollister, Kemper, and Maynard, 1984), for example, dedicate their attention to experimental tests of human resource programs. The Police Foundation and the Crime Control Institute in Washington, D.C., have undertaken tests of police patrol strategies and alternative ways of handling domestic violence (Sherman and Berk, 1984). Organizations that cast a wider net in their applied social research, such as Abt Associates, have done fine experimental tests of alternative ways to reduce the costs of day care programs for preschool children and to find effective methods of nutrition education (St. Pierre and Rezmovic, 1982; St. Pierre et al., 1982). Rand's health insurance experiments are well known (Brook et al., 1984). SRI has had considerable experience in the negative income tax arena (Robins et al., 1980; Robins and West, 1981). These are supplemented often and displaced at times by university-based groups.

CONTROL AND CONSTRAINTS. An important lesson of Conner's (1977) study of twelve field experiments is that controlling the randomization process counts heavily in a successful social experiment. Control is no less important in medical randomized trials, of course. Friedman, Furberg, and DeMets (1985), for example, were careful to encourage blind randomization in drug effectiveness experiments that might otherwise be easily subverted by medical specialists involved in the trials. The lack of control over randomization accounts at least partly for failures of TV experiments in El Salvador (Hornick et al., 1973), the Roos, Roos, and McKinley (1977) trials in health services, and the Bickman (1985) tests of nutrition programs for the elderly and others.

The mechanism for exercising control varies considerably. In the IRS taxpayer compliance experiments described by Perng (1985), centralized control over randomization is a natural part of the administrative process. More loosely coupled social systems are more typical, however. The need for control in looser contexts has led to the use of centralized random assignment (by telephone) in the work/welfare tests that Gueron (1985) describes. That is, welfare program staff provided some client information to MDRC, and assignment to alternative regimens was made from random number tables constructed to generate blocks and groups. Telephone-based blind assignment was also used by Goldman (1977) in experiments on how to reduce time in court with pretrial hearings. The Police Foundation's approach has been less direct in that police officers were responsible for assigning on the basis of a "randomization pad." But surveillance was possible to ensure adherence to the rule (Sherman and Berk, 1984).

Exercising control also implies limits on control. A physician's relinquishing direct influence over the treatment of a patient, for instance, presents a major ethical problem. The same problem, and tension over diminished or shared professional power, is evident in judicial experiments (Goldman, 1977), police experiments (Sherman and Berk, 1984), educational experiments, and others. Exclusionary rules are crucial to discretion for the courts (for example, the pretrial hearings experiments), to program staff (for example, the Minneapolis Domestic Violence Experiments) or to ensure compliance with statute (Breger, 1983) or regulation. The main lesson of all this is that exclusionary rules must be specified beforehand or as early as possible in the experiment.

RESOURCES: TIME AND MONEY. No general information has been compiled on how much experiments have cost. No journal articles or books have reported detailed analysis of their costs. This prevents benefit-cost analysis of individual experiments and comparing relative costs and benefits across disciplines (e.g., Mosteller and Weinstein, 1985). All this is despite the Social Science Research Council's efforts, among others, to encourage such reports (Boruch, 1976) and complaints of economists, such as Nobel laureate Theodore Schultz (1982) that economists do no benefit-cost analyses of their own work. There are a few exceptions, notably the Abt Associates' analysis of day care experiments. The experiment itself concerned whether relaxing federal regulations on the credentials of the day care staff would have negative effects on children. The results were used to alter regulations. The use resulted in the experiment's paying for itself in less than five years.

Special Design Issues

There are a variety of issues involved in experimental and quasi-experimental design that are likely to be important in compliance work. Some of the issues have already been discussed. A few deserve more attention and they are discussed here.

UNITS OF RANDOMIZATION AND ANALYSIS

The units of randomization can at times be chosen so as to facilitate field tests. To judge from the educational research, for example, students within classrooms cannot be randomly assigned to one of two or more regimens. In contrast, the unit that can be feasibly randomized may consist of a group of individuals—a neighborhood, a family, a classroom, entire schools, hospitals, or other institutions.

In fact, the tactic of randomizing aggregates has been exploited to execute experiments in Colombia, where small, randomly assigned geographic sectors have been used to estimate the effects of preschool and nutrition programs, and in Nicaragua, where classrooms were assigned to alternative regimens to estimate the effects of radio-based mathematics education. Bickman's (1985) tests of children's health education and school improvement incentives involved random assignment of schools; his tests of nutrition education for the elderly involved assignment of sites to alternative regimens.

That the choice of unit can indeed be difficult is clear from Sherman and Berk's (1984) consideration of alternative units for randomization in the Minneapolis Domestic Violence Experiment: days, precincts, cases within individual officers' workloads, officer within treatment versus officer across treatment. Their resolution was randomizing case handling method within officer. It appears to have worked very well, without appreciable loss of experimenter control. As Lind (1985) points out, there are similarly difficult choices in court experiments, too, notably in deciding whether individual cases or related cases ought to be taken as the unit.

The choice of unit seems relevant to compliance research. That is, individuals within local office, local office, taxpayers, small groups of taxpayers within strata, and so on, may lend themselves differentially to experimentation. In fact, the compliance experiments about which we know use only the individual taxpayer as the unit of randomization and analysis. This is the right unit given the objectives of the studies reviewed earlier on delinquent accounts, simplification, and so on.

Individuals do not present themselves for random assignment all at once, of course. The little bunches that appear may themselves be randomized. A variation on this theme is time-bound quota sampling used by Hillsman-Baker and Rodriguez (1979) in their court experiments. Single-case randomized assignment was unacceptable to lawyers involved in the tests, but there were no objections to quota sampling when there were more cases than could be assigned to treatments. The investigators randomized time segments that determined how large a quota could be expected. In consequence, the first intakes in a segment were assigned to treatment until the quota was filled; the remaining intakes were assigned to control. Segments of different lengths were randomly arranged over person-work-hours to reduce periodicity.

Periodicity and "suitable" number for randomization within subgroup can be manipulated within reasonable limits. And they influence feasibility and integrity of randomization. For instance, Collins and Elkin (1985) take seriously the question whether to randomize within groups of four individuals (to each of four treatments) or to randomize within groups of sixteen. Either approach was feasible given the client flow; either could achieve numerical balance across treatments. The sixteen-member subgroup was chosen eventually to make subversion of the randomization very difficult. That is, it is easier to anticipate where particular patients will wind up when groups of four are randomized in sequence than it is in the case of sixteen. The tactic of randomizing within what is, in effect, a time block is not unusual. See for instance, Hahn (1984) on acoustic experiments with airport birds.

The stage at which randomization occurs is also a research design parameter for able managers of field tests. So, for example, randomized assignment of all individuals eligible for special services for the chronically ill may not always be sensible prior to eliciting their consent to participate in the trials. Random assignment after eligibility screening and after consent is elicited generally reduces the sample and the generalizability of results. Despite this, the screening is sensible if the object is to get accurate results at slight reductions in generalizability. So, for example, Bickman, among others stresses the need to delay random assignment until the last possible stage of an endeavor, mainly to avoid complicated attrition problems.

REACTIVITY AND VALIDITY OF THE EXPERIMENTS

Reactivity here refers to an experimental subject's awareness of the experiment and the effect of that awareness on his or her behavior. So, for example, an individual who knows the pill is experimental may be inclined to feel positively or negatively about it, regardless of the pill's physiological effect. The feeling undercuts efforts to assess actual medical effects.

Because individuals react in a variety of unpredictable ways to their awareness, it is common practice in medicine to use placebos and double-blind measurement. That is, the volunteer patient in a clinical trial is kept unaware of which of two potentially effective drugs is being administered. Those responsible for measurement are also blind to types of treatment.

Awareness can plausibly be expected to affect validity of social experiments. But accommodating the problem is usually more difficult. Furthermore, the matter becomes very complicated if one considers awareness at each stage in the experiment from the random assignment through process and eventual measurement of response.

Two broad questions are pertinent to this threat to validity of randomized tests: Is the threat plausible? Is its magnitude likely to be substantial? What can be done about reducing and estimating the threat's magnitude in the settings in which it is plausible?

Is the threat plausible? Clearly we can categorize compliance studies into those in which

• Reactivity effects are implausible;

- Reactivity effects are unpredictable; and
- Reactivity effects are plausible and likely to be great.

Settings in which reactivity effects are least plausible include all those in which the subjects of research do not know they are involved in an experiment. As a practical matter this includes all experiments in which the treatments are a matter of small changes in administrative or bureaucratic processes that are not terribly visible to the public. Some examples include:

- Tone, frequency, length, and style of telephone calls and reminder letters to delinquents or other subgroups, as in the Accounts Receivable Treatments Study;
- Character of questions asked of a national probability sample in a poll about the IRS, as in the randomized response experiment; and
- Single-shot, fast turnaround experiments in which word about the experiments cannot get out quickly, as in the Schwartz-Orleans experiment.

The experiments that are most likely to involve reactive effects include those in which: (a) subjects are aware that their treatment is different from others, and (b) the difference is regarded as important enough to engender differences in behavior.

For instance, a randomized test of the effect of amnesty programs on tax delinquents may engender distress or anger among control group members who have not been offered amnesty or who regard amnesty as unfair to honest taxpayers. That distress may lead such individuals to resist further, to seek remedies to perceived unfairness in the courts, or to take some other action.

What can be done to reduce the threat of reactivity? An obvious option is to choose to do only those experiments for which plausibility of occurrence and magnitude of reactivity are likely to be low.

The next option is to capitalize on strategies that actively reduce the threat. In particular, one may: avoid publicization of the experiment till it is complete, refrain from informing subjects that they are in an experiment, design the experiment so that its conduct is fast and its visibility low ("stay low and keep moving").

The IRS Research Division has, in fact, avoided publicity in earlier tests so as to avoid distortion of results, notably in the Long Range Tax Forms Simplification Study (IRS, 1983).

Regardless of which option is chosen, it is sensible to estimate the magnitude of the reactivity. In particular, it seems sensible to design a side experiment whenever possible to determine whether and how awareness influences behavior. This requires that at least one subsample be unaware of the experiment and that awareness be measured.

For instance, the IRS's (1983) Long Range Tax Forms Simplification Study included a control group that was unaware of any experiment. The return rate of taxpayers in each of the three experimental groups did not differ appreciably from this group's rate, suggesting that the experiment was not reactive in this particular respect. Similarly, Schwartz and Orleans included both a placebo group and an untreated control to understand the placebo effects of the experiment on taxpayers (no significant effect evidently appeared).

COUPLING EXPERIMENTS TO SURVEYS AND QUASI-EXPERIMENTS

Randomized experiments can be coupled to longitudinal surveys and panel studies. The purposes of this "satellite" policy include: calibration of nonrandomized experiments, more generalizable randomized experiments, and better methods for estimating program effects.

Longitudinal studies and surveys such as the TCMP based on well-designed probability samples are clearly useful, for management and policy, in understanding how individuals (or institutions) change over time. For example, longitudinal studies avoid the logical traps that cross-sectional studies invite, such as overlooking cohort effects, in economic, psychological, and other research. Cross-sectional studies are useful for crude trend analyses.

Both types of survey designs are often pressed, however, to produce evidence that they cannot support. Of special concern here is evidence about the impact of a compliance program on groups that a longitudinal or cross-sectional study happens to include. In employment and training work, for example, the Continuous Longitudinal Manpower Survey has been justified and supported primarily on grounds that we ought to understand what happens to the human resources pool. Its secondary justification is that it can help understand the effect of special programs—in youth employment, training, and so on. This secondary claim is unwarranted. Longitudinal and cross-sectional surveys are often not sufficient to permit us to estimate the effect of programs designed to, say, affect reported income of individuals who happen to be members of a survey sample, the crime rates of these people, and so on.

That the claims made for longitudinal surveys with respect to evaluating effects of programs can be misleading is clear empirically and analytically. The most dramatic recent empirical evidence stems from Fraker and

Maynard's (1985) comparisons of program effects based on randomized experiments against effects based on nonrandomized data, notably the Continuous Longitudinal Manpower Survey and the Current Population Survey (but see Heckman, Hotz, and Dabos, 1987). Earlier evidence in different arenas stems from the Salk vaccine trials, health services research, and others (see Boruch, 1976, for a listing).

Randomized experiments, by contrast, permit one to estimate the effects of projects with considerably more confidence. Indeed, reports of the National Research Council's Committee on Youth Employment Programs (Betsey et al., 1985), the Institute of Medicine's (1985) report on testing medical devices, and others are emphatic on this account. A major shortcoming of experiments, one not shared by the large-scale longitudinal studies, is their limited generalizability. That is, a set of experiments might be feasible in only a half-dozen sites, and those sites may not necessarily reflect national characteristics.

The implication is that we ought to invent and try out research policy that couples the benefits of longitudinal studies, i.e., generalizability, with those of experiments, i.e., unbiased estimates of program effect. See Farrington, Ohlin, and Wilson (1986) for a recent treatment of the idea.

The policy recommended here is akin to science policy on satellite use. The satellite, like the longitudinal or continuous cross-sectional survey, requires enormous resources to emplace and maintain. But scientists who design special-purpose work can obtain access to part of the satellite to sustain their investigation. Just as a physicist may use the satellite as a vehicle for limited, temporary investigation, the policy recommended here would allow the social science researcher to use the longitudinal survey infrastructure as a resource and as a vehicle for conducting prospective studies.

This strategy engenders some obvious difficulties. For instance, learning how and when existing survey samples can be augmented for experiments or how and when subsamples of the main sample can be drawn off for experiments is not clear. Nor is it clear how to design the side experiments so as to avoid invidious demands on or damage to the main study. How real these difficulties are needs to be understood if any progress is to be made in this area. The best way to find out presumably is by trying the strategy out.

The policy element gets beyond simple scientific traditions of data sharing (Fienberg, Martin, and Straf, 1985). It is considerably more debatable and more important in principle. Access is likely to be feasible, for example, for only a few projects, perhaps only one every year or two, on account of the sheer difficulty of coupling studies to an already complex longitudinal enterprise. It deserves some thinking in the context of the TCMP.

Iterative Experiments: Sequence and the Laboratory-Field Interface

A single-shot study, randomized experiment or otherwise, rarely produces results that are definitive or durable. It fails to be definitive often for reasons of imperfect execution and, more important here, because if done well it will raise new questions as well as answer older ones. In the social and behavioral arena, its results will be durable to the extent that laws and society change. A compliance program emphasizing threats, for example, may be cyclically effective as taxpayers grow less bold and more bold over time. Degradation of project effects occurs in long term tests of youth employment programs (Betsey et al., 1985) and elsewhere. One would expect some cycling and some degradation of the effectiveness in compliance work.

The point, of course, is that a single-shot study may be useful for a problem at hand, but a sequence of experiments is more likely to yield results that have some generalizability in time. And, with the right designs, they will have generalizability with respect to populations of interest to the revenue services. Coupling of experiments and panel studies, as described earlier, is one way to ensure a more or less orderly sequence. Other approaches are possible.

The interface between laboratory test and field experiments constitutes one aspect of iterative research. The idea is to cross-walk between laboratory and field periodically. The purpose is to capitalize on the inexpensive, controlled conditions of a laboratory at times and to exploit the field to verify laboratory work.

Such cross-walking is not uncommon in research on jury decision making. Indeed, the IRS, in collaboration with private contractors, has used the strategy to understand how to simplify tax forms and whether laboratory-based results, on error rates and taxpayer burden, for example, hold up in large-scale field tests.

In short, it doesn't take much wit to understand that sequence and a laboratory-field interface are sensible features of any experimentation policy. It takes considerably more, however, to determine how, how much, and when these features can be exploited.

BLOCKING VARIABLES AND SPECIAL TARGET GROUPS

Certain groups of individuals may deserve special attention in experiments for two reasons. First, such groups may be especially interesting, because of their noncompliance rate, say, and so may be labeled high priority for attention. Second, and more important here, one group may react to a treatment regimen in ways that differ appreciably from another group's reaction. For instance, the Schwartz-Orleans results suggest that low-income taxpayers react in one way to appeals to moral conscience and high-income individuals react in another.

Other, more recent studies also suggest that interactions between program type and person type are important and ought to be recognized in design work. Paid tax preparers, for instance, were very likely to choose conventional forms rather than experimental forms in the 1983 IRS Long Range Tax Forms Simplification Study. The individual taxpayers chose the (assigned but voluntary) experimental forms at a much higher rate.

A similarly conservative choice strategy is also evident in subgroups of individual taxpayers. Lower-income, "married filing separately," and head of household filers were more likely than others to opt for the usual 1040A instead of the alternatives in this study.

Schwartz and Orleans found tantalizing evidence for the idea that the attitudes of the highest socioeconomic class of taxpayers are notably affected by reminders about legal sanctions against tax compliance. The lower three classes, by contrast, were not affected appreciably. The lowest class category was affected most by appeals to moral conscience to judge by their responses to open-ended inquiries about reasons why taxpayers might report all income of a certain kind.

Findings on employed versus self-employed taxpayers seem no less relevant to understanding which groups may lend themselves well to experimental tests of compliance programs. Small businesses are of special interest, of course, in that their noncompliance rate seems high; the self-employed are often small business owners. Moreover, the Schwartz-Orleans work suggests that appeals to conscience rather than sanctions are likely to have a remarkable effect on compliance.

Quasi-Experimental Designs

"Quasi-experimental design" here means a plan for collecting data that will yield estimates of program effect but does not include the randomized assignment of individuals (or entities) to one of several alternative regimens. These designs are labeled "quasi-experimental" in the educational, social, and psychological research literature and in some biostatistics work (Campbell and Stanley, 1963). Some of the designs are not different in principle from those employed in econometrics and biometrics.

Only two such designs are considered here. They are demanding but are most likely to generate good estimates of the effectiveness of programs or projects. The two designs are regression-discontinuity approaches and time-series approaches.

Other designs can produce defensible estimates of program effect, but the circumstances under which they do are more special and their assumptions are more demanding (see, e.g., Glass et al., 1975; Rossi and Freeman, 1981; Campbell and Boruch, 1975).

DESIGNS BASED ON PROGRAM ALLOCATED IN STRICT ACCORD WITH MEASURABLE NEED: REGRESSION-DISCONTINUITY

Randomized field tests are not always feasible. When people, groups, cities, or regions are assigned to receive services in strict accord with measurable need, however, a reasonable alternative design can be exploited. The design requires measurement of at least two points in time, on a sample of both service recipients and nonrecipients. The approach, developed by Donald T. Campbell (Riecken et al., 1974; Trochim, 1984) works in the following way.

The need of regions or individuals is first measured; for example, compliance level is measured for each of (say) fifty sectors. The least compliant sectors are assigned to receive program services strictly on the basis of their measured level of compliance. For example, only the three with the lowest compliance rates receive program services or other treatment. Once the program has been emplaced and has had an opportunity to exercise notable influence, all sectors are measured again.

The estimate of the program's effect hinges on the assumption that there is normally a strong, simple relation between compliance levels from one year to the next. To the extent that the program disrupts that relation, e.g., enhances the compliance rates in the areas subjected to special attention, the program can be said to have been effective. The estimate of program effect is then judged relative to a projection based on one prior measure and, as important, the assignment of sectors on the basis of measured need or merit.

In the simplest case, the "strong simple relation" constitutes the null condition—i.e., the standard against which program effects are judged. In the absence of a special program effect, the relation between before and after program observations is regular and, in this case, linear. If introduction of the program engenders a simple additive effect, then a disruption of the relation will appear. The effect of the program is reflected by the size of the discontinuity.

This design is not yet commonly used. But is has substantial merit on technical grounds; the logic and statistical models reflecting the logic have been articulated well, by Trochim (1984), for instance. If the relationship of needs from one period to the next is strong and the program is assigned strictly in accord with need, the design is at least as good, on technical grounds, as a randomized test. Its feasibility will be greater in some cases. See Trochim (1984) for illustrations and Rubin (1977) for a thoughtful analytic treatment.

TIME-SERIES DESIGNS

In some program areas, good archival data are available to address particular interests. For example, accurate monthly records on the level of certain kinds of compliance may be available. The existence of such records makes a time-series approach to estimating program effects possible.

In particular, individuals, organizations, or other entities in a target area are monitored at successive points in time before the program is introduced. The new program is put into place, and the individuals or entities are again monitored. The estimate of program effect is normally the difference between the level of compliance, for instance, following introduction of the program and the level evident prior to its introduction. The standard of comparison in this case is historical: a prediction, based on prior data, about what compliance would have been without the new program.

Such historically based comparisons have merit to the extent that records are uniformly accurate and the time series is free from peculiar and poorly understood variation. To the extent that the quality of the records varies, or that factors other than the new program or project exercise unknown or incalculable influences on compliance, then estimates of the program's effect will be ambiguous at best and misleading at worst.

Controlled experiments and time series are not inimical. They can be combined in an evaluation. The main point is that the randomized experiment sets up a contemporary empirical standard for judging the effect of a program. Effects are based on comparing a group of people who participated in Program A against an equivalent group who participated in

Program B. The time series involves a historical standard and assumption that is sometimes less tenable: that the behavior of the area or group under examination can be predicted confidently from earlier behavior alone.

Because time-series analyses depend heavily on archival records whose quality is uniformly good and collected over a long period of time, the approach is adaptable only in particular areas and often not in new contexts.

Good illustrations of time-series analyses of social data are not hard to identify: e.g., Glass et al. (1975), Nelson (1973), McCleary and Hay (1980), and Box and Tiao (1975). To determine the effectiveness of new, stringent laws governing drinking while driving in some parts of the United States, for example, time-series data on traffic accidents, arrests, and the like have been used. Variations in the quality of crime records and temporal variation in the definition of crime make it more difficult to use conventional administrative records for determining the effects of new laws on crime rates, but some attempts have been successful, e.g., estimating the effect of more severe sentences on carrying an unlicensed pistol in the state of Massachusetts.

Analogous approaches to estimating the effects of new laws have been undertaken in Denmark. For example, the effect of relaxing pornography laws in Denmark was established in part by examining time-series data on sex-related crime rates. The Kutchinsky studies are especially conscientious because he recognizes that variation in legal definitions of crimes, cultural attitudes, and propensity to report crime is considerable, and he documents the extent to which these are plausible influences on the outcomes.

Some Crude Ideas About Field Experiments in Taxpayer Compliance
EDUCATION AND EXPLANATION

Explaining what tax revenues are used for is held to be important by some as a device for increasing revenues. For instance, the Massachusetts Department of Revenue puts stock in the idea that voluntary compliance is enhanced by telling taxpayers that revenues are used for the Office of Children, the state police, homeless shelters, prison systems, environmental quality engineering, and other systems. How much effect this has is not clear, although some effect is plausible. The state of Massachusetts does not know how much effect explanations of this kind have, despite the importance attached to them. Experiments using the individual as the unit of randomization seem feasible in view of precedents such as Schwartz and Orleans and Perng.

Educating small businesses seems important from work in Massachusetts under Ira Jackson's leadership, work by the U.S. Congress's Joint Committee on Taxation, and others. The percentage of revenues voluntarily reported as a function of revenues that should have been reported is less than 50 percent according to the joint committee's report. So-called businessmen's kits and other educative consumer services directed at small businesses seem worth trying out. In particular, it is not clear how to best inform and remind new small businesses.

Randomized tests using businesses as the unit may be warranted to test out an array of telephone, letter, and document-based advice. Similarly, accountants and firms that service small businesses might be regarded as a legitimate target population insofar as they provide poor or ambiguous advice to clients. These entities would then be the unit of randomization.

MONEY AND REWARDS

The idea of creating explicit well-advertised rewards for taxpayer compliance has been taken seriously by the state of Massachusetts, among others. For instance, the state puts considerable stress on prompt refunds and advertises the fact. Rewards such as this are relative, of course; taxpayers who grow accustomed to fast refunds may in time be less affected by this incentive.

Determining whether and when new kinds of monetary rewards have an effect on compliance seems important. One can conceive of a lottery, for instance, to ease the pain of being (randomly) audited. Small controlled tests of lottery-based reward in this and other contexts would help to establish whether the lottery-based rewards decreased indifference, hostility, or gratuitous criticism. (Deciding whether such attitude changes lead to more compliance is a separate matter for research.)

ASSISTANCE AS REWARD

At least some individual taxpayers use the IRS to store cash in a sock. That is, they declare no deductions, have a maximum federal tax withheld, and usually wind up with a refund (without interest). This "enforced savings" strategy is of some benefit to the taxpayer, but it does reduce the amount of money available during the year.

This phenomenon seems not to have been explored empirically. It is likely that IRS assistance can help taxpayers understand how to take deductions properly and why it is in their interest to do so. Experiments with individuals or small regions might be undertaken to determine what kind of assistance works and whether such assistance changes either attitudes toward the IRS or behavior.

SIMPLIFICATION

Tests of alternative tax forms lend themselves naturally to randomized experiments. That such forms may lead to better compliance is plausible and important if we judge by the work of the IRS and the states of Massachusetts and Pennsylvania. The individual taxpayer or couple are most pertinent for randomization. Formal randomized experiments on the topic seem not to have been conducted or published by state revenue offices.

This is in contrast to the IRS's (1983) efforts to undertake and report on forms simplification. This early effort was not executed completely, but it did demonstrate the hazards of randomized field experiments with volunteer subjects—i.e., a 10 percent response rate of participation in tests of forms.

ATTITUDES

The state of Massachusetts, among others, stresses the importance of changing attitudes in the interest of voluntary taxpayer compliance. This is an especially challenging matter since the relation between measured attitude and actual behavior is often not empirically explored. When the correlation is estimated in field surveys, it is often puny—e.g., correlations of less than .10 between work ethic attitudes and actual work behavior among youth involved in employment programs.

Still, the matter is important to the extent that attitudes reflect actual behavior and attitudes are easier to measure. Experimentation seems feasible on a small scale, at least, if we use Schwartz-Orleans as a model. Indeed, the Schwartz-Orleans work suggests that remarkable attitude change and behavioral change resulted from their special treatments. (Attitudes were deduced from normative response to open-ended inquiry, not standardized-item questionnaires.) Experimental tests of attitude change devices seem most pertinent to those taxpayers whose behavior is least verifiable—e.g., the self-employed—but only if experiments on other groups support the notion that attitudes reflect actual behavior.

MANIPULABLE VARIABLES MORE GENERALLY

Nagin's (1986) statement of the revenue office's missions and the Klepper-Nagin (1987) work make a nice little general guide to what variables might be manipulated in randomized tests.

(a) Providing the means for compliance, as in simplifying or stream-lining forms, and the information need to comply, as in revising instruction manuals, invites randomized tests of alternative forms, instruction manuals, and related client services.

(b) Developing organization capacity to process returns invites experimental tests of alternative approaches to training revenue office staff members and of office procedures including communications, command and control, and so on.

(c) Identifying noncompliers and bringing them into compliance invites field experiments that yield better identification schemes and various ways to encourage compliance.

(d) Contributing to statutory changes that make the tax system better invites tests of experimental policies, procedures, or regulations that may eventually become law.

All this is a bit too abstract to be very helpful, of course. But Nagin's model helps to build a speculative research agenda around the idea of systematic experiments in compliance.

References

Aitken, S.S., and Bonneville, L.
 1980   A General Taxpayer Opinion Survey. Prepared for Office of Planning and Research, Internal Revenue Service, March 1980, by CSR, Inc., Washington, D.C. (Contract No. TIR-79-2)
Betsey, C., Hollister, R., and Papageorgiou, M., eds.
 1985   *Youth Employment and Training Programs: The YEDPA Years.* Washington, D.C.: National Academy Press.
Bickman, L.
 1985   Randomized field experiments in education. *New Directions for Program Evaluation* 28:39–54.
Blumstein, A.
 1983   Models for structuring taxpayer compliance. Pp. 159–172 in P. Sawicki, ed., *Income Tax Compliance: A Report of the ABA Section on Taxation, Invitational Conference on Income Tax Compliance.* Washington, D.C.: American Bar Association.

Boruch, R.F.
  1976   On common contentions about randomized experiments. Pp. 158–194 in
         G.V. Glass, ed., *Evaluation Studies Review Annual, 3*. Beverly Hills, Calif.:
         Sage Publications.
Boruch, R.F., and Cecil, J.S.
  1979   *Assuring Confidentiality of Social Research Data*. Philadelphia: University
         of Pennsylvania Press.
  1983   (eds.) *Solutions to Ethical and Legal Problems in Social Research*. New York:
         Academic Press.
Boruch, R.F., Dennis, M.L., and Greer, K.D.
  1988   Lessons from the Rockefeller Foundation's experiments on the Minority
         Single Parent Program. *Evaluation Review*, in press.
Boruch, R.F., McSweeny, A.J., and Soderstrom, J.
  1978   Bibliography: randomized field experiments for program planning, devel-
         opment and evaluation. *Evaluation Quarterly* 4:655–696.
Box, G.E.P., and Tiao, G.C.
  1975   Intervention analysis with applications to economic and environmental
         problems. *Journal of the American Statistical Association* 70:70–92.
Box, J.F.
  1978   *R.A. Fisher: The Life of a Scientist*. New York and Chichester: John Wiley
         & Sons.
Brook, et al.
  1984   *The Effect of Coinsurance on the Health of Adults: Results from the RAND
         Health Insurance Experiment*. Santa Monica, CA: Rand Corp.
Breger, M.
  1983   Randomized social experiments and the law. Pp. 97–144 in R.F. Boruch
         and J.S. Cecil, eds., *Solutions to Legal and Ethical Problems in Applied Social
         Research*. New York: Academic Press.
Campbell, D.T., and Boruch, R.F.
  1975   Making the case for randomized assignment treatments by considering the
         alternatives: six ways in which quasi-experimental evaluations in compen-
         satory education tend to underestimate effects. Pp. 195–296 in C.A. Ben-
         nett and A.A. Lumsdaine, eds., *Central Issues in Social Program Evaluation*.
         New York: Academic Press.
Campbell, D.T., and Stanley, J.S.
  1963   *Experimental and Quasi-Experimental Designs for Research*. Chicago: Rand
         McNally.
Chelimsky, E., ed.
  1985   *Program Evaluation: Patterns and Directions*. Washington, D.C.: Ameri-
         can Society for Public Administration.
Collins, J.F., and Elkin, I.
  1985   Randomization in the NIMH treatment of depression collaborative re-
         search program. *New Directions for Program Evaluation* 28:27–38.

Conner, R.F.
  1977   Selecting a control group: an analysis of the randomization process
         in twelve social reform programs. *Evaluation Quarterly* 1(2):195–
         243.
Corsi, J.R.
  1983   Randomization and consent in the New Mexico teleconferencing experi-
         ment: legal and ethical considerations. Pp. 159–171 in R. F. Boruch and
         J.S. Cecil, eds., *Solutions to Ethical and Legal Problems in Social Research.*
         New York: Academic Press.
Corsi, J.R., and Hurley, T.L.
  1979a Attitudes toward the use of the telephone in administrative hearings.
         Administrative Law Review 31:247–283.
  1979b Pilot study report on the use of the telephone in administrative fair
         hearings. *Administrative Law Review* 31:485–524.
Dennis, M.L.
  1988   Implementing Randomized Field Experiments: An Analysis of Criminal
         and Civil Justice Research. Ph.D. dissertation, Psychology Department,
         Northwestern University.
Farrington, D.P.
  1983   Randomized experiments on crime and justice. *Crime and Justice: An
         Annual Review of Research* 4:257–308.
Farrington, D.P., Ohlin, L.E., and Wilson, J.Q.
  1986   *Understanding and Controlling Crime: Toward a New Research Strategy.*
         New York: Springer-Verlag.
Federal Judicial Center
  1983   *Social Experimentation and the Law.* Washington, D.C.: Federal Judicial
         Center.
Ferber, R., and Hirsch, W. Z.
  1982   *Social Experimentation and Economic Policy.* Cambridge: Cambridge Uni-
         versity Press.
Fienberg, S.E., Martin, M., and Straf, M.L., eds.
  1985   *Sharing Research Data.* Committee on National Statistics. Washington,
         D.C.: National Academy Press.
Fienberg, S.E., Singer, B., and Tanur, J.M.
  1985   Large-scale social experimentation in the United States. Chapter 12 in
         A.C. Atkinson and S. E. Fienberg, eds., *A Celebration of Statistics: The ISI
         Centenary Volume.* New York: Springer-Verlag.
Fraker, T., and Maynard, R.
  1984   *The Use of Comparison Group Designs in Evaluations of Employment-Related
         Programs.* Princeton, N.J.: Mathematica Policy Research.
Freund, P.A.
  1968   Legal frameworks for human experimentation. *Daedalus* 98:318.
Friedman, L.M., Furberg, C.D. and DeMets
  1985   *Fundamentals of Clinical Trials.* Littleton, Mass.: PSG Publishing, Inc.
Gilbert, J.P., Light, R.M., and Mosteller, F.
  1977   Assessing social innovations: an empirical base for policy. Pp. 185–242 in

W.B. Fairley and F. Mosteller, eds., *Statistics and Public Policy*. Reading, Mass.: Addison-Wesley.

Glass, G.V. et al.
1975   *Design and Analysis of Time Series Experiments*. Boulder, Colorado: Colorado Associated University Press.

Goldman, J.
1977   A randomization procedure for trickle-process evaluations. *Evaluation Quarterly* 1(3):493–498.
1985   Negotiated solutions to overcoming impediments in a law related experiment. *New Directions for Program Evaluation* 28:63–72.

Gordon, G., and Morse, E.V.
1975   Evaluation research. *Annual Review of Sociology* 1:339–361.

Gray, B.H.
1975   *Human Subjects in Medical Experimentation*. New York: John Wiley & Sons.

Gueron, J.M.
1985   The demonstration of work/welfare initiatives. *New Directions in Program Evaluation* 29:5–14.

Gueron, J.M., and Nathan, R.
1985   The MDRC work/welfare project: Objectives, status, significance. *Policy Studies Review* 4(3).

Hahn, G.J.
1984   Experimental design in the complex world. *Technometrics* 26(1):19–31.

Hargrove, E.C.
1981   The bureaucratic politics of evaluation: A case study of the Department of Labor. In H.E. Freeman and M.A. Solomon, eds., *Evaluation Studies Review Annual 6*. Beverly Hills, Calif.: Sage Publications.

Heckman, J.J., Hotz, V.J., and Dabos, M.
1987   Do we need experimental data to evaluate the impact of manpower training on earnings? *Evaluation Review* 11(4):395–427.

Hendricks, M.
1981   Service delivery assessment: Qualitative evaluations at the cabinet level. In N.L. Smith, ed., *New Directions in Program Evaluation* 12:5–24.

Hillis, J.W., and Wortman, C.M.
1976   Some determinants of public acceptance of randomized control group experiments. *Sociometry* 39:91–96.

Hillsman-Baker, S.B., and Rodriguez, O.
1979   Random time quota selection: An alternative to random selection in experimental evaluation. Pp. 185–186 in L. Sechrest et al., eds., *Evaluation Studies Review Annual, 6*. Beverly Hills, Calif.: Sage Publications.

Hollister, R.G., Kemper, P., and Maynard, R.A.
1984   *The National Supported Work Demonstration*. Madison, Wis.: University of Wisconsin Press.

Hornick, R.O. et al.
1973   *Television and Educational Reform in El Salvador*. Stanford, Calif.: Stanford University Institute for Communication Research.

Institute of Medicine
  1985 *Assessing Medical Technologies.* Committee for Evaluating Medical
        Technologies in Clinical Use. Washington, D.C.: National Academy
        Press.
Internal Revenue Service
  1983 *Long Range Tax Forms Simplifcation Study.* Research Division, Tax Forms
        and Publications Division. Washington, D.C.: U.S. Department of the
        Treasury.
Kinsey, K.A.
  1984 Survey Data on Tax Compliance: A Compendium and Review.
        American Bar Foundation Tax Compliance Working Paper 84-1, Decem-
        ber, 1984. American Bar Foundation, Chicago.
  1987 Theories and models of tax evasion. Criminal Justice Abstracts 18.403:
        Revision of American Bar Foundation Tax Compliance Working Paper
        84-2, December 1984. American Bar Foundation, Chicago.
Klepper, S., and Nagin, D.
  1987 The Role of Tax Practitioners in Tax Compliance. Unpublished paper,
        Department of Statistics and School of Urban and Public Affairs,
        Carnegie-Mellon University.
Lempert, R.O.
  1984 From the editor. *Law and Society* 18(4):503–504.
Levine, R.J.
  1981 *Ethics and Regulation of Clinical Research.* Baltimore and Munich: Urban
        and Schwarzenberg.
Light, R.J., and Pillemer, D.B.
  1984 *Summing Up: The Science of Reviewing Research.* Cambridge, Mass.: Har-
        vard University Press.
Lind, A.
  1985 Randomized experiments in the federal courts. *New Directions for Program
        Evaluation* 28:73–80.
Lipsey, M.W., Cordray, D.S., and Berger, D.E.
  1981 Evaluation of a juvenile diversion program: Using multiple lines of evi-
        dence. *Evaluation Review* 5(3):283–306.
Loftus, E.
  1985 To file, perchance to cheat. *Psychology Today,* April:35–39.
Long, S.B.
  1981 Social control in the civil law: the case of income tax enforcement. Pp.
        185–214 in H.L. Ross, ed., *Law and Deviance.* Beverly Hills, Calif.: Sage
        Publications.
Matt, G.E.
  1988 Fraud and Error in Three Federal Programs: Aid to Families with Depen-
        dent Children, Food Stamps, and Individual Income Tax Returns. Ph.D.
        dissertation, Psychology Department, Northwestern University.
McCleary, R., and Hay, R.A.
  1980 *Applied Time Series for the Social Sciences.* Beverly Hills, Calif.: Sage Pub-
        lications.

Meier, P.
  1972   The biggest public health experiment ever: The 1954 field trial of the Salk poliomyelitis vaccine. In J.M. Tanur, F. Mosteller, W.H. Kruskal, R.F. Link, R.S. Pieters, and G. Rising, eds., *Statistics: A Guide to the Unknown*. San Francisco: Holden-Day.
Mosteller, F., Gilbert, J.P., and McPeek, B.
  1980   Reporting standards and research strategies for controlled trials: Agenda for the editor. *Controlled Clinical Trials* 1:37–58.
Mosteller, F., and Weinstein, M.C.
  1985   Towards evaluating the cost-effectiveness of medical and social experiments. In J.A. Hausman and D.A. Wise, eds., *Social Experimentation*. Chicago: University of Chicago Press.
Nagin, D.S.
  1986   The Tax Administrator's Model of Tax Compliance. Report prepared for the Conference on Tax Compliance Research, Padre Island, Texas, January 15–17, 1986.
Nelson, C.W.
  1973   *Applied Time-Series Analysis*. San Francisco: Holden-Day.
Nelson, R.L., and Hedrick, T.E.
  1983   The statutory protection of confidentiality of research data: synthesis and evaluation. Pp. 213–236 in R.F. Boruch and J.S. Cecil, eds., *Solutions to Ethical and Legal Problems in Social Research*. New York: Academic Press.
Perng, S.S.
  1985   Accounts receivable treatments study. *New Directions for Program Evaluation* 28:55–62.
Riecken, H.W. et al.
  1974   *Social Experimentation: A Method for Planning and Evaluating Social Programs*. New York: Academic Press.
Rivlin, R.M.
  1971   *Systematic Thinking for Social Action*. Washington, D.C.: The Brookings Institution.
Robins, P.K., Spiegelman, R.G., Weiner, S., and Bell, J.G.
  1980   *A Guaranteed Annual Income: Evidence from a Social Experiment*. New York: Academic Press.
Robins, P.K., and West, R.W.
  1981   *Labor Supply Response to the Seattle and Denver Income Maintenance Experiments*, Menlo Park, Calif.: SRI International.
Roos, L.L., Roos, N., and McKinley, B.
  1977   Implementing randomization. *Policy Analysis* 3(4):547–559.
Rossi, P.H., Berk, R.A., and Lenihan, K.J.
  1980   *Money, Work, and Crime: Experimental Evidence*. New York: Academic Press.
Rossi, P.H., and Freeman, H.
  1981   *Evaluation: A Primer*. Beverly Hills, Calif.: Sage Publications.
Rubin, D.B.
  1977   Assignment of treatment group on the basis of a covariate. *Journal of Educational Statistics* 2:1–26.

Schueren, F.
  1985 Methodologic Issues in Linkage of Multiple Data Bases. Prepared for the National Research Council Panel on Statistics for an Aging Population, September 13.
Schultz, T.W.
  1982 Distortions of economic research. Pp. 121–134 in W.H. Kruskal, ed., *The Social Sciences: Their Nature and Uses.* Chicago: University of Chicago Press.
Schwartz, R.D., and Orleans, S.
  1967 On legal sanctions. *University of Chicago Law Review* 34:274–300.
Severy, L.J., and Whitaker, J.M.
  1982 Juvenile diversion: An experimental analysis of effectiveness. *Evaluation Review* 6(6):753–774.
Shadish, W.R., and Cook, T.D.
  in press Evaluation of social programs. In B.B. Wolman, ed., *International Encyclopedia of Psychiatry, Psychology, Psychoanalysis, and Neurology* (First Progress Volume). New York: Aesculapius Press.
Sherman, L.W., and Berk, R.A.
  1984 The specific deterrent effects of arrest for domestic assault. *American Sociological Review* 49:261–272.
  1985 Randomized experiments in police research. *New Directions for Program Evaluation* 28:15–25.
St. Pierre, R.G., and Rezmovic, V.
  1982 An overview of the Nebraska Nutrition and Education Training Program evaluation. *Journal of Nutritional Education* 14(2):61–66.
St. Pierre, R.G., Cook, T.D., and Straw, R.
  1982 Evaluation of the Nebraska Nutrition and Education Training Program *Evaluation News* 3(1):67–69.
Trochim, W.M.K.
  1984 *Research Design for Program Evaluation: The Regression Discontinuity Approach.* Beverly Hills, Calif.: Sage Publications.
Witte, A.D.
  1987 Tax compliance research. Pp. 101–109 in *Proceedings of the American Statistical Association: Survey Research Methods Section.* Washington, D.C.: American Statistical Association.

Appendix C: Symposium on Taxpayer Compliance Research

National Academy of Sciences/National Research Council
Commission on Behavioral and Social Sciences and Education
Committee on Research on Law Enforcement and the Administration
of Justice
Panel on Taxpayer Compliance Research

AGENDA
SYMPOSIUM ON TAXPAYER COMPLIANCE RESEARCH

January 15–17, 1986
Conference Room A
Padre Island Hilton Resort
South Padre Island, Texas

Wednesday, January 15

8:30 a.m.	CONTINENTAL BREAKFAST
9:00 a.m.	Welcome and Introductions
	Ann Witte, Symposium Chair

9:15   Roundtable I. *What we need to know: Political and administrative perspectives.* (Panel Report Outline II.A, V.)

Jerome Kurtz, Chair

Discussants:

Ira Jackson (Steven Klepper/Daniel Nagin paper)
Paul McDaniel (John Scholz paper)
John Wedick (Synthesis)
Eugene Bardach (Synthesis)

Authors:

Steven Klepper and Daniel Nagin
"The Tax Administrator's Model of Compliance"

John Scholz
"Political Context of Tax Administration"

Panel Commentators:

Walter Blum
Alfred Blumstein

12:15 p.m.   LUNCH

2:15 p.m.   Roundtable II. *The individual incentive model: Costs and
benefits of compliance.* (Outline section III.A.1–3)

Harvey Galper, Chair

Discussants:

Daniel Nagin (Robert Kagan paper)
Steven Klepper (Joel Slemrod paper)
Thomas Coleman (Synthesis)
Paul McDaniel (Synthesis)

Authors:

Robert Kagan
"Visibility of Violations and Tax Compliance"

Joel Slemrod
"Complexity, Compliance Costs, and Tax Evasion"

Panel Commentators:

Walter Blum
Stewart Macaulay

5:15 p.m.   ADJOURN FOR THE DAY

Thursday, January 16

8:30 a.m.   CONTINENTAL BREAKFAST

9:00 a.m.   Roundtable III. *Extending the individual incentive model.*
(Outline section III.A.4.)

Richard Schwartz, Chair

Discussants:

Daniel Rubinfeld (Howard Margolis and Suzanne
Scotchmer papers)

Richard Nisbett (John Carroll paper)
Ira Jackson (Synthesis)

Authors:

John Carroll
"Role of Uncertainty in Compliance Decision-Making"

Howard Margolis
"Taxpayer Noncompliance and the Problem of Collective Action"

Suzanne Scotchmer
"Extensions of Theoretical Modeling of Tax Compliance"

Panel Commentators:

Jerry Green
Jerome Kurtz

12:00 p.m.   LUNCH

2:00 p.m.   Roundtable IV. *Social influences.* (Outline section III.B.)

Richard Lempert, Chair

Discussants:

Felice Levine (Robert Kidder/Craig McEwen paper)
John Carroll (Robert Cialdini paper)
Howard Erlanger (Third Parties)
Roger Plate (Synthesis)

Authors:

Robert Kidder and Craig McEwen
"Normative Pluralism and Compliance Research"

Robert Cialdini
"Social Motivation to Comply: Intrinsic Rewards and Social Influences"

Panel Commentators:

Sidney Davidson
Richard Nisbett
Barbara Yngvesson

5:00 p.m.   ADJOURN FOR THE DAY

6:00 p.m.   Reception and Dinner
               Conference Room B

Friday, January 17

8:30 a.m.	CONTINENTAL BREAKFAST

9:00 a.m.   Roundtable V. *Future Research*. (Outline section IV, V.)

Alfred Blumstein, Chair

Discussants:

Daniel Rubinfeld (Robert Boruch/Peter Schmidt papers)
Harold Grasmick (Seymour Sudman paper)
Felice Levine (Synthesis)
Fred Goldberg (Synthesis)

Authors:

Robert Boruch
"Experiments and Quasi-Experiments in Context of Tax Compliance Research"

Peter Schmidt
"Statistical Considerations in Modeling Taxpayer Compliance"

Seymour Sudman
"Observational Techniques for Tax Compliance Measurement"

Panel Commentators:

Jan Kmenta
David Linowes

12:00 p.m.   LUNCH

1:00 p.m.   ADJOURN SYMPOSIUM—Authors and invited participants depart for airport

Appendix D: Panel on Taxpayer Compliance Research

ANN DRYDEN WITTE (Chair), Department of Economics, Wellesley College, and National Bureau of Economic Research, Cambridge, Massachusetts

EUGENE S. BARDACH, Graduate School of Public Policy, University of California, Berkeley

WALTER J. BLUM, School of Law, University of Chicago

ALFRED BLUMSTEIN, School of Urban and Public Affairs, Carnegie-Mellon University

SIDNEY DAVIDSON, Graduate School of Business, University of Chicago

HARVEY GALPER, Peat Marwick Main & Co., Washington, D.C.

JERRY R. GREEN, Department of Economics, Harvard University

JAN KMENTA, Department of Economics, University of Michigan

JEROME KURTZ, Paul, Weiss, Rifkind, Wharton and Garrison, Washington, D.C.

RICHARD O. LEMPERT, School of Law, University of Michigan

DAVID F. LINOWES, Institute of Government and Public Affairs, School of Public Policy, University of Illinois

STEWART MACAULAY, School of Law, University of Wisconsin

RICHARD E. NISBETT, Institute for Social Research, University of Michigan

JOHN W. PAYNE, Fuqua School of Business, Duke University

RICHARD D. SCHWARTZ, School of Law, Syracuse University

BARBARA YNGVESSON, School of Social Science, Hampshire College

JEFFREY A. ROTH, *Study Director*
JOHN T. SCHOLZ, *Senior Research Associate*
GAYLENE J. DUMOUCHEL, *Administrative Secretary*
TERESA E. WILLIAMS, *Administrative Secretary*

Biographical Sketches

ANN DRYDEN WITTE is professor of economics at Wellesley College and research associate at the National Bureau of Economic Research. In her research, she applies microeconomic theory and econometric techniques to the study of various social issues, including tax compliance, law enforcement, crime, housing markets, and day care. She has authored or edited seven books including *Predicting Recidivism Using Survival Models; Advances in Applied Micro-Economics; An Economic Analysis of Crime and Justice;* and *Beating the System: The Underground Economy.* Witte has served as chair of the American Economics Association's Census Advisory Commission and has been a member of numerous professional and advisory committees, including the panel's parent Committee on Research on Law Enforcement and the Administration of Justice and the American Statistical Association's Committee on Law and Justice Statistics. She is a fellow of the American Society of Criminology, a trustee of the Police Foundation and the Law and Society Association, and an associate editor of a number of professional journals. She received a B.A. from the University of Florida, an M.A. from Columbia University, and a Ph.D. in economics from North Carolina State University.

EUGENE S. BARDACH is professor of public policy at the Graduate School of Public Policy, University of California, Berkeley. He has written on policy and program implementation and especially, in recent years, on the implementation of health and safety regulation by all levels of government. His books include *The Implementation Game: What Happens After a Bill Becomes a Law; Going by the Book: The Problem of Regulatory Unreasonableness* (with Robert A. Kagan); and *The Skill Factor in Politics: Repealing the Mental Commitment Laws in California.* He is currently writing a book on ethics and public policy. He received a B.A. from Columbia University and a Ph.D. in political science from the University of California, Berkeley.

WALTER J. BLUM is the Edward H. Levi distinguished service professor at the University of Chicago Law School. He has served as trustee of the College Retirement Equities Fund and as consultant to the American Law Institute Federal Income Tax Project. From 1960 to 1966 he served on the Advisory Committee for Studies of Government Finance at the Brookings Institution and was a member of the Steering Committee of the Administrative Conference Project on the U.S. Internal Revenue Service (1974–1975). Since 1947 he has been a member of the Planning Committee of the

University of Chicago Law School Federal Tax Conference and since 1948 has been legal counsel to the *Bulletin of the Atomic Scientists*. He is a member of the American Bar Association, the Chicago Bar Association, the American Law Institute, the Chicago Federal Tax Forum, and the American Academy of Arts and Sciences. He is the author of *The Uneasy Case for Progressive Taxation* (with Harry Kalven, Jr.); *Public Law Perspectives on a Private Law Problem* (with Harry Kalven, Jr.); *Materials on Reorganization, Recapitalization and Insolvency* (with Stanley A. Kaplan); and *Readjustments and Reorganizations* (with Stanley A. Kaplan); as well as numerous articles in the fields of federal taxation, insurance, corporate finance, and bankruptcy.

ALFRED BLUMSTEIN is dean and J. Erik Jonsson Professor of urban systems and operations research at the School of Urban and Public Affairs of Carnegie-Mellon University. He has had extensive experience in both research and policy with the criminal justice system since serving the President's Commission on Law Enforcement and Administration of Justice in 1966–1967 as director of its Task Force on Science and Technology. His research has covered many aspects of the operation of the criminal justice system, with special attention to prison populations and sentencing, and has involved extensive research on criminal careers. Blumstein was a member of the panel's parent Committee on Research on Law Enforcement and Administration of Justice from its founding in 1975 until 1986. He served as chair of the committee between 1979 and 1984 and has chaired the committee's panels on research on deterrent and incapacitative effects, on sentencing research, and on research on criminal careers. Blumstein has served since 1979 as chairman of the Pennsylvania Commission on Crime and Delinquency, the state criminal justice planning agency for Pennsylvania. He has also been a member of the Pennsylvania Commission on Sentencing since 1986. His degrees from Cornell University include a baccalaureate in engineering physics and a Ph.D. in operations research. He was president of the Operations Research Society of America in 1977–1978 and was awarded its Kimball Medal for service to the profession and society in 1985. He is currently the president of the Institute of Management Sciences and a fellow of the American Society of Criminology and was the 1987 recipient of the society's Sutherland Award for research contributions.

SIDNEY DAVIDSON is the Arthur Young Distinguished Service Professor of accounting at the University of Chicago. He is a certified public accountant and holds B.A., M.B.A., and Ph.D. (in business administration) degrees from the University of Michigan. He is the author or editor of several books and many articles on accounting, economics and finance. He was president of the American Accounting Association in 1968–1969 and vice president of the American Institute of CPAs in 1986–1987. He was elected to the Accounting Hall of Fame in 1983. He has served as a consultant to the U.S. Department of the Treasury and the Securities and Exchange Commission.

HARVEY GALPER is a principal in the accounting firm of Peat Marwick Main & Co., resident in its Washington, D.C., office. His prior positions include senior fellow at the Brookings Institution (1982–1987), senior public finance resident at the Advisory Commission on Intergovernmental Relations (1981–1982), and director of the Office of Tax Analysis of the U.S. Treasury Department (1976–1981), from which he received a meritorious service award. He has also served on the staff of the Urban Institute and has taught at Dartmouth College, the University of California, Berkeley, Yale University, and the Georgetown University Law Center. He has authored or coauthored more than forty articles in public finance, wrote *Assessing Tax Reform* with Henry Aaron in 1985, and edited *Uneasy Compromise: Problems of a Hybrid Income-Consumption Tax* with Henry Aaron and Joseph Pechman in 1988. He is a past member of the board of directors of the National Tax Association–Tax Institute of America and currently serves on the editorial board of the *National Tax Journal* and on the advisory group of the commissioner of the Internal Revenue Service. He received a B.A. from Dartmouth College and M.A. and Ph.D. degrees from Yale University.

JERRY GREEN is the David A. Wells Professor of political economy at Harvard University. He has served as chairman of the Department of Economics at Harvard and as chairman of the National Science Foundation's Information Science Advisory Panel. He is a research associate of the National Bureau of Economic Research, a fellow of the Econometric Society, and an overseas fellow of Churchill College, Cambridge University. He has written over seventy articles published in economics journals and has edited several collections of papers. His book, coauthored with Jean-Jacques Laffont, *Incentives in Public Decision Making,* was published in 1979. He has held a Woodrow Wilson dissertation fellowship (1969–1970), and a National Science Foundation postdoctoral fellowship (1971–1972), has been a fellow of the Center of Advanced Study in

Behavioral Science (1980–1981), and is currently a John Simon Guggenheim memorial fellow. He has been the recipient of the J. K. Galbraith Prize for teaching in economics (1980) and the distinguished alumni award of the University of Rochester (1984). He is founder and editor of *Economic Letters*. He received a B.A. and a Ph.D. in economics from the University of Rochester.

JAN KMENTA is professor of economics and statistics at the University of Michigan, specializing in econometric models and methods. His research has involved a variety of theoretical and applied econometric problems. He is a fellow of the American Statistical Association and of the Econometric Society and associate editor of the *Journal of the American Statistical Association* and of the *Review of Economics and Statistics*. His publications include *Elements of Econometrics; Evaluation of Econometric Models* (coedited with James B. Ramsey); and *Large Scale Macro-Econometric Models: Theory and Practice* (coedited with James B. Ramsey). He received a B.Ec. degree from the University of Sydney, Australia, and M.A. and Ph.D. degrees in economics and statistics from Stanford University.

JEROME KURTZ is a partner in the law firm of Paul, Weiss, Rifkind, Wharton & Garrison, resident in its Washington, D.C., office. He has served in the U.S. Department of the Treasury as commissioner of internal revenue (1977–1980) and as tax legislative counsel (1966–1968); he received that department's Alexander Hamilton Award (1980) and its Exceptional Service Award (1968). He has taught tax law and policy as a lecturer at Villanova University (1964–1965) and the University of Pennsylvania Law School (1969–1974) and as visiting professor of law at Harvard University (1975–1976). He served as chairman of the tax section of the Philadelphia Bar Association (1975–1976), a member of the executive committee of the tax section of the New York State Bar Association (1981–1982), chairman of the special committee on tax shelters of the tax section of the American Bar Association (1982–1984), and president of the Center for Inter-American Tax Administration (1980). He is a member of the Federal Income Tax Project Advisory Group of the American Law Institute and a fellow of the American College of Tax Counsel. He received a B.S. from Temple University and an LL.B. from Harvard University.

RICHARD O. LEMPERT is professor of law and sociology at the University of Michigan. He received an A.B. degree from Oberlin College, a J.D. from the University of Michigan Law School, and a Ph.D. in sociology from the University of Michigan. He is chair of the Committee on Research on Law Enforcement and the Administration of Justice. He has served as editor of the *Law and Society Review* and as a member of the executive committee of the Law and Society Association. He is coauthor of *A Modern Approach to Evidence* and *An Invitation to Law and Social Sciences*.

DAVID F. LINOWES is professor of political economy and public policy and Boeschenstein Professor Emeritus at the University of Illinois. He is also senior advisor to the Institute of Government and Public Affairs. Linowes is chairman of the President's Commission on Privatization. He served as chairman of the President's Commission on the Nation's Energy Resources and from 1975 to 1977 as chairman of the U.S. Privacy Protection Commission. He was a founding partner of Laventhol and Horwath, a worldwide management consulting firm. He headed economic development missions for the U.S. Department of State and the United Nations to Turkey, India, Greece, Pakistan, and Iran in the late 1960s and early 1970s. He is the author of *Managing Growth Through Acquisition, Strategies for Survival, The Corporate Conscience,* and *The Privacy Crisis in Our Time.* Linowes is a member of the Council on Foreign Relations.

STEWART MACAULAY is Malcolm Pitman Sharp Professor of the University of Wisconsin. He is a member of the Commission on Behavioral and Social Sciences and Education (CBASSE). He was president of the Law and Society Association and associate editor of *The Law & Society Review.* He is coauthor (with Lawrence Friedman) of *Law and the Behavioral Sciences,* one of the first collections of teaching materials in the field. His "Non-Contractual Relations and Business: A Preliminary Study," published in 1963, is still widely cited and reprinted. More recent publications include "Private Government," "Law and the Behavioral Sciences: Is There Any There There?" and "Images of Law in Everyday Life: The Lessons of School, Entertainment, and Spectator Sports." He received A.B. and LL.B. degrees from Stanford University.

RICHARD E. NISBETT is professor of psychology at the University of Michigan and program director at the Institute for Social Research. His research interests include judgment and decision making, inductive reasoning, and attitude change. He is coauthor or editor of seven books, including *Human Inference* (with L. Ross) and *Induction* (with J. Holland, K. Holyoak, and P. Thagard). He is the former director of the cognitive science program of the University of Michigan. In 1982 he was awarded the Donald Campbell Prize for distinguished research in social psychology by the American Psychological Association. He received a Ph.D. in social psychology from Columbia University.

JOHN W. PAYNE is professor of business administration at Duke University. He is director of the Center for Decision Studies at the Fuqua School of Business and area coordinator for the management and organizational behavior faculty. He has published forty articles and book chapters dealing with the psychology of decision making. He is an associate editor of several journals in management science and decision research. He received B.A., M.A., and Ph.D. degrees in psychology from the University of California, Irvine, and was a postdoctoral fellow in cognitive psychology at Carnegie-Mellon University.

JEFFREY A. ROTH, who served as the panel's study director, is study director for the Committee on Research on Law Enforcement and the Administration of Justice. His interest is in the policy uses of social research, especially in the areas of taxpayer compliance, criminal careers, and pretrial release. He is a member of the American Society of Criminology, the Law & Society Association, the American Economic Association, and the American Statistical Association. He received B.A., M.A., and Ph.D. degrees in economics from Michigan State University.

RICHARD D. SCHWARTZ is Ernest I. White Professor of law at the College of Law and professor of sociology and social science at the Maxwell School of Syracuse University. He is the former dean and provost of the Faculty of Law and Jurisprudence at the State University of New York, Buffalo, and was founding editor of the *Law and Society Review*. He was a member of the Committee on Research on Law Enforcement and the Administration of Justice. He is interested particularly in the sociology of law, criminal law and society, and administrative regulation; a current focus is public participation in environmental protection proceedings. He received B.A. and Ph.D. degrees in sociology from Yale University.

JOHN T. SCHOLZ, research associate for the panel, is associate professor and director of the graduate program in political science at the State University of New York, Stony Brook. His primary research and publications have focused on enforcement and compliance aspects of regulatory and tax policies, particularly the Occupational Safety and Health Administration and the Internal Revenue Service. He has also written on other aspects of regulatory policy, and co-authored *Nepal: Profile of a Himalayan Kingdom*. He received a B.A. in government from Harvard University and M.A. and Ph.D. degrees in political science and an M.S. in environmental economics from the University of California, Berkeley.

BARBARA YNGVESSON is professor of anthropology in the School of Social Science at Hampshire College. She has written widely on informal social control, dispute processing, and the interpretive theory of law. Her research has been carried out in Sweden and in the United States and has focused on the interplay of local and official understandings and practices. She is currently completing a book on the negotiation and transformation of local conflicts by officials and citizens in an American criminal court and the implications of this negotiation for understanding of the social construction of law.

Appendix E: Committee on Law Enforcement and the Administration of Justice, 1987–1988

RICHARD LEMPERT (Chair), School of Law, University of Michigan

ALBERT J. REISS, JR. (Vice Chair), Department of Sociology, Yale University

ANTHONY V. BOUZA, Chief of Police, Minneapolis Police Department

JONATHAN D. CASPER, Department of Political Science, Northwestern University, and American Bar Foundation, Chicago, Illinois

JACQUELINE COHEN, School of Urban and Public Affairs, Carnegie-Mellon University

PHILIP COOK, Institute of Public Policy, Duke University

SHARI S. DIAMOND, Department of Psychology, University of Illinois at Chicago, and American Bar Foundation, Chicago, Illinois

DAVID P. FARRINGTON, Institute of Criminology, Cambridge University, England

ROBERT KAGAN, Department of Political Science, University of California, Berkeley

MARK H. MOORE, Kennedy School of Government, Harvard University

JOHN ROLPH, The Rand Corporation, Santa Monica, California

KURT L. SCHMOKE, Mayor, Baltimore, Maryland

JAMES F. SHORT, JR., Social Research Center, Washington State University

PATRICIA MCGOWAN WALD, U.S. Court of Appeals for the District of Columbia Circuit

STANTON WHEELER, Yale Law School, Yale University

BARBARA YNGVESSON, School of Social Science, Hampshire College

ANN DRYDEN WITTE (ex officio), Chair, Panel on Taxpayer Compliance Research; Department of Economics, Wellesley College, and National Bureau of Economic Research, Cambridge, Mass.

JEFFREY A. ROTH, *Study Director*

TERESA E. WILLIAMS, *Administrative Secretary*

Index

Abt Associates, 358–359, 360
Accountants. *See* Tax practitioners
Accounts Receivable Treatment Study
   (IRS), 241–242, 342, 356, 363
Adjusted gross income (AGI), 44, 105, 319
Age, 81; compliance levels and, 8, 133–135,
   329; and social sanctions, 157; and tax
   practitioner use, 174
Agency Practice Act of 1965, 35
Aggregate cross-sectional data base. *See*
   Project 778
Aggregate unreported taxable personal
   income, *fig.* 42
Aguayo v. *Richardson*, 243, 348
Albany, N.Y., 167
Alimony income, 29, 60
Allingham, Michael G., 80–82, 83
Altruistic acts, 124
Ambiguity, 22, 26, 27, 81, 88; perceptions
   of, 128–129; tax practitioners and, 175.
   See also Complexity
American Bar Association (ABA), 169, 252;
   Commission on Taxpayer Compliance,
   20; ethical standards, 193–194; and
   research, 17; Tax Section, 16
American Bar Foundation, 68, 190, 195
American Civil Liberties Union, 357
American Institute of Certified Public
   Accountants (AICPA), 16, 176,
   193–194
American Medical Association, 169
Anthropologists, 77
Arthur Young Foundation, 17, 252
Attorneys, 35. *See also* Tax practitioners
Audit-based compliance measure, 222–223,
   224, 231–232
Audits: cost of, 30, 31; DIF and, 186;
   interactive strategies, 83, 84–86;
   multiperiod dynamic model, 83,
   86–87; perceptions of, 54, 74–75;
   random, 83–84; rate of, viii, 6, 30, 72,

81, 97–99, 102–106; in research, viii,
   23–24, 93–96, 102–106; revenue yield
   from, 30–31; selection strategies,
   83–86; taxpayers and, 71–72, 90,
   327–328; TCMP, 2, 49, 58, 66–68, 308,
   309, 316, 317. *See also* Enforcement, tax
   law

Banks, 26
Barter, 92
Behavioral decision theory, 152
Boruch, Robert F., ix, 339
Bounded rationality theory, 155–156, 160
Bouza, Anthony V., 392
Brackets, tax, 182
Brandeis, Louis, 348
Brookings Institution, 341
Budget deficits, 16, 47
Bureau of Economic Analysis (BEA),
   44–45
Burke, Edmund, 339
Business expenses: extent of
   noncompliance, 43, 52, 54, 59, 61, 64,
   65; perceptions of, 132

Calibration experiments, 356
California, 159
California Welfare Rights Organization v.
   Richardson, 348
Campbell, Donald T., 341, 368
Capital gains income: extent of
   noncompliance, 26, 52, 60, 63,
   107–108, 115; overreporting, 26, 52, 60,
   63, 70 n. 9
Carroll, John, 152
Cash income, 44–45, 107
Casualty losses, 61
Catfish farmers, 167
Censored normal regression model, 318–319
Census Bureau, 45, 46, 214–215, 218, 228,
   235, 343, 350